Portuguese Colonialism, Food, and Society in Goa

Portuguese Colonialism, Food, and Society in Goa

1900–1961

Maria de Lourdes Bravo da Costa

BLOOMSBURY
NEW DELHI • LONDON • OXFORD • NEW YORK • SYDNEY

BLOOMSBURY INDIA
Bloomsbury Publishing India Pvt. Ltd
Second Floor, LSC Building No. 4, DDA Complex, Pocket C – 6 & 7,
Vasant Kunj, New Delhi, 110070

BLOOMSBURY, BLOOMSBURY ACADEMIC INDIA and the Diana logo are trademarks of Bloomsbury Publishing Plc

First published in India 2025
This edition published 2025

Bloomsbury Academic India
An imprint of Bloomsbury Publishing Plc

ISBN: HB: 978-93-61315-89-3; eBook: 978-93-61317-43-9
2 4 6 8 10 9 7 5 3 1

Typeset by Integra Software Services Pvt. Ltd.
Printed and bound in India by Replika Press Pvt. Ltd

For my dear parents, Maria Madalena Fernandes e Costa and Jaime Bravo da Costa, my best friend and husband Leonel, daughters Linette and Loraine, sons-in-law Mauro and Ajay, and grandchildren Neil and Dia.

Contents

Tables

Acknowledgments

This book is the result of my research for a degree in Doctor of Philosophy. I had the desire to obtain one for some years, which could materialize only after I retired from service as Assistant State Librarian at the Krishnadas Shama State Central Library, Panaji, Goa. It is with immense gratitude that I thank the Almighty, who blessed me with good health and permitted me to make this research a reality. It is also with His blessing that I am publishing my thesis.

I wish to place on record my thanks to my guide, Prof. Remy Dias, who with his suggestions and guidance led me through the research with innovative ideas in writing the thesis. The discussions and the perceptions offered by him during my research helped me to understand new perspectives of history and his encouragement helped me with its completion.

I thank the members of the Departmental Research Committee (DRC) of Goa University. Prof. Nagendra Rao, who helped by advising my research and writing, as well as Prof. Varsha Kamat, who made valuable suggestions during the DRC presentation of my papers.

My deepest gratitude to all my friends who were part of my journey and encouraged me in my research by having discussions and sending literature on the subject that is not available in Goa. Prof. Susana Sardo, Prof. Isabel Alonso, and Prof. Paula Meneses contributed valuable suggestions and supported my work right from the beginning. I thank my colleague Dr. Parag Porobo for the discussions and inputs during my research. Prof. Rosa Maria Perez and Dr. Sandra Ataíde Lobo made valuable suggestions. I also thank the members of the group Pensando Goa, especially Professors Helder Garmes, Robert Newman, Duarte Braga, Cielo Festino, Cibele Aldrovandi, and Marcelo Assunção, for their contributions and guidance. I am grateful to Ms. Melita Fernandes Colaço who took the time to go through my drafts, thanks to José Lourenço for his assistance with the manuscript, and to Prof. Smitha Bhandare Kamat for translation from Konkani to English.

I acknowledge the assistance of the staff of Krishnadas Shama State Central Library, Panaji, Goa, and especially of the Rare Books and Local History Section, who continue to be a part of my journey as both a professional and a research scholar in the institution. I am grateful to Ms. Maria Ana Paiva for her help in whatever way to make my work a little lighter. To Sneha Malkarnekar, Vassanti Naik, Sudha Karmalkar, Siddhesh Gaude, and Gurudass Ajgaonkar a big thank you. So also, to Alzira de Souza, Dr. Pedro Pombo, Dr. Sushila Fonseca, Ms. Pia Rodrigues, Ms. Lilia (Bunota) Sousa, and Ms. Marina de Souza for their input and help. I also wish to extend my thanks to Ms. Blossom Medeira, Director of Archives, Goa, and Ms. Aruna Dias and Ms. Lalita D. Naik for their help with the computer work.

I appreciate the help extended to me by the staff of the different libraries in Goa, Lisbon, and Coimbra. Thanks to the staff of the Department of History and Academic Section (Ph.D.) of Goa University. My thanks also to Mr. R. Chandra Sekhar, publisher, Academic Books, Bloomsbury Publishing House, for his support with the publishing process.

I wish to express gratitude and thanks to my family, without whose encouragement and support I would not have been able to complete this work. The devoted backing of my best friend and husband Leonel das Merces Rodrigues made it possible for me to do my research and successfully finish the project. Similarly, the unstinted support of my daughters, despite their busy lives, Linette da Costa Rodrigues and Loraine da Costa Rodrigues, and sons-in-law Mauro Menezes Mathew and Ajay Aravind, not forgetting the good wishes of my grandchildren, Neil and Dia Aravind. To all others, my relatives, friends, and well-wishers, who were keenly following the travails of my research and writing the thesis, a big thank you. God bless you.

Maria de Lourdes Bravo da Costa

Abbreviations

BIJCE	*Boletim Informativo da Junta de Comércio Externo*
BO	*Boletim Oficial*
DL	Diploma Legislativo
FG	*Free Goa*
GT	*Goan Tribune*
MNE	Portugal, Ministério de Negócios Estrangeiros

Glossary

abcari/abkari Revenue accrued from toddy tapping and related industries.
Acção Católica A Catholic association of lay people.
acçionistas Shareholders.
addao A mock war dance performed by tribals during the harvest festival.
add-mass A dish prepared from bones from which most of the meat is removed and has some left on them, therefore called add-mass, i.e., bones and meat.
Administrador das Comunidades Officer appointed by the government to administer the functioning of the Comunidades of each taluka.
agarbati Incense sticks.
aksal A gravy made with small fish, onions, and cocum skins cooked in water.
alças A profit accrued from subleasing the fields of the village community.
alças de bate Buying under this denomination the rice at a cheaper rate from the poor to later sell at a higher rate on behalf of the Fazenda.
alcistas Syndicates of persons who specialized in taking the lands of the village community on lease at the annual or triennial auction.
Alvorada Music played at dawn to announce a festive day.
arrematação Triennial auctioning of the estate of the Comunidades.
avel Flattened rice, also called *poha*.
balchão A preserve made of fine shrimps, also a dish made with prawns or pork using the preserve.
bhatkars Landowners or landlords.
Bikareamchem jevonn Symbolic meal for the poor.
boias People who belonged to the Sudra caste and who served in carrying palanquins.
Boletim Oficial Government Gazette.
candil A variable measure. In this case, it is equivalent to 160 liters.
canjee Rice cooked in extra water till soft.
capo Jackfruit of the hard type.
Caró-asgo A variety of rice cultivated in Goa.
Caró-Quendalo/Quendalo A variety of rice cultivated in Goa.
chikol Sludge or mud.
Chonchery A variety of rice cultivated in Goa.
chouriço Sausage.
coddo A bamboo mat for storage of dry paddy.
compromisso A contract.
Comunidade Association of *gaunkars* of each village in Goa.
Confrarias Confraternity of brotherhood of the Christian community.
consoada Sweets and savories prepared for Christmas in Goa.

Contribuição Predial Tax imposed at the rate of 12 percent of the gross rural produce by the Portuguese government from the 1880s onward.
copito Small wine glass.
cuddas The club-houses where the Goan emigrants lived in places like Bombay.
dai A flat spoon made of a single piece of wood, used to stir the batter while cooking Goan sweets.
danto An instrument like a rectangular fork, used to plough the field.
decreto Decree.
Diploma Legislativo Legislative Diploma.
dispensa Storeroom.
dodol A sweet made of coconut juice, palm jaggery, and rice, a specialty for Christmas.
donno A small container made of leaves of selected trees, used to serve eatables (plural *donnes*).
fama A religious observation a day before the novena of a feast starts.
fest Feast.
fogeter The person responsible for making and lighting the fireworks.
foros Rent.
fosnem Petard, firework.
freguesia Parish.
Gaudi, Gaudo, Gawda A tribe of Goa. Many of the Gawda tribe worked as *mundkars* of the *bhatkars.*
Gaunkari, Gauncarias Association of *gaunkars*. The Portuguese called it Comunidade.
gaunkars Male descendants of the original settlers of the villages in Goa through the male lineage.
godchem A generic name for teatime sweets made of jaggery and coconut.
gutto A planed plank used to level the soil.
interessados The interested parties in a Comunidade.
khazans Reclaimed sea-land for cultivation susceptible to inundation during tides.
Kurumbi, Curumbi A tribe of Goa.
laat A tin used for irrigation.
lanços Lands at the time in the existing form of a lease by parcels.
Legislação do Estado da India Compilation of Legislation.
Mahars Basket weavers.
mandares A savory prepared for Christmas from pumpkin and raw rice, both ground together.
mann Equivalent to 16 kilos.
manos Sluice gate.
Mazania Temple association.
mordomo A patron responsible for defraying the expenses of a feast.

mundkars Tenants working on the landed estate of the individual private proprietors, especially in the coconut plantations.
nalli Petards, firework.
onde Small ponds (singular *ondo*).
opa-mursa White surplice and red cape worn by the clergy and by lay people with particular liturgical ministries at worship, such as members of the Confraternity.
paili Four poddis are equivalent to one paili, which is equivalent to 3.993 liters.
para Pickle of dry fish like mackerels, kingfish, streak fish.
pensão Onus on a property.
pez Canjee.
podd A volumetric measure for grains.
podgué An earthen container to carry rice or canjee.
Portaria Notification or an order.
Portaria Provincial Provincial notification or an order.
ranpin Female cook.
rendeiro Toddy tapper.
reudeo Residue of pieces after extraction of fat.
rogddo Grinding stone.
sacador(es) Revenue-farmer(s) or tax collector(s).
Sacadoria Office of the tax collector.
salves Marian antiphons. A hymn is sung at each novena in praise of Mother. Mary. Salve Regina, means Hail Queen.
sopocar Rent collector.
sorodio Kharif crops.
Tambry-patny A variety of rice cultivated in Goa.
tangas One rupee had 16 tangas.
tisreo Clams.
tollem Age-old rain-fed reservoirs of water, dating back to the pre-Portuguese period.
touxem Cucumber.
Ufaar A religious ceremony.
urid A type of lentil.
vangana Rabi crops.
vann A hole made with laterite stones for pounding cereal, chilies, etc.
vigia Guards of the plantation in the lands of the Comunidade.
vonn A specialty sweet made of coconut juice, palm jaggery, and boiled gram dal.
xit-coddi-ani-nustem Fish-curry-rice.
zagor A comic representation in Konkani by rural amateur artists; rudimentary theatre in Goa.

Introduction

> *At this time of day the curumbin women used to put* podgué *full of steaming broth or boiled rice, the turbid, gummy water strained away, into bamboo baskets, along with dried fish for lunch, and leave them on the dung-covered floor by the door. Now, however, dark-grained millet ambil replaced large, ochre-streaked grains of rice in the péz. About two years ago the rice started getting scarce, and in its place young millet and yellowish bajri was boiled in the old pots of blackened clay. The men and women who worked in the rice fields had almost forgotten the taste of it, and children, in the lean and uncertain harvest of those years, themselves recalled secretly munching on golden stalks.*[1]

This passage is taken from the novel *O Signo da Ira*, which presents the appalling conditions and suffering that the poor had to experience due to the unavailability of rice which is the Goan staple food. The scarcity of rice was due to various factors studied and analyzed in this book which uses food to show the deprivation and struggles of the people in Goa during the last sixty-one years of Portuguese colonial rule. The reasons for this suffering were varied. The importance of food in the ethos of Goa is discussed through the major aspects of this connection. Food is not only essential for the existence of mankind but also an important element in the sociocultural, traditional, economic, and political conditions of a place.

This study focuses on the key features of the food history of Goa and its impact on colonial Goan society, economics, and politics for the period from 1900 to 1961. It is not a study of culinary art, even though Goa has its own unique cuisine resulting from a host of various rulers over the centuries, with the last colonizers, the Portuguese, having had the most significant influence on the food habits of Goans. It is a history of insufficiency and abundance—primarily the insufficiency of rice and the abundance of alcohol.

An analysis of literary and academic works indicates that there is a gap in studies related to Goan history, in that there is a need for a sustained study of the food history of Goa, to understand the influence of colonization on the subject people. Food, cooking, diet, and eating habits allow us to understand better the complex issues of cultural change and transcontinental cultural flow during the colonial regime, and the challenge undertaken here is to research the food history of Goa from the early twentieth century. In what way has food been crucial in the context of Goan society during the last six decades of Portuguese rule of this land, and also in subsequent years? Did issues of food directly impact the community? Was the availability of the produce so exclusive to the people of the territory that it shaped their history in a particular way? For example, rice varieties that are cultivated (such as corgutt) are home-grown types intricately linked with the region's ecology and the survival of the local communities. The coconut types are also exclusive to some areas, for instance, the varieties from Benaulim and Calangute villages are well known. Social life, religion, trade, social institutions, and caste stratification of the people of Goa, as well as other diverse aspects of Portuguese Goa, have been analyzed and studied extensively by scholars. Anthropological and ethnographical studies of this community have been covered in many of these works. Food plays a vital role in the sustenance and well-being of people. Food has signified both substance and symbol through the ages. It holds multiple meanings to different sections of society and is also a form of communication between groups in society. Its place in the sociocultural and economic life of any social structure, including that of Goa, requires deeper searching to illuminate the history of this region from a different perspective. On one hand, food binds the citizens of a society while on the other it divides them. Various literary forms, proverbs, theater, folk songs and stories, and novels in Portuguese, Konkani, and Marathi, all indicate the anxiety within society, centered on food, food production, distribution, and access. These also motivate the need to discuss issues like scarcity of food, deprivation, struggles, etc., for the region through the ages.

This study puts together a wide-ranging food history of Goa from 1900 up to 1961 when it was liberated by the Indian army. It highlights the travails of the subalterns as they strived to make both ends meet for most of the year, as shown by the diverse folklore of the region, government rules and regulations, and the press. The poor suffered due to the insufficiency of rice in the territory. This shortage was used as a tool by the landlords, the Comunidade, and the government for their benefit and to the detriment of the underprivileged masses. The landlords exploited the *mundkar* and poor farm laborers, who were not paid their rightful dues. A *mundkar* is a person allowed to stay on the property of the landlord with the obligation of working for him for little or no wages. Besides, the landlords often collaborated with the government to raise the price of the local rice so that they would sell it at a profit, though it meant that people would have to buy it at a price even higher than the imported rice which was actually cheaper. This was done by imposing a surcharge tax on imported rice. The government favored this protectionist idea as it would benefit from this tax surcharge. This situation created an atmosphere where politics were played using rice by those interested in gaining an upper hand over the others, that is, the *mundkars* and the poor.

Like any other nation in South Asia, Goa's economy was based on agriculture and was influenced by the local climate, antiquated farming practices, and the unequal distribution of agricultural resources. The payments were made using the produce, mainly rice in the case of Goa. Thus, the metaphor of food serves as a vehicle for expressing several significant concepts related to power, sharing, and redistribution.[2] The example of the metaphor of rice in the novel *O Signo da Ira* has been discussed by me elsewhere.[3] According to Arjun Appadurai, in an agrarian system, the shares in the agricultural product—particularly food grains used as a form of payment—were the primary means of simultaneously expressing the relationships of cooperation and solidarity between patrons and clients, as well as their subordination and domination over one another.[4] The food shaped local power relations and the sociocultural processes, which are reflected in the novel *O Signo da Ira*.

Appadurai argues that food in South Asia can serve two diametrically opposed semiotic functions and serve to indicate and construct social relations characterized by equality, intimacy, or solidarity; or, it can serve to sustain relations characterized by rank, distance, or segmentation.[5] This argument shows the different class structures or inequality existing among the *bhatkar* and their dependents. On the feast day, lunch is served at *bhatkar* Ligôr's house to his guests who include the upper caste, *sudra-mundkars*, and the *curumbis-mundkars*. The latter are at the lowest in the social structure and therefore served the meal in the garden and the second in the corridor of the house. While the *curumbis* are served rice with fish curry and kokum on banana leaves, the others eat *sarapatel* and *sannas*.[6] The upper-class guests have lunch along with the host in the house.

Literature allows us to analyze the intricate interaction between the body, subjectivity, and societal systems that govern consumption. At the same time, food may signal "wealth or power, cultural difference or a sense of belonging, status and identity in terms of rank, and moral standing."[7] Scholars have equated food to language and consider it as exclusive a human behavior as language. According to Claude Lévi-Strauss, "Cooking, it has never been sufficiently emphasized, is with language a truly universal form of human activity: if there is no society without a language, nor is there any which does not cook in some manner at least some of its food."[8]

Appadurai has also discussed another type of literature: cookbooks. According to him, Indian cookbooks written in English and aimed at an Anglophone readership pose some intriguing issues related to understanding how a national cuisine is constructed under contemporary conditions.[9] He argues that cuisines are constructed and language and literacy, cities and ethnicity, and women and domesticity are some of the concerns cookbooks imply and create.

Similarly, Massimo Montanari argues that "[l]ike spoken language, the food system contains and conveys the culture of its practitioner; it is the repository of traditions and of collective identity."[10] He also argues that food can be looked upon as "an extraordinary vehicle of self-representation and of cultural exchange—a means of establishing identity, to be sure, but also the first way of entering into contact with a different culture."[11] Massimo states that it appears easier to eat the food of the "other" than to understand their language. However, he correctly concludes that food can act as a bridge between cultures far more than spoken language alone, opening up cooking techniques to all kinds of innovation, cross-pollination, and contamination.[12] According to Clifford Geertz, every component that makes up a culinary culture is interconnected, including every ingredient, dish, meal plan, and meal structure.[13]

Numerous authors have used food-related story descriptions in their novels, essays, poetry, dramas, and other works of fiction, both in the past and in the present, due to the importance of food in daily life. Anca-Luminiţa Iancu and Alexandra Mitrea's work depicts the importance of literature in expounding the role of food in day-to-day living, as well as the numerous interpretations by various writers.[14] In the introductory essay, the editors discuss the role of books in laying the base for foodways' history.

As Roland Barthes effectively remarks, food represents a system of communication that allows us to create, share, and transform meaning with other people.[15] Lévi-Strauss further stressed this idea, pointing to the relations between food systems and sociocultural identity,[16] as well as totemic relations. Scholars have also emphasized the important function that food plays in modeling and reflecting specific value and meaning systems. For example, today we not only eat food but also discuss and describe it, using social media we spread information that gives meanings and values that influence our culinary experiences.

In *Food Cultures across Time: Flavors and Endeavors*, food and its scarcity have been prevalent themes in literature, everyday life, and intercultural conversation. This anthology presents literary and cultural depictions of abundance, scarcity, and consumption in general, to demonstrate how they inform and modify one another. The volume contends that literary and cultural goods contribute to the formation of food cultures, investigating how our social and ethical relationship to literary texts and cultural artifacts reflects our response to issues surrounding food production and consumption.[17] At the same time, food may signal "wealth or power, cultural difference or a sense of belonging, status and identity in terms of rank, and moral standing."[18] The book has two parts: the first is devoted to novels and the second to essays on food. The first examines the nuances and complexity of food in society and attempts to map food cultures and food pathways in fiction by examining issues related to eating in the works of writers from as varied a range of nations as possible. It also explores subjects such as comfort/discomfort fiction, depictions of food and the female body, and the intersections of class, racism, and identity through food. The subtle parallels between food and fiction have a significant role in creating literary experiences, acting as a memory mediator, the way that food's absence causes dislocation, confinement, and trauma, and presenting translation challenges.[19]

The second reflects some of the typical classic examples of a community which shows that the process of making unique food represents the people and their culture. In this category, we have two essays.[20] Visan discusses the syllabub, tracing its development by examining how culinary information about ingredients and recipes is arranged in lexicographical entries in British and French dictionaries and encyclopedias of the time. Miller writes about the history of the *frutta Martorana*, an Italian marzipan sweet by analyzing the dish's provenance, composition, application, and significance within societal and religious frameworks. Miller further highlights the links between art and food by viewing the *frutta Martorana* as a work of art.

The distinctiveness is also demonstrated when I write about Goan curry (uman) arguing that it contributes to the uniqueness of Goan cuisine. Its value to the community is reflected wherever the diaspora settled, since they continue to cook it daily, and others mimic their preparation.

The Goans who migrated tried to maintain their identity through the food they cooked. For example, the first-generation Goans, who traveled to Beira in Mozambique, directly from Goa, maintained the uniqueness of their preparations. The reason was the know-how and availability of ingredients, like coconuts, tamarind, chilies, and spices as Mozambique was a tropical country. Let us take the example of the preparation of *uman*, the Goan coconut curry. The uniqueness was maintained as all the ingredients, including the abundant fish, were available. The interviews on *caril* (curry) with D. Fatima from Ilha de Mozambique[21] and others highlighted in a study on the Goan community in Maputo, Mozambique,[22] show how the uniqueness was maintained in preparing the Goan curry.

We are aware that a large number of immigrants, particularly first generation, maintain close connections with their place of origin through relatives, friends, remittances, participation in events and festive occasions, and occasional trips. However, migrant culinary canons often develop following their own dynamics that are not necessarily the same as their cuisine of origin: the context, the external pressures, and the internal structures are not the same.[23] But in the case of Goans who migrated to Mozambique this interaction did not take place.

After the independence of Mozambique, when the Goans left for Portugal, they continued to cook the same quotidian and festive food. This was facilitated by the enterprising Indians who had set up shops and were known as "Loja de Indianos" (Indian Store), especially in Lisbon city, where ingredients for Asian cooking were available. The Goans from Beira, organized annual reunions called *Encontros dos Goeses da Beira* (Reunions of the Goans of Beira) from 2000 onward. In these get-togethers, Goan food was served to those attending the event. Interestingly, *sarapatel* became the exemplary dish for these get-togethers, when it was served at supper. I attended one such full-day event in May 2017 as a guest of my relative.[24] Snacks included Goan croquettes and samosas, and lunch was Portuguese food served at the table. After an afternoon of music and dancing, in the evening supper was served with *sarapatel* as the main dish, which was eagerly looked forward to and relished by those present.[25]

Taste, including aesthetic taste, has been viewed as a corporeal experience rather than a cognitive one. However, corporeal taste creates narratives and organizes memory, similar to Marcel Proust's "involuntary" or associative memory, and arouses memories. Body and mind are thus not distinct.[26] Proust's book, in seven volumes, was a work of fiction and not an academic exercise. The episode involving the tea-soaked madeleines brings up memories of the tea-soaked cake he shared as a child with his aunt. This triggers Proust to experience involuntary recollections of his former childhood home and surroundings, including the town he resided in.

Food history is a recent pursuit of research. It shows the concerns and working procedures of new history, but it is still a field to be explored: an incomplete business that raises more questions than answers, and it has a symbolic value.[27] In an essay, F. Braudel writes at the start that the food history sector is one among other areas of research and historical understanding, and therefore shows the same repetitious regularity as others.[28] According to Braudel, studies of the general cultural habits of the people need to be done. This need was felt since earlier the playfield vied with what was outstanding or outlandish, like the tables of royalty or the elite. They considered theirs as the systems of food and therefore resistant to any change.[29]

The environments in which people live and what they consume are associated with "certain" components unique to an area and are also continuously influenced by imports from other places. Goa would be such a thought-provoking example. It preserves its traditional food ecology, which is fish, curry, and rice. However, over the years it was influenced by various rulers and people who lived here, having been a vital entrepôt and business hub at that time. The conquest of this land by the Portuguese effected many changes in the Indian subcontinent, which were very profound in Goa where they ruled for more than 450 years (1510 to 1961). The Portuguese were responsible for bringing to the continent and carrying to other parts of the world many diverse plants which changed the food habits of the people living in those areas.

Ethnographic studies document food customs over the years. They show that the consumption of food is planned according to a powerful symbolic code: the rituals of preparation and meal, the calendar of traditions (festivals, Lent), and the techniques of eating (etiquette at the table) consist of strong elements of sociocultural proof of identity and can thus suggest the fair title of "food sociability," according to Braudel. He holds that "these material systems disaggregate before the eyes in favour of the standardization of normal life and of leveller enculturation, multiform and belligerent. It is crucial to study what remains, the process of their disorganization and rearrangement: the observation would open the way to the psychology of food, which is a logical completion of the study in progress."[30]

The food of a people depends on their geographical conditions. Goa is in the Konkan region of India and has a long coast. This has mainly been an agricultural state during the historical period under study, where the main cultivated produce was rice. Coconut trees are grown aplenty in the state, and the coconut is very central to the Goan diet. It is used generously by households, be it for the making of curry, or vegetarian dishes, or its extract as cooking oil. In the latter form, it is also used for medicinal purposes.

The coastline of Goa is over 100 km long. Besides its main rivers Mandovi and Zuari, a number of other small rivers, rivulets, and water bodies provide people with plenty of fish. Thus *xit-coddi-nustem* (fish-curry-rice) has formed the staple diet of a vast section of Goan people through the ages. The Brahmin diet excludes fish as they eat only vegetables and pulses. There are others who live in and close to the hilly regions, who cultivated ragi (nachni–*eleusine coracana*), which, along with rice, was consumed by them throughout the year.

This book explores the politics of rice by the *bhatkar* (landlord), the Comunidades (village communities) of Goa, and the government, who all wished to have power over the people, especially the poor. *Gaunkari* was a system of agrarian associations prevailing in Goa, which were later renamed by the Portuguese as Comunidade. Under this system, the colonial regime transferred the control of cultivable land and fish ponds to these associations. Paddy fields were leased by them for cultivation through auction and the locals could then bid for them. However, only the privileged *gaunkars* were allowed to participate in the auctions. These were for a specified period (either yearly or triennially) and the tenant cultivator could bid again after the lapse of the lease. The lessee had to pay the annual rent in kind to the Comunidades. They then sold the produce through auction, which would help them pay for the specified socioreligious duties, the government dues, and other expenses. The surplus was distributed to their members, known as *gaunkars*. The *acçionistas* and *kulacharins* were also given some money, and the shareholders, if any, were paid.

Crops in Goa

There are two crops of rice raised in Goa. One is the *sorod* or *kharif* crop which is cultivated during the monsoons and the second is the *vangana or rabi*. In the novel, *O Signo da Ira* (1961) by Orlando da Costa the story pivots around the *vangana* crop. Costa has used rice as a metaphor to show the different facets of the lives of a Goan *bhatkar* and *mundkar*, as well as the latter's sufferings.[31] The emphasis is on how rice cultivation and production in Goa are simultaneously a symbol of vital importance for the survival of the subalterns and an instrument of *bhatkar* power.[32] Said in another way: it is based on rice that social dynamics were established. Whoever controlled and dominated its production, somehow dominated the social system.[33]

Considering this, it was crucial to research the current system of field leasing by the *bhatkars* and the Comunidade, as well as the regulations pertaining to the latter, which played against the interests of the tenant cultivators. A large percentage of the cultivable land was under the Comunidade system, managed by the *gaunkars*. Cultivable lots were auctioned only to the *gaunkars*, who in turn sublet to the actual tillers at a higher price, thereby fleecing the latter. The Comunidade had created an auction system that favored them and not the cultivator. This was done through *alcistas*[34] who were paid *alçãs*[35] by the Comunidade. Even during the pre-liberation era, the system was so prevalent that requests to prohibit it were made to the government. This was because, in most cases, instead of actually cultivating the fields, the lessee would sublet them to a cultivator via an oral contract and benefit by a 100 percent, which harmed both the cultivator and the Comunidade.

The various measures in use by the government to help in making rice available for the whole year have also been debated; for example, the hiring out of fallow lands and making them feasible, as well as restoring the land by reestablishing the Comunidade of Assolna, Velim, and Ambelim.[36] The government initiated a Rice Campaign (Campanha de Arroz) to get better production of rice using new ways and means of cultivation. However, these measures did not yield the desired results. According to Jose Conceição Almeida's remarks in *Aspects of the Agricultural Activity in Goa, Daman, and Diu*, if cultivable fallow land in each taluka was available for agriculture, more than half would be converted to cereal-bearing crops. There would have been an increase in the 44,699 Ha area under paddy cultivation to around 92,367 Ha.[37] Aiming to resolve the financial problems faced by the territories, the government introduced a sur-tax on imported rice, which was enforced as a protectionist measure. For the successful execution of these measures, several Diplomas Legislativos or Portarias were published. These were in fact counterproductive, as rice and other goods became costlier, affecting the common man. Still worse, it rebounded on the exports of local products like coconuts, areca nuts, salt, dry fish, mangoes, and other sundry goods, which lost their market as they had to pay high duties, thus making their goods costlier to the Indian consumer. However, the authorities insisted on continuing with the tax despite public objections since it was profiting from this surcharge, at the cost of the Goan consumers.

The Congresso Provincial da Índia Portuguesa was established by the Goan intelligentsia to deal with matters that directly affected the economic and social development of Goa. The core issue to be discussed was agriculture in Goa since rice deficiency was felt throughout the period of study. The Primeiro (First) and the Quinto (Fifth) Congresso were devoted to its improvement, with a focus on rice cultivation. The Segundo (Second) Congresso was devoted to emigration and its related problems. It was not only men who migrated, but women also followed. With people leaving Goa in hordes to get jobs since they were not available in the territory, emigration became a major issue. The main reason for people to migrate was the need to feed and sustain themselves and their families.[38] The majority of Goan migrants sought to overcome deprivation by working as helpers and cooks in restaurants and as housemaids and ayahs. The latter amounted to about 3,000 in number. These kinds of jobs essentially assured them of regular meals. The Census of 1921 gives the number of landlords as 7,004, *mundkars* 35,110, and laborers 49,686, which shows the disparity in social and economic levels. The Census of 1931 shows that agricultural laborers numbered 121,962, whereas those living exclusively on their own income were 9,369. These numbers corroborate the disparity shown in the earlier Census of 1921. The second Congresso also had many papers on improving agriculture. They discussed the need for agricultural credit services for the farmers to acquire loans as money lenders extorted a very high interest, sometimes as high as 50 percent. The Congresso argued that even if there was goodwill on the part of the Goan intelligentsia, the government was lethargic in taking action on the proposals and in enforcing the laws enacted to implement them.

Issues concerning the Comunidades were discussed and the proposal by the government for their disentailment was opposed by the delegates. Suggestions were made that the sublease of the rice fields should be prohibited. Since the well-off who sublet had the extra land to profit from, there was a need to fix the maximum number of plots that each individual could lease. The *sacador* and *vigia* who were responsible for collecting dues from the cultivators exploited them by imposing their own conditions. Changes were suggested to the Code of Comunidades to free the cultivators from such exploitation.

Some lands were owned by the *bhatkars* (landlords). They usually used the *mundkars* to cultivate the fields. The owner *bhatkar* made the *mundkars* work hard to till the land in order to get a good rice crop. They were generally paid in kind with rice. This mode of payment traditionally depended on the terms laid down by the *bhatkars*. They could entrust the land for cultivation to the *mundkars* and in return get rice as reimbursement for it. Or they could provide the land and also provide the seeds, and get rice as payment. Or the *bhatkar* could just hire the *mundkars* to cultivate the land and give them rice in return. In any of these alternatives, the *bhatkar* would be the beneficiary and the poor *mundkar* who worked tirelessly would be the loser. Moreover, everyone's fate would depend on a good harvest. It was very essential, as the payment in kind would be directly related to the harvest and sufficient production of rice.

This book also looks into the distinctiveness of Goan rice that is used for cultivation, and the reason for this selection. Goa's exclusive ecosystem has fertile and productive land around the river called the *khazan*. These are saline floodplains along Goa's tidal estuaries. There are also the *morod* (uplands) and *kher* (midlands).[39] For example, *caró-asgo*, *caró-quendalo*, or just *quendalo*, is cultivated where saltwater affects the fields.[40] *Chonchery* is used for sandy terrain.[41] And *tambry-patny* rice is cultivated on the mountain slopes and in the plains.[42]

Food Archives, Food Memories

The extensive literary sources available in the Krishnadas Shama Goa State Central Library, Goa Archives, and other libraries of Goa, as well as the Centro de Estudos Sociais and Biblioteca Pública in Coimbra, and the Biblioteca Nacional, Biblioteca Pública, Biblioteca da Sociedade de Geografia, and Hemeroteca, all in Lisbon, have been data-mined for developing a narrative of Goan food history for the period under study. The work also assesses the policy of the Portuguese government and that of British India. Most of the goods were imported from the neighboring territories, a greater part of which, by the beginning of the twentieth century, was under British rule. Goa depended almost entirely on the import of goods. Although goods came from far away in Europe and other places, the prices were not too expensive. This was possible due to the policy of the Portuguese government to impose low taxes on imports and also to raise the salaries of the staff. Did these policies benefit a certain section of society to maintain an affluent lifestyle?

Another direct link to food is the study of the memories it evokes amongst people. When a particular food is consumed, the taste allows them to build their personal and community history through memories of the past. This topic is in the early stages of research and therefore no well-defined and straightforward literature can simply be examined to assess the current state of the field of food and memory. Besides, both are multidisciplinary subjects. So, to write this chapter various resources have been used: history, anthropology, sociology, folklore, literature, etc. The literature review had to go beyond Goa-related books. I referred to a few books that have been used as indicators in this field, to draw the theoretical assumptions. These include those of David Sutton, Marcel Proust, and C. Counihan.[43] John H. Mace, professor of psychology writes that these comprise the most common happenings, characterized by their element of surprise, as they appear to come into consciousness on impulse.[44] Studies also suggest that such occurrences are especially convincing and recurrent in relation to one's sense of smell.[45] These were applied to the Goan scenario in eating fish, curry, and rice—the Goan daily meal—bringing to mind past involvements evoked by the senses of taste and aroma. The Goan *xit-coddi-nustem* (fish-curry-rice) can be like the madeleines and lemon tea of Proust.

Several folk stories or memoirs have been read in which food brings back memories. We have the author Lucio Rodrigues[46] eating mangoes, as well as the story of a mother awaiting the arrival of her son and family from far away Africa, who peps up their visit with several Goan dishes and, of course, the mango. Another story tells us about the gluttony of the son-in-law who is offered an assortment of Goan sweets and then gets up in the middle of the night to sneak into the kitchen to lay his hand on one sweet that he had declined to eat but actually wanted to taste. This behavior can be connected to the greed in demanding an *ojem* by the groom's family who insists on having several sweets and fruits for personal consumption and distribution to relatives and neighbors on occasions like weddings, festivals, etc.

David Sutton's *Remembrance of Repasts. An Anthropology of Food and Memory* offers a theoretical account of the interrelationship of food, memory, and ethos. In this book, Sutton writes about how the "food of memory" is also the "memory of food." He provides many paradigms to connect both, which have been debated here using Goan instances. Sutton's work is supported by both ethnography and literature.[47] He deals with many of the varied occurrences that we brand as memory. For example, how the seasonal food cycle forms "prospective memory" by initiating one to look forward to past events.[48]

This phenomenon of the seasonal food cycle was applied to the summer months in Goa. The mango is the king of the Goan fruits, with its reputation not only for its taste but as also for being the most desired, and the stories around it—full of memories for Goans, rich or poor—have been discussed using literature and memoirs. In his reminiscences in the essay "Pink and Green," the author Lucio Rodrigues gives an enthusiastic account of the mango.[49] The tilling of the fields, the harvesting, and the procedure of getting the rice ready for consumption have also been discussed. This is done by the womenfolk who use special preparation tools and techniques. As they work, they sing folk songs, which shows that these can serve as cultural artifacts for ethnographic appraisal and collective memory. In fact, Sutton makes an appeal for ethnography that starts from the principle that food is not simply another topic that "symbolizes" identity. He stresses that ethnography should challenge us to rethink our methods, assumptions, and theories in new and productive ways.[50]

Using literature and folklore, the cycle of food and the preparations made to get ready for the rains are studied. The end requirement of the latter was to have sufficient food for the family throughout the wet season.

Sutton claims that hunger is an excellent memory motivator; when individuals are hungry, they think of food. In *O Signo da Ira*, Orlando da Costa describes the plight of *mundkars* who must endure starvation since they are elderly and unable to work. They have to go door to door begging for handfuls of rice. Both remembering and forgetting trigger reminiscences. The *mundkars* of Ligôr recall a time when they had much to eat, and it saddens them to see the rice barns empty.

It is not only the act of eating that brings memories but also the production of food. In the introduction titled "Anthropology, Food and Modern Life," the editors Jakob A. Klein and L. Watson[51] agree with Sutton that there is a need to investigate ethnographically and theoretically how cooking skills are performed, developed, and transmitted, often in highly gendered ways. So, under the production of food, the Goan curry is discussed vis-à-vis the curries of different communities.

Mnemonics, nostalgia, and remembrance are also used to bring back memories about food. Food and food events appear to serve an important memory role as they remind individuals of previous episodes, prior states of social connections, and previous debts and claims. The mnemonic function of food events is probably linked to the sensory and emotional immediacy of food consumption and the semiotic virtuosity of food is enhanced by its mnemonic utility. The examples of a turkey and a pumpkin are explored to discuss this feature.

Studies on the diasporic or expatriate population that have suffered displacement often focus on food-related nostalgia. Sutton highlights how the tastes and scents of a past homeland might temporarily transport diasporic people back to a time when their lives were not broken up. As a type of memory "nostalgia," according to Holtzman, has multiple meanings, both broadly and in relation to food. Some food writing, especially that which does not come from the field of anthropology, depends on the popular idea of sentimentality for a bygone age, using food as a symbol for memories of family and childhood.[52] Food-centered memoirs are one genre in which food-centered recollections are expressed. Some Goan authors have written elegies to their favorite dishes in the form of songs, essays, verses, or prose. These include *godshem*, *sarapatel*, and *consoada*, as well as fish-curry-rice, the epicurean *chouriço* that evokes powerful memories in the émigrés.

The tradition of picnics and the advantages of the spring waters for the treatment of illnesses have been documented in the *dulpod E TeTollsam' Zori' Barik Gogo.*[53] This *dulpod* is entirely about the memories of people who went for baths to the springs. Picnics as annual outings are reminiscent not only to those in Goa but to the diaspora who looked forward to being present as these were meeting points of the community. This custom was carried along by them and they even arranged picnics wherever they settled.

It has been suggested that ritual is a potent place to develop food-centered memory and food-centered forgetting. Masses are said in remembrance of a deceased Catholic after their passing. These are said after seven days, a month, and a year, and then once a year after that. Many families host a special lunch in memory of their departed loved ones on the month's mind.[54] The dead are believed to be represented by beggars or poor persons and therefore this lunch is called *bikareamchem jevonn* or "beggar's lunch."

To add to the senses of smell and taste, I have discussed the role of the other senses of touch, sight, and hearing, to evoke memories. The act of trying to find if the fruit was ready to eat by feeling the softness of mango is an instance of touch. We looked at the colors of fruits to check if they were ripe, and the child heard the songs that the mother or grandmother sang as he or she was fed.

Food in Religious Rituals and Festivities

Food is a part of rituals and traditions that have been observed by people for years. Three religious celebrations of the Goan Catholic community have been analyzed. A study of the traditions of the people and the practices of food offerings present in the celebrations of these three feasts is highlighted, namely, the Feast of Santa Ana (St. Anne) at the Church of Santa Ana, Talaulim, the Feast of Our Lady of Annunciation at the Chapel of Our Lady in Siridão, both in Tiswadi taluka, and the Feast of Holy Cross at Nerul, in Bardez taluka. One important area of correspondence is the arrangement and method of celebrating the church's ceremonial calendar feasts.[55] For example, the feast at the church can only be celebrated by the *gaunkars*. Similarly, only they can serve as the feast's *mordomo* (patron/ president). Another example of Hindu consciousness among Catholic *gaunkars* is the harvest feast in Santa Cruz village, Tiswadi. During these festivities, they solely serve vegetarian meals.[56]

In this context, I have used an appeal to Santa Ana that asks for favors, published in the *Almanach Indo-portuguez para o Anno de 1886*,[57] which goes with and rhymes with some of the votive gifts to the Saint. This appeal helps us reconstruct the tradition of the past followed by the residents of the village before they were converted. The gifts to Santa Ana differ according to the vows made by the devotees. There are curious invocations to the Saint made by newly married couples and others who are childless, lamenting over the emptiness in their marriage. They beg Santa Ana to grant their appeal while touching the gift to the feet of the Saint's statue.

The reason why the feast is commonly known as *Touxeachem Fest* is discussed using the ecosystem of the village. The study showed that it was customary to offer to God the first produce of the season in thanks, which for the agriculturists of Talaulim would be the vegetables they cultivated, that included the *touxem* (cucumber) and the lentil *urid*, to the deity of the village.

The feast of Our Lady of Annunciation is commonly known as *Pezechem Fest* (Feast of Canjee). The Dempos, a well-known industrialist family of Goa, offer *pez*, a rice gruel, to the devotees on this occasion. The study shows that this was an act of philanthropy by the landholder, possessor of almost the entire village, who felt that he should provide a meal to the visitors who came from far and wide, keeping in mind the travails of the devotees, with many of them traveling all night by foot, bullock carts, and canoes. In the past, eateries were not a part of the model of a city, leave aside in villages that were inhabited by poor fisher folk and toddy tappers who lived by their hard work. Why was *pez* selected? The common people had it as their first meal daily in the morning and it gave them sufficient nutrition and strength to do their daily work. Another reason for offering the *pez* could be an "obligation" on the property that the Dempos inherited from the previous owners. The present owners of the property may have had to honor a pledge, a *pensão* that they may have acquired when they purchased the property from the earlier owners, the Dominicans, who in turn might have been the landlords either by purchase or by being gifted, along with this onus.[58]

The *Tisreachem Fest* is one more example of a feast that is associated with Goan culture, traditions, and the ecosystem. The study of this feast was centered on fieldwork and oral cultural practices. I attended the feast to capture the arrangements for the preparation of the main dish prepared by using *tisreos* (clams) to serve the devotees—*tisreachem sambarem*—and to also observe the other festivities. This feast shows the significance of using the local resources available to the villagers. Instead of depending only on agricultural produce they looked to the sea to obtain food without any money. The extraction of the clams was done without any costs, as no tools were required, and these were available on the shore during low tide. Another tradition observed in the celebrations of the feast is the coming together of neighbors from very early in the morning to help in preparing the *tisreachem sambarem.* This shows the cultural practices of living in communal harmony. The serving of seasonal fruits demonstrates that people rely on nature not just for their everyday needs but also for celebrations.

Borrowing to celebrate festivities and the resultant indebtedness is reviewed using literature, writings by various columnists in the local press, and the traditions abided by the people. Ligôr *bhatkar*, the main protagonist in the *O Signo da Ira*, the short story "O'Salutaris" by Lucio Rodrigues, and the vernacular press, *Porjecho Adar*, especially the comments of the columnist Costa Bir, are used as references to show that feasts were not only for pleasure and celebrations. They entailed much more for the people in general, especially for those who had to defray great expenditure as the *mordomo* of the feast. Here I would like to allude to Cristovam Fernandes from Panjim, a well-off businessman who was a *mordomo* twice for the feast of St. Thomas at Sao Tomé ward and spent lavishly, which led him to a financial debacle. The journalist Luis de Menezes was at the time a committee member of the chapel and decided that in the future no person would be *mordomo* more than once. This example leads to a discussion on how serving alcohol in various celebrations—religious or otherwise—has increased drinking in Goa.

Alcohol Consumption in Goa

The consumption of alcohol was not socially acceptable because it was harmful to the health of the consumer. But by the start of the twentieth century, it had reached levels that could be considered an "epidemic." The Congressos Provinciais (Provincial Congresses) had to include alcohol consumption and related topics as the main focus in the Sétimo Congresso (Seventh Congress), as alcoholism became a major problem for Goan society. The intelligentsia and professionals in various fields that gathered at this academic event discussed the many problems affecting the alcoholic and suggested solutions to overcome this vice. The endemic problem of alcoholism in Goa and its harmful consequences are discussed in this book. It was a rot deeply rooted in society, recognized by some while others ignored it as something not happening in their backyard. These others included the colonial government, which incidentally was the main beneficiary of this vice with the advantage of collecting high revenue taxes from *sura* (toddy), collectors, and alcohol producers.

The elite and intellectuals too felt that it did not affect them and that it was only a problem of the poor laborers, though some had begun criticizing the authorities. Even when the Conferência Sanitária (1914)[59] took place there was only one paper on alcoholism, titled "Sugestões para Combater o Alcoolismo em Goa," by Hipólito Policarpo Pegado, and references to it in another two papers.[60] As the title suggests it was a battle against the vice of alcoholism. The other two were "O Saneameto Rural da India Portuguesa na sua Relação com a Organisação Administrativa," by J.J. Roque Correia

Afonso,[61] and "A Tuberculose," by A. Filipe Pinto Cordeiro who wrote that there should be a fight against alcoholism which is accountable for the spread of tuberculosis.[62]

But, unexpectedly, the Congresso Provincial da Índia Portuguesa (1916–31) which had as its aim to solve Goa's problems when it was established never included alcoholism in its agenda. In the Second Congresso, three papers connected to the subject of alcohol were presented. The first two were on *abkari*, and assessment of taxes, and the third on how to solve the vice of alcoholism: A. Teodoro Miranda, 'Regimen of *Abkari* for the District of Goa'[63] and Azarias Condorcet Lobo '*Abkari* in Goa: Before the Anglo-Portuguese Treaty in India'[64] while L.M. Condorcet Pereira, "Anti-alcohol Campaign."[65] The Congresso was held on January 27, 1918.[66] However, the intellectuals and elite awoke from their apathy to organize one independent session in the Sétimo Congresso (1927). The need arose as even the elite had now joined the bandwagon of alcoholics.

At the Congresso Provincial, it was revealed that statistically the Catholics were more involved in drinking. Such claims had also been made in the past. The contention was that the introduction of Christianity by the Portuguese into Indian society which later came to be known as "beef and wine" Christianity, for the first time familiarized the people with a culture that was in essence Western.[67] For the Portuguese, wine drinking was a part of their social and religious ceremonies. Alcohol as food and medicine in general, and in Goa in particular, and the struggles of the alcoholics are discussed. The latter makes use of literature—the book *Tales of Goa* by Berta Menezes Bragança.[68]

At the Congresso de Acção Católica (1933) held at Old Goa, Baronio Monteiro made an ardent reference to alcoholism in the paper "Alcoholism and Tobacco," and referred to the Catholics and requested the patriarch to take action and guide the congregation onto the right path. Monteiro also founded the Liga Economico-Social da India Portuguesa (Economic-Social League of Portuguese India) (1931), Liga Anti-Tabago-Alcoolica (Anti-Tobacco-Alcohol Society) (1932), and Liga de Temperança (Society of Tolerance) (1934).

The patriarch of the Archdiocese of Goa assured that he would look into the matter and issue a pastoral letter. However, only a newsletter was handed out to all the parishes asking the priests to help regulate alcoholism. As a follow-up to the newsletter, there were adverse comments made in the newspapers, especially by Hegdo Dessai of *O Bharat*. The patriarch, therefore, handed out a Carta Pastoral and asked the priests to follow it and bring it to the notice of the devotees by reading a translation in Konkani to the people attending service in the church.[69] Reactions in different newspapers and from individuals regarding alcoholism are discussed, which point out the government's apathy in taking any action. Even though some regulations were issued after the Congresso Provincial's suggestions to the government, they were not executed. Many newspapers, both local and metropolitan, took up the matter and wrote about the threat. Several people also spoke up about this issue.

Although the battle to control alcoholism was taken up by the Church, the intelligentsia—Catholics and Hindus alike—and others, it was observed that not much was done by the government to put an end to alcoholism. The primary cause was the requirement for taxes on the produced and sold alcohol, which were crucial sources of cash for a region that had little throughout the 1950s—apart from Goa's mining industry, which helped tide away the difficult situation created by the economic blockade implemented by the Indian government on the Portuguese territories.

The Embargo

The last chapter of this book analyzes how the Goan populace was severely affected by politics. After India gained independence in 1947, problems cropped up between Goa and the newly independent country formerly colonized by the British, who incidentally were allies of the Portuguese.[70] The prime minister of India, Jawaharlal Nehru, asked Portugal to leave her territories of Goa, Daman, and Diu. The prime minister of Portugal, António de Oliveira Salazar, refused point-blank, as he considered them to be "extended territories of Portugal" and not colonies. As diplomatic attempts failed to yield any positive results, India tried other means. The only feasible alternative for Jawaharlal Nehru, who held on to the Gandhian policy of nonviolence, was to use an economic blockade and this was formally imposed in 1955. Earlier there had been attempts to deny access and sporadically block the flow of food or remittances to Goa. Sarto Esteves writes that after the freedom fighters liberated the territories of Dadra and Nagar Haveli,[71] India replied by imposing an economic blockade.[72] However, a formal economic blockade was imposed by Nehru in July 1955, by stopping the trains traveling beyond Castle-Rock. Although it was told that the suspension was provisional, the line was not restarted until after the annexation of the territories by the Union of India. Accordingly, the trains ran only between Mormugao and Sanvordem in Goa.[73] In order to support its decision, varied notifications were published by the Government of India. The results of the blockade were felt by the emigrants' families since their remittances were stopped and they did not have money to buy commodities even if they were available. The Portuguese government did try to overrule this imposition by starting an air transport, TAIP, to fly in merchandise from Pakistan which became the entrepôt between Goa and other European countries. Food was also transported from Portugal and other colonies, and these, especially Mozambique, profited from such dealings.

Rice politics were at the forefront during this period, with both countries using it—one to stop and make difficult the supply of the essential staple and the other to make all attempts to make it easily accessible to the Goan people. The local papers do not give a precise picture of the dilemma of the people who endured hardships. Food and money were unavailable without the flow of remittances. On the other hand, a lot of tinned and bottled packed food products and different kinds of fruits alien to the Goan consumers made their appearance in the Goan market, altering their diet many a time with easy accessibility for those who had money. The blockade also gave rise to trafficking when food was smuggled into Goa and foreign imported goods were taken illegally across Goa's border by *contrabandistas*.

The local newspapers were not able to write about what was actually happening as they were gagged by censorship. Therefore, the Goan newspapers based in Bombay, the *Goan Tribune* and *Free Goa,* which began publication with the sole aim of supporting the freedom movement of Goa, wrote against the Portuguese rule in Goa. By researching these, a picture can be drawn of the struggles faced by the common folk. Non-receipt of remittances and the difference in money from rupee to escudo caused a lot of misery to the emigrants and their families. There are no editorials that write about the deprivations faced by the people. But the very fact that there were preparations made by the government to transport and distribute the food in a regulated manner, with limited quantities made accessible for purchase by individuals, reveals the ongoing crisis. The government took measures to import food from other countries through different means of transport to bypass the blockade. People altered their eating habits as they could easily access the various imported products. The local media was full of advertisements for tinned stuff replacing fresh products for cooking, like *tomatada* (tomato puree) and olive oil. *Bacalhau* (dried codfish), which is typical of the Portuguese diet, also flooded the market. Fruits, pulses, butter, cheeses, alcohol, etc., made their entrance in different varieties and trademarks. Advertisements in the newspapers were used to allure people to change their food habits. For example, frozen chicken was promoted, as well as food enhancers like Maggi.

Methodology and Sources

This is a historical study on food that also covers ethnography, anthropology, and other pertinent aspects, and is, therefore, an interdisciplinary work. In undertaking the study of food history, different resources were analyzed in addition to oral history data gathered by interviewing various persons. Since a large number of the traditions observed in Goa are not documented, fieldwork research coupled with interviews and personal experiences with practitioners of agriculture and people of the region was used to analyze and come to conclusions.

The information collected was analyzed from a historical point of view. This is presented in the following chapters. Chapter 1, "Rice, the Perennially 'Insufficient' Goan Staple: A Study of *O Signo da Ira* (The Sign of Wrath) and Other Historical Literature," discusses the insufficiency of rice, its cultivation, and the problems faced by the tenant cultivators and the *mundkars*. As the title suggests, literature is used to argue on this subject. "Food, the Memory Connector: A Study of Goan Folklore and Other Forms of Literature" is a chapter that studies the connection of food with memories which bring back nostalgic experiences, and this is done using Goan folklore and literature. "Feasts and Traditions: Borrowing to Celebrate Festivities, and the Resultant Indebtedness" is a chapter that discusses three religious celebrations using food connected to them. I have argued in this chapter that feasts were not only about celebrations but could also lead to the indebtedness of those who borrowed for the festivities. In the chapter "The Drink That 'Cheers' but Brings Tears," I have examined the outcome of the unlimited production and consumption of freely available alcohol, and the government's lethargy to overcome the problem of alcoholism. The last chapter is on "The Economic Blockade and the Pangs of Hunger," in which I look at the new perspective of how food was used as a tool by the Indian government to pressurize the Portuguese to hand over the territories.

It is clear from the chapters that each one is a separate case study on a particular subject. So, the literature review encompasses a vast number of documents that I have used to make my arguments and draw a conclusion.

I referred to historical as well as anthropological sources, and carried out fieldwork. Konkani proverbs, folk songs, theater, stories, cradle songs, those of toddy tappers (Render-*gitam*), of *Kunnbis* (*kunnbi-geet*), *fugddi* and *dekhnni* dances, and novels in Portuguese, Konkani, and English have been accessed to show the agitations in the society centered on food and food production, distribution and access, food scarcity, deprivation, conflicts, etc.

Of importance were primary sources like various *Anuários Estatísticos da India Portuguesa* and *Anuários Estátisticos do Ultramar*, which are reports of the government about the territory in general and statistical details helpful for analysis. The *Census Reports* were also important sources for the population as well as various activities in the territories. Various codes of the Comunidades were referred to for the rules and management of the institution as well as changes that occurred during the years. Several sources with published documents like *Collecção de Bandos*, *Leis Peculiares das Comunidades Agrícolas*, and *Bosquejo Histórico das Comunidades* were of importance to analyze the issues of the Comunidade. The *Boletim Oficial* (Government Gazette)[74] and *Legislação do Estado da Índia*[75] for the study period were important sources for various legislation issued by the government and official notices. Two reports were carried out soon after the liberation of Goa. The *Techno-Economic Survey of Goa, Daman and Diu*[76] by the National Council of Applied Economic Research to undertake a benchmark survey of the newly acquired territories is very important as it gives the status of Goa before 1961. The other is the *Report of the Goa Land Reforms Commission, 1964*,[77] a study of the land problem in Goa. The second is also a very important source for land usage, detailing some of the Comunidade rules about the lease and rent policies of the fields.[78]

Similarly, there are a few other studies that have helped with the study of Comunidades and consumption in Goa including *The Socio-Economic History of Goa with Special Reference to the Communidade System: 1750–1910* by Remy Dias.[79] Two essays—*Some Aspects of the Consumption History of Estado da India: 1900–50*[80] and *Consumption History of the Estado da India* by Remy Dias[81]—were important sources for the consumption history and alterations in the diet after the Anglo-Portuguese Treaty of 1878. *Abolim*,[82] Lucio Rodrigues's collection of essays on folklore, folk tales, and legends that reflect the Goan ethos was referred to for this study. His well-researched essay on *dulpod*, *mando,* and *dekhni*, the Goan folksongs, as well as some very interesting traditions, are a part of this collection. It is an important source for understanding the Goan past. *Undra Muja Mama*,[83] a compilation of various *dulpods*, the folk songs of Goa, by Jose Pereira, Micael Martins, and António Costa is important as it reflects the culture and is descriptive of traditional Goa, especially the life of Christians in the past.

The primary source also included primary archival data from a vast number of newspapers and periodicals in Portuguese, English, Konkani, and Marathi languages which are referred to as "archives of the people."[84] The information and happenings reported, besides writings by various contributors, allowed me to study and get the broader spectrum of happenings and their aftermath for the period of study. The news covered was general and political too, and the periodicals were also a platform for polemics. They were published in Goa and Bombay and included the papers in exile, *Free Goa* and *Goan Tribune*. The vernacular press, which was started with the aim of keeping in mind the proletariat and helping the downtrodden, the emigrants, and others was also an important contemporary source. Several journals were referred to in order to read the modern trends in food history. These were supported by ethnographical studies which border on anthropology and provide explanations.

Structure

Chapter 1—"Rice, the Perennially 'Insufficient' Goan Staple: A Study of *O Signo da Ira* (The Sign of Wrath) and Other Historical Literature"

This chapter describes the politics of rice, the insufficiency in production, and the reasons for the same. Orlando da Costa's *O Signo da Ira* is analyzed to show how rice cultivation and production affected the subalterns. It also studies the prevailing system of renting out the fields by the *bhatkars* and the Comunidade, and the laws regarding the latter which acted to the disadvantage of the cultivators. Measures taken by the government to increase the yield and taxes imposed are discussed.

Chapter 2—"Food, the Memory Connector: A Study of Goan Folklore and Other Forms of Literature"

The connection of food with memories of past experiences is examined here through Goan folklore, stories, theater, *dulpods*, cradle songs, and other cultural forms. The senses of taste, touch, sight, and smell can trigger elaborate memories of childhood and adulthood events, especially for the diasporic Goan community, who yearn for the food and flora of their homeland.

Chapter 3—"Feasts and Traditions: Borrowing to Celebrate Festivities, and the Resultant Indebtedness"

This chapter deals with three popular feasts of Goa, namely, the Feast of Santa Ana at the Church of Santa Ana, Talaulim, the Feast of Our Lady of Annunciation at the Chapel of Our Lady in Siridão, and the Feast of Holy Cross at Nerul. The foods associated with these feasts are studied to investigate their religious, cultural, ritualistic, economic, and geographical links. The chapter also discusses the indebtedness caused due to borrowing by the celebrants of the feast to keep up with the traditions.

Chapter 4—"The Drink That 'Cheers' but Brings Tears"

The problem of alcoholism and the politics of the government toward this issue are covered in this chapter. It shows that the increasing number of taverns and the production of alcohol were responsible for deepening alcoholism among the downtrodden and also the well-off. It also shows that the government failed to take constructive measures to ease the burden of the families who suffered physically, mentally, economically, and socially due to this vice. Though the Church tried to work out a solution by sending pastoral letters to be implemented to end this malady amongst the Catholics, who incidentally were in the majority addicted to the vice, this was not successful. Nor could the intelligentsia find success through discussions and proposals to stop alcoholism. They were successful in getting some laws enacted during the Congresso Provincial, but the government did not implement them to satisfaction as it would lose significant revenue.

Chapter 5—"The Economic Blockade and the Pangs of Hunger"

This chapter examines the political situation between the Portuguese and the Indian governments after the independence of India. The attempts to diplomatically end the stalemate having failed, India imposed an economic blockade on the Portuguese territories. The banning of food articles from the neighboring Indian territories led to the introduction of various food items including a lot of preserved foods that came in the form of tins, bottles, etc., from different parts of the world, which profoundly altered consumption patterns. The blockade also brought misery to people who suffered because of the unavailability of food, especially rice, as remittances from their relatives were blocked.

Conclusion—The final chapter summarizes and revisits the findings of the study.

The chief argument of the book is that people struggled to survive as rice, the Goan staple, was insufficient for the entire year, bringing suffering to the people. The main reason was that the local production was sufficient for just under six months and the government's efforts to increase production were unsuccessful. The implementation of the programs was not effective due to the lethargic attitude of the administration. This worsened during the period of the economic blockade. I have argued that there was a change in the consumption pattern during the blockade with new imported food products introduced in the market, which included fruits and vegetables that were largely consumed by the colonialists, the wealthy elite, and the government employees whose salaries saw a big raise. I have also argued how the stopping of remittances by the Indian government led to the suffering of families in Goa who were dependent on this cash flow, and that the blockade was counterproductive as it was supposed to destabilize the Portuguese administration, and not the people. Another argument focuses on the abundance in the production of alcohol and the growing number of taverns, which increased alcoholism in the territory. This was again to the benefit of the government which dragged its feet to counter this malady as it would lose a significant volume of revenue from tax collection. I have also dealt with the senses of touch, sight, and hearing to show that food and memory were also connected through them and not only through taste and smell as discussed by most scholars in this field of food history.

Through the chapters of this book, the reader can explore the powerful role of food in the last decades of colonial Goa—especially the tiny grain of rice—in exploiting the working masses, enforcing class hierarchies, evoking memories of pleasure and yearning, causing celebration along with crushing debt, destroying the socioeconomic fabric of society through alcoholism, and in a blockade that choked the colonial regime and the people.

1

Rice, the Perennially "Insufficient" Goan Staple: A Study of *O Signo da Ira* (The Sign of Wrath) and Other Historical Literature

Introduction

Rice, the staple food of Goa, was in demand by all the households for daily consumption. What was problematic was its unavailability in enough quantity throughout the year, and therefore the need to import it. This situation created an atmosphere where those interested in gaining an upper hand over the masses could play politics using rice. It was not only the *bhatkar*, even the government and its adversaries used rice to attain their political objectives.

Goa, during the period under study, was predominantly an agricultural region. Rice is the main crop in Goa, consumed with fish curry, and constitutes a vital part of the Goan diet. This diet did not change with the Portuguese takeover of Goa. On the contrary, it was carried over to Portugal and other Portuguese colonies by the emigrant Goan and other Portuguese citizens who made it part of their quotidian food.[1] Rice was consumed four times a day by those who could afford it, as breakfast *canjee*, midday-*canjee*, fish-curry-rice for lunch and dinner, or just as *canjee* at dinner.

The landed gentry who owned paddy fields were economically better off. However, there were others who toiled in the fields and shared the produce with the owners, whose land they tilled. For the tillers, it was essential that the harvest was good, or else they would have less to eat for the year. Moreover, they would be indebted to the field owner who was little concerned about any bad harvest. Orlando da Costa's historical

The title *The Sign of Wrath* has been adopted from the English translation of *O Signo da Ira* by D.A. Smith (Saligao: Goa 1556, 2017).

novel *O Signo da Ira* has as its central theme the sufferings of the *mundkars* (tenant cultivators) at the hands of the *bhatkar* (landlord/field-owner), with rice cultivation as a subplot.

Goa has historically been a rice-deficit territory. In fact, trade and commerce in Goa from 1900 to 1961 were chiefly for the purpose of procuring the much-needed rice.[2] In earlier centuries, when the population of the territory was lesser, rice produced locally was perhaps enough for consumption, but later as the numbers increased, rice imports became essential.[3] There was an increase in the population in the first half of the twentieth century.[4] During the early nineteenth century there was much demand from Goa for the Canara rice. The rice cargo came to Goa from Basrur, Mangalore, Honnavar, Kalianpur, and Ponnani.[5]

Insufficiency of Rice Production

There were several factors responsible for the low production of rice. The chief factor was the inadequate area for paddy cultivation and the inaction to increase this coverage (Table 1.1).[6] The system of land holdings and outdated methods of cultivation were other factors. A large percentage of the cultivable land was under the Comunidade system managed by the *gaunkars*. Cultivable lots were auctioned to the *gaunkars*, who in turn sublet them to the actual tillers at a higher price, thereby fleecing the latter.[7] To make matters worse, the lease period was fixed at three years, which caused a lot of hardship to the lessee, who was tied up with few benefits, if any, as well as the liabilities, which were many, during the lease period.[8] Later, there was an increase in the period of the lease to six years.[9] The Portuguese government accepted that the locally grown cereal was sufficient for only five to six months of the year.[10]

There were other reasons why the territory was short of rice. Nature's vagaries often affected the production. Rice cultivation depended on the monsoons. The cultivation of *sorodio* (kharif) is entirely dependent on the monsoons. If the rains were not regular or were deficient it would cause a drought-like situation. On the other hand, excessive rain would inundate the fields, destroying the standing crop. In such instances, the tenant cultivators faced great losses. The *bhatkar* would not lose anything, for even when the production fell short, the tenant had to unfailingly pay the *bhatkar* the contracted share, leaving the former with a meager rice stock for family consumption.[11]

Table 1.1 Rice cultivation in hectares and percentage

Sorodio	38,629	86
Sorodio and *Vangana*	5,602	13
Vangana	468	1
Total	44,699	100[13]

[Source: *Report of the Land Reforms Commission, 1964*. Panaji: Government Printing Press, 1964, 12]

About 14 percent of the fields would be cultivated to raise a second *vangana* (rabi) crop.[12] There was no attempt to increase the cultivable area beyond this small percentage. What was the reason for this attitude? It was probably aimed at controlling the marginalized tenant cultivator. If there were enough crops for everyone the tenant cultivators would not be dependent on the *bhatkar* for sustenance.

It was important to increase the area under *vangana* cultivation as there was always hope of getting a good harvest, with the fields being irrigated manually with water from the ponds. Hence the poor would pray for the rains so that the *bhatkar*'s pond overflowed and they could have a good crop.[14] But, would they enjoy the produce? The landlord would take his share and also demand the unpaid balance for the previous years, if any, and thus take away almost everything.[15] There were also instances where the landlord would deny the farmer his rightful share and sometimes even lie that the paddy had been robbed. Such treacherous behavior of the *bhatkars* is exposed in the novel *O Signo da Ira.*[16]

Moreover, the laws, instead of helping the tenant cultivators, were often detrimental to their legitimate interests. Examples of these were the different laws enacted by the government during the period of study with reference to the lease of the Comunidade's agricultural land.[17] Another case was the rice shortage in 1938, which caused a great outcry.[18] The Portuguese government put restrictions on rice imports in order to "protect the locally grown rice" and "help the *bhatkars*" get a higher price for their produce. However, the outcome of this ill-conceived measure was a large-scale shortage of rice. To meet the rice shortages, it was suggested that *nachinim* (millet) cultivation be enhanced. *Nachinim* is a viable substitute for rice and has more nutritive value. But no concrete steps were taken in this direction.[19]

During the Second World War, Goa again faced food scarcity, primarily due to the limited supply of rice from British India. Rice could not be sourced from other areas either, on account of the tense global circumstances. Thus, even though Portugal had declared its neutrality, the effects of the war adversely impacted Goa which was dependent on British India for its food requirements.[20] The effects of the war led to voices of dissent being raised. The local Portuguese language periodical, *O Heraldo*, reported on the food scarcity on August 21, 1942. Protests were raised about "neither sugar nor kerosene" being available in the market. The government imposed restrictive measures to regulate the sale of consumables and created zones for this purpose.[21] Rationing of rice became the order of the day.[22] There was wanton smuggling and hoarding of stock by the traders, who wanted to benefit by raising prices. This compounded the woes of the people.[23]

Land Classification, Ownership Patterns, and Harvesting Water Resources

Agricultural lands in Goa can be classified into three categories: *morod* (uplands), *kher* (midlands that are sandy, close to the sea-shore), and *khazan* (saline floodplains along Goa's tidal estuaries) lands.[24] *Morods* are situated on high lands, with poor soil quality. As these areas are rain-fed, only the *sorodio* crop is possible. Yields are low, with a production of just seven to eight *khandil* per hectare.[25] *Kher* lands (situated between the morods and khazan) are best suited for rice cultivation and production is eighty *khandil* per hectare. The *khazan* is reclaimed from the sea by erecting bunds and sluice gates. Such reclaimed land is generally below the high tide level. The sluice gates assist in regulating the flow of seawater during the tides.

The area under paddy cultivation was 18,000 Ha, 17,500 Ha, and 9,200 Ha for the *khazan*, *kher*, and *morod* areas, respectively. *Khazan* and *kher* lands collectively comprise about 80 percent of the cultivable area under rice cultivation.[26] Besides these three main types of rice lands, there is one more, the *kulne* lands, which are highlands mostly located in the midst of forest areas, but their acreage is limited. *Kulne* areas are fertilized with the ash of dry wood and foliage; however, the yield is meager.[27]

The *vangana* was cultivated only in the midlands, i.e., the *kher* lands, which are closer to the water bodies. *The Techno-Economic Survey* records that two crops were grown in pre-Liberation Goa, on an area of only 5,600 Ha, mostly of the *kher* and *khazan* type.[28] It also mentions that only the *vangana* crop is grown in certain areas, where due to the bad drainage and consequent flooding of the fields during monsoon season no *sorodio* crop is possible. This crop covers about 467 Ha.

Vangana lands are irrigated by three types of water bodies: wetlands, freshwater lakes, and ponds. Besides the rivers, there are numerous wetlands, both natural and man-made, used for irrigation. The most important are the wetlands of Carambolim, Chimbel, Mayem, Cacora, and Calafur (Santa Cruz).[29] These are large tracts of low-lying areas that are used to store rainwater.

Freshwater lakes called *tollem* are age-old rain-fed reservoirs of water, dating back to the pre-Portuguese period.[30] These are man-made reservoirs that store the rainwater for agricultural activity during the non-monsoon months. Most of these are semi-permanent water bodies and qualify as wetlands, as stated by Cowardin.[31] The *tollem* water is used to irrigate the *vangana* crop in low-lying areas.[32] A full-length wide and deep trench meanders through the *tollem*, which facilitates the draining of water collected from the upper areas and the surrounding fields into the river during the monsoons. The trench is deeper and wider near the sluice gate. Thus, this part of the wetland remains water-laden throughout the year, and the rest of the area is used for the cultivation of the *sorodio* crop. The harvest of *sorodio* in the first week of September is soon followed by damming of the water in the wetlands i.e., the *tollem*. These are also used as traditional aquaculture tanks. The fish in the *tollem* is harvested in mid-April by the highest bidder following an auction.[33] For instance, many people flock to Curtorim village in Salcete taluka to buy freshwater fish caught at the Angoddi *tollem*.[34] Even at present, the sale of freshwater fish is a big draw.[35] Most of the fish is dried and salted, and *para* (fish pickle) is made for consumption in the rainy season when fresh fish is not available due to the rough seas.

Since the *tollem* was not completely dried the shallow water was used by the farmers for cultivating beans, watermelon, radish, onion, chili, etc. Farmers dug up small ponds called *honde* (singular *hondo*) at various places in the wetland for agricultural purposes. Steps led down to the pond to fetch water with a pitcher. In some places where the water level was deeper, a *laat* was used for irrigation—a tin was tied to a bamboo stick which was dipped into the water and pulled up.[36]

Today, 22 varieties of high-yielding rice seeds introduced from other states are cultivated in Goa. The traditional 35 varieties, which were specific to the Goa region, are no longer grown.[37] Felipe Neri Xavier, in a monograph, gives details of the know-how of cultivation and the seeds used according to the terrain.[38]

It would be interesting to know the ownership of land area available for agricultural purposes in Goa (Table 1.2).

Table 1.2 Land under different owners

Ownership	Area in Ha	Percentage
Private proprietors	176505.8964	53.757
Government	103083.2667	31.658
Comunidades	36623.5001	11.383
Hindu temples	9391.1299	2.875
Christian religious associations	926.1299	0.283
Municipalities	12.8836	0.004
Santa Casa da Misericordia de Goa	115.9527	0.036
Under litigation	12.8836	0.004
Total	326671.6863	100.00[39]

[Source: J.C. Almeida, *Aspects of the Agricultural Activity in Goa, Daman and Diu* (Panaji: Government Printing Press, 1967), 17]

From the above, it is seen that a major part of this area, that is, about 54 percent was held by private owners and constituted chiefly of the paddy fields, coconut groves, and cashew plantations. Next follows the area owned by the government which was largely forest areas.

It is commonly believed that a greater part of the agricultural area was owned by the Comunidades. These are presently in possession of about 11 percent of the total cultivable area.[40] However, in Tiswadi, Salcete, Bardez, and Mormugao talukas the Comunidade holds a greater area of the paddy fields.[41]

A.R. Padoshi analyzes the trends in the agrarian pattern of Goa using "operational holding," which is the area of land that the cultivator cultivates even when he may not be the owner.[42] In this particular case, the author is using the area of land owned and self-cultivated by the cultivator plus the area leased and this is more pertinent for the understanding of the economics of farming. It will give a more accurate measure of agriculture since the operational unit is the actual unit of production. The economies of scale are more directly related to the size of cultivation holdings rather than to ownership holdings. Similarly, for understanding the disparities in the distribution of land and income among cultivators, the concept of operational holding is more relevant than ownership holding. The data used by Padoshi regarding the distribution of holdings by size groups for

Table 1.3 Distribution of holdings by size groups in Goa in 1960

Area in Ha	No. of holdings	% total	Area covered in Ha	% total
0–0.1	7,746	29	350.48	4
0.1–2	14,709	57	8,021.00	11
2–4	1,672	6	4,790.14	6
4–20	1,757	7	14,464.75	23
20–100	354	1	14,367.50	22
100 and above	81	–	21,376.64	34
Total	26,319	100	63,370.51	100

[Source: A.R. Padoshi, *Agricultural Development of India*. Bombay: Himalaya Publishing House, 1991, 25]

the year 1960 is from the *Techno-Economic Survey*.[43] However, this data pertains only to the talukas of Tiswadi, Bardez, and Salcete.

Table 1.3 shows the distribution of holdings by size groups for the year 1960 and reveals the important features of the agrarian pattern of Goa before 1962–3.[44]

Thus, it is seen that the agrarian economy of Goa before 1961 was numerically dominated by relatively small and micro holdings. The private agricultural property is excessively divided, and this division goes on increasing every day, due to successive divisions because of inheritance, consequently increasing difficulties for the small rural proprietor, especially since very few cultivate the fields on their own. Out of the total number of holdings, as many as 85 percent are found to be less than two hectares each (i.e., less than five acres each), thus indicating a large number of smallholdings.[45] These units were economically unviable and most cultivators lived a hand-to-mouth existence. Landlords of vast continuous land are very rare, except for the Comunidades which as discussed were primarily responsible for the existing rice production in Goa.

The Enigmatic *Bhatkar–mundkar* Relations

Many authors have written, in various languages and literary genres of the territory, about the *bhatkar–mundkar* relationship. All of them have portrayed how the *mundkar* is ill-treated and exploited by the *bhatkar*. For example, R.V. Pandit (1917–90), in his Konkani poetry book *Mhojem Utar Gavddeanchem* (I am a Gaudo, 1967),[46] has a poem *Pausa, pausa, io re io* (Rain, rain, come, do come), describing the sadness and anxiety of the tillers, praying to God for rain and for an abundant rice harvest, so that they would have enough for the year and could pay off the *bhatkar*'s dues.[47] In Lucio Rodrigues's (1916–73) short story, "It Happens" (1954),[48] the son of the *bhatkar* sexually exploits the *mundkar*'s daughter. To protect her son's interests, the *bhatkan* (bkatkar's wife) forces the girl's mother to send her daughter to Bombay. Lucio draws a picture of Goa where instead of the perpetrator of the crime being punished, it is the victim who is evicted and uprooted from Goa.

João Agostinho Fernandes (1871–1947), the pioneer of Konkani theater, wrote original plays addressing the social relations of the *bhatkar*, particularly in *Batcara-I* (1904), *Batcara-II* (1905), *Kunnbi Jaki-I* (1934), and *Tandlanchem Kestaum* (1944). Vimala Devi, (1932–) in the book *Monção* (1962) includes two short stories—"Ocaso" and "Venus and Its Arms"—portraying the same type of exploitative relationship. This chapter examines the novel *O Signo da Ira* (The Sign of Wrath) (1961) by Orlando da Costa (1929–2006), who dedicated part of his work to the action of social and human conflicts in Goan society, including among them the problems faced by the *mundkar* at the hands of the *bhatkar* who was described as autocratic and arrogant, mistreating and exploiting them. The author uses metaphors to show abundance and poverty represented by *bhatkar* and *mundkars*, respectively.[49]

The dilemma faced by the *mundkars* is the central point of the novel. However, there is another focus: the cultivation and production of rice and the dependence on it for subsistence by the *mundkar*. There are two central aspects of the work: first, the portrait of the miserable daily life faced by the *mundkars*, and second, rice production, with its unequal distribution and importance for their livelihood.

The *bhatkar* made the *mundkars* toil the land and paid them in kind. Traditionally this model of contract depended on the stipulations laid down by the *bhatkars*. They could give the land for cultivation to the *mundkars* and in return get rice as payment, they could provide the land and the seeds and get rice as payment, or the *bhatkar* could just employ the *mundkars* to till the land and give them rice in return. In any of the options, the *mundkars* would be the losers and the *bhatkar* would benefit. Moreover, the dependency on a good crop was crucial since the payment in kind would be directly related to a good harvest and production of rice.[50]

As stated earlier, in Goa some fields are cultivated twice a year: the *sorodio* during the monsoons and the *vangana* during the winter season. If the *sorodio* does not give a good yield the farmer hopes for a good harvest during the *vangana*. The *sorodio* is at the mercy of the monsoons, and the tillers often suffer a loss of standing crops due to flooding or drought. Farmers hope to make up for such losses in the *vangana* crop, when fields are irrigated with water from water bodies like ponds, lakes, tanks, spring water, rivers, and rivulets. Besides, there is hectic agricultural activity in the form of multi-cropping with the cultivation of vegetables or fruits.[51]

The story of *O Signo da Ira* is set in the 1940s. The main plot centers on the *bhatkar–mundkar* relation and the *vangana* crop. In a note, the author states that the facts about the land and the nature in which it was integrated and expressed and the complex tenure system favoring the "haves" as against the "have-nots" are portrayed truthfully as they existed at that time.

Orlando da Costa depicts the exploitation of the *mundkars* by the *bhatkars* who make them toil hard on the land. The *bhatkars* use their expertise and knowledge to cultivate the fields. What it takes to prepare and cultivate the fields is not just a physical activity but an act enmeshed in customs and traditions understandable in totality only to the rural folk. As was the practice then, the *mundkars* were paid in kind for the labor, i.e., rice, which allowed them to have their basic meal of rice *canjee* or rice-curry. Therefore, the *mundkars* pray and hope the crop will be abundant and that there will be enough for their sustenance. However, the *bhatkar* Ligôr cheats them of their payment. He takes the rice that would have been their payment and sells it on the black market. To cover up his misdeed, he tells the poor *mundkars* that the rice was robbed at the rice mill.

The *mundkars* had hoped for a good crop, for the earlier years had been bad due to incessant rains and a shortage of seeds.[52] There were also rumors of war, the first signs of which appeared in 1942. To overcome the shortage, the government used to import rice from Burma, which was now occupied by the Japanese.[53]

Costa wrote the novel drawing from his memory, using the experiences of his time in Goa from childhood through adolescence. He was eighteen years old when he left Goa. In an interview,[54] he mentioned that the need to write this first novel on the realities of Goa was a profound call, which he felt and accepted. He gave the reasons for writing it as civic since it was the appeal of Goa and her people that had a strong influence on him. According to him the perspectives with which he faced this reality at that time and the relations that defined local society were coherently directed by a markedly materialistic social vision as well as deep humanist roots.[55]

Costa as an adolescent had a sensibility that helped him to remain attentive, sometimes curious, and open to seeing things happening around him. This allowed him a certain closeness with nature, and a grasp of certain aspects of social life, like solidarity, on the one hand, and a critical tendency, on the other.[56]

He made various attempts at writing the novel over the course of years. However, it materialized only later with the political happenings in Goa and the struggle for freedom gaining momentum. Also, his contact with the Communist Party and other leaders of the independence movement of African Portuguese colonies may have influenced him in the writing of this novel. His description of the *bhatkar–mundkar* relation shows his Marxist views and socialist attitude toward the injustices by the rich against the poor. The book was published a few months before the Liberation of Goa which took place on December 19, 1961.

O Signo da Ira (The Sign of Wrath)

The story of *O Signo da Ira* borrows its template from the *bhatkar–mundkar* land relations in Goan society. The focus is on the elite landed gentry, in this case, the *bhatkar* Ligôr, and his *mundkars*, the subaltern Kunnbis who toil the soil for the benefit of the master. Orlando da Costa was influenced by the Portuguese neo-realist writers who tried to interpret the mores of society using the art of thinking. Their arguments were dialogs of reality and most of them focused on the lives of the tillers. *O Signo da Ira* illustrates the main concerns of neo-realism perfectly, as it was a movement committed to revealing the present in its harsh and naked reality, with its social injustices and gender inequality, while also suggesting corrective measures to build a better future.

Costa has used the need for food as a parameter to show how the rice cultivated by the *mundkars* was used to control them. He shows how they are obliged to give away even their daughters and granddaughters for a handful of food much needed for their subsistence. Natél, a young girl in her teens, is asked by the *bhatkar* to be sent to work at his place. Her grandfather knows what this means. It is not only the burden of hard work in the house but also implies that the girl would be sexually abused by the landlord and lose her virginity. Yet her grandfather is ready to accept the *bhatkar*'s fiat, even if unwillingly, as he knows that she would at least have a square meal at the *bhatkar*'s house and a place to stay when he dies.[57] The story revolves around *bhatkar* Ligôr and his *mundkars* Pedru, Jaqui, Gustin, Kitru, Bostião, Coinção, Natél, Rumão the tavern owner, Portuguese soldiers, and others.

At the beginning of the novel, the preparation for the cultivation of the rice field for *vangana* is described. As there have been no rains, the men start work on the fields by irrigating them with water from the *tollem*. They open up trenches for watering the rice fields. The areas that are closer to the *tollem*, the midland fields, would be irrigated by the water flowing through the pathways specially made for this purpose, and then tilled and readied for cultivation. The monsoons in Goa are active from June to September.[58] After the monsoon there would be no water for irrigation of the fields, therefore every village had at least one *tollem*.[59] The farmers would cultivate the second crop of rice from November.

There were rules to be followed for the management of the *tollem*. First, the monsoon paddy cultivated in this area had to be harvested within a certain fixed date. The sluice gate then had to be closed to allow the *tollem* to fill with rainwater. Xavier writes that the closing of the sluice gate of the Comunidade of Morombim-o-Pequeno *tollem* had to begin on August 29.[60] Thus, the closing of the gate, and the subsequent bountiful collection of rainwater, was the responsibility of the Comunidade. There were times when the monsoon crop of rice paddy was not fully ripened for harvesting, and the farmers would move an application to the authorities, the Administrador das Comunidades, not to close the sluice gate and to allow them a few more days to harvest the paddy. A maximum of two to three days was then granted.[61] Closing the gate in time was important because if there was no sufficient rainfall, it would not be possible to dam sufficient rainwater for the *vangana*.

As already mentioned, in the Comunidade of Morombim-o-Pequeno, in the village of Merces, the opening of the *tollem* had to be closed on September 3. Mr. Venancio João, seventy-six years old,[62] a *gaunkar* of the village Morombim-o-Pequeno, recollected an incident that took place during the Portuguese regime. A farmer tenant, Mateus Barreto, who was also a *gaunkar*, mistakenly sowed seeds that took longer to ripen. As per the rules, the sluice gate was closed on the chosen day.[63] To the farmer's bad luck, the rains started to fill the *tollem* and inundated his field. However, the paddy stalks were not completely submerged, so he used canoes and managed to harvest the crop. Therefore, those who cultivated the *sorodio* in this area had to be very careful, lest they suffer damage and lose the crop.

The *vangana* cultivation in Orlando's novel is important to the *mundkars*, who have not had sufficient rice for two years owing to bad harvests caused by excessive rains and insufficient seed. They hope that rice produced during this time will enable them to have a square meal a day till the next crop is harvested. The *mundkars* are pained to see no paddy in their hovels. They have only the ladyfinger (okra) and beans produced in the kitchen gardens. The *ambil* (gruel) made of *nachinim* (millet) grown around their huts helps stave off their hunger.[64]

The *mundkar* women pray to the Almighty for a good crop, using a sheaf of paddy kept in the oratory or near the saint's image in the house: *"Saiba, tende piedade de nós!"* (Lord, have pity on us!).

These crises where the means of subsistence, the daily rice, was not available occurred a number of times due to the famines in Goa and also in India, from where rice was procured to cover the deficit of production. Such a problem arose during the First World War. In 1918 the monsoons were very erratic and insufficient, not only in Goa but also in British India, and the agricultural yield was poor. There were apprehensions that the price of rice and other commodities would be excessively high. There were also worries that British India might stop exporting rice to Goa. This had happened once earlier when the British governor stopped exports due to insufficient production.[65] The Portuguese government then felt the need to form a committee to handle the crisis of subsistence faced by Goa. Thus, a committee was appointed which was asked to urgently study any means to provide a solution.[66] Although it made various proposals, it does not seem to have succeeded in implementing them. One suggestion was that the Comunidade should jointly pool in resources in cash which would be used to buy food. The main emphasis was on buying rice, which was the staple for the people, and distributing it through outlets specially set up for this purpose. It was pointed out that the purchase of rice should be done as early as possible and in sufficient quantity, as there could be an increase in the price of rice or even a ban on its export. Instead, the governor went ahead and bought rice at a high price without taking into consideration the suggestions of the committee.[67] This action of his led to the sale of rice at a higher price, and affected the consumer, especially the commoners with limited financial resources.[68]

The much-anticipated *vangana* crop represents the collective hope of the *mundkars*. The newly married couple, Quitrú and Gustin, are *mundkar* of *bhatkar* Ligôr, they hope that the *vangana* of the year will relieve them from deprivation and uncertainties. The wife hopes that their yet-to-be-born child will grow without hunger.[69] The child will be born soon after the *vangana* harvesting, and they hope there will be enough rice for the lactating mother.[70] However, Gustin is speechless when told that the yield has been good, but there is no paddy in the house.[71]

Bostião, who is secretly in love with Natél, Jaqui's granddaughter, looks forward to an opportune time to express his feelings and place his marriage proposal before him. He decides to approach Jaqui after the field has been cultivated. On second thought, he decides to wait until after the harvest time. Bostião ruminates: "After the harvest, paying off the debts, we get married."

In reality, the *vangana* is the restorative hope for everyone who lives in that village, for themselves, and for Gustin and Quitrú who are expecting their first child. Bostião knew that the *vangana* represented all the expectations he could have, the little that life gave to humble men like him, to the population of Kunnbis in times of love and death.[72]

It is important to note that during difficult times such as those portrayed in the novel thousands of poor Goans crossed the Goa border at Colem in search of jobs. It was not only men who emigrated, but women also followed.[73] There was actually a shortage of domestic workers because a sizable number of girls emigrated out of Goa to earn a more rewarding wage. This was not welcomed by the landlords who ended up not having enough workers or having to pay more due to the labor deficit.[74] Goa had minimal opportunities, without industries to generate enough jobs. As most of the people were agricultural workers for whom there were only seasonal jobs and work paid in kind, they had to find other odd jobs during the rest of the year.[75]

Costa also writes about the elderly *mundkars* who, unable to toil, had to beg every Saturday, at the *bhatkar*'s and other wealthy houses, in the hope of receiving a handful of rice. The prayer was repeated from door to door: "*Noman Morie, Noman Morie* ..." (Hail Mary, Hail Mary). A handful of rice was offered to the beggars who prayed for graces for themselves and the wealthy owners. However, when the rice production was not satisfactory alms were given in coins with which they could hardly buy any food.

The Metaphor of Rice

Orlando da Costa uses rice not only as the main source of wealth but also as a bargaining chip that is central to the narrative of *The Sign of Wrath*. This vital asset is also used in the exercise of power by men over women. The most dramatic example relates to Ligôr *bhatkar*, the young Natél, and Coinção.

Coinção, Pedru's youngest daughter, is twenty years old. According to tradition, when there were no male children, the youngest daughter bore the responsibility of caring for the parents. In this case, Coinção cared for her bedridden mother and alcoholic father. Knowing her predicament, no man came forward to marry her. Aware of this, Coinção proposed to go to Ligôr *bhatkar*'s home instead of Natél, so that the latter could marry Bostião, and also as a way of escaping loneliness and gaining some food. Coinção was aware of the fate of *mundkar* women who lived in Ligôr *bhatkar*'s home and knew that she was going to lose her virginity. But what difference would that make? She didn't have the love of any man. And perhaps the *bhatkar* would eventually find a boy to marry her ... so she thought.

In the narrative, *bab* Ligôr first sees Coinção on the feast day at his house and decides that she should come to work for him, ordering her to do so before the end of the year, even without the knowledge of her agreement with Natél. Once at the *bhatkar*'s house, Coinção is sent to the old storeroom between the barn and the attic, away from the facilities of the other maids. Behind this room stand the latrines. When she enters the room, she feels lonely and frightened, in the middle of a lot of worn-out things, looking at the old attic and smelling the strong odor of raw paddy. She knows that she will have to do the most difficult of jobs: apply cow dung to the ground, take paddy to the mill for husking, and carry out other chores like washing the toilet bowls of the old and sick. She would have to take her meals alone, away from the others. But to compensate for these drawbacks she feels that at least she will not suffer the pangs of hunger.

Thinking about what she left behind—the huts, Natél, Quitrú, her father walking in the middle of the night like a soul from another world, her mother whining on the floor-mat, and Rumão, the owner of the tavern, who had approached her, eager with desire, on a night when he took her father home totally drunk, leaving her with unforgettable sensations—Coinção has a heart full of anguish and restlessness. On her knees, her cold fists sink into a heap of rice, and with her head drooped, the anguished Coinção bites a mouthful of the unhusked paddy.[76]

It is at this moment that rice also becomes a kind of emotional catalyst in the submissive destiny of Coinção at the mercy of the will of Ligôr *bhatkar*. The moment of greatest sexual violence happens when *bab* Ligôr enters the barn with a lamp in his hands and throws Coinção onto the paddy which is spread on the floor. She is stunned by Ligôr's violence and coldness. She expected at least a word from him, but none was uttered.[77]

The sexual aggression against the character takes place literally on a heap of rice, a symbolic way that the narrator finds to show the connection between rice production, the characters' behaviors, and the power relations between them. Crushed by the silence, Coinção feels devastated and the harsh contact with the unhusked grain evokes in her a longing for the life she had before she came to the *bhatkar*, and a yearning for a gentler touch. The acrid smell of the paddy makes her feel like sneezing. That is when, under the increasing weight of Ligôr overpowering her, the rice beneath seems to wince, her head falls back, her eyes close, and the first tears of intense pain and grief pour forth.[78]

The landlord's cruelty toward the *mundkar*, now subordinated and fragile, continues to be exposed by the author. He describes the moment when Ligôr approaches Coinção to find out if she had any physical relationship with Rumão, after he learns that the latter was suffering from leprosy. He finds her lying naked on the mattress and wakes her up by stamping his foot on her thigh, communicating his intention that he had not come to sleep with her.[79]

Another aspect of the violence is seen when the men go to the tavern and Rumão informs them that the paddy has been stolen. One can see only sadness and suffering in the eyes of the *mundkars*. All their dreams have been crushed![80]

On hearing such heartbreaking news, the *mundkars* gather and go to meet the *bhatkar*, who tells them that the rice was stolen at the rice mill. The truth is that the corrupt Ligôr saw an opportunity to make money from selling the rice on the black market. In this way he would have additional money, which he badly needed to pay off his debts, partly acquired as the main celebrant of the annual church feast. He had earlier pawned off all the fields he had inherited from his ancestors, except for the current one, with rumors going around that the same has been mortgaged too.

Instead of trying to mitigate the sufferings of the *mundkars*, *bhatkar* Ligôr cynically suggests that they endure hunger for a few more months, and adds that the lack of rice was not a new phenomenon, as the same situation had recurred in the past. However, some *mundkars* gather the courage to retort and ask what their children's fate would be. To calm them down, he promises a handful of rice for the children from a portion he had in the barn for his family's consumption. The men look at him with a new spark—until then never seen—which the narrator leaves to the reader's imagination on whether it represents revenge, hate, or protest.[81]

Coinção, who sleeps in the attic of the barn, knows there is enough rice for a few months. She wants to help her people and sends a message to the *mundkars* that she will siphon off some rice to satisfy their needs. They plan on how to steal the rice. Bostião proposes that he will carry away the rice in the middle of the night. It is necessary to find a safe place to keep it, for distribution among everyone later. The place chosen is the tavern of Rumão, who in the meantime has been arrested for illegally trading in petrol smuggled from the Portuguese army by a soldier.

At that point, there is a tragic twist in the plot. When Rumão is arrested, they discover he has leprosy. When Father Antu visits him in prison, Rumão confesses that he had touched Coinção in pitch darkness. The priest, who was aware of Ligôr's immoral activities and knew about Rumão's interest in Coinção, informs the *bhatkar*. Angered by the knowledge that the leprosy-tainted Rumão had touched the maid, and though he was also aware of her virginity, Ligôr threatens Coinção and says he will resolve the matter. Unaware of what the *bhatkar* was referring to as she is ignorant of Rumão's condition, Coinção fears that he knew of the help she had given the *mundkars* to siphon off the rice. The poor girl is found dead the next day. Was it a murder or a suicide?

In the meantime, the Portuguese soldier who used to sell smuggled petrol kills Rumão and burns down the tavern to eliminate any evidence against him. The stolen rice hidden there is also reduced to ashes. Thus, all their tribulations are in vain. The desperation in the prayers of Quitrú, as they try to put out the flames devouring the rice, which they had managed to obtain with such difficulty and secrecy, shows that for these humble characters of the novel, rice was critical for survival. "*Saibá*! (Lord!) What will become of us!" "Why did you curse that rice that is ours, *Saibá*?"[82]

The "Hollow" Debates of the Provincial Congresses

The objective of the Congresso Provincial da Índia Portuguesa, when it was established, was to deal with matters that directly influenced the economic and social development of Goa. The core issue was agriculture in Goa, and the first session of the Primeiro Congresso was devoted to its improvement, with a focus on rice cultivation.[83] Its importance can be gauged from the thirty-one papers presented in the first session.[84] Suggestions had been made to the government to take over and distribute the properties belonging to the Comunidade to those who had interests in them. A paper by Leandro Pereira on "Desamortização dos terrenos" (Disentailment of Properties) did not favor such a closure, and suggested the continuation of ownership of the Comunidade's lands at the time in the existing form of a lease by *lanços* (parcels).[85]

One of the delegates of the Primeiro Congresso, F.X. Teodoro de Miranda, proposed the establishment of an agricultural credit system in the paper titled "Crédito Agrícola" (Agricultural Credit). Miranda strongly felt that for the progress of agriculture, it was vital to raise capital to fund the tillers. He suggested that a cooperative movement was the most efficient way to provide agricultural credit.[86] The importance of agricultural credit is seen in the several papers on this topic, which shows that external funding was an essential need for the cultivator to undertake the work in the fields.[87] This was required as most did not have adequate income and they needed loans. The money lenders from whom they had to borrow extorted high interest rates from them, which most of the time they were unable to repay. In a paper presented in the Segundo Congresso Provincial, the writer informs that the interest rates from private money lenders were as high as 50 percent or more.[88] He suggested that local bodies like the Confrarias and Mazanias should be allowed to give loans, as in the past, to spare the borrowers the burden of paying high interest on loans and the bureaucratic hurdles that led to delays. It is to be noted that there was no provision to prorogue the date of payment of *foros* (rent) to enable them to harvest the paddy. This is one of the reasons why people preferred to take loans from a moneylender, even though they had to pay high interest.[89]

The lease of Comunidade assets for agricultural activities was of great concern to the cultivators as it was critically linked to their sustenance. There were three papers on this issue. Jose Joaquim J. de Brito Ferrão, in the paper titled "Arrendamento nos campos comunais" (Lease in the Communal Fields), suggested that the subleases of the rice fields of the Comunidade should be prohibited.[90] Since the well-off sublet the extra land to profit from it, there was a need to fix the maximum number of parcels that each individual could lease.[91] According to the Code of Comunidade (1904), "each litigant can lease any number of parcels, by providing payment in equal installments when the value of the lot exceeds 1000 rupees."[92] This was also an important topic, with four papers on this subject.[93] Auctions meant much more than just bidding for the land. Over the years it had created endless disagreements and fights between opponents and even created long-time enmity between individuals and families.[94]

"Alterações ao Código das Comunidade" (Changes to the Code of Comunidades),[95] as the title suggests, proposed changes to the Code of the Comunidade (1904) to get rid of some of its office functionaries, as they exploited the cultivators. It suggested the suppression of the office of *sacador* and *vigia*.[96] These two could cause and indeed were causing, problems for the cultivators as they collected the dues from them. While doing so, they often imposed their own dubious conditions.[97]

The *sacadores* (tax farmers or revenue collectors) were individuals appointed by the Comunidade to collect the taxes and other dues from the cultivators, and their office was called the *sacadoria*. This office was auctioned every year in December and the charge was assumed at the beginning of January. The *gaunkars* of the village usually served as *sacadores* for their village. Since the job involved the collection of money, they had to furnish an adequate guarantee for the discharge of their duties without causing any loss to the Comunidade. The work was awarded to those who offered their services on payment of the least premium by the Comunidade and agreed to fulfill the conditions of the office. Since they were not paid any salary, they would exploit their authority by collecting extra money from the cultivators. The debtors of the *sacador* included all the bidders and lessees of the estates, the people entrusted with the watch and ward duties of the rice fields and coconut groves, and the other renters of the Comunidade together with their respective guarantors.[98]

The office of the *sacador* was introduced by the Portuguese in 1735 when the collection of rent and taxes was first enacted. The *Regimento* of that year instituted the *sacadoria*[99] headed by the *sacador* who was directly and personally responsible for all the rents and taxes. The *vigias* were guards of the plantation on the lands of the Comunidade. The cultivators could take away the harvest from the threshing grounds only with their permission. The *vigia* and *sacador* abused their restraining powers, which caused grave problems and losses to the cultivator who could not lift the paddy if he was not allowed to do so. Many a time the harvest was left to rot on the ground.

The main concern of the authorities and the cultivators was to reduce the cereal deficit and be self-sufficient in rice production. Two papers were discussed to overcome the deficit and find means and ways to reduce the shortfall of rice in Goa.[100] The rice deficit and how to overcome it was always on the minds of the people. Therefore, the Quarto Congresso held in 1921 was fully focused on this problem, with eight papers presented on it.[101]

The president of the Segundo Congresso Provincial in his inaugural speech, while reviewing the proceedings of the Primeiro Congresso Provincial, emphasized the importance of rice in Goa, calling it the "O pão do índio" (Native's bread). He strongly recommended an increase in the cultivable area and proposed that the government should provide its land for the purpose.[102] In this Congresso too, there were papers on agriculture and again three papers on agricultural credit, which shows how much importance was laid on agricultural loans.[103] Money was scant and greatly needed, not only to buy seed and labor, but also especially to pay the inflated rents.

Alçãs, *Alcistas*, and "Farcical" Public Auctions

Most of the inconveniences obstructing the growth in agricultural output arose from the system of leasing agricultural assets of the Comunidade.[104] The rice fields and other lands for cultivation were either distributed or allotted to the *gaunkars*. This distribution was done either annually or every three years through a public auction called *arrematação*.[105] Since only the *gaunkars* could bid, other cultivators had to take on the fields through subletting from those who bid in the auction. It was important to the bidders, who were well-off individuals making money by subletting, as well as to the cultivators. An auction would be discussed at social functions, and by the press as well as the writers of the time. It promoted chicanery, intrigues, and petty politics. The Comunidade had created a system of auction that suited them and not the cultivator. This was done through *alcistas* who were paid *alças* by the Comunidade. The government had laid down rules for the auction and one of them mentioned that *gaunkars* should not connive among themselves to bid and obtain land at a lower price, for which they would be prosecuted, indicating that such irregularities were indeed prevailing.

Those who offered the highest rent from amongst the *gaunkars, cuntocares,* and other *interessados* (the interested parties) got the rice fields and other cultivable lands beside the other estates of the Comunidade. However, it may be noted that only the *gaunkars* were admitted to offering a bid directly. The participation of the *interessados* was limited to offering bids at the public auction of Comunidade lands only through the *gaunkars.*[106] The right to bid was also given to *gaunkars*, *jonoeiros*, and other *interessados*, who were less than twenty-one years but over fifteen years, in the *arrematação de varzeas* (rice fields auction) of their respective Comunidade without even the authorization of their parents or guardians, provided that they furnished adequate guarantees.[107]

The literature of the time which writes about the auctions includes the novel *Jacob e Dulce* by Francisco João da Costa (GIP)[108] and the short story "Jacob e Carapinho" by the same author.[109] A lively discussion is depicted in *Jacob e Dulce* during the wedding of the chief protagonists, regarding the taxes imposed by the government.[110] Those present at the reception also discuss the scarcity of fish, problems of markets, and the triennial auction of the Comunidade.[111]

The *mando* writers did not lag behind in focusing on such an important subject and the politics behind it. The *mando* "Kurhtrech'm arrematasaum-om"[112] gives glimpses of how the auctions functioned. To ingeniously outsmart their rivals, the elites played caste politics by using the Mhars (or Mahars), members of the scheduled caste, to do the bidding in the Comunidade of Curtorim which was dominated by the Brahmin caste (Arnaldo de Menezes believed it to be an affront as potent as a curse).[113] This auction brought a lot of excitement and was celebrated with fireworks by the *non-gaunkars.*[114] However, the high price quoted by the successful bidder fleeced the poor cultivator. For wider dissemination, the auctions were publicized in the newspapers, and in this particular case, it was notified in the newspaper *A India Portugueza*.[115] The *Boletim Oficial*[116] which was the official organ of the government also published such notices.

The *mando* "Kity'm munn sanguchem lokako" by Francisco Menezes, probably written between 1906 and 1910, also discusses the auction held in Curtorim village, the granary of Goa.[117] According to him, the auction brought unrest amongst the people. He writes about two individuals who manipulated the proceedings in their favor. They insisted on an auction "of the sixth" and were successful in gaining the lease of the fields to the consternation of the goldsmith Ori, who was cultivating them earlier.

The auctions as already mentioned were a money-making racket, as the norms laid down benefited the *gaunkars* who sublet the fields to others at a higher price. The amount accrued in this transaction allowed some of them to live at the cost of the actual cultivators. Those who bid for the agricultural lands and sublet them to others were known as *alcistas*, as the difference between the rent lease they paid to the Comunidade and the amount they received after subleasing was called *alça*.[118] They were mostly capitalists and formed syndicates specialized in taking the lands of village communities on lease at the annual or triennial auction. The expression *alça* or *alcista* was also used in the pejorative form to label a person as an exploiter. The author Costa (GIP) uses it to degrade the character of Fr. Sertório Dantas, a relative of the main protagonist Jacob Dantas.[119]

This kind of system where only a few privileged persons could bid at the auction had to have repercussions. This system deprived the tillers of enjoying the fruits of their labor. Those who wished to cultivate the fields for their individual and family sustenance were at the mercy of the *gaunkars* who were allowed to bid for an unlimited number of fields as long as they were the highest bidders. They acquired the fields in order to sublet to those who were the actual cultivators, but at a much higher price. This system prevailed only in Goa and not in any other Portuguese colonies. *Alcista* is a person in India, who is paid a *tença* (profit) called *alça*.[120] This is defined as "presente que se dava ao medianeiro em algum negócio; lucros."[121] *Tença* also means "income" in India.[122] The *Glossário Luso-Asiático* defines *alça* as "a word used with peculiar meaning to show a profit which is accrued from subleasing, and sale of small objects (sundry) of the village community."[123] As the system was pernicious to the people in general, Marquês de Pombal, the prime minister of King D. José had ordered it to be abolished.[124] However, its banning was not successful and it prevailed even in the twentieth century in the pre-Liberation period. It was resented by the people so severely that the local press was compelled to request the government to prohibit it.[125]

In view of this criticism, the government decided to take action against the *alcistas* by issuing a Portaria (notification) to solve this scourge. This was required considering that in the majority of cases, the lessee did not cultivate the fields and simply sublet them to the cultivator via an oral contract and the lessee then enjoyed the profit. It was a known fact that in such transactions the lessee made a profit of 100 percent to the detriment of the cultivator and the Comunidade.

One measure to end the anomaly in the auction and lease would be to give fields on direct lease to the cultivators liberating them from *alcistas* who lived a parasitic life at the cost of the poor cultivator. Therefore, the governor-general issued Portaria no. 813[126] in 1930, based on the proposal of the Inspecção das Comunidade (The Inspection Committee of the Comunidade). The governor made provisions to oversee the activities, and ordered to have in each taluka a committee nominated by the administrator of the respective taluka.[127] The committee was entrusted with the duty of ascertaining the average income gained by leasing the parcels in the various Comunidades, the profits accrued on the same parcels when subleased, and the overall amount misappropriated from the income of the Comunidade's stakeholders and subsequently of the government, annually. In the same manner, the amount by which the state was deprived in the annual settlement of contributions was also to be ascertained.[128]

Subcommittees were formed at the *freguesia* (parish level) to help the Taluka Committees. Both committees had to be installed within eight days[129] and submit the report within ninety days.[130] A report detailing the actual state of affairs in each Comunidade, along with maps showing the denominations or designations of the *lanços*, the average amount for which they were leased, and the approximate amount by which they would be subleased, had to be submitted to the Inspecção das Comunidade.[131] Nevertheless, the subletting continued, as the system of leasing the fields was incorporated in the Code of Comunidade of 1933. The earlier Code of 1904 had been revised by a Diploma Legislativo, which had even then retained the system of the lease of lands by public auction.[132]

In 1937, there was a revision to the Code of 1933 vide Diploma Legislativo no. 966,[133] which while introducing certain further changes in the administrative setup, retained the system of lease of lands by public auction that existed in the Codes of 1904 and 1933. However, the revision required that persons intending to bid for the lease of lands in the auction had to furnish security. The majority of the cultivators were not in a position to furnish the required security. Consequently, only *gaunkars* or those having economic resources could bid in the auctions. Thus, it often happened that a single individual with resources and influence obtained a large number of agricultural land parcels, and sublet them to tillers on payment of *alçãs*.[134]

We have seen that a Portaria was issued in 1930 in a bid to stop the *alcistas*.[135] However, the Diploma Legislativo no. 966 of 1937, with its provision that the bidder must furnish security, continued to benefit financially well-off individuals. To prevent this abuse and eliminate the middlemen Governor Jose Cabral then passed the Diploma Legislativo no.1035 dated December 23, 1938, which prohibited subletting, required renters to cultivate lands directly, and made some other provisions for better management of the lease.

However, the story of *alcistas* and *alçãs* also had another side. When discussions were going on to eliminate the middlemen through the Diploma Legislativo of 1938, not everyone blamed the *alcistas* as ambitious and exploitative. The newspaper *A Vida*, which had published several articles on the various aspects of the problems of rice since its inception,[136] carried a comment saying that the *alcista* guaranteed the income of the Comunidade[137] and reported that many poor people, widows, and those who could not make prompt payments were helped by the *alcista* as he would directly pay the Comunidade.

There were also others who defended them. Camilo Severino Rodrigues wrote a series of articles in *A Vida*, wherein he expounded why and how the system of *alçãs* became a part of the Comunidade lease system.[138] In the beginning, the Portuguese maintained the autonomy of the Comunidade, but over the years when the government required money for expenses, it began to demand a compulsory tribute by claiming the right of direct ownership of lands by the king of Portugal and maintaining that the *gaunkars* were simply renters. Thus, *coxi vorodo*, originally a voluntary contribution, was continued as a compulsory tribute. The villages were also getting depopulated due to migration, which led to the neglect of cultivation of the lands. Some, though apprehensive of sharing their status as *gaunkars*, surrendered their *tangas* (shares) to others. With the transfer of shares, the number of outsiders having a right to participate in the income of the Comunidade increased, which gave rise to frequent disputes and created disharmony in the village. Gradually the Comunidades were deprived of the autonomy they had enjoyed, and their approach progressively changed. With the neglect of the cultivation of fields and the *gaunkars* migrating, the Comunidade did not have enough revenue to pay the *foros* to the government and look after the infrastructure of the village, and therefore at that point had to borrow to make the payments.[139]

Though there were shareholders who were investing in buying shares, they did so only to enjoy the benefits of the income they would accrue annually.[140] Many of them being outsiders, not *gaunkars*, were not interested in the management of the institution.[141] Since the income was from agricultural land through the lease, the Comunidade felt that it would be better to have single or more individuals, the *alcistas,* take on the lease of the fields and then sublet them to make a profit. The onus of paying the Comunidade fell upon the *alcista*, who had to make good the lease payments, whether the crop production was satisfactory or not, since he was the direct lessee. Of course, the system also led to abuse and extortion of the cultivator by the *alcista* as already discussed.[142]

Now the bidder (alcista) became a sort of broker for the cultivator and assumed the responsibility for the income, non-cultivation of the fields, and all the liabilities listed in the Comunidade Code. He also assumed the consequences of the defaults of the cultivator and had to endure the difficulties in dealing with the bureaucracy. And finally, the bidder guaranteed the safety of what in its nature itself is unsafe—the successful cultivation of the fields. To the comment made that "[t]he alcista is an immoral person, born of the excesses of ambition," Rodrigues presents the other side of the issue. According to him, the *alcista* was the product of the shareholder's carelessness, whose only interest in the Comunidade was to go there once a year to receive his income. He concluded that the income paid to shareholders resident outside the village was money that came out of the village, never to return, and that the results of "absentee-landlordism" had brought about the impoverishment of the villages.[143]

The Diploma Legislativo of 1938 was supposed to be a progressive legislation, as it prohibited the subleasing of agricultural fields and made it mandatory for the lessee to personally cultivate them. However, to protect its interests, the government included the clause that the lease amount of the fields should not be less than what was already being paid earlier.[144] Thus, the rent that the cultivator had to pay directly to the village community would be the same as, if not more than, what he had to pay under the previous system to the middlemen. It was also found to be ineffective in practice as the direct tillers, who had the influence to secure low rents for the lands leased by virtue of their having previously cultivated them, managed to retain the fields. However, this state of affairs led to proportionately higher rents for other lands, since the aggregate rent on the paddy lands held by the Comunidade was not to be less than that obtained in the previous auction.[145]

The implementation of the clause that there should be no subletting was criticized by Tristão Bragança Cunha who argued that although the government had stopped the services of the middlemen (who lost the benefit of collecting alça from the lessee), it did not benefit the cultivator as the government fixed a higher rent and thereby made the cultivator pay more money to the lessor.[146] In the end, it was the government that actually benefited, by getting a higher tax collection from the Comunidade.[147] The government did this as it was beneficial to the administration, in order to raise the land tax.[148] Further, the rent was fixed in an arbitrary manner, to be accepted by the cultivators without any possibility of reduction.

There were other orders related to leases, auctions, and payments, but the government did not succeed in curbing the malpractices of the influential *gaunkars* and others.[149] There were quite a few changes in the Code of Comunidade, 1933, depending on the need and practical implementation. The government, therefore, proposed a new code to encompass all the changes made after the date of promulgation and to fulfill the demands of those times, for which a committee of experts was appointed to give recommendations. This materialized on April 15, 1961, when a new Código das Comunidade, 1961 was promulgated.[150] However, the pernicious auction system was reintroduced in this new Code of 1961. The rent paid by the actual lessee or the tiller of the soil before Liberation and especially after the auction held in 1961 in many cases exceeded 50 percent of the estimated gross production. After the Liberation of Goa, representations were made to the new administration, which at the time was under the military governor, that the auctions of 1961 were detrimental to the cultivators as the bidding was done hastily and that the bids were higher than the reserved price fixed based on the *calculo* (assessment).[151] The military governor considered these representations and passed orders effecting changes to benefit the cultivators. For example, on September 12, 1962, the governor ordered that the rents payable by the lessees of paddy fields of the Comunidade should not exceed 50 percent of the assessment.[152] The Code is still in use at present, after the Liberation of Goa on December 19, 1961, with further amendments made by the government to suit its interests.

Campanha de Arroz (Rice Campaign)—An Exercise in Futility

The economic problems faced worldwide in the 1920s and 1930s did not spare the Estado da Índia which also reeled under the effects of the First World War and the Great Depression.[153] To overcome these economic problems measures had to be taken to make the territory self-sufficient in rice production. Toward this aim, the government initiated a campaign called Campanha de Arroz (Rice Campaign) and issued a Portaria in this regard.[154]

A Junta Central (Central Committee) was created to implement the Portaria, with the Inspector of Comunidade as its chairman. Its scope included the collaboration of the official technical agricultural stations in Goa to help in the improvement of agriculture. To enact this Portaria, some of the fields belonging to the Comunidade were used to experiment with new methods of rice cultivation. They were also asked to work on a project wherein the uncultivated and unused land would be used to conduct the experiments. For example, the Comunidades in Ponda taluka were asked to release the land which they had in their possession, including hillocks that were not cultivated.[155] The land was grouped into two categories: (1) for the cultivation of rice, (2) land used for other types of cultivation, and remaining land not suitable for agricultural exploration.[156] The government also decided to reestablish the Comunidade of Assolna, Velim, and Ambelim and revoked the Administração Rural (Rural Administration) of these villages through a Diploma Legislativo.[157] This would be effective from January 1, 1932, and the fields would be given again on lease.

The Campanha de Arroz by itself, though promoted with good intentions, would—if successful at all—take time to achieve the goal of having enough production of rice to overcome the shortage and stop the import. Therefore, the government needed to take other parallel measures. The Portuguese government had convened a conference, the Conferência Económica, to discuss various economic problems faced by its territories.[158] The government aimed to protect and guarantee the home product, which had competition from imported goods, by not only providing an assured market but also with recompensing prices, keeping in mind the interests of the producers as well as consumers. It was decided that such measures should first be taken in connection with rice which was imported even from Rangoon (the erstwhile capital of Burma, today Myanmar) and Sind in India, at a very low price.[159] This resulted in a loss to the *bhatkar* for whom selling at the price of imported rice was not viable and also to the Comunidade which could not sell their rice at a higher price causing reduced *zonn*[160] to the *gaunkars* and dividends to the shareholders. Besides, the government also lost revenue which it would have accrued from the Comunidade as tax.

In order to solve the problem of the unavailability of rice, the government of Goa decided to implement the article in the Diploma Legislativo and organized the Conferência Económica in Goa. This conference convened for the first time on March 6, 1931, at Panjim. One of the points discussed at the session was the suggestions asked by the governor, regarding the protection and cultivation of local rice.[161] He had invited public opinion regarding what measures should be adopted to protect local cultivation and wanted to know if it was advisable for the government to impose a variable tax on imported rice.[162] Luis de Menezes, the editor of the *Diário da Noite,* who was against such a move, wrote: "It is about rice, and the major part of the people of Goa is known to live only on rice. The question of rice for the people of Goa is a question of life or death."[163] *Diário da Noite* reports the comments of Vicente Barbosa, Bernardino Camilo da Costa, and José Inacio de Loyola, all belonging to the landed gentry. Each one of them had differing opinions regarding the imposition of tax. Barbosa opined that a very heavy tax ought to be imposed: eight *tangas* per *kandil,* and that the price should be uniformly fixed at eighteen rupees, for both imported and locally grown rice. On the other hand, Bernardino Costa proposed a medium tax and suggested that the income accrued from it should be given as prizes to the cultivators. Loyola suggested that a cooperative society of the Comunidade should be established to import rice, and that the profit from the sale of imported rice should be used to facilitate the export of coconuts to Europe. On weighing these three proposals it can be noted that the people as such would gain no advantage. On the contrary, they would have to buy rice at a higher price. The tax would not benefit the common folk but would give the government a net return of twelve lakh rupees, making it the highest beneficiary.

However, from the reports of proceedings, it is clear that the proprietors would also benefit. When Bernardino da Costa, along with V. J. Figueiredo, proposed an increase in the tax, he argued that there was no reason to be scared to implement such taxes as the money was required by both the government and the landlords. His statement made it very clear whom he was defending, as he questioned whether the landlord and the government employees should perish. According to him, if this tax was not implemented the landlords would not be able to cultivate the lands. If they did not cultivate, there would be no revenue for the government, and the state in turn would have no money to pay for its staff.[164]

V.J. Figueiredo added to this argument by saying that this tax was not for the benefit of the *bhatkar* but for the benefit of the poor people as he claimed that if the *bhatkars* were not to cultivate there would be no work for them. Luis de Menezes ironically remarked on the comments made by Costa and Figueiredo: "I don't know who is speaking the truth!" He also took a jibe at the *bhatkar* who accrued benefits of the *alça* by subletting to the cultivators the fields they acquired at the auction, as henceforth they would have to directly cultivate them.[165]

The proposal to tax imported rice was not well received as it would only favor the government and a few landlords at the cost of the majority of the people. The press debated in the papers and most of them were against this proposal as it was unfavorable to the people. The *Diário da Noite* carried excerpts from different local newspapers that included *A Terra* and *Anglo-Lusitano* which opined that the tax was not viable.[166] The proponents also discussed and defended the tax in the press.[167] Vicente Alvares proposed to impose a tax on rice and to lower the export tax on coconut. He also suggested offering a bonus, so that the price of coconut would reach forty rupees for 1,000 coconuts, which was the price fixed by the British government.[168]

The debate over the tax continued appearing in the local press, but in spite of the majority opposing it, the government went ahead and announced a "tax surcharge" on imported rice to balance the price difference between the imported and local rice by issuing a Diploma Legislativo called "Sôbre-taxa de equilíbrio."[169] The government justified the surcharge by citing:

> It is necessary to ensure that the effects of the economic crisis are mitigated. Considering that this objective could be achieved using a set of measures and first of all, it would be important, to ensure local production, in competitive conditions, not only a safe market but also more rewarding prices, within the harmonious limits of interests of the producer and the consumer. Considering the importance of rice in the life of the people of the territories, arrangements for it had to be determined first.[170]

The Diploma Legislativo "established and imposed a variable rate called 'surcharge tax for equilibrium' on the import of both types of rice for consumption, without the husk and with husk."[171] This tax would be equal to the difference between the cost of local production and the cost of imported *kandil* of 160 liters after it was cleared from the Customs' warehouse.[172] This tax would remain effective for as long as the existing agricultural crisis continued. In 1931, the year of the issue of the diploma, the tax would be 14 *tangas* for rice with husk and one rupee fourteen *tangas* without husk.[173]

It was quite a large amount. The tax would also apply to the rice already imported before this diploma was implemented and was lying in the warehouse of the Customs Department.[174] Another diploma correlated to the one on surcharge tax was published on December 30, 1932,[175] which also suggested the formation of a fund, "Fundo do Fomento." It would be used to improve agriculture and award prizes to the farmers, thus aiming to incentivize them.[176] Further, money from this fund could not be used for any other purpose than what has been laid down in the diploma.[177] This clause was reiterated in a subsequent Diploma Legislativo issued in 1934.[178] Rice that was imported for seeds was exempted from any surcharge tax; however, a declaration had to be issued by the authorities in this regard and produced by the importer.[179]

The diploma also allowed the government "to curb any abuse or speculation by limiting and fixing the prices."[180] Measures were also recommended to prevent an unjustified increase in the price of rice, with and without husk, wholesale, and retail, in order to avoid any increase in the cost of living.

The government also had the power to limit the import of rice, which created problems due to the unavailability of rice.[181] This also shows the politics of the government which sought to gain control over the people by regulating the supply of this staple food and benefiting the local proprietors and businessmen, and even indirectly encouraging the black market, while claiming to help the locals. As mentioned, two other orders were issued regarding this surcharge tax.[182] Diploma no. 615 modified the variable tax called "sobretaxa de equilibrio" on the import of rice for consumption with and without husk.[183] Thus, we find that though the aim was to reduce the price of the staple and lower the cost of living, on the contrary taxes were imposed to increase the price of rice to protect the landowners and benefit the government.

The surtax was not well received by the majority and was criticized in the press as benefiting only the government and the *bhatkars* or at least the big landowners among the latter. In fact, the association of landowners from Salcete sent a representation to the Municipality opposing such a move. They claimed that after the Diploma Legislativo was implemented the laborers increased their salary by 20 to 40 percent, which prevented the cultivators and the landlords from carrying out any kind of work in the fields or coconut groves. Since no work was undertaken by the landlord due to the rise in wages, the laborer was left unemployed and deprived of a regular salary.[184] However, the government which was also looking for extra revenues was not moved by such criticism and proceeded to implement and maintain the tax, despite the repercussions to the export commodities from Goa. For example, in retaliation to the surtax on rice, the British Indian government imposed a heavy tax on coconuts from Goa affecting the revenue of the *bhatkars* and exporters, leaving them in a dire state. In this regard D.D. Kosambi writes:

> When the total yield seems to reach sufficiency—which is what the official 1937 figures are supposed to prove like other reports before

> them—a duty was put upon the British rice imports always necessary for feeding Goa. This brought a very heavy retaliatory customs duty upon all food products from Goa to British India and (along with the 1929–33 depression) ruined the market for one of the principal exports to British India, coconuts.[185]

However, the remark by Kosambi that the tax was imposed because there was sufficient production of rice—as seen from the Goa government's report—contradicts the intention of the diploma which states that it was to solve the current financial problem faced by the territories. This same objective was also published in the other two subsequent amendments to this order issued in 1932 and 1934, emphasizing the protection of the local rice growers' cause, as the need of the hour.

The reports may not be truthful about the existing problem for the reason that they could have been manipulated according to the government's directives, which had pledged to improve and solve the situation through the improvement of agriculture using the surcharge tax.

Secondly, Kosambi refers to the report of 1937—although he doesn't identify and specify it—and the surcharge tax was implemented from the date it was issued on October 23, 1931. Besides, if there was sufficient rice produced in Goa to satisfy the needs of the people, there would not be a demand for rice in the first place. Reports on this appeared in the press too. Though freedom of expression was restrained due to the prevailing censorship[186] some writers courageously expressed their views to reveal the truth and the indifference of the government toward solving the problems of the people. The surcharge was solely to benefit the government—by way of taxes—and the landlords who had rice in their stock and could not sell, as it was more expensive than imported rice. Unsold rice meant that the *bhatkars* would be left with the stock in their storerooms.

Undoubtedly, the main reason for imposing the tax was to accrue revenue for the government and to sell the rice of the landlords. It was never revoked, as later during the economic blockade period imposed by the Indian government in 1955, the surcharge resurfaced, as has been discussed in the chapter "The Economic Blockade and the Pangs of Hunger." A parallel can be drawn here, regarding the export of local goods to British India, with the action taken by the government of India when it stopped importing Goa's produce like coconut, areca nut, mangoes, etc., to make the 1955 blockade successful.

By imposing the surtax, the government made the staple food of the working class costlier, without realizing that they were moving in a vicious circle. Costlier rice would provoke a further rise in wages and therefore additional expenses in the cost of production while also lowering the purchasing capacity of the consumer. However, some individuals wrote in favor of the surcharge. One of them defended the higher price fixed as well as the quantity of rice imported by the government, maintaining that it helped the cultivator and the landlord, and in this case also the Comunidade. He further added that those who do not cultivate and depend on imported rice are few, less than one-third of those who cultivate.[187] But the ground reality was different since the majority of those who cultivated did not have enough to eat as the area under cultivation was small and they would have to buy rice to feed their families.

This protectionism of the government has been discussed and criticized by Tristão Bragança Cunha in his essay "Rice Problem in Goa," which proves the argument that it was not "when the total yield seems to reach sufficiency" that the surtax was imposed. In fact, the colonizers did not regret the almost-famine conditions that existed among the people in Goa since their only objective was more and more revenue for the state. Cunha remarked that this scandalous increase in taxes was but another example of the failure of the government to resolve Goa's rice problem. He discussed the enhancement of the taxes and tariffs on the products that were imported from British India, as according to him the Portuguese government considered that the neighboring British India territory was another distant country and not one on which they depended fully, even though the greater part of the foodstuff most indispensable to the life of the people in Goa came from there.[188] Similarly, the export of local produce was mainly to neighboring India. And most importantly, the money in the form of remittances to the local budget, amounting to over ten million rupees, which helped to balance the economic bankruptcy of the state, also came from British India.[189] In spite of all the evidence for the need to maintain a lower tariff on imports as well as exports by Goa, the local government enhanced these to the detriment of the people, who had to buy goods at higher rates.

Cunha wrote several articles in which he discussed and criticized the Portuguese government. In one, he critiqued the decision to impose customs tariffs, since these were to be paid both from the country of origin (the exporter) and also by those importing it at the country of consumption. In another article, he explained in detail the surcharge tax on rice.[190] To prove his point he prepared a table to show the amount of tax that had been collected and benefited the government for a period of seven years from 1931 to 1937.[191] Table 1.4 gives details of the tax collection for this period.

Thus, it is observed that besides this huge sum of thirty lakh rupees, the money paid by the consumers due to the excessive profits permissible

Table 1.4 Tax collection from 1931 to 1937

Year	Super-tax in Rs.	Ordinary tax in Rs.
1931	71,181	1,77,460
1932	4,03,286	1,93,030
1933	4,88,779	2,34,704
1934	5,87,684	1,84,644
1935	68,850	2,10,000
1936	1,05,519	1,15,800
1937	1,05,438	1,24,561
Total	18,30,737	12,41,119

[Source: T.B. Cunha, *Goa's Freedom Struggle,* Bombay: Dr. T.B. Cunha Memorial Committee, 1961,124]

to the merchants under the system of permits also created misery for the common man. Further, rice became expensive as a consequence of these heavy duties and profits realized, and to make it worse, rice which was almost the sole food of the Goan people had to be imported in large amounts from neighboring British India, where it was obtained at Rs. 6 per bag. The cost in Goa was Rs. 13 per bag and sometimes Rs. 16 thanks to profiteering by merchants.[192] Though it was decreed that the surtax money collected under the pretext of protection to local rice would be allocated for development, augmentation, and production, or even for decreasing the cost of cultivation, it appears that not much was utilized.[193] On the contrary, this high burden had only contributed to make local rice production even more expensive. Cunha even suggested pulling down customs barriers which he termed as "asphyxiating" the Goans and surprisingly proposed restoring the controversial Customs Union with India, which he said "in our evil hour, we had been forced to renounce."[194]

Rice deficiency was felt throughout the period of study and the newspapers were quite vocal about the issue, criticizing the government policies that were against the common folk and favored the landlords. Whenever any new legislation and measures were taken regarding rice or rice-related issues, that did not benefit the people, there would be a reaction not only from the editors but also from columnists and others. As already mentioned, *A Vida* regularly carried articles on rice matters. The editor of *A Voz da India*, Antonio Sequeira wrote about the problem of rice on the first page, as the people had no rice and the government's measures were not people-friendly. For instance, the government decided not to requisition rice from *sorodio*, as they would import rice from British India, which unfortunately was also in crisis and did not have rice for export as they needed it for their own consumption. Another measure was to stop rationing when there was no sufficient rice.[195] Both these decisions went against the people as they led to a scarcity of rice. In the chapter "Economic Blockade and Pangs of Hunger" rice problems have been dealt with for that period (1955–61).

Thus, we have seen how the *bhatkar*, the *gaunkar*, and the government used rice to subjugate the subaltern *mundkars* and tenant cultivators. The first two had the agricultural land in their possession and the third enacted laws to favor them. The efforts of the elites who prioritized the rice problem during the various Congressos conferences as well as the government's efforts to increase the rice output, whether by establishing the Conferência Económica or the Campanha de Arroz, failed to improve the availability of rice. The "Sôbre-taxa de equilíbrio" imposed by the government on imported rice, with the objective of protecting local rice production, did not benefit the common folk either, as they then had to buy rice at a higher price. On the contrary, it benefited a few powerful landlords, the Comunidades, and the government, the latter being the major beneficiary.

2

Food, the Memory Connector: A Study of Goan Folklore and Other Forms of Literature

Introduction

This chapter analyzes the folk literature of Goa, showing how the *dulpods*[1] and other forms of literature convey memories that symbolize the local identity connected to food—a representation that bonds people and family together.

Academic works related to Goa on this subject are very sparse. Even otherwise, there are not many studies directly related to food and memory, especially self-defined works that can be referred to evaluate this theme readily.[2] However, a few books have been used as studies in this field, notable among which are those of Marcel Proust, David Sutton, and Carole Counihan. Proust's book was a work of fiction and not an academic exercise.[3] His "episode of the madeleine" laid the foundation for studies on this subject. The novel narrates the story of a young boy's journey through life. An incident of eating tea-soaked madeleines reminds him of his childhood practice of eating tea-soaked cake with his aunt. This arouses involuntary memories in Proust that enable him to remember his past childhood home and his surroundings, including the town he lived in. He uses this trope of sensations reminding him of previous experiences throughout the novel. The madeleine incident shows the power of food to evoke some of the deepest memories.

J. H. Mace in *Involuntary Memories*[4] writes that there are at least three different contexts within which involuntary memory arises.[5] The most common occurrences are those happening in everyday life and in everyday mental functioning. They give the impression that they come into conscious awareness naturally.

Olfactory information memories are more expressive than those associated with signals perceived through other sensory systems like verbal or visual information.[6] Common daily practices connected to the olfactory senses for a Goan could be eating a daily meal of fish, curry, and rice, bringing to mind an experience suggested by the sense of taste and smell.

The Symbolic Importance of Food in Local Identity

Some authors have dedicated their work to understanding the importance of food in the development and strengthening of local identities. David Sutton's *Remembrance of Repasts* offers an account of the inter-relationship of culture, food, and memory. Sutton shows how the "food of memory" is also the "memory of food." By questioning links between food, consumption, and memory and using them in enlightening ways, he makes a case for his main statement: that the food-memory connection is different from other memory connections, and that the constructed relationship between food and memory is culturally specific and cross-culturally variable.[7]

People feel strongly about the things they eat, as food is essential to life. Yet the things we eat often seem utterly prosaic. When food is consumed, unlike other material goods, its concrete substance is gone. But the consumption of food is linked socially to all else in life and the mind, including previous and future acts of consumption. Although consuming makes it disappear, food binds time.[8] Sutton adds that if "we are what we eat," then "we are what we ate" as well.[9] His work deals with many of the diverse facets of what we call memory. For instance, the seasonal food cycle shapes prospective memory by inducing one to look forward in reference to past events.[10]

This phenomenon of the seasonal food cycle is evident in Goa. The summer season brings a variety of fruits that people eagerly wait for, such as mangoes, *kandans* (wild blackberries), kokum, *jambhalam* (Syzygium cumini), *jangama, zamang* (Flacourtia cataphracta), and *churnam* (wild berries). However, it is the mango, the king of the Goan fruits, that easily evokes memories for those who lived in Goa.

The coconut tree
The coconut tree produces vinegar,
Sugar, wine, and oil;
Water, wood and filaca

It's a kind of milk.
...

From the part that is inside
The coconut, the curry is made[11]

The importance of the coconut tree in the Goan scenario can be gauged by the number of trees that dot the entire territory, planted by the *bhatkar* to earn income. Incidentally, the *mundkars* were not allowed to plant coconuts or mango trees near their residential areas, as these two gave good returns for the *bhatkar*. The coconut tree was seen as a provider of sustenance for the family as no part of the tree was wasted—the fruit and sap (toddy) for consumption, the rest as artifacts, fuel, or rafters for the house.[12] The coconut tree was important to the government and fetched good revenue through the export of coconuts and dry copra to British India. Most importantly, the revenue accrued on the sale of palm *feni* was substantial.[13]

The alcohol cess was the highest revenue earner for the government, as argued in the chapter "Drink That 'Cheers' but Brings Tears," and the maximum collection was on palm *feni*. Many villagers were employed to extract toddy, and quite a few families depended on this trade. Besides *feni*, the toddy was used to make jaggery, which was the sweetener for Goans.[14] Toddy was also used to leaven bread.

The toddy tapper had to climb the tree thrice a day, in the morning, afternoon, and evening, to extract sap.[15] Such an important profession[16] merited a *dulpod* that reflects the activity of the *render* (toddy-tapper). There is the toddy-tapper with a sharp knife in one hand and a gourd pot in the other. The poet calls upon the toddy-tapper to climb the tall coconut tree briskly. "If the earthen pot on the top of the tree breaks, do not worry," he says, "but take care of the gourd pot." After all, it's in the gourd pot that the toddy-tapper collects the toddy, which is an important revenue earner.[17]

The coconut kernel was not only the basic ingredient in curries; it had various other uses, both culinary and in rituals. In Goa, on the occasion of laying the foundation stone of a new house, pieces of raw coconut along with coconut jaggery are served to the guests. This is symbolic, as both represent the *godchem vonn*,[18] the sweet savory served during a traditional Goan meal like *bikareamchem jevonn*.[19] In the past, Goa observed many rites, at birth and death. The distribution of *sou disache chonne*[20] to the relatives and neighbors continues to be followed, though with less frequency.[21] It was believed that on this day the child's destiny would be written, as in the proverb *Sotven boroilolem tem zalem* (what destiny has written will happen).

According to folklore, the sixth day from the birth of the child was shrouded by some mysterious danger of which none spoke, but all knew and understood. On this crucial day, a wake would be held till midnight, with members of the family, relatives, and neighbors taking part in the vigil, and special precautions being taken against the imaginary danger lurking in the background of superstitious beliefs.[22] Many Catholic families celebrated the *ladainha* (litany) in honor of Mother Mary, seeking her blessings to ward off any disaster.[23]

Coconut is used as an ingredient not only in curry but also while preparing vegetables and some dishes that require gravy. It is also used for preparations in various *goddechem* (sweet dishes), where coconut is the main ingredient along with jaggery, which is why *merenda*—the evening tea snack—is also called *jagrada*—from Portuguese *jagra* for jaggery. In a short story, Lucio Rodrigues writes about a greedy son-in-law who is served some *goddechem* on a table, like the traditional *pudde*,[24] pancakes, and *shir-vohio* (rice vermicelli).[25] There are other *goddechens* made with lentils and beans that are boiled and added to the jaggery-coconut mixture.[26] Food cooked in coconut oil has a distinct flavor, and the oil is also used for medicinal purposes. Tender coconut, with its soft and jelly-like kernel, is a favorite delicacy. Tender coconut water is used as a refreshing and soothing beverage and is given to patients who cannot eat solid foods. In emergencies, it even substitutes for glucose saline.

Mango, the Favorite

Lucio Rodrigues, in an essay titled "Pink and Green," gives a lucid account of mango through his experiences which connect the past to the present.[27] No Goan who has lived in Goa must have missed the experience of relishing a green mango the way it is traditionally eaten. This is how Rodrigues describes his experience, to which many can relate: "the greenest of the green, which you stuff with chilies and salt and spices, and smacking your lips crunch away the hot and pungent delicacy. It is a kind of cocktail. Full of pep in it."[28]

There was also another method of eating a raw mango that many would recollect. It was stuffed with only green chilies and salt and then compressed. The tender mango should not have developed the stone so one could cut through the soft undeveloped seed. Also, the mango for this "cocktail" had to be from specific trees. Grafted trees did not give fruit suitable for this enjoyment. It was only the tender ones, but not of all trees. It was the *khuntt*, which grows on its own from discarded seeds, not from the grafts.[29]

For those who are familiar with mangoes, it is easy to grasp the intricacies of their varieties. There is no better way to differentiate between the types of mangoes than in vernacular Konkani: *Ambo* is for the mango, the bigger size, which can be cut and includes fruits of the grafted trees; and *ambli* is for the smaller variety used to make pickles. The latter's pulp, when ripe, is traditionally sucked through an opening at its top.

Green tender mangoes were in demand early in the season, before the stone developed, to preserve in salt brine and make pickles to be consumed especially during the monsoons as an appetizer, when there was no fish or to accompany *canjee*. This salted mango was consumed with *canjee* when a patient could not have spicy or fried food. Interestingly, the tavern owners would keep slices or small pieces for their clients' pleasure. To prepare these mangoes, large *boião* (porcelain containers) were used, in which these were added to concentrated salt brine with some red chilies. These salted mangoes could be served directly or pickled with stuffed masala (mixed and ground spices), and were called *boriello*.

There were at least a hundred varieties of mangoes in Goa, and favorites depended on the tastes of individuals.[30] But how they were eaten depended on the variety of the mango. Malcorada was a favorite of most and usually cut into slices and eaten, but a child would enjoy eating the mango as a whole, with the mango pulp spread over their hands, mouth, and face and the juice dripping right down to the elbows.[31]

The mango season was looked forward to by the migrant Goans from Bombay and Africa, who actually planned their vacations to enjoy these fruits. In "They Come and Go," the story is told of an old mother who eagerly waits for her son and his family's visit to her after five years.[32] They are coming from Nairobi, and the year is 1939 when people traveled on long journeys by ship. When the mother receives the letter informing her about the arrival of her son, she replies that she is waiting anxiously for them to come and also asks the son to inform the children that there are a lot of mangoes that year.[33] The mother also makes preparations for their holidays, and to recreate a typical Goan holiday, she goes to the Friday fair at Mapusa and brings the necessary provisions—chilies, onions, green mangoes, chicken, etc.[34] The emigrants, besides eating the fruit during their stay, would also take with them mangoes, pickled raw mangoes, and chutneys of the ripe ones for their consumption as well as for gifting to friends and relatives who looked forward to satisfying their nostalgic yearnings.

Mango was also a revenue earner. Even though it was seasonal, its export was substantial. The economic blockade was detrimental to the export of mangoes, causing loss to the *bhatkar*. On the other hand, a reference in the *Goan Tribune* newspaper relates how the mango came to the rescue of the poor people during the same period. During the summer months, people could fill their hungry stomachs with the delicious mangoes and jackfruits, which were cheap because of the inability to export.[35]

The importance of the fruit to the landlord is portrayed by Leslie de Noronha in the novel *The Mango and the Tamarind Tree*, in which the Albuquerque family uses the mango as a cash crop, with the landlady having converted rice fields into mango plantations, as they would provide the much-desired revenue.[36] In fact, Peter Nazareth's pertinent comment on the novel shows the importance of the mango for the Goans, be they poor or rich—"the mango … was an abundant staple for the poor masses, yet also a profit-making staple for the enterprising wealthy class."[37] Noronha describes how the mangoes were also used to make *mangada* (mango jam), which was a delight for the youngsters as well as older family members.[38] The importance of the mango as a commercial crop made the owners take good care of the crop, to avoid loss of revenue.[39]

It is not only Leslie de Noronha who wrote about the mango; there are others who extol its importance. Way back, we had João de Melo de Sampaio (1832–1909), a Portuguese *descendente* (descendant) born in Goa, who wrote a long poem in praise of mangoes, describing the attributes of a few of them. Melo de Sampaio claimed that the mango from Goa was the best and definitely better than any fruit from Portugal or Brazil, the latter having many, or for that matter than any other fruit in the world.[40]

> Portugal has beautiful fruits
> In Brazil, there are also
> But like our Goa's
> No other land has them[41]

Melo de Sampaio compares the aromatic and tasty Xavier, a mango with the perfume of roses, and adds that a bunch of roses cannot surpass its aroma, as the mango is equivalent to a thousand buds of the flower.

> The Xavier is all aroma
> Of a thousand flower buds[42]

The Goan mango raised nostalgic feelings amongst the emigrants. Manohar Rai Sardessai, who was in France for some years, did not forget to sing praises of the mango.[43] This is the last of the five stanzas of the poem "The Goan Mango":

A hymn of joy
A song of fragrance
The wealth, the pride
Of Goa the Golden
The Goan Mango

Rice Cultivation

There were two methods to cultivate the rice paddy fields. One was by sowing the dry seeds for germination. The other was by using the pre-germinated seeds for raising seedlings transplanted onto the field. These seedlings could be raised in two ways: dry and wet nurseries.[44]

The dry nursery system was mostly followed in the villages where the fields retained humidity and had water availability during the month of May, which was important as the seedling beds had to be watered. This method is known in Konkani as *xavier* or *xeier*, which means *xev* (humidity).[45]

In the case of a wet nursery, no sooner had the first rains arrived and water collected in the fields, the farmer was ready to start the work of preparing the seedlings. Before being taken to the field, the sprouted seeds had to be separated from one another, and this method was called *rou modpak*, or else the seedlings would be clumped together in the soil. As the buffaloes moved the plow, the laborer would sow the seeds in the furrows.

Before the introduction of the transplantation method, fields were cultivated using directly sprouted seeds, and the method was called *ompac*. For that, a *danto*, a wooden agricultural tool resembling a giant rectangular fork, was used to plow the field for sowing.[46] One worker would walk behind the plow to sow the seeds. Another person would use a *gutto*, a planing plank, to level the soil. The manure used before the cultivation consisted of ashes, cow dung, and fish waste. The laborers harvested the paddy when the panicles turned yellow, and threshing would then be undertaken by them.

Once the paddy was well dried and cleaned, it was stored in a *coddo*, a mat made of bamboo sticks, which was treated with cow dung to protect it from any insects. The *coddo* had perpendicular and parallel sticks woven to form a mat. The amount of paddy stored within could be measured by the circumference of the *coddo*. Before using it for storage, a dry grass layer would be placed at its bottom to keep out moisture that could spoil the paddy.

The process of getting the rice ready for consumption by the women, using special preparation tools, techniques, and songs, shows that these can serve as cultural artifacts for ethnographic enquiry and collective memory. In fact, Sutton makes a plea for ethnography, as discussed in the Introduction.[47]

Provisions for the Monsoons

Another important task for the Goans was to arrange provisions for the monsoon. For the period of study, Goa had no proper roads and no adequate public transport, which meant limited mobility from the village to the city or from one city to another. There were markets in the main town with shops selling groceries, but the ones in the village were not well provisioned. In addition, in the village, there might have been only one shop monopolizing the business without any competition, and that shopkeeper would not store a selection of expensive goods as most were perishable.[48]

Consequently, housewives had to plan to store the required food items, which included various spices, rice, onions, dry fish, coconuts, etc. The Catholics preferred to consume *ukde tandul* (boiled rice), in which case paddy had to be boiled and sun-dried before husking. The Hindus did the husking of the paddy without boiling it, and the rice was called *suroi tandul* (polished rice). In the past, husking was done manually as there were no commercial power-driven rice mills. Hence, almost all the houses had their own *vann*, a pounding hole. The women of the household, sometimes with the help of the neighbors, husked the rice with a wooden pestle called a *mussoll*. Landlords who had a large quantity of paddy to make rice had several *vanns* and employed persons to do the work. Some *dulpods* tell us about this, inspired by this age-old household activity. In the first one, the girls sing:

> Hoist the crooked flag, O boatman.
> let's go to Divar.
> We are girls from Divar,
> good pounders of rice.[49]

In another *dulpod*, the pounders try to lighten their work by striking the pestle to the musical rhythm of *Sho*! *Sho*!

> *Sho*, *sho*, Joana,
> the pestle does not pound
> the middle mortar.
> *Sho*, *sho*, *sho*,
> ...
> The pounder women
> have finished their pounding.
> The sifter women are sitting in a row.[50]

Once the rice is husked, it needs to be cleaned by removing the chaff with the *sup* (winnowing basket) and fan, made of woven palm leaf. We have another verse for this important activity in another *dulpod*[51]: "*Maia-maim sifts the rice, putting it in the hollow of the winnowing basket ...*"[52] After this activity, the rice is ready for consumption and stored in wide-mouthed containers called *vail* (made of clay).

For those who had no properties, coconuts had to be plucked or bought and stored.[53] During the monsoons, it would be difficult to climb trees. To fry and cook, the housewife needed oil, which in the past was extracted from dry coconut (copra). Vegetable oil was not usually available or commonly used. The Catholics used pork fat to cook, which was extracted at home or purchased from pork meat vendors. At home, the oil was extracted by heating the pork fat. After extraction, a residue of small pieces of fat would be left behind, which were called *reudeo*. They were crispy solids and very tasty, and enjoyed by many, especially kids. There is a reference to fat in the *dulpod Aum-um Tori Cherh'm ga Lanom*, where a young girl, Maria Santan, suggests sarcastically to a would-be groom that if he wants to be successful in finding a match, then he should apply some fat to his mustache. "Rub some lard on your moustache. Go, find a match [look for a bride]," which shows that fat was an important cooking component in the kitchen.

The *dispensa* (storeroom) of a well-provided house had to be stocked with condiments needed for day-to-day cooking. These were generally purchased at the weekly or annual fairs.[54] The best-known fairs were the Friday markets of Mapusa and Banastarim. In the month of May, many religious feasts were celebrated throughout Goa, and many had fairs where various items, including spices, were sold. Among the popular ones were the Feasts of the Holy Cross in Santa Cruz village, the Ascension of Jesus at Panjim, and the Holy Spirit at Margao. People flocked to the fairs to buy their required annual provisions. Therefore, these feasts were also known as "The Feast of Provisions."[55]

At the fair, one could buy spices, onions, chilies, dry kokum, mango rinds (sollam), and other requirements for the monsoons.[56] The Panjim fair had temporary stalls selling piles of onions, dry red chilies, turmeric, kokum, and mango *sollam* (dry rinds of the fruits). On the covered footpath of the *Praça do Comércio* were stalls with spices stored in huge jute bags and displayed for selection by the client in a *cail*, a metal container. All this was nicely arranged in rows so that people could easily see and evaluate the goods before buying. In the evenings, there were small electric bulbs that illuminated the spices. Buying these was a very meticulous and important job for the housewife.[57]

Red dry chilies were another important item in every kitchen. The Hindus bought the *botão*, grown mostly in Harmal, Pernem, and the *kolcha* or *lambat* from Canacona, normally by volume, using the local measures of *pod* or *paili*.[58] The Catholics went for the fat and long chili from Aldona, which were bought in hundreds.[59] It is interesting to know the way they were counted: in fives, and each five made one *fadda*. So, in a hundred there were twenty *faddes*. To every twenty *faddes*, another one or two were added as a bonus. To keep track while counting a large number, a chili was kept aside for every counted hundred.

Onions were cultivated only during the dry season because otherwise, the rains would spoil the crop. There were other important items that needed to be stored. The onions were bought by weight and usually in *manns* (a unit of 16 kilos). In order to store them, the onions were tied up and suspended from a horizontal bamboo. The best place for this was usually the kitchen, where the smoke from the wood fire helped in preserving the onions. For hanging, the onions were plaited with dry paddy grass.in a particular manner.

Since fish was scarce during monsoons and Goans needed the *toca-boca*, an appetizer to accompany the rice and curry, they consumed dried salted fish. This was bought at the market or made at home by salting and drying fresh fish or purchased from annual fairs. The feast fair at Margão was well known for its wide choice. This salted fish could also be pickled to make *para*.[60] To break the monotony of dry fish, various pickles and sweet chutneys were made of mangoes, *tendlis* (gherkins), brinjals, limes, etc. The work to get the provisions ready was carried out by the women of the house, who in this way ensured the subsistence of the family during the monsoons.

The Month of May

In summer, which spans from March to May, it is not only the availability of various fruits that brings back memories, but there is much more to this season. The well-known *dulpod Avoi Maiatso Muinnom Paulo Lagim* captures the essence of the importance of this month for the housewife.[61] The first stanza of the *dulpod*:

> Mother, the month of May is approaching.
> And I haven't done a thing.
> The roof must be re-tiled, awnings must be set up.
> I just don't know what to do[62]

Though she speaks about getting the roof ready, the first line of the *dulpod,* "Mother, the month of May is approaching and I haven't done a thing!" indicates that there are more nuances to this than just the work on the house. It is a month that keeps the housewife very busy because she must prepare for the ensuing monsoons.

The work of re-tiling was usually carried out by the youngsters of the ward. This task would begin at dawn before the sun rose to protect them from the heat. The boys alternated from house to house until most of the houses were re-tiled. The only payment made was offerings of seasonal fruits like jackfruits, mangoes, pineapples, and other eatables for the youngsters.[63]

Another important activity of the household in preparation for the monsoons was the storage of firewood. Large logs were separated from cut firewood, coconut husk, shells, leaves, etc.[64] Besides firewood, the villagers also collected and stored dry leaves. Leaves would be collected from the adjoining estates or hillocks.[65] This practice is described in the *dulpod, Te Kombea Sadari Josefin Fuim go Gelolem,*[66] in an exchange between a mother and daughter:

> Mother: At the cockcrow, Josefin, where did you go?
> Daughter: I went into the forest to gather firewood.

Coconut husk, coconut shells, dried cow dung cakes, sawdust, paddy husk, etc., were also used as fuel and stored by the people.[67] The city-dweller too had to arrange for fuel. By mid-May, arrangements had to be made to buy wood and store it. Wood was purchased by weight in *mann* or by volume.[68]

Hunger—A Memory Stimulant

According to Sutton, hunger is a great memory stimulant; when people get hungry, they remember the food. In *O Signo da Ira,* Orlando da Costa narrates the plight of the *mundkars* who have to endure hunger because they are old and cannot work. They have to go begging from house to house for a fistful of rice. There was an underlying understanding that humility (of the mundkar) and charity (of the bhatkar) would enable the poor *mundkar* to get some food to overcome hunger. This was one of the reasons why Bostian joined the other beggars.

Old age caught up with her, and as she could not continue to work, the only option left for survival was the one taken by the other elderly *mundkars*—the weekly routine of begging every Saturday in the city of Margao.[69] The *bhatkar* and the rich would offer a handful of rice to them in exchange for reciting the prayers—"*Noman Moriê, Noman Moriê …*" (Hail Mary, Hail Mary …), as the poorly dressed group moved from house to house.

However, during the Second World War, the production of rice was not satisfactory, so for the old who went begging, life was dreadful because they were not given rice by the *bhatkar*, but instead, a few coins, which could hardly buy any food for them. For the poor, the money would not help; it was so little. On the other hand, the rice, even if it was a small quantity, would be divided for the days of the week. This would be achieved by cooking it in extra water and drinking it in the morning and munching a few rice berries at noon. At night, to overcome the hunger, the poor would snuggle their stomachs against the beaten floor of the shack.[70]

Goa, like many places, had beggars seeking alms. There were days earmarked for them to visit the houses. It was Saturdays for the cities of Panjim and Margao. In Merces, it was on a Wednesday, Santacruz on a Thursday, and so on. They were usually aged people who could not work and probably had no one to look after them. They moved in groups of two or more and would stop at the door or window and call out with a "*Bai go, esmol gal*" (Madam, give me some alms) or "*Baba re, esmol gal*" (Sir, give me some alms). For them, begging was the only means of sustenance.

Both remembering and forgetting bring back memories. In Orlando da Costa's novel, Ligôr's *mundkars* recall the past when they would have sufficient to eat. But over the last five months, their despair had grown because the granaries remained empty and only okra (lady's fingers) and beans had grown in their gardens. Millet had carpeted the scorched earth around the huts. The humble *mundkars* had to silently carry on with life. While the elders endured this pain, children with jaggery-smeared bellies and famished eyes snapped dry *brindão* husks and roasted tamarind seeds between their teeth.[71] It made them sad to see the rice container empty. It was only *ambil* that allowed them to resist hunger and help them survive.

The *Curumbin* (Kunnbi) women remembered how they would prepare baskets of food with *podgué* full of steaming *canjee* or boiled rice along with dried fish for lunch and would leave them by the door for those working in the fields. For about two years, the rice started getting scarce, and the millet *ambil* and the yellowish *bajri* replaced the grains of rice in the preparation of *péz* (canjee). "The men and women who worked in the rice fields had almost forgotten the taste of it, and children, in the lean and uncertain harvests of those years, themselves recalled secretly munching golden stalks."[72]

Deprivation and plenty are reflected in the *dulpod Ago Fulambai* (*Ful/ Fulambai*), and it is presented through the making of *pattoios*.[73] These are prepared with raw rice that is soaked overnight and ground into a dry batter, which is then spread on a turmeric leaf.[74] It is filled with a mixture of tender coconut and jaggery, halves folded to close, and then steamed. In the *dulpod*, the girl is asked to put the filling sparingly, indicating that they do not have enough of the mixture to add more. It is sung with the following lyrics: "Put a little of the sweet, minced coconut here, a little there."[75] However, plenty is seen in the priest's family, which is well-off and has a sufficient filling and can therefore make lots of *pattoios*, extending the making throughout the night.

> And the padre's family's daughters-in-law
> Were preparing sweet *pattoios* all night long, flower girl!
> Padre take please sweet *pattoios*.[76]

Food and Colonial Memory

It is found that eating is not the only source of bringing back memories. The way the food is made is an important factor too. For instance, when more people joined in the cooking, there were possibilities for improving and getting better results. The age-old adage of "too many cooks spoil the soup" did not apply here. The new approach suggested for studying and investigating cooking skills is through ethnography and theory.[77] This examines how cooking skills are achieved, developed, and communicated. It is also applied to the gendered ways. Another evolving aspect in the area of ethnographic enquiry is that of the distance between the processes of making and cooking.

Sannas, a local bread, was made only occasionally, during a formal repast for a feast or some grand celebration. It can be termed a "heritage food," which is sometimes most closely tied to collective memory and is symbolic of the local identity. Indeed, many studies successfully emphasize the symbolic importance of food without reference to its bodily experiences.[78] *Sannas* was not a quotidian item on the menu and would be a suitable example to bring memories of its preparation with its own procedures and the meal that was served to go with it on the feast day, to which the family and guests looked forward. Some were made with a mixture of jaggery and coconut added to *sannas*, which were served for evening tea. During the Portuguese regime, toddy was available in plenty, especially in the villages. People would go to the palm grove where the toddy was extracted to buy the virgin sap, and they would ensure that it was not mixed with the stale stock in the house or with any water.

The feast repast, which was eaten along with *sannas,* had to include *sarapatel* or *cabidela.* To prepare these dishes, a female piglet would be slaughtered (males would always be allowed to grow into adulthood and then sold or slaughtered for a good price). Most Catholic families reared pigs and poultry, both for personal consumption or for sale. Fresh pig's blood mixed with vinegar was a requirement in the preparation of both *sarapatel* and *cabidela*, especially the latter. Both these dishes, originally brought by the Portuguese from their country, took root in Goa, with spices added to give a local tinge, and today are identified as Goan specialties, along with *vinha de alhos*, *assado*, and *feijoada,* to name a few.

What has remained of Portuguese origin is only the name, with the Goan *sarapatel* or *cabidela* having transformed altogether into a unique dish identifying with the community and prepared as a festal food.[79] This tradition was also carried by the expatriates, as can be seen from the statement made by a Mozambican Goan who acknowledged that it was unthinkable not to make exclusive Goan food.[80] While the Portuguese version has only pig's blood and as condiments garlic, pepper, and bay leaf, the Goan dish comes with many spices that include chilies, garlic, ginger, cumin seeds, turmeric, pepper, cloves, and cinnamon all ground together to form a paste.[81]

Goan Identifying Marker—"The Curry"

The Goan curry—the *caril* of Portuguese, the *koddi* of Catholics, and the *uman* of Hindus—is an important dish that adds that zing to the cooked rice and gives identity to Goan food. Garcia da Orta makes one of the first references in Portuguese sources to the *caril* when he describes the coconut in the *Colloquios*.[82] He tells that the juice of the coconut is used to make a caril with birds and meat.[83] Cecilia de Souza writes: "Fish curry is a bond that unites all communities; with rice, it is the emblem of Goan hospitality, the symbol of pot-luck."[84] An interesting description is given about the curry in the *Annaes Marítimos* (1842): "[C]urry is a sauce made of spices, grated coconut, and shrimp, or fish, which is tossed over rice cooked with unsalted water; it is a family dish, or national, that makes its appearance in all dinners: and in the most profuse and even festive, always forms the last cover."[85] In the novel, *The Mango and the Tamarind Tree,* Leslie de Noronha writes about the preparation at Raoul's home in Goa, which shows its difference from the curries available in restaurants abroad: "then came the grinding of each spice separately: Raoul shuddered when he thought of the neutral, tasteless gooey concoctions of bottled spices, sultanas, and raisins that passed for curry in restaurants abroad decorated like sets for a musical extravaganza."[86]

In a study on the community in Maputo, Mozambique, Marta Vilar Rosales transcribes a comment by a Goan about their curry, which shows that even the diaspora continued preparing it in its original form: "[R] egarding what you said about European families always eating curry on Sundays, I remember perfectly well a store of an Indian in Lourenço Marques (Maputo) that sold spices and that had a huge European clientele that didn't understand anything about it." And he sarcastically comments: "Europeans knew how to buy spices! It's not like my wife, who makes the spices here at home. She asks for so much of this, so much of that, and the spices are made here at home. Europeans used to arrive at the store and ask for curry powder. And he had something prepared that was called curry powder."[87]

It is not also the "curry" that Maria Paula Meneses writes about in her paper, in which she uses the Mozambican curry, a national dish, to connect to the food and memory of the indigenous people.[88] According to Rosales, while discussing the curry being the national dish in Mozambique, the Goan families report that it is, in fact, an imitative development that emerged from a mimetic process by other social groups that also included the colonial elites who introduced it in their quotidian practices. Another of the interviewees, while talking about food, commented: "On Sunday there was always curry. The other non-Goans did it too, but by imitation."[89]

In her interview with D. Fátima, a native woman from the Island of Mozambique (the island where the first Goans landed in the sixteenth century), Meneses asked her how she would cook the curry. After describing the preparation, the lady also comments on the Goan curry, which, according to her, is different from the native Mozambican, which is served with fish and vegetables. For her, what people meant by "curry," when they went to a restaurant or looked for in the books about how to cook it, was the one that was prepared in the past by the Goans that lived in Mozambique, and that remains as a memory for those who experienced the colonial period.[90]

The curry is prepared in different ways, depending on the ingredients used. However, the basic components of a Goan curry are the coconut and the chilies. The chili was introduced into India by the Portuguese, and this spice constitutes the most important ingredient in modern curries.[91] The Sanskrit books of cookery, which cannot be of any considerable antiquity, contain many recipes for curry without this ingredient.[92] Its preparation was a daily affair for a housewife, who would start with husking and breaking a coconut. After grating the coconut kernel, she would grind it on a stone along with spices, depending on the kind of fish she was going to add to the curry.

The ground mixture would then be mixed with water in a clay vessel and boiled on a slow wood fire until it thickened and acquired the desired consistency.[93] The taste of the curry also depended on the freshness and quality of the fish, prawns, or shellfish added during the preparation, as it would enhance the taste of the curry. When fish was not available, people prepared curry without it, which was called *sovrak* or *ankvar coddi* (spinster curry).

The art of preparing a delicious curry was not everyone's cup of tea. Some people prepared a tastier one than others, with the same ingredients. As the saying goes, the person should have "the touch" to prepare a tasty curry. This touch is called in Konkani *hath-gunn*—a quality of the hand that is something special! Sutton makes a pertinent comment in this regard by pointing out that though the basic ingredients used were alike, he was surprised at how important small variations (say, in the spices) were what made the difference in the way people thought about how to prepare it. This, according to him, was a highly individualized way of preparing that gave uniqueness to the food.[94]

Different souring agents are used depending on the type of preparation. Tamarind is used in the majority of the curries. Tamarind trees abound in Goa, and people bought fresh pods, which were available seasonally during the summer. Other souring agents were the dried peels made from kokum fruit. These were added particularly for curry prepared with mackerels, sardines, *peddi,* or *kurlie. Teflam*, an aromatic seed, was also added to this curry.[95] Fresh skin is also used to make a sweet beverage called *xarope de brindão*, or kokum syrup. It is a very tasty and healthy drink, especially during summer. During the Portuguese regime, due to the limited availability of aerated and other beverages, kokum syrup was served to guests. Another refreshing drink offered to guests was the *orchata* made with almonds and sugar. The almonds were substituted by cashew nuts as they were easily available and cheaper.

Kokum is also used to prepare *funttikaddi*, a concoction with water, salt, and green chilies, to which *karipata* (curry leaves) or coriander leaves are added. Another variation, *solkaddi,* is made using coconut juice instead of water. This drink supplements the curry and also acts as a digestive—a must at the table of Hindu Saraswat and Brahmins, who end the meal with the *kaddi.*[96] Some patients were advised by doctors not to consume curry, but instead, have a lighter preparation called *aksal.*[97] Another traditional dish using kokum is the *solantullem*, a preparation of pork meat, which is a specialty of South Goa.

Yet another souring agent is the sundried salted raw mango, the *ambeachim solam.* These enhance the flavors when added to prawn curry. During mango season, fresh-cut raw mangoes are added along with the mango stone to the curry. The best *solam* are made with raw mangoes, which are mature and have a fully developed stone. The latter is halved and also dried like the slices. The stone is specially used to make the *sambarechi coddi.*

In the period of study, many houses had a *bilimbi* tree in the kitchen garden, and its fruits, *bilimbis,* were used as souring agents for making curries, especially for preparing prawn curry. *Bilimbis* are also used to make pickles, and a favorite one is with prawns, called *balchão de bilimbim.* However, these have a short shelf life. Another fruit added as a souring agent is the *ambaddo* (hog plum), which is seasonal.[98] The forgotten and less-used *vatamba*[99] fruit gives a distinctively delicious taste to the curry.[100] The trees grow in the *kullagars* (areca nut plantations) in Goa and bear roundish fruit (two to four inches in diameter), irregularly shaped and of yellowish color, which is sweetish and sour in taste.[101] It is used mostly in fish curries for its sourness and has better health value than tamarind as it is less acidic. It can also be used in chutney preparations.

In *The Mango and the Tamarind Tree*, Leslie de Noronha tells that although the Albuquerque family had Westernized food when entertaining guests, for their daily lunch, rice and curry were their main dishes. He gives a long description of how the curry was made at Raoul's mother's house. He narrates the incident of the new maid who was making the curry without the supervision of Rosa Maria (the housekeeper), who would usually check every step as she wanted things done meticulously in her own way and regarded the preparation of the curry as her prerogative.[102]

However, the keys to the storeroom were with Rosa Maria, who had overslept, and therefore the vinegar was unavailable. So, the new maid took a handful of tamarind pods and squeezed them until the thick, sour, sticky, blackish-red juice ran through her fingers, leaving the fibrous dry pulp. She then poured the juice, a crude souring ingredient customarily used by the villagers, into the curry.[103]

The curry has its own class hierarchy. Nuances in the way curries are prepared show social status. Amongst the Catholics, besides the spices already mentioned, dry coriander seeds are added in the making of prawn curry. However, in the rural context, people use coriander seeds along with other spices for both fish and prawn curries. But more pronounced is the difference in the way coconut is used between the landed gentry and others. Since the former have coconuts in abundance, they extract the milk from the kernel. The others grind it fine. It was said that a number of landed families who were miserly would use the remains of the coconut after extracting the juice to prepare curry for their servants' consumption. That there were differences in preparing curries for the employees was also revealed by Noronha: "[T]hese were her basic ingredients. From these, by endless permutations and combinations, of the blending, and quantities of each, she could turn out hundreds and hundreds of curries of different flavors, from a suave, virile curry for the family table to a rough, pungent-as-hell full-bodied curry for the servants' meal."[104]

To make a Goan curry, vinegar was not used, nor was there all that elaborate frying of spices and grinding with coconut milk as described by Noronha. That points to his imagination in writing the novel. At the beginning of the novel, he tenders an apology to "all those whose homes and kindness he misused by exaggerating their lunch menus."[105]

The tamarind and vinegar controversy is intended to validate the title of the book, and more importantly, to show the difference between the landed gentry and commoners by using the mango and the tamarind tree to represent them, respectively. The latter, though an important component of Goan food preparations, is deprecatorily categorized by Noronha as an egalitarian ingredient, "a crude souring ingredient customarily used by the villagers." The vinegar also reflects the economic status, as it is a by-product of coconut trees, which were owned by the landed gentry.

The privileged and those who could afford it used to prepare it at home because it was needed for cooking meats, gravies, masalas (especially one of red chilies and spices, called "tempero do recheio", used for stuffing fish), and for *para,*[106] pickles, chutneys, and other preparations that needed preservatives. Vinegar is used only by Catholics, while Hindus and Muslims dislike its strong odor and acidic taste.

The Hogs and the Goan *chouriço*

Ladis da Silva writes about the pigs: "[N]o matter where you went, in the villages and paddy fields of Goa, one sees them nosing happily, emitting soothing grunts of contentment."[107] In the olden days, many would be seen roaming around the wards eating plants and fruits. During the mango season, they would be around to relish the ripe mangoes that fell from the tree. They would create a nuisance during rice cultivation by destroying the crops in the fields. It was prohibited for pigs to move around in the cities. If anyone wanted to rear them, they had to be kept inside closed precincts within the outer walls. The owner would have to pay a fine if pigs were found in a public place. Another important task allotted to the pigs was eating the leftovers. They were environmentally friendly scavengers. According to Silva, the "history of hogs in Goa goes back to the Portuguese conquests." However, it is well known that pigs were present on the Asian continent from ancient times, much before the arrival of the Portuguese, and their meat was even consumed by people. Of course, what the Portuguese introduced was the preparation of pork dishes as mentioned earlier, and most importantly the art of making sausages, *chouriço—churisas* or *linguiças de Goa* for Silva—one of the most cherished foods in Goa, as well as by expatriate Goans. Silva laments its inaccessibility in foreign countries: "Unfortunately, for many obvious reasons, these spicy, juicy, and highly palatable delicacies do not reach many in various countries of the world."[108] According to him, "the demand for genuine 'Goa sausages' is preposterous!"[109]

It is not only Silva who reminisces about the sausage and its quality. There are others like Frank Simoes, a writer who lived in Bombay and originally hailed from Saligao, Bardez in Goa. He writes an essay on the Goan *chouriço*, "A Sausage with Soul."[110] He feels that the Goan sausage prepared in Goa had no competitor. He comments on those prepared in Bombay: "the over-spiced, under-flavored Bandra sausage, the sad-sack Dhobi Talao sausage, other unsavory offerings from Marve, Bassein and points north. No contest."[111]

The penchant for *chouriço* is shown by another Frank. The well-known Frank Moraes, the first Indian editor of the *Times of India* in Bombay, was born and brought up in Santa Cruz, Bombay. Incidentally, Frank Moraes's family was originally from Santa Cruz, Tiswadi, Goa, and it shows in his yearning for Goan food. In an article titled "Jackfruit and Sausages" by Dom Moraes, his son, a poet and writer,[112] pens that when he was back from Oxford after he finished his studies, he did not know what to do. His father told him to go to Goa and spend some time there, which would help him to decide. And Frank, who had not been to Goa for many years and was feeling nostalgic about the jackfruit and Goan sausages, told Dom, "You can bring some things back for me from there. As many Goa sausages as you can carry, and a jackfruit. It's what all Goans eat."[113]

The *chouriço* was an ideal food for the housewife, very handy when a guest walked in unannounced. It was easy to cook and could be served in different ways—fried, plain boiled, or with potatoes and onions. It was also added to the rice to make sausage rice (sausage pulao). When used while cooking in stews, *guisado*, and croquettes, it enhanced the taste of these dishes and gave that special zing. A pertinent comment from an emigrant from Mozambique, now in Portugal, highlights the importance of the sausage in giving that special touch to Portuguese cuisine: "[W]e Goans give a Goan touch to the Portuguese cuisine. It is something gone over and improved. For example, if a traditional Portuguese *feijoada* takes a *chouriço* from India, made with spices from there, it tastes fantastic. Whoever says a *feijoada*, says also a *dobrada*. A Goan-style *dobrada* is something extraordinary."[114]

The conflict between the Portuguese and Goan kitchens, wherever the former's cuisine got integrated into family practices, was with the "Goan taste." This happened as it experienced adaptation through the use of spices, vegetables, and fruits. We have already seen this happening with the *sarapatel, cabidela, chouriço,* and other Portuguese food in Goa, and the diaspora community did not lag behind. The researchers found that the families who were interviewed did not consider the integration of many Portuguese influences on the "Goan gastronomic heritage" as a risk to its wealth and originality.[115]

The Goans adapted Portuguese cuisine to their tastes and created their own cuisine, altogether dissimilar from the original, only retaining the name and that too sometimes, with a different orthography. This was unlike the British, who made the Indian cooks gradually alter and simplify the Indian recipes to suit their tastes.[116] A very common snack is *pão com chouriço* (sausage bread), which can also substitute for a meal. During the annual novenas of St. Francis Xavier held at the Basilica in Old Goa, women and some men are found selling *cheris pao* (chouriço-pão). It is common to see devotees after mass devouring the tasty snack. It is a must for many undertaking this annual pilgrimage.

This Goan sausage is the counterpart of the Portuguese *chouriço*—a sausage also known as *linguiça*. The Goan variety is made of pork pickled with various spices and vinegar, stuffed in the dried gut of cattle. The sausages are then sun-dried or smoked by keeping them over a fireplace. A string of small sausages is a familiar sight in the markets of Goa, differing from the Portuguese ones, which are usually long and large in size. During the summer, sellers do brisk business with the emigrants, who buy a substantial quantity to take with them, and the locals for their consumption at home.[117]

Mnemonic for Remembering

Remembering the past when someone looks at a thing and connects it to some happening or event is a person's ability to bring back memories. Food can also be used as a mnemonic, like any other thing or happening. Interestingly, Sutton used food as a reminder, as visits to his parents' friends gave him an opportunity to learn a new and thought-provoking culinary delicacy. So, whenever his parents asked him if he remembered a particular person whom he had met a couple of years ago, his response was to ask them what they had for dinner.[118] This kind of connecting food to the memory and events of the past is everyone's prerogative.

Take, for example, an affluent person in Goa. Seeing a turkey would connect it to some wedding reception, where the bird, stuffed and dressed, was the pièce de résistance at the buffet table. While remembering the wedding, he would also recollect the bride and the groom, their parents, how the function was held, and many other details related to the event. But for a farmer who raises turkeys, it would be a bird that earns him some money when he sells it, or as food for his family. However, the same farmer looking at a pumpkin would recall memories of the Christmas celebrations as he would recollect how the creeper trailed on the roof of his outhouse with a bountiful crop, and of how the best and the biggest was selected for making *mandares*.[119] He remembers how it was carefully nurtured and, when ready, removed and kept carefully till the time it needed to be cut. And how, after keeping a portion for his own preparation, the remaining would be distributed to relatives and neighbors to make *mandares* for Christmas. Many adults will remember that as children they had to take turns with siblings or other family members to shoo off the crows when the *mandares* were being dried.[120] These are served deep-fried or roasted on charcoal embers and stored in tins to be served as and when required.

Weddings were important events in Goa, and these celebrations had their own charm. The wedding nuptials were usually held in the morning. The receptions were held at home; only a few rich families could afford a club or hotel. Some would have a reception in the church premises, which had a parochial house with a decent room and a veranda where invitees were served snacks or other eatables and drinks.

The reception at home entailed preparations such as putting up a *mattov* outside the house and getting the floor ready for couples to dance.[121] This was done by watering the mud floor for two nights and then beating it hard with a *batedor*. A layer of cow dung was applied for a better finish. The band was the village brass band, which came by noon and had to be served a good lunch before they played for the reception. They ate the best and were well-fed and did not have to wait for the wedding to get over to dine, as is the practice today.

The affluent ones would have a buffet layout, while other families served various dishes on quarter plates. The number depended again on the financial status of the family. A society wedding that did not go for a buffet service would have at least three, if not four, types of plated food: a *caldo* (clear soup), fish, usually in mayonnaise, and a third of meat or rice. The meat could be a stew or assorted snacks like samosas, croquettes, and a sandwich. Rice was served as *arroz refogado.*

In the village where the people had to stretch their limited finances to feed the guests, the *arroz refogado* was the only dish. Some might have added a ham sandwich or a meat stew. Why the choice of rice? It was served because it was substantial food and presumed that it would satisfy the guests, unlike the fanciful snacks of today, which do not satiate hunger. And perhaps it was economical for the hosts too.

The slaughter of a pig was common in the village on the occasion of a wedding since it would cut the expenses for the family. When a pig was slaughtered, the family, more often than not, had enough to prepare for the family dinner. At this dinner, guests were served *sarapatel*, *add-mass*, and *assado,* amongst other dishes.

The older generation reminisces about the gourmet style of serving the *arroz refogado*. In a cup, a mixture of cooked vegetables, carrots, peas, and cooked pieces of sausages was added by one person. The cup was then passed on to another, who would add rice, press it down with a spoon, and then turn it onto a quarter plate. The additions were not only taste enhancers but also gave a beautiful appearance to the rice.

Christmas was the time for special food. People looked forward to making their favorite sweets and savories that are an integral part of a Goan *consoada*.[122] *Pinaca*, *dodol*, *doce de grão*, *neureos*, etc., were prepared. The *neureos*, which are a must for the festival, are a remnant of Hindu tradition. Every household will include these, whether made of coconut or a different flour mixture. The various sweets and savories were placed on a tray and served to the visitors.

Many families, especially in the village, made *oddes* of rice flour. These are like *puris*, round puffed bread made of flour and deep-fried in oil and served as an accompaniment instead of bread. However, the *oddes* are crispy and smaller in size than *puris* and can be stored for days if properly packed in an airtight container. *Cormolam*, *bebinca*, *teia de aranha*, *bática*, *bolinhos*, marzipans, and *cocada*[123] are some other Goan sweets. Many make a Goan halwa from wheat flour and coconut milk. The privileged delight is the queen of desserts, the *bebinca*, a multilayered sweet prepared with egg yolks, coconut milk, and sugar, and baked in layers using *ghee* (clarified butter).

Nostalgia and Remembrance of Food in Goan Literature

Food-centered nostalgia is a recurrent theme in studies of the diasporic or expatriate population who have experienced displacement. Sutton emphasizes the longing evoked in diasporic individuals by the smells and tastes of a lost homeland, providing a temporary return to a time when their lives were not fragmented. Holtzman comments that as a form of memory, "nostalgia" has several different senses, generally and with respect to food. Some food literature (particularly outside anthropology) relies on a lay notion of sentimentality for a lost past, viewing food as a means for recalling childhood and family. Food-centered reminiscence is articulated within genres of food-centered memoirs (writings).

Yet, in contrast to viewing nostalgia as a re-experiencing of emotional pasts, it may also be seen as a longing for times and places that one has never experienced. Arjun Appadurai characterizes this as "armchair" nostalgia—a nostalgia without lived experience—suggesting that in late-capitalist consumerism "the merchandiser supplies the lubricant of nostalgia" and the consumer "need only bring the faculty of nostalgia to an image that will supply the memory of a loss he or she has never suffered."[124] This could be one reason why the expatriate Goans' next generations, who have never experienced nor been to Goa, are interested in buying items to prepare Goan food from shops that sell spices and items which are unique to Goa. They connect these items to their identity, like an umbilical cord with Goa. The statement made by one of the interviewees confirms this argument: "In Africa, my mother cooked Goan food very well. She liked very much what she did and got us accustomed to Goan food. It seems to me that it is my umbilical cord with Goa. And I think it's not just me."[125] The sensuousness of food does not fully explain the widespread "armchair nostalgia" surrounding many foods, nor how rarely eaten "heritage foods" are sometimes those most closely tied to collective memory.[126]

The recent concern with transnational identities has put the issue of nostalgia on the theoretical table.[127] However, the obvious link between food and nostalgia has produced only some intriguing descriptive material.[128] Even if there is no theoretical explanation, food obviously has the ability to bring back nostalgic feelings and remembrance, especially if it made them happy in the past and is not accessible anymore.

A few Goan writers have written odes to their favorites—in prose, verse, and song. We have already seen how the *chouriço* evoked memories amongst the emigrants. Far away from Goa, the poet and writer Adeodato Barreto (1905–37), who lived in Coimbra, Portugal, reminisces about the Christmas celebrations in his homeland.[129]

> I am longing for the *consoada*, the *fuguéus*.
> …
> Where in the kitchens, in the pots,
> Smelling of oil, fat *oddes* sing.[130]

Alfred Rose (1932–2003), a famous and popular *tiatrist* (theater personality), actor, and singer of the Konkani stage, sighs that he no longer can eat his favorite *goddxem* and sings an elegy to this sweet dish in the Goa of the past as discussed earlier, which again shows us the importance of the *merenda* to connect food and memory.

> ***Goddxem***
>
> Mother used to make *goddxem* and serve me. She would make *vonn* and place it on the table. The sight of that *vonn* of jaggery would arouse my tongue. She would fill this belly with *ale-bele*. And sweeten this mouth with *filos*. She would make *tizan* of millets and give strength to my body.[131]

Rose remembers his school days when, after coming home, he would eat these sweets for evening tea made by his mother, which made for a wholesome snack.

Another nostalgic poem, an elegy to *sarapatel* that is ingrained in our culture and tradition, has been dedicated by Philip Furtado (1951–2020). He lived in Bombay and in the poem "Sorpotel," he reminisces not only of *sarapatel* but also of its significant accompaniment—the local bread *sannas* and the Goan alcohol *feni*, albeit of cashew.

> ***In Praise of Sorpotel***
> …
> But for us who hail from Goa

> There's naught like *sorpotel*!
> . . .
> There's none whose mouth won't water
> When you talk of *sorpotel!*
> And, oh, for Christmas dinner,
> . . .
> We could, as they can in Goa,
> Have a bottle of *cajel*
> And toddy-leavened *sandnam*
> To go with *sorpotel*![132]

There are at least ten books of Konkani proverbs, the best being *Florílegio dos Provérbios Concanis* (1922) by Sebastião Rodolfo Dalgado and *Enfiada de Anexins Goeses* (1931) by Roque Bernardo Barreto Miranda. There are around 3,500 Konkani proverbs, and many deal with food. *Ami tumi iekam, xitan kelim lokam* (we are one, divided though by rice) indicates the churnings in a Konkani society centered on food and food production. The proverb also underlines issues such as food scarcity, deprivation, conflicts, etc., for the region.

There are several folk stories or memoirs in which food brings back memories. We have Lucio Rodrigues, the author, eating mangoes, as well as the story of a mother waiting for the arrival of her son and family from far away Africa, who peps up their visit with several Goan dishes and, of course, the mango. Another story tells us about the gluttony of the son-in-law who was presented with an assortment of Goan sweets and then rose in the middle of the night to sneak into the kitchen to lay his hand on one which he had refused to eat and now wanted to taste. This behavior can be connected to the greed in demanding an *ojem* by the groom's family, who insist on having several sweets and fruits for personal consumption and distribution to relatives and neighbors on occasions like weddings, festivals, etc.

Emigration

The Goan housewife needed money for domestic expenses, and the emigrant's wife would eagerly await the remittances promised by her husband, who had migrated to Bombay for work. Not only money but even a letter or information about his whereabouts was longed for. Such a situation amongst the emigrants' wives was not rare. Many times the lonely men would seek solace in other women and, not being able to support both, would keep the wife, who was far away from him, in the dark. The second stanza of the *dulpod Avoi Maiatso Muinnom Paulo Lagim* gives subtle insights into the lives of the emigrants.

> My husband went to Bombay promising to send me money
> What shall I tell you? He has not even sent a letter
> Where has he got to, where has he gone?
> I just don't know what to do

Emigration was most often the cause of a temporary separation between husband and wife. Sometimes he would go to work on a ship. In those days, the journeys were long, and they would be apart for years. The wife would wait for the return of her husband, who, in some cases, never made it back home, leaving the wife a widow, sometimes with small children, to fend for herself. The separation imposes an emotional strain on the two and endangers the bond of fidelity in the marriage. But it is not only the husband who falls into temptation and takes a mistress away from home. The wife in Goa may have her paramour. Rodrigues writes about a *dulpod* where the poet counts with surprise the number of children that the woman has: one, two, three, four, and more, and it is strange because the woman's husband has been away from home.[133]

Picnic

Summertime was not only about work but also enjoyment for some and health care for others. Many went on holiday to the beachside for a change, which was called *mudansac gela* in Konkani. Being a part of the lifestyle of the privileged, the social columns of the local press informed readers about many of those who went for *mudança* and the names of the vacation places. Well-off families would book houses for their annual holidays. Others would raise temporary shacks or use the verandas of some houses to spend the night.

Summer was also the time when people would go for a picnic to enjoy an outing in the realms of nature. It would provide an opportunity for the emigrants who were on their visits home to meet up with others. This trend of going for picnics was carried on by those who organized picnics, wherever they settled, even in modern times.[134] The places selected could include any of these: a beach, near a riverfront, a scenic spot over a hillock, in some property, at a spring, or even in a palm grove in the village. Goa was known not only for her beautiful beaches but also for springs, with many being famous for their medicinal properties, where people would go for a bath to cure their ailments.[135] A well-known and historic account of such a cure is linked to the priest William Robert Lyons,[136] an Englishman based in Bombay, who suffered from a skin ailment and was frustrated because he could not get cured. He was advised by a friend to visit Goa and have a bath at the Pomburpa spring. After a few visits to the spring, he started improving and was cured. For this reason, Fr. Lyons decided that he would not return to Bombay and stayed back in Goa. This decision was beneficial to the people of Goa because when Fr. Lyons established a school at Siolim, he laid the foundation for education in the English language in Goa.[137]

The tradition of picnics and the benefits of the spring waters to cure ailments have been recorded in the *dulpod E Te Tollsam' Zori' Barik Gogo.*[138] This *dulpod* differs from others by being entirely devoted to one subject—the recollections of people who went for baths to the spring.

> The springs at the Tollsam fountain are small. The body hardly gets wet
> People bring their lunches (bakreo-butio) (lit. chapatis and rice balls)

The lyricist complains that the flow of the Tollsam fountain is small and that it is not enough to wet the body. The poor flow is probably indicative of the severity of summer, which dries up the source of the spring, or it could also be due to poor maintenance of the spring. But despite this, people still visited it, carrying with them *chapatis* and rice.

Obviously, whatever was taken for lunch had to be practical and something easy to carry. What better food than *chapatis* and a container with rice, curry, and probably dry salted fish and *chepnentli ambli* or *tor* (salted raw mango) or pickle. The rice and its accompaniments were stuffed in a *buti* (tiffin called buti, plural *butio*). Placed within the stuffed rice was a small glass bottle with curry. The *ambli*, *tor*, or dry salted fish, and if available, fried fish, was kept on the rice, sometimes wrapped in a banana leaf. Many a daily wage laborer also carried the *buti*.

Rituals of Remembering and Forgetting through Food

Ritual has been viewed as a strong site for building food-centered memory and food-centered forgetting. After the demise of a Catholic, masses were said in memory of the person on the completion of seven days, one month, and one year, and subsequently every year. The practice of offering on the seventh day was stopped after the mass on a funeral day was introduced in the late sixties. At the month's mind, many families serve a special meal in honor of the deceased.[139] They are represented by beggars or poor persons, and therefore this meal is called *Bikareamchem Jevonn* (Beggar's Lunch). According to Munn and Battaglia, "[M]ortuary feasting is a particularly important arena for memorializing and forgetting through food, viewed in some instances as a context that creates a space of temporary memorialization, after which the person can be (at least publicly) forgotten."[140] The stress in this kind of literature is for the most part on food's role not in remembering the dead but in their forgetting. Munn argues that mortuary rites serve the function of a "temporary memorialization," but, in fact, "when the mourning is over, the chief mourners will return to the activities of daily life and forget … the dead."[141]

Both as a symbol and as a social practice, these are ceremonies for the remembrance of the dead, and a special meal is cooked for sharing with the poor, the neighbors, and relatives, making it a community of the living.[142] A special meal is prepared, and the food that is most important in terms of mortuary symbolism is the sweet dish, *vonn*.[143] Other food includes rice, curry, vegetables, fish, bananas, and bread. The repast includes *sambarechi coddi*, a special curry made of various spices (sambar) along with onions, garlic, and ginger, all sundried, then fried in oil and powdered. In addition, grams and vegetables—gherkins and pumpkin—are cooked and added to grated coconut mixed with *sambar* masala. Some fried fish is also served. Mortuary food is also observed on All Souls' Day when *vonn* is prepared with the presumption that the family souls will visit the house on this day.[144]

The *bikareamchem jevonn* is also served on some other occasions, like housewarmings and the marriages of sons or daughters. This tradition is followed to appease the dead in the family and to wish the couple a happy married life.

In the afternoon before serving lunch, a rosary is recited for the souls of the departed family members. This meal is served on a large bamboo mat, which is laid out in the hall for the guests. The beggars are served by the mother of the groom. Before starting the meal, some more prayers are said for the welfare of the bride and groom and their families. The meal is served on a *patravalli*, a plate made by stitching together jackfruit leaves with the ribs of a coconut palm leaf. It is a grand layout with an array of meat dishes: chicken, beef, and the ever-present pork. Vegetables, fish, rice, pulao, and the *vonn* as dessert also feature in this repast. Bananas, bread, liquor, and *beedis* are also served. Before serving the meal, all the food cooked for lunch is placed on a *patravalli,* including bread, banana, and *beedis*, the last made of *dumpty*—tobacco leaves wrapped in a dry jackfruit leaf, conical in shape. This plate is then kept outside the house, and only after the crow starts eating from the plate are the guests served.[145] There are variations in the food that is prepared. For meals in memory of the dead, no meat is served; however, as already written, the one on the occasion of the wedding has a number of meat preparations.

Touch, Sight, and Hearing

The most convincing answers, after having discussed many studies, show that the sensuality of eating transmits powerful mnemonic signs, mainly through smells and tastes.[146] However, this answer also has its limitations, as the scholars tend to emphasize forms of bodily memory compatible with Western views of food and the body. They also stress the pleasant smells and tastes of good food. Not much attention is paid to other types of sensualities, less gourmet and sometimes less pleasant, which include the parameters of fullness, energy, lethargy, hunger, sickness, or discomfort.[147] Another observation is that both taste and smell have been emphasized to explain the connection between food and memory. This approach has left aside the other senses of touch, sight, and hearing, though these also play an important part in bringing back memories. Some examples show how effective these three are in constructing memories.

Several distinct sensations are communicated to the brain through specialized neurons in the skin to realize the sense of touch. These include different sensations like pressure, temperature, light touch, vibration, pain, and more. These properties can bring back memories and help recall the past. Softness is also used to check whether fruits are ripe, for example, chickoo (sapota), custard apple, papaya, musk melon, etc.

Seremetakis's reflexive montage aims at developing a memory of the senses. For instance, the exchange of saliva in the masticated bread that passes from grandmother to the child's mouth.[148] In Goa, where rice is the staple food, the baby's first solid food is *canjee*.[149]

The grandmother or mother serves *canjee* in a *vatli*, a metal plate made of *pitui*, a brass alloy, and feeds the baby. To make it easier for swallowing and easy digestion of the batter, she mashes the soft rice grains by pressing them between her fingers and shaping them into a small ball, then dips it in a little sugar to make it more palatable. Pressing the soft rice grains with her hands until it turns into a batter is an experience of touch, as is the act of feeding the child with her hands—lending a touch to the action—which is reminiscent to any child who was fed in this way and to the adult feeding the child.

Eyesight can be equally successful in bringing back memories. Youngsters, especially boys, would go around seeing if they could find ripe fruits to eat and relish. The ripeness of fruits was known through their colors. Typically, they changed from green to other tones of ripe fruit. Green guava turns lighter or yellow, whereas *candam* (wild berry) turns from green to black when it is ripe. On the other hand, a mango could be yellow, red, or a mix of both red and green, as in the case of the "Monserrate" and "Nicolau Afonso" varieties.[150]

Mangoes also bring back memories of those days when young boys went looking for ripe mangoes, to pelt stones using a catapult or directly pelt stones at them if one had a good aim. Then there were the kids who waited under the mango tree for the breeze or the squirrel and the crow that pecked at one to throw down the ripe fruit. No sooner was the thud of the falling mango heard than the kids would rush to pick it up before anyone else did, or still worse, a pig took it away.

Mothers and grandmothers must find ways to get children to eat their food. It is not always easy to feed them, and the ladies have to try to lure them with a song.

> One handful from the plate,
> Handpicked lovingly from the fields
> and farms of a maternal uncle,
>
> Dipped in the sweet coconut milk.
> Finish it off in one go,
> Finish it off—*haap*![151]

Another song is about an imaginary crow, where the mother or grandmother is calling the bird, "*Kaudea, kaudea io, io, Kaudea, kaudea io, io, iem chit tucague—haap*." (Crow, crow, come here, come here, take this handful of rice—*haap*.) The intent is to instill fear in the child that the crow will take away the food, and as a result, the child would open their mouth to receive the food.

Although there is no direct literature on Goan food and memory, this connection between the two has been shown using different literary forms like novels, folklore, poetry, and even songs. Besides taste and smell, which have been emphasized by most scholars in this field, the other senses of touch, sight, and hearing have also been shown as strong connectors between food and memory.

3

Feasts and Traditions: Borrowing to Celebrate Festivities, and the Resultant Indebtedness

Introduction

The Portuguese had an impact on the religion of the Goan community as well as its cultural and social life. Religious celebrations amongst the Catholics follow the liturgical calendar of the Roman Catholic Church. The missionaries instituted these feasts in the churches in the early conversion period.[1] Besides, there are also celebrations at the numerous crosses that adorn the countryside. These normally take place during the month of May as the Catholic Church celebrates the Feast of the Holy Cross on May 3.[2]

Feasts are times to celebrate, with festal food to entertain the family and guests. This may vary according to the festival. Interestingly, some of the food, fruits, or vegetables connected to certain feasts offered—by the devotees and for the devotees—have gained importance and impacted the celebrations in ways that have even surpassed the names of several Saints, Our Lady, or a Cross. In this chapter, we examine the customs of people in connection with religion and food, with a focus on the traditions followed in the celebrations of three feasts: the Feast of St. Anne at the Church of Santana, Talaulim; that of Our Lady of the Annunciation at the Chapel of Our Lady in Siridão, both in Tiswadi taluka; and the Feast of the Holy Cross at Nerul in Bardez taluka.

Many aspects of Catholic social structure and organizations remain similar to those of Hindu caste society.[3] Even after conversion, caste has been an important organizing principle among Catholics. It influences the distribution of rights and privileges in the organization of feasts within the church. One significant area of correspondence is the organization and manner of celebration of the feasts of the ritual calendar of the church.[4] For example, in most churches, only the *gaunkars* are allowed to celebrate and be the *mordomo* (patron or president) of the feast. Another instance of

Hindu consciousness is the harvest feast celebration at Santa Cruz village in Tiswadi, where the *gaunkars* serve only a vegetarian repast on this occasion.[5]

The Feast of Santa Ana (Saint Anne)

In Goa, there are six churches devoted to Saint Anne.[6] This study covers the celebration of Santana (Santa Ana) at Talaulim Church in the village of Talaulim in Tiswadi taluka. The Feast of Santa Ana was celebrated on July 26 until the new Synod decreed that feasts should be moved to the nearest Sunday. According to certain biblical narratives, Ana married Joaquim and for long years endured ignominy and suffered the social opprobrium of sterility. After having prayed ardently in old age, she miraculously gave birth to a girl, named Maria.[7]

The feast of the church at Talaulim is also popularly known as *Touxeanchem Fest* (Feast of Cucumbers), as these fruits are offered to Saint Ana by the devotees. Talaulim once had *gaunkars* of the Comunidade, most of whom no longer live in the village. However, some of them do come to celebrate a novena or the feast as the *mordomo*. The *gaunkars* of this village were all Brahmins.[8] There is an interesting story of how the church was dedicated to Santa Ana.[9]

After dedicating the hermitage to Santa Ana, it was upgraded to a church. The present church was built in 1695.[10] This large and beautiful church catered to around 12,000 people, who included Portuguese *fidalgos*, businessmen, and natives residing in the village at that time. In 1783, the village was devastated by an epidemic. It is said that its population diminished to just 400 souls, who also left for other villages for their own safety from the plague.[11] After the Liberation of Goa in December 1961, the government declared the church a protected monument until 1994, following which it was listed under UNESCO Heritage Monuments.

The religious customs or popular religious expressions are as old as humanity. They express community traditions or group expressions of religion rooted in the social nature of man. Many of these customs were based on *do ut des*, that is, "I give so that you might give." The neo-converts to Catholicism continued with some of their previous practices and followed partly the Hindu pantheon of gods and goddesses alongside the Catholic rites, rituals, prayers, and precepts.

This is observed during the Feast of Santa Ana, where the offerings to the saint are cucumbers, making the feast popularly known as *Touxeanchem Fest*. On this occasion, hundreds of devotees gather to pay homage to the saint and individually pray and beg according to their needs, for a child, a life partner, or any other favor. Curious traditions are followed by them, which seem to be centuries old. It is important to note that the devotees are not only Catholics, but there are also Hindus, the majority of the latter belonging to the tribal Gawda community.[12] This strange, religious-cum-folklore tradition seems to have captured the imagination of the devotees who believe that Santa Ana is miraculous and spiritually very powerful.

On the feast day, after the Mass, the faithful queue up to make their offerings; these could be *touxem* (pepinos/cucumbers), *urid dal* (lentil), *manilha* (bangle), *colher* (spoon), *agarbatti* (incense sticks), flowers, candles, and coconuts.[13] The offerings are made depending on what the person desires, to seek the intercession of the saint for the quick and timely realization of their heart's wishes.

For instance, a petition to Santa Ana to request favors is published in the *Almanach Indo-portuguez para o Anno de 1886* by C.C. Philalete Castelino,[14] which matches and rhymes with some of the votive offerings to the saint.[15] This petition helps us recreate the tradition of the past followed by the inhabitants of the village before they were converted and how the Portuguese, as dominant colonizers, appropriated the tradition followed by the Hindus.

The following interesting invocations to the saint are made by newly married couples. They go near the statue and offer a tender *pepino,* imploring for a male child: *Tóma pepino, dá cá menino* (Take a cucumber, give me a boy).

The request is to grant the couple a bonny boy in exchange for the offering of a cucumber. Many Goans, like some other Indians, believe that a boy is a prized possession and is regarded as the light of the house.[16] Married couples who desire a girl child, since there are only boys in the family, offer a *manilha*: *Tóma manilha, dá cá filha* (Take a bangle, give me a daughter).

It is not only for children that one goes to the Church of Santa Ana on the festive day. Some unmarried girls, desirous of a suitor, visit the church and pray reverently, offering *urid*: *Tóma urid, dá cá marid* (Take lentil, give me a husband). On the other hand, the bachelors offer a *colher,* saying: *Tóma colher, dá cá mulher* (Take a spoon, give me a wife).

This tradition was observed only at Talaulim, Goa. Joseph Barros, in a paper presented at a history seminar in 1991, titled "Religious Tradition at St. Anne's Church,"[17] concludes:

> An eminent social scientist-cum-biologist was asked to elicit his opinion on the above cited couplets. If the same were only for literary

> rhymes or if they could connote or denote something more than that. The view expanded was that the tender "pepino" in the present context be symbolically viewed as phallus or linga of the Hindu mythological lore, the bangle, and the elliptical shape of the spoon as the yonic symbol, that is, *pudendum muliebre*, the symbol under which the Hindu female is worshipped in India. The tiny cereal (lentil) "urid" could symbolize the male procreative sperm.[18]

Referring to Barros's conclusion of "poetic imagination or whether reads in it some symbolic imagery," and clarifications in the paper he presented, it does not give a motive for the theory of appropriation, for the reasons explained here. Why was *touxem* selected as a popular name for the feast and not the other offerings? It is observed that there are other offerings like the *urid* (lentil), the *manilha* (bangle), and the *colher* (spoon). The answer is in the ecology of the village. Talaulim village has fields and hillocks, and the villagers, being agriculturalists and agricultural laborers, had to make the best of their land for sustenance and survival. Rice cultivation was extensive in the village. However, the hillocks had also to be used and made economically viable.

The portion of the hilly area, which was feasible to cultivate rice, was used for paddy. On the remaining sloping portion, the farmers planted vegetables, taking advantage of the monsoons. This plantation was called *malyan mohvo.* Long narrow trenches were cut in the ground, keeping space between them for planting seeds. These would be sown on the edges of the trenches, either on one or both sides. The sowing was done before the rains. The main crops planted were cucumbers, varieties of gourds, lady's fingers, melons, and lentils (urid and moong).[19] The cucumbers would be ready for plucking and sale by July so that by the time the feast came around, there were plenty of them.

It was normal to offer to God the first produce of the season in thanksgiving, which for the agriculturists of Talaulim would be vegetables like cucumber and the *urid*, to the goddess of the village, namely, Satteri. A book of homilies in Konkani printed in Goa in 1658 titled *Jardim dos Pastores* by a Jesuit, Fr. Miguel de Almeida, who was rector of both the Colleges of St. Paul and Rachol, reveals the benefit from the gifting of the new crop in the text *Primitias frugum terrae tuae offeres in domum Domini dei tui, Exodus 23*, which firmly states that "we do not lose what we offer to God, rather on the contrary we gain advantages thereof."[20] The system of offering continues with rice, during big celebrations through the harvest festival, when a sheaf of rice is offered to the deity, by both Catholics and Hindus. The latter observed on the second day of Ganesh Chaturthi when a new sheaf of rice was seen offered to Lord Ganesh. A few grains of unhusked rice were added to the *pais*, the sweet made of rice, milk, and sugar and presented as *nivedya,* the symbolic offering to the deity, especially cooked on a festive day.[21] A couple of sheaves were tied to the *mattolli* (ceremonial hanging of local vegetables and fruits). The first fruits or firstborn, from a plant or animal, play a special role. Earlier, they were considered to be divine; then it was believed that they were created by the gods and were offered as thanksgiving or sacrifice, either to the god or to the chief.[22]

It is not only through prayers and offerings that the farmers seek blessings from the Almighty for a good crop. An example is given of the lower classes in Sattari, Valpoi, who perform a ritual to obtain a good harvest: "The lower classes in Sattari (North of Goa) make a *mutthoi*: a *gaunkar* breaks a coconut, kills a young fowl, and mixes a little cooked rice with the blood of the fowl; then he sprinkles it over the field and immediately harvests a fistful of ears of paddy."[23] The offering was for gratitude and thanksgiving and presented to the deity, which thereafter—by touching the image—would become blessed for the devotee and would be considered as *prasad*[24] and distributed and eaten by the members of the household. So, this tradition of offering to the deity was observed by the people much before the Portuguese arrived. Rui Gomes Pereira writes that the ancient temples in the village of Talaulim did not leave any vestiges and it was not known if the deity was transferred to any other temple.[25] Amongst the ancient temples, there was one devoted to Satteri, the Mother Goddess, who is also the Earth Goddess.[26] On observing the tradition of Talaulim from an anthropological angle, it appears that the pre-Catholic traditions have been superimposed and merged carefully with Catholic veneration of the saint according to the pieties of the time, or maybe the neo-converts to Catholicism continued some of their pre-conversion practices together with Catholic rites and prayers.

Pezechem Fest and the Goan *Canjee*

In the village of Siridão, on the Sunday after Easter Day, the Feast of Our Lady of Annunciation is celebrated. This feast is popularly known as *Pezechem Fest.* The name is derived from the *canjee* (rice gruel), which is *pez* in the Konkani language. This tradition is rooted in this village, which was prosperous in the past with many houses, but after the people moved out of the hamlet, it consisted only of coconut groves.[27] It was also popular for summer vacations of the landed gentry and well-off citizens from Panaji and adjoining areas. The *pez* is offered by the Dempo family.

The inhabitants of the village are Catholics, Hindus, and Gawdas. Many of the villagers are employed in the traditional work of fishing and toddy tapping. However, a sizable number of Catholics have migrated to France, and some others work on the ships. Of late, taking advantage of Portuguese citizenship offered by the erstwhile rulers, many have migrated to the UK.[28] The emigrants come for the feast to have a grand celebration with their family and friends, even though it is not that of the patron of the village church.[29] The feast is also known as that of Jesus Nazarene as it celebrates the Annunciation of Our Lady of Nazareth. However, on this occasion, the Catholics celebrate the mystery reported by St. Luke.[30] The chapel dedicated to Our Lady of Annunciation is perched on a hillock with a beautiful view of the sea. On the feast day, a life-size image of Ecce Homo is kept for public adoration. So, it should not come as a surprise that people started referring to the feast as "Jesus Nazare."[31]

The Feast of the Annunciation was attended not only by the folk from Siridão, but also by people from all over Goa and elsewhere, like Sawantwadi. Many devotees from Bardez, Salcete, and Ilhas, especially women, used to come on pilgrimage to pray and pay obeisance to Jesus of Nazareth.[32] People came in hundreds by bus, canoes, or on foot, accompanied by musicians on the eve of the feast day. The households in Siridão extended their hospitality to them even if they were total strangers. It is said that no visitors to the house, including strangers, were refused a meal on the feast day or vespers.[33] In the past, the transport system was inadequate, and therefore commuting from one place to another was difficult and tedious. It would not be possible for people coming from afar to reach for the Mass, which would take place early in the morning. They would travel before the feast day and would spend the night on the verandas of the houses, with the locals giving them food and hospitality.

The Preparation of the *Pez* (Canjee)

A well-known tradition observed to date by the people attending the feast is the consumption of *pez,* which is distributed free of cost to all who wish to partake of it. Some people make vows that they will attend the feast and have the *pez* if their prayers are granted. Vinayak Khedekar writes about this feast in the book *Eco-culture Goa Paradigm*:

> The entire ritual has a natural atmosphere, and no pandal is erected. The serving is done in big-sized *done*—bowls of banana, or by using any big sized leaves. For serving, a broad coconut shell ladle

> with a bamboo handle is used. A Hindu family supplies the required quantity of rice. The Hindus do the cooking and its distribution. The rest of the feast is organized along Christian lines.[34]

Contrary to Khedekar's observation, while there was no formal *pandal* (a large open-sided temporary pavilion), there was an enclosure called *matov* made traditionally with braided coconut leaves called *mollam*. The *pez* was served in *maitulas* made of clay. Using *donnes* made of leaves was also traditional in religious ceremonies and otherwise, as these could be easily discarded and the leaves were freely available.[35]

Kensor Menezes, whose family used to help cook the *pez*, and her daughter Maya Gauns were interviewed. Kensor is from the village of Nauxim, located in Bambolim, but a part of the Curca panchayat. She belongs to the Gawda community of Goa. Her name indicates that her family was converted to Christianity and then reconverted to Hinduism.[36] Kensor was married to Custodio João, popularly known as Kistud, who hailed from Siridão and was a *mundkar* of the Dempo family. He looked after the properties of Dempo, functioning as a supervisor, and made all the arrangements whenever the landlord wanted to celebrate the traditional festive occasions. The *pez*, though served for a Catholic feast, was prepared by Hindu Gawdas, and people from all religions partook of it. Kensor informed that Custodio, along with two other male *mundkars*, Vitorino and Francisco, was responsible for cooking the *pez*. Thus, on the feast day at three in the morning, a fire was lit to start cooking the rice.

Kensor described how the preparations for cooking the *pez* were done days before the feast. Around six women were employed to do the groundwork, which included collecting the firewood and leaves to be used to cook the rice. They also had to collect the green leaves of the coconut tree for making *mollam*.[37]

Work on preparing an enclosure would start a few days before the feast. The enclosure would be used to cook and serve the *pez*. The men folk plucked raw mangoes, sliced them, and served them to the people along with the *pez* as an appetizer. Kensor said that seven temporary fireplaces using three stones for each were also erected, and seven large copper vessels were placed on these fires. Was there any particular reason or explanation for that particular number of vessels? Kensor did not know the reason. However, Vinayak Khedekar writes:

> Elderly villagers rely on the legend of SaptMatrika—Seven Mothers mentioned in ancient Sanskrit literature. The seven cooking pots used in the Peaje Fest also symbolize the seven sisters. The legend is

> quite prevalent in Shirdon village. Peaj is cooked on seven *chullhass*, specially made for this purpose. Seven large copper vessels are used to cook the large quantity of rice and this is distributed to all devotees.[38]

However, Kensor explained that the *pez* for distribution to the devotees was not cooked in all the vessels. Only three were used for cooking in large quantities. In the remaining four, a small portion of rice was cooked symbolically.

The *mukadam* (supervisor) of the landlord would buy the required quantity of rice and hand it over to the men to cook. Ten *cuddoes*[39] of rice were used for the *pez*. The type of rice is *ukkdo,* the local boiled variety. The cooking was exclusively done by the three men, Custodio, Vitorino, and Francisco, who were the *mundkars* of Dempo, and the women came only to help with the fire and to bring the required water. In the olden days, it was women from Siridão who helped. Today, those from the neighboring Palem village are entrusted with the work.

After attending the Mass, the devotees partook of the *pez*. Earthenware sellers used to make *maltis*, small clay plates which devotees bought to have the *pez*. In the past, before serving the people, the *pez* was first offered at the *xim* (demarcating village line) for the protector of the village, the Rakhandar, and other spirits.

The expenses for preparing the *pez* are borne by the Dempo family, who owned most of the land in the village. The other landlords are the Mascarenhas and Waglo families, who own a small percentage of the village land, and neither clan follows any tradition of offering any meals to the *mundkars*. However, Balchandra Vaglo told of how his family sponsored a litany of a cross found on their property. Those present at the celebrations were the toddy tappers who collected the sap from the coconut trees of the estate. But why was this tradition particularly followed by the Dempos? One of the explanations put forth is that this *pez* is given to honor a *pensão*, which was probably established by the original landowner. What is a *pensão*? It is a type of "periodical payment." In the past, some persons who had no heirs or, in an act of philanthropy, bequeathed property or gifted money to the church, with certain conditions which had to be fulfilled. The conditions would range from a certain number of Masses to be said in the benefactor's memory and that of his family or even in the memory of the forgotten and wandering souls. Some others would ask to offer oil, which was used to light the lamps in the church or chapel. If the condition laid down was not honored, it was said that the spirits of the dead would protest and something untoward would happen. People were therefore cautious while buying properties and would shirk from buying those which had a *pensão* because they were afraid that if the wishes of the departed donor were not fulfilled, it would bring them bad luck.[40]

The Dempos owned a house in Panjim[41] where the needy and poor could seek food and shelter.[42] Panjimites were witness to the serving of meals there every afternoon.[43] The *bhat* performs a *puja* every day as the Dempos have a *shaligram,* and the *nivedya* is rice and *ros*, a lentil curry.[44] On a special visit to the house to collect data, the manager was interviewed and asked what quantity of rice was cooked for the daily *puja*. He said it was five *podds.*[45] According to the religious traditions, a set amount of rice needed to be cooked every day to present as *nivedya.*[46] Five *podds* was quite a large quantity, and it was distributed to the poor after the family and staff had their share. Meals to the beggars have been stopped since January 2016. However, food continues to be cooked as *nivedya* and is partaken by the staff.

It seems that the Dempos wished to fulfill the needs and obligations included in the *shastras* so that they were blessed by the gods through the alms offered by them. The daily ritual of serving meals to the needy, or an annual offering to the dead, is included in the *shastras*.[47] The offering of the *pez* on the feast day can also be considered such a ritual offering.

Tisreachem Fest and Its Connection to Ecology and Culture

The *Tisreachem Fest* is another example of a feast that is connected to Goan traditions, culture, and ecology. This study was also based on fieldwork and oral cultural practices. Nerul, in Bardez taluka, is a coastal village surrounded by the River Mandovi. The inhabitants of this village comprise both Hindus and Catholics.

Most of the villagers were once agriculturists or agricultural laborers. A minuscule percentage was in service, either government or private. There was also a sizable community of fisherfolk, which was natural with such an extensive riverbank. There were several large landholders, the *bhatkars* and *mundkars,* in the village. The economy was agrarian in nature. There were no industries, except for the rice husking mill and some shops, like in any other village of Goa. Many migrated and became financially well-off. The villagers cultivated rice during the monsoon and winter seasons. Fishing was another important activity. Many fisherfolk would also cultivate fields to supplement their incomes. Animal husbandry was also dominant amongst them, with cows, buffaloes, goats, hens, and pigs reared as domestic animals for personal consumption, with any surplus being sold. The villagers knew how to use the available resources and live within an economical and sustainable ecosystem. In fact, the community's economy in those days was based on the availability of local products and the exchange of goods, as cash flow was limited.

Our Lady of Remedios is the patron of the main church. The village has several chapels[48] affiliated with the church, and some public crosses. Many of the residential houses too have a cross in their compound. The month of May marks the end of the summer season in Goa, a time of vacation for school children and celebrations for families. This is the time when Goan emigrants from the neighboring cities of India, especially from Bombay, return to their homes to enjoy a hard-earned holiday along with their families. So, one observes that many of the feasts of patrons of churches, chapels, and family crosses are celebrated in May. In Nerul, the feasts of various chapels and crosses, private and public, are celebrated with the singing of *ladainha* (litany).[49] A unique preparation of *tisreos* (clams) called *tisreachem sambarem* is a must for a couple of chapel feasts, which has given the celebration the popular name *Tisreachem Fest*. Other food items may be included depending on the individual celebrating the feast.

Tisreachem Sambarem, a Sublime Delicacy

The choice of *tisreo* for serving during the celebrations was a natural one. The best qualities of *tisreo* in the Bardez taluka are from Nerul.[50] The adjoining village of Verem also had a good yield. And the best part was that there was no need to buy them. These were available in abundance to those who were willing to search for them on the river bed. Therefore, there was easy access as well as free availability of *tisreo* for a village where nearly half of the population had to work hard to make both ends meet.

The villagers lived as a community and worked for one another in their agricultural fields as well as on odd jobs at home. When religious celebrations or social functions like weddings or birthdays came around, the neighbors from the ward would join hands to help one another in the preparations and cooking of food. As a large quantity of *tisreo* was required to serve at the feast, relatives, neighbors, and others joined to search and gather the clams.[51]

Community and Ecological Cultural Practices

The cultural practices of attending the feast are observed not only by the residents but also by their children and extended families. Those not living in the village make it a point to attend the litany. Earlier, only the males had the privilege of celebrating the feast, but later the married daughters were also offered this option.

The feast was looked forward to by the people of the ward as a community celebration, which is reflected in the manner the *tisreo* are prepared. Ms. Luisa Nazareth was the *mordomo* in the year 2018, as in the past she had made a vow to celebrate the feast in the name of her son. In the chapel of St. Anthony in Bati ward, those interested in commemorating the feast have to approach the committee members for permission. If there is no pending request from another person wanting to celebrate, the request is granted the same year. Otherwise, the requester has to wait for his or her turn. The waiting periods depend on the number of requests from interested people.

There is another Goan cultural practice that has almost died out. There used to be a *ranpin*, a lady cook, who came to the house to cook and oversee the kitchen preparations. Later, men also got into this line of work. The *ranpin* was supported by neighbors and relatives who came to help from the village.

The neighbors brought their own tools. Fortunately, this cultural practice has still remained in this particular celebration, where one finds ladies of the ward coming together to help clean the clams, grate the coconut, and grind it, with a *ranpin* present to oversee the preparation. She was also responsible for preparing the important *sambareacho temper* (masala). Women came with graters, knives, and kitchen boards to help in the cooking of the *tisreo*. The Goan grater is made of a wooden bench of low height, to which is attached a long knife-like blade that ends with the grater. The blade is used to open the shells and cut vegetables or slice the onions. The grated coconut is ground in an electrical food processor. In the past, they used to grind it on a *rogdo* (stone grinder).

The preparations start with a man breaking around eighty coconuts. A woman washes the *tisreo* to remove the sand from the shells. Then, in another group, each one of the ladies takes a portion of washed clams in a small bucket with water, and they start opening them. After a sizable quantity is opened, it is added to a container with clean water. This process is followed until all are washed. They are then put in different containers and kept covered. Alongside, a couple of ladies grate the coconuts. This is then ground, not very fine, but a little coarse in thickness. Attention has to be paid while adding water for grinding. No excess water is to be added. It has to be just enough to have the required consistency as the gravy has to be almost dry.

In the meantime, two stone fires are readied in an open space outside the house, and huge vessels are placed on them to cook the *tisreo*. The cooking starts with adding the chopped onions and tomatoes to hot oil and frying them until golden. The cooking of the clams is in two steps. First, the ground coconut is mixed with the fried onions and tomatoes. Then the masala is added and mixed well.[52]

After the incorporation of the masala, the *tisreos* are added to this coconut mixture. Care is taken that the clams do not separate from their shells. Sugar and coconut palm jaggery are added to enhance the taste.[53] Thereafter, in the next cooking step, small portions of this coconut and *tisreos* mixture are put into smaller vessels and cooked. This way, the possibility of the food getting burnt or stuck to the bottom of the vessel is avoided when cooking in large quantities. After cooking, these smaller quantities are added back to the large vessel and further cooked until the entire coconut and *tisreos* mixture is ready. A large wooden spoon is used to mix and shake the *sambarem*. It is called a *dai*, having a large flat surface for mixing and a long stick for holding.[54]

The masala is tedious to prepare and takes a couple of days to be ready. It is heavily spiced with around thirteen spices. These are dried in the sun for days. Onions, ginger, and garlic that go into its making are also dried. Each of the ingredients is then fried individually in oil and powdered. Since it is a large quantity, it is taken to the village grinding mill. In the olden days, some might have powdered them at home in a *vann*, which consisted of an iron container placed in a hole in the ground.[55] The spices were pounded with a big wooden stick called a *mussol*. A well-prepared masala can last for months if stored properly.

Two Chapels and Two Celebrations

In the evening, the people converged near the chapel of St. Anthony in Bati ward[56] to sing the litany and say the prayers. This chapel is not included in the *Anuário de Arquidiocese de Goa e Damão para 1955*.[57] It is one of the many that were raised by the devotees from the crosses existing in the villages. The Augustinian religious order had a *casa do campo* (summer house) at Bati and a chapel attached to it, which was dedicated to the Holy Cross. When the Augustinians had to abandon the house, the statues of Santa Luzia and São João Evangelista existing in the chapel were taken to the chapel of S. João Baptista at Calangute, and the baptismal font was transferred to the existing chapel at Bati.[58] The place where the chapel of the Augustinians existed is marked by a cross.[59] The cross existing in the chapel of St. Anthony is probably the one that marks the chapel of the Augustinians.

It is the responsibility of the *mordomo* to make all the arrangements and take care of all expenses in connection with the feast. Following the litany, prayers were recited repeatedly, invoking different reasons and names of people who should benefit from the prayers. After the prayers, hosannas in thanksgiving were sung. People then queued up to pay obeisance to the images in the chapel. On the way out stood a table on which *donnes* with *tisreo sambarem* were arranged. Each person picked up the *donno* and bread, which were kept in a large basket. Some people sat to eat and enjoy at the chapel, while others took the food home. No alcoholic beverages were served. Napoleão Sousa, who is from Bati ward and whose family has celebrated the feast quite a few times, said that this cultural practice of serving the clams is more than 150 years old. The bread was included in the offerings to the guests somewhere down the years, and it continued to be a part of the meal.

The second feast is at Fortawaddo, where there is a small chapel by the wayside, known as the Holy Cross Chapel.[60] We attended the feast after the one at the Bati ward. Here, the chapel is also bedecked with lights and other ornaments, and a pandal is erected. Again, it is the responsibility of the *mordomo* to make all the arrangements and cover expenses in connection with the feast. The people from the ward also participate in celebrating the feast with great pomp.

How was the feast celebrated at this chapel, and did the ward members request celebrating to fulfill vows made by them? The feast of the chapel, in this particular ward, was celebrated democratically by every house in rotation. Here too, a *ranpin* would oversee the preparations of *tisreanchem sambarem*. In this chapel, mangoes and jackfruit were also served to the guests. Every *donno* contained *tisreo*, jackfruit (the hard variety called capo), and a mango. Besides these items, boiled grams were served to those present, along with a slice of cake to sweeten the mouth. For those who enjoyed *feni,* the *copito* would do the rounds, while others could enjoy a soft drink. No bread was served, and the preparation was almost dry so that to eat, a person could pick up the clams with their fingers.[61]

On the feast day, celebrations started with a litany in the evening. Prayers were said to thank and request blessings on the *mordomo,* family, and all the people of the ward. The next morning, a Monday, a Mass was said, and in the evening, a litany was held. While the novenas are celebrated by the people of the ward in a group of three members per novena, the *fama*, vespers, feast, and the celebrations of the following Monday were the responsibility of the *mordomo*.[62] Angeline Barreto from Fottawaddo was interviewed. She is in her late sixties and now goes as *ranpin* to prepare the *tisreachem sambarem*. She claimed that she had learned to cook on her own. It has been more than forty years that she has been preparing the *tisreo* and does not charge any money for cooking.

In keeping with the Goan cultural practices of communal harmony, we find that the Hindus of Nerul, Pilerne, and Verem join together to celebrate the Feast of The Cross on May 3, the day of the Holy Cross.[63] This cross is situated in the middle of the fields in Nerul. The religious celebrations are similar to those followed by the Catholics. Participation in the litany is from all religions, with the prayers being recited by the Catholics. Lots of food is offered by the celebrants. Interestingly, they too serve *tisreachem sambarem* as one of the food items.

A religious cultural practice observed by the villagers is that of Ufaar, an offering of a gold miniature clam to the Sea Goddess. Every year, the authorities of Dev Dadeshwar Temple at Maima Wado in Nerul auction the rights to collect money from villagers to make the offering. The person who gains the rights from the auction then collects donations by going around the village. Both Hindus and Catholics contribute to making the gold clam. This offering is done on an auspicious day, on a Sunday after Mahashivratri. The plate of offerings of the gold clam also contains puris, coconut, *supari* (areca nut), *paan* (betel leaf), and some sweets. The locals gather at the temple to say the prayers and thereafter go to make the offerings, which are placed in the sea. After the performance of Ufaar, the locals start going to the river to collect the clams. This activity goes on till the end of July. This observation of Ufaar continues to date. In the past, when many people used to go to collect the clams, there were days earmarked for each ward so that all could share in the bounty. Today, this practice is not followed.

The Feast of the Holy Cross shows the importance of making use of the available resources by the villagers. Even today, neighbors walk in the early morning to help in preparing the *tisreachem sambarem*, showing Goan cultural practices and how they lived in communal harmony. The serving of seasonal fruits shows that villagers depend on ecology not only for day-to-day survival but also when celebrating. Fruits like mangoes and jackfruits are abundantly available during the summer months.

The food served is a symbolic representation of the authentic Goan culinary trait. The *sambarechi coddi* is symbolic of Goan food. Besides, the use of natural resources is rooted in the culture. The cultural practices of serving the *tisreachem sambarem* overlap with the cultural identity of the villagers, considering its social and cultural importance despite the introduction of various other foods later.

This tradition of offering the clams at a Catholic religious observation—the *ladainha*—acquired the popular name *Tisreachem Fest*, and people believe that the name has a religious connotation. An article was written by a columnist,[64] who quotes Fr. Bolmax Pereira, the then vicar of Nerul Church, as saying that *Tisreachem Fest* cannot be associated with any Christian or religious feast as there is neither a specific day for celebrating it, nor does it have any religious significance. Pereira further adds that it is just an opportunity for the people to come together. True, the name *Tisreachem Fest* does not have religious significance, but the celebration has, as it is associated with the litany at the Holy Cross Chapel, which is a Catholic religious observation. Besides, though it doesn't have a fixed day in the liturgical calendar, it is held annually on the second Sunday of the month of May, where devout devotees who perceive that the Cross is a miraculous one come to thank for the favors bestowed on them and implore for protection or pray for their needs. It is also a tradition that when a child is born in a family at Bati, the family celebrates the litany.[65] In the same article, comments on the celebrations are made by another writer.[66] According to him, shellfish were abundant in Nerul and Verem, and therefore, since "the locals were mainly fishermen, they decided to dedicate a day of thanksgiving for the abundance of tisreo."[67] As already written and discussed, the celebration is a litany at the Holy Cross Chapel at Bati ward, where the residents are mostly Catholics and no fisherfolk lived there; therefore, the celebration has no connection with the abundance of *tisreo*.[68] However, there are Catholic fishermen at Danddarim ward who are not connected with the celebrations at Bati or Fottawaddo.[69] The role of the *tisreo* is only as food.

Borrowing to Celebrate Festivities and the Subsequent Indebtedness

These festivities, beyond the church rituals and popular traditions, had more to them than was apparent. People needed money to celebrate with family and friends. Those who did not have money borrowed to bear the expenses, thus creating a financial burden that was difficult to overcome for those with limited incomes. But still worse were those who eagerly looked forward to being the *mordomo* of the feast, '*mordomo* in Konkani means "president.""[70] He was the person who bore most of the expenses of the feast, which involved religious rituals as well as other traditions. It was an honor, and many an aspiring villager keenly waited for his turn to celebrate the feast.

Depending on the churches and rules laid down by individual Confrarias and Comunidades, the *mordomo* also had to celebrate some other not-so-solemn feasts that were part of the church rituals. Besides these rituals, there were the church decorations, the brass band which played for the vespers, and the *alvorada* on the morning of the feast day.[71] The band also had to play before and after the solemn feast Mass and during the procession. Almost all important feasts had to be accompanied by fireworks and *foznem* (petards). There was also music during the novena days played by two Mahars, with the bugle, snare drum, and a drum, who also had the duty to light the *foznem*.[72] This was done before and after the novena Mass in the morning and evening and *salves*.[73]

In many of the churches, celebrations of the Feast of Our Lady were also accompanied by fireworks during the novenas and the vespers. The different wards of the village sponsored the expenses on a particular day. However, the vesper was the prerogative of the *mordomo*, which meant that he had to spend money, whether he had it or not, to observe and maintain the traditions. Still worse was the mania to outdo the earlier ones in having a grand affair. "Perhaps, no event in rural life gives a fitter occasion for the manifestation of personal lavishness among Goans than the village *festa*, with its novenas, salves, and vespers."[74]

The guidelines for the celebrations of the feast may vary from church to church and would also depend on its patron. Traditionally, the feast's *mordomo* was a *gaunkar* of a village Comunidade, and they had to be members of the church or chapel confraternity.[75] However, not every *gaunkar* could be a *mordomo*. There was a hierarchy amongst them in some of the Comunidades, and this hierarchy was also maintained in the Confrarias. But there were also other Confrarias, which were exclusive to a particular caste, in what Leopoldo da Rocha called *exclusivismo confrarial* (Confraternity's exclusivism), which means that to ingress in these associations, the right is reserved to a certain class or category of people.[76]

Many *gaunkars* looked forward to celebrating the feast of the village, but since there were many aspirants, their desire would sometimes not be fulfilled. Those who were lucky went out of their way to celebrate the feast, to the extent of borrowing to pay for the expenses. The example of Ligôr *bhatkar* in *O Signo da Ira* shows to what extremes a person can go to satisfy his pride. Orlando da Costa writes that the landlord was looking forward to being the *mordomo* of the Feast of Our Lady of Immaculate

Conception, on December 8 at the Church of the Holy Spirit, Margao, so that he could show his greatness as a *bhatkar*. Despite Ligôr's debt and dire financial conditions, he did not shy away from celebrating the feast with great pomp, like no one else before him. He also considered himself lucky that he could achieve this honor before he was fifty years old: "… seemed to ignore the ruin left behind it all, wrought by his decline in those recent times of privation and discontent. He had mortgaged everything that necessity demanded of him to save his family's honour. Now, striding gravely under the festive arches that surrounded the square, he thought that his family's honour had been invested in him."[77]

The expenses also included food and drinks that were served to the guests. The *bhatkar*'s house was full of *mundkars,* and his servants moved about carrying and serving dishes of food and drink.[78] And the ostentatious celebrations did not end at the house, as Ligôr tells the *mundkars*: "Eat here, then at nine o'clock go watch the fireworks I've arranged for in the church square."[79] Contrary to what was always done, Ligôr had moved the display of fireworks from the night of the vesper to the feast day itself.[80] He had surrounded himself with clever excuses and made pledges to make it happen, as this simple innovation would be enough to raise the expectations and curiosity of everyone for whom the festivities were being held. He also knew that this was the last opportunity he had in life to be the *mordomo* of a feast, "A feast worthy of a great Brahmin lord," he thought."[81] Manú Foguetêr had assembled one of the most spectacular firework displays, to which there was nothing comparable in recent years.[82]

Watching the fireworks, people commented, "It's to impress the other Brahmins of the brotherhood and the *paclé*!" In fact, people already knew that he had been forced to mortgage a great deal of his property to celebrate the feast.[83]

However, Ligôr knew the price of vanity that he felt at that moment, to satisfy his ego, to maintain his honor, and to leave a lasting impression in the memories of everyone—a memory that could not have been forgotten except with the passing of many years so that, even in death, his name would be respected and would not be mocked. Despite all the reverses he had suffered since the war started, he had managed to maintain his credit and impose his will.[84]

According to tradition, one's prestige was measured by the variety and abundance of the fireworks. Therefore, those who wished to outdo others had a larger outlay of fireworks and gunpowder, even at the risk of incurring debt.[85] A *fogeter* was the local manufacturer of fireworks about whom Lucio Rodrigues ironically comments that he was the rural precursor of the modern maker of rockets, missiles, torpedoes, bombs, and warheads. His services were indispensable whenever public or private gala celebrations were to be held. The pride and magnificence of the Goan celebrating an event depended upon the *fogeter*'s genius.[86] It is on such occasions that he reveals his genius as an artist in fireworks. Rodrigues comments that they became a status symbol, a mark of personal affluence and largesse.[87]

Rodrigues narrates a story to illustrate how a person is ready to spend money to show off. Told with wit and humor, it shows the Goan psyche in particular, through an unknowledgeable person. Salu, Pedro's neighbor, celebrated the feast of the village patron saint with great pomp. Nothing was spared; the most famous preacher from Old Goa was engaged to deliver the sermon during the novenas, for morning and evening Masses.[88] The village resounded with the sound of *foznem* (petards), and after the *salve*, the band played ballroom music outside the church, followed by fireworks. On the day of the feast, the pomp and splendor reached their climax. Old Salu, clad in a white surplice and red cape, joined the procession and walked proudly, while Pedro looked at him with admiration. At the time the priest began the *O Salutaris,* Pedro pricked his ears and said to himself, "What a great honour to have his name thus sung in praise by the choir and the faithful. I will celebrate the feast next year," he decided on the spot.[89]

If Ligôr is an example of a *bhatkar* in penury going all out to celebrate the feast just to show his status, that of the common man was no different. In this case, vanity alone might not have been the main reason for borrowing, but the different rituals and traditions that went along with the celebrations, which had to be strictly followed, led the *mordomo* to financial losses. A news item carried in the paper *Porjecho Adar*,[90] writes that the Feast of Saint Lourenço was celebrated with great pomp at the church at Sinquetim, Aguada, by the "president" of the feast, Francisco Lopes, and remarks that when the procession with the saint returned to the church, he observed the tradition of lighting twenty-one *nalli* (foznem).[91] The news shows how traditions were important and needed to be observed as laid down. In this case, the number and timing of lighting the *foznem* were specified.

The Harvest Festival of the Comunidade of Taleigão and Its Numerous Traditions

The harvest festival of the Comunidade of Taleigão is an example of how rigorous the traditions are to be followed by the *mordomo*, a privilege set aside only for the *gaunkars* of the first *vangor*, which consists of nine families.[92] It is laden with traditions and rituals that are spread over four days. The festival begins on August 21, the first such celebration in the Tiswadi taluka. The other villages of this taluka celebrate it on August 24, or on a Sunday after that date.[93] This privilege was given by Afonso de Albuquerque to the *gaunkars* who, at great risk to their lives, helped him and his soldiers overcome hunger by offering them food when their ships were anchored on the Mandovi River, as the Aguada sandbar[94] was closed for maritime traffic, waiting to sail for safety.[95]

Any male member of each *gaunkar* family does the harvesting by rotation on August 21. A procession starts from the church and is accompanied by the *gaunkar* celebrating the feast, who wears the *opa-mursa* (surplice and cape) of the confraternity of St. Michael, the patron of the church. Along with him are the parish priest, other *gaunkars*, members of the fraternity, and devotees. They wind through the fields to a location that the Comunidade of Taleigão has marked for this purpose. A ceremonial red umbrella is carried to protect the *gaunkar* and the priest. The *gaunkars* and confreres carry the statue of the patron St. Michael in the procession. In the past, the entourage was accompanied by the *addao*, a group of Gawda villagers, fancifully attired and holding decorated bamboo poles in their hands, which represented swords. They used these to fight a mock battle.[96] One of the *gaunkars* would hold the Portuguese flag, which according to legend was given to them by Afonso de Albuquerque. On the feast day, a certain number of *foznem* had to be lit before, during, and after the service. For example, when the procession left for the fields, when it reached the spot where the new sheaf was harvested, on their way back, and before and after the Mass. There was a formal lunch offered by the *mordomo* to his guests on the last day of the celebrations, on August 24. During the repast, *foznem* were lit at various intervals of time.[97]

On the following day, August 22, *avel* (flattened rice), which symbolizes the local produce, is distributed to all the *gaunkars* in the village by going to their houses. Each *gaunkar* is entitled to one *podd*, and a widow receives half a *podd*. The ringing of church bells and burning of firecrackers announce the beginning of this distribution. The *mordomo* or his representative is also entitled to the ceremonial umbrella and is accompanied by the band of the Mahars.[98]

On August 23, *avel* is ceremoniously offered to the parish priest by the *mordomo*. The grand finale of the four-day festival is on August 24. It is on this day that he and a committee of *gaunkars* carry *avel* and a sheaf of paddy stalks to the Se Cathedral, where a High Mass is celebrated.[99] On this occasion, the Chapter of the Cathedral used to be occupied by the Canons, twenty-four in all, and after the Mass, each one of them was given a measure of *avel*. On their return from Old Goa, the entourage would go directly to the palace of the Adil Khan (present old Secretariat) in Panaji, and the governor was handed the fresh sheaves and *avel* by the *mordomo*. At this ceremony, the *addao* performed for the authorities and the public opposite the palace.

Thereafter, the entourage paid a visit to the patriarch, who was also offered the paddy stalks and *avel*. Opposite the patriarch's palace, the *addao* also performed before they returned home, dancing along their way. On this day, the *mordomo* had to offer a sumptuous lunch to the entourage/committee. The lunch consisted of twelve varieties of cooked food. Like any Comunidade affair, this too is a male-dominated event. Only sons can harvest the new sheaves, and only male *gaunkars* are part of the entourage that participates and partakes at the table on August 24. The *mordomo* has to religiously follow norms laid by the Comunidade. For example, the burning of petards has to be done at a particular interval of time. If not complied with, any *gaunkar* can lodge a complaint against the *mordomo* of the feast for not observing the specified norms. The traditions are followed to this day.

Borrowing and Its Outcome

Many lived according to their means, so there were no savings, and even if there were any, they would not have been sufficient to pay the expenses of celebrating a feast. The only alternative left was to borrow. Then, this loan had to be eventually repaid. At what cost? Would it be possible to do so without troubling the family, which would have to bear the brunt of deprivation? The payment of the loan would reduce the availability of money. This would mean less buying power for their day-to-day needs of sustenance, leaving aside luxuries, and it could affect the health of the family. Besides, there would not be enough money to pay for the education of the children. Those having grown-up daughters would need money to get them married. For all these necessities, the only option would be borrowing more or selling valuables or properties, and further digging the grave of indebtedness.

The vernacular press criticized this problem as it became a serious issue for the community. Costa Bir, a noted businessman from Margao and a columnist with the *Porjecho Adar*, took on the mission of educating the masses and advised people to stop wasting money on the celebrations of the feast. He wrote that the times had changed and explained that in past decades the expenses for the feast celebrations had cost much less. As an example, the price of *foznem* and a *couso* (one gallon) of *feni*, which in the past cost one rupee each, was given. It was pointed out that at present the cost of the Mass and that of the *couso* of *feni* had increased to ten rupees. Those who spent their hard-earned money to celebrate the feast to satisfy their desire to be considered important men were criticized. In reality, he opined, the commoners were just imitating the rich.[100]

Criticism was also made about the proletariat who were not ready to acquire a loan to educate their children, but to celebrate the feast, they were ready to take a loan and even sell their gold ornaments. There was indeed a *compromisso* that laid down the traditions to be followed for celebrating the feast.[101] However, there was a need to change it, as the *compromisso* was old. Since the time it had been implemented, many changes had taken place, which influenced the celebrations. Most importantly, the prices of things had increased, making the feast celebrations costly. Another suggestion was that the Comunidades should celebrate and bear the expenses of the church feasts. Costa Bir proposed that changes should be encouraged by the religious authorities, and he felt that the priest should tell the devotees not to spend unnecessarily.[102] Of course, he commented that this proposal is a difficult one since the priest or the church itself is the beneficiary.

If one thinks that these feasts were only for joy and celebrations, they are wrong. They meant much more for the people in general and especially for those who paid for the expenses as the *mordomo* of the feast. The people also looked forward to dressing up in their best outfits, spending money to make new ones, and cooking and serving the best of the food, even if they had no money, as they wanted to join in the celebrations with great pomp and show. Usually, a feast was a once-in-a-year event, and they did not want to miss flaunting their clothes and jewelry on that occasion. In the case of the *mordomos*, for many of them, the feast eventually brought misery and suffering for themselves and their families, as some of them did not actually have enough money to pay for the expenses. But the show had to go on. The only way to achieve this was through borrowing or taking a loan. To repay those loans, many even sold their property.

So, as seen, feasts were not only joyous celebrations, but they also brought suffering to some people. To maintain the traditions and to honor their names and that of the families, the *mordomos* of the feast wasted their hard-earned money. Those who borrowed for the expenses had to work hard to repay the loans, living in indebtedness and anxiety. The family remained in anguish until the loan was repaid, which was a tardy process given the prevailing financial situation.

4

The Drink That "Cheers" but Brings Tears

Introduction

Alcoholism was a deep social problem for the Goan community at the beginning of the twentieth century. It had adverse effects on the consumers, their family members, and the community as a whole. The problem was increasing every year, and yet the government wasn't seen to be doing much about it, probably fearing a loss of revenue for the state exchequer.[1]

For the Portuguese, wine drinking was a part of their social and religious observances. Alcohol that was produced in Goa before their arrival was for personal consumption and only for occasional festivals. However, with the introduction of Catholicism, many more religious festive occasions arose. So, occasions like birthdays, christenings, weddings, *ladainhas*, and chapel and church feasts were celebrated with copious amounts of alcohol. Even at sad times like funerals, alcohol was served.

With its churches in all the villages and towns, a multitude of chapels, and numerous community crosses, Goa witnessed celebrations almost throughout the year. If these were not enough, there were also crosses in houses and personal properties, where *ladainhas* or feasts were celebrated.

There were other reasons for the rise of alcoholic addiction in Goans. For instance, the wages of a laborer were often partly paid in kind with *feni*. Other vices, like gambling, also led to alcohol addiction when players consumed liquor.

Some studies claim that people consume alcohol more often when it is locally produced and available to the drinker. So, availability becomes an important parameter in this case too. The interrelationship between the availability of alcohol and the extent of alcoholism can be applied to Goa, which produces *feni* from coconut palms as well as cashew apples in large quantities.

Alcohol produced in Goa was not only enough for local consumption but was also exported to the neighboring territories of British India, bringing substantial revenue to the government. During the tenure of the Anglo-Portuguese Treaty, the new taxation regulations introduced on alcohol substantially benefited the Portuguese government. Therefore, they did not change the tax structure even after revoking the Treaty.[2]

Alcohol as Food and Medicine

The substance that we today consider poison and bad for health was, ironically, once believed to be an elixir to help solve health problems. Doctors and hospitals recommended it to treat diseases, and laymen also used it as traditional medicine. There was no gender or age difference in this. Everyone—men, women, and even children—was prescribed alcohol to alleviate sickly conditions.

Interestingly, alcohol was not thought of as harmful to health. In fact, it was encouraged to drink. In ancient tradition, wine and beer were considered food, imbibed by the sick when solid food could not be tolerated.[3] When alcoholic spirits became available, these too were accepted by the sick, substituting solid food.[4] The medical profession and the laity viewed it as appropriate nourishment both for debilitated persons and for those who refused to eat in times of sickness.[5] According to Roe, the decline of the use of alcohol as a wonder drug was due to the practice of dietetics, the scientific study of food and its effects on health. Food was shown to influence positively the recovery from acute and chronic disease. Prescriptions of wines and liquors could be discontinued only when proof emerged that alcohol was not beneficial. Until then, alcohol kept being prescribed.[6] Even though Roe's study focuses on Western medicine, more specifically in the UK, alcohol was used in treatment in other parts too, and was included in the pharmacopoeia of the time. It was and is still used in medical practices in Goa.[7]

So ingrained was the medical tradition of alcohol in therapeutics that it did not die out until about the 1920s. Indeed, the reaction against the use of alcohol as a drug only began in the early nineteenth century and parallels the development of the Temperance Movement.[8] The early supporters of the movement first began to question the need for alcohol as a restorative of health, and later supporters instituted clinical research with the objective of demonstrating that alcohol could be deleted from pharmacopoeia and eventually removed.[9] However, to date, alcohol is used in many medicines as a tonic and solvent for other ingredients, especially in cough syrups, where it also acts as a tranquilizer.

Doctors in Goa did not seem to be lagging behind in prescribing medicines imported from overseas, which contained alcohol as one of their components. Advertisements in the local papers show that tonics containing alcohol were regularly advertised to cure various ailments. Huxley's "Ner-Vigor" is prescribed as a fortifying tonic for weakness, loss of nerve strength, weakness of blood, and depression. Another one is "Sanatogen Tonic."[10] "Vinho Tonico EFKA," a Tonic Wine is advertised as "the bigger and better than the other Tonic wines." This red wine with added herbs or compounds like iron salts was strong and sweet. In those days it was thought to have medicinal benefits, though now considered otherwise.[11]

"Wincarnis," another popular wine, was considered as a tonic drink to cure all ills, one that would provide strength and energy to those of a nervous disposition and cure a whole range of disabilities by building up the nerve forces. A "Wincarnis" advertisement extolled the wine as "the key to the enjoyment of life," as "it gives a strong constitution, it is the food of the blood, the life-giving fluid which carries vitality and vivacity wherever it flows."[12] Besides the imported wines, there were also locally manufactured "Vinocarnis." One was manufactured by Paulino Dias (1874–1919), a doctor and pharmacist who owned a pharmacy in the city of Nova Goa (later Panjim), where he made several medicinal concoctions.[13] He was also a well-known poet. In advertisements in the newspaper *O Comércio* of 1909, he promoted his own Vinocarnis.[14] "Take the Great medicine, which is ideal for anyone to recover energy. Wine of Meat of Dr. Paulino Dias."[15] The other manufacturer was Costa and Company, which continued to manufacture it even into the 1980s.Vinocarnis became very popular throughout the world, with many other countries manufacturing it. This proliferation led a businessman seller Heitor Peres to advertise emphasizing that he was selling "Wincarnis. Wine of life," from the original manufacturer Coleman from Norwich and to "beware of imitations."[16]

Antonio Peregrino da Costa said that it was difficult to know what the right dose for the improvement of health was when it was known that alcohol is "a bad food, a food that is detestable." He quoted Lauder Brunton and B. Sanderson, who affirmed that "alcohol is not a necessity; a man lives better without alcohol: even in small doses there are nutritional changed disturbances."[17] According to Peregrino da Costa, alcoholism is hereditary and can give rise to the next generation of alcoholics in the family.[18] And this problem, unfortunately, can also be carried by women alcoholics, especially those who breastfeed babies. He gave an example of a family of a baker who lived in his neighborhood in Aquem. The parents were alcoholics and had seven children: "Three suffered from tuberculosis and died, one was an idiot, and another suffered from nephritis." On the other hand, a *boia* who abstained from drinking led a long life.[19]

In Goa, alcohol, especially palm and cashew *feni*, was used for medicinal purposes. It is not necessarily consumed but also used for local application, such as an antiseptic to disinfect the area to be treated or as an analgesic to relieve pain. It could be used for the area for injection, a wound, during childbirth, or to treat the umbilical cord when antiseptics were unavailable. It was also used for joint pains and bone setting.[20]

A few drops were added to the baby's bathwater as protection against the common cold. After the bath, a person would dip a finger in the spirit and gently rub it on the baby's tongue to cleanse and protect it from a cold.[21] *Feni* is also used as an anti-flatulent to treat stomach disorders; its ingestion and rubbing on the belly of a person help loose motions to subside. It is used to de-worm children by applying it to the head and stomach, and for grinding various ingredients to make pastes to be used for the treatment of worms. Pastes are also made to cure other ailments like swelling, pains, and orthopedic complications. Either palm or cashew *feni* is used to grind the herbs and spices. A popular paste for local application for pains or swelling was made of cumin seeds ground with palm, which is used even today, as well as some barks or roots of trees with medicinal properties are scrubbed on a stone with it and the mixture is applied to the area to be treated. A warm concoction of cashew and sugar is used to cure a cold.[22] A small dose of palm was recommended in the 1930s by a well-known physician of the times to those who suffered from malaria. This was to be taken before dinner to ward off any shivering that might be caused because of the infection.

The belief that alcohol actually increases the resisting power of the body to the poisons of certain diseases and is good for health was a wrong notion. This assumption was debated by many, especially by those in the Temperance Movement. It was also debated by participants at the Sétimo Congresso Provincial. A paper authored by Peregrino da Costa[23] is discussed and often cited by Correia Afonso in his report,[24] proving the argument that alcohol is bad for health even in small quantities. In fact, he argued that one way to enter the regular diet of an individual was supposed to be its dietetic and medicinal value. To some extent, it was correct; however, there was nothing more unscientific than the way this vulgar conception was formed. For example, according to Peregrino da Costa, the small dosage of alcohol taken as *ração* (a gram of alcohol contains 7 calories), though a source of energy like other food, was bad food, as it destroyed the organs in the body to various levels and destroyed the albuminoid substances of the organism and increased the elimination of nitrogen.[25] It also disturbed the processes of internal oxidation and altered the function of the stomach, liver, brain, etc. Alcohol was, therefore, a harmful and damning luxury food.

Alcohol as *Ração* for the Laborers

It was a tradition in some villages in Goa to pay the laborers in cash and also give them a dose of alcohol, which is known as *ração*. For some of them, it would be an initiation into drinking alcohol, to which they would become addicted after regular consumption. Why was this *ração* given to the laborers? Was it to enhance their power or energy to work? Or was it benefiting the landlord monetarily? Or was it a deliberate way to get them addicted and thereby have control over them?

Studies show that after consuming alcohol, on the first day the performance increased, but from the second to the third day it started reducing.[26] In fact, it was found that those who did not consume alcohol worked better than those who consumed it.[27] In the manufacture of *feni*, the landlord was given a certain quantity in kind by the lessee of the coconut trees from which the toddy was extracted, depending on the contract. The same would apply to those who leased the hillock from where the cashews were plucked and used for *feni* distillation. Sometimes the landlord himself would directly undertake the distillation. Consequently, the landlord would have a good quantity in stock, which he used to partly pay the wages in kind and thus pay less in cash. This arrangement financially benefited him but not the laborer, who, after regular consumption of alcohol, became addicted and subjugated to the landlord.

Medical science says that even the first glass can lead a person to addiction. If taken regularly, it gets into the system, the habit becomes difficult to shake off, and the person becomes an alcoholic. This kind of dependence was widespread in Goa, with the poor Goan laborer spending part of his wages, if not all, on satisfying his addiction. Further, when not paid in kind, he spent part or sometimes the entire wages on buying alcohol, to the detriment of his family. Since all the money was spent in a tavern and there was nothing left to buy food, it brought misery to them. It was still worse when he did not work. The laborer would purchase alcohol on credit, and the debt went on increasing because he had no means of paying.[28]

Berta Menezes Bragança (1911–93) touches deeply sensitive chords as she narrates a family's misery due to alcoholism in a poignant story "Debts Were Paid"[29] in her book *Tales from Goa*. It tells how a man can be driven to commit unimaginable deeds that bring misfortune to the entire family.[30] This is the story of a poor family that migrates to Goa from Karwar, as they were told by a Goan cook who worked there that in Goa one could earn well and nobody experienced hunger. Allured by this information, the parents, along with their children—a six-year-old boy, and two girls, aged five and one and a half—come to Goa. The truth is bitter for them when they realize how hard it is to get a job, and that the odd jobs are barely enough to buy food to survive. When there is no work, the husband idles away his time at a tavern watching men playing *tablam-fer*.[31] The tavern owner demands that the player who loses pays up in kind with palm *feni*. After watching for some time, he also joins the gamblers and becomes addicted to the game. When he has no money, he asks for credit from the tavern owner. Unable to repay his dues and driven by despair he gives away his child, without the knowledge of his wife, to the tavern owner who has no children. The wife is heartbroken and frantically searches for her child, ending up going insane. The father repents, and unable to come to terms with his action, commits suicide. This story shows how the greed and astuteness of the tavern owner led to the addiction and misery of a family. And of how idleness and other vices like gambling can also be responsible for alcoholism.

Alcoholism and Vices

That alcoholism and vices go hand in hand is also portrayed in a poem by an anonymous poet who writes that when a person becomes an alcoholic, he gets attracted to playing cards. According to him, alcohol and cards have a very close relationship and are responsible for destroying fortunes, homes, and families, and he advises that people should stop drinking. The poem is *Ixtt bebdicaiêcho vortouta khêll cartancho.*[32]

Gambling Is a Friend of Drunkenness.

When a Man gets the vice of drunkenness
He promptly yearns to play with cards
Under the hammer of liquor
He shuts his eyes and loses his money.

In the play of drink and cards
True relationships are naught to be found
Man! Use your mind and think
And correct yourself a little.

Drunkenness brings beggary upon a respected family
Wickedness wreaks old age upon youth
The yoke of debt falls on the neck of the drunkard
And raises clouds of darkness in his mind.

Man's heart burns with liquor
His body aches, his heart shudders
The limbs of his body are torn with weakness
His chest is parched, the voice turns hoarse.

Man, please think and see
How your wife and children suffer
Swollen eyes come staggering
Your children's curses will cause sores in your heart.

Alcohol is also known to have an effect on the brain. People could lose their sanity and be influenced by immoral attitudes, even leading to criminal acts by the alcoholic. It destabilizes the thinking of those who may not have the strength to control their perverse instincts. In this context, Berta Menezes Bragança gives us another example where alcohol is responsible for the death of a friend. In the story titled "Surrender," a man kills his friend over a discussion about the money he owed him, after having some shots of *feni* in the tavern. Before entering the tavern, they had amicably settled the matter, but the rounds of alcohol they drank roused vicious instincts in them, and they started quarreling, leading to the death of one of the friends. The killer laments with remorse that it was the *feni* that killed his friend: "If only they had not gone into the liquor-shop! It was the liquor-shop, the feni that had done it all. It was the feni that had murdered his friend. Not he; no, no, not he. Never again would he go into a liquor shop. Never, never taste that vile liquid again."[33]

By the beginning of the twentieth century, the consumption of alcohol in Goa had reached a level that could be considered an "epidemic." However, it was not seen as one by the government authorities, who looked at alcohol as a revenue earner for the state coffers. Some individuals did raise concerns and wrote about it. Alberto Osório de Castro, a well-known writer of the time, spared no effort to study the various problems faced by the community and tried to overcome them. He sent a proposal to the Junta Geral de Província to curb alcoholism.[34] He concludes it with, "There are known ways of combating alcohol consumption. Let's be human! That the greed of the yield from the *sura* of the palm tree does not seal the eyes of intelligence and of the heart. Alcoholism is the scourge of society, and this scourge sheds its purulence on all classes."[35]

Conferência Sanitária (1914) and Congresso Provincial (1916–31)

It was in 1914 that a Provincial Sanitary Conference was held to celebrate the seventy-second anniversary of the formal Escola Médico-Cirúrgica de Nova Goa.[36] This acted as a catalyst for future academic endeavors. The conference was not only an academic exercise; it tried to inform and clarify, in general and to the government in particular, important health problems and therefore "the material and moral well-being of the territory, the best and highest interests of this land."[37]

At the Primeira Conferência Sanitária, 1914 (First Sanitary Conference, 1914), many scientific papers related to health problems and administration were presented by doctors, administrators, and others. These were published in two volumes.[38] However, there was only one paper on alcoholism titled "Sugestões para Combater o Risco do Alcólismo em Goa," by Hipólito Policarpo Pegado, who was a military doctor of the rank of Captain (Capitão médico).[39] According to Pegado, it was the lifestyle of the people that led to alcohol consumption by family members. He gave the example of the laborers who visited the tavern at the end of the day or on a holiday and took their children along, giving them a little spirit to deworm them or because they asked for a sip. This practice tended to become a habit and create future alcoholics.[40] Years later, in her paper at the Sétimo Congresso, Ermelinda Stuart Gomes also corroborated Pegado, mentioning "the horrible habit of parents of taking children to the tavern to 'wet the tongue.'"[41] This habit seems to have been well-entrenched among Goans, as written in a poem titled "Teeth of Wine" by R.V. Pandit:

In Goa
Some children
Learn to drink
Before their teeth are born

And then …
When Wisdom teeth are born
These teeth
are of alcoholic wisdom,
that grind themselves.[42]

Pegado also pointed out that alcoholism was considered the harbinger of and a detrimental influence on the cause of many diseases. Indeed, a chronic alcoholic offered a fertile field for the tuberculosis bacillus and several other diseases, and no organ or viscera in the body escaped its destructive action, especially the liver, kidneys, and brain. The proof lies in the number of deaths due to tuberculosis, as seen in the statistics, which show a higher mortality directly or indirectly related to alcoholism. Tuberculosis of the respiratory system has a total of 239 deaths, out of which 167 are males and 72 are females. It also shows that the children who died of TB included eight infants less than a year old (five males and three females), two one-year-olds, and two between four and nine years of age. Table 4.1 gives details of deaths due to tuberculosis in the respiratory system.

There were a sizable number of deaths due to cirrhosis: 277 in total (174 males and 103 females). It interestingly shows that there were 46 deaths among children of less than one year of age (28 males and 18 females). There are also deaths among the other age groups in children. Cirrhosis can be caused by hepatitis or alcohol consumption. The statistics do not show any entry under hepatitis, so we can presume the deaths due to cirrhosis are alcohol-related. The sizable number of children below one year confirms the fear that it may have been related to alcoholic nannies and mothers feeding the children. Table 4.2 gives causes of death due to cirrhosis.

Pegado discussed another important cause of alcoholism, that of *amas de leite* (milk nannies). There was a system where nannies were engaged to look after newborn babies. Many of them also offered the service of feeding the babies. This was possible if the nanny had recently given birth to a child. This service was solicited in cases where the mother of

Table 4.1 Deaths due to tuberculosis in the respiratory system

Age	Male	Female	Total
Adults	167	72	239
Children below 1 year	5	3	8
1 year	2		2
2 years	–		–
3 years	–		–
4 years	1		1
5–9 years	1	–	1

[Source: Government of Goa, Daman and Diu, *Statistical Year Book, 1961*. Panaji: Government Printing Press, 54–7]

Tuberculosis of other forms: adults: total 23 (10 males, 13 females), children of 5–9 years: total 3 (2 males).

Table 4.2 Causes of death due to cirrhosis

Age	Male	Female	Total
Adults	174	103	277
Children below 1 year	28	18	46
1 year	9	12	21
2 years	8	14	22
3 years	7	6	13
4 years	2	3	5
5–9 years	3	3	6

[Source: *Statistical Year Book, 1961*, 54–7]

the newborn was not too well or did not have enough milk to breastfeed her baby. But there were also many well-off ladies who, despite being healthy and capable of nursing their babies, refused to feed them under the pretext that it would change their physical shape and beauty. Many of the nannies could have been addicted to alcohol. It is in this context that Pegado refers to the nannies as being potential carriers of alcoholism and infecting the infant. When they fed the babies, alcohol got into the babies' bodies. This could cause convulsions similar to epileptic and meningitis attacks. It was observed that these symptoms stopped when feeding was discontinued. Later, the child could also manifest problems like gastrointestinal disturbances and certain symptoms of chronic alcoholism, such as nightmares, nocturnal tremors, and nerve sensitivity disturbances. It would be interesting to connect Pegado's comment to the death statistics shown above.[43] Surprisingly, the cause of death of a number of children was due to cirrhosis. However, Pegado's comments on alcoholic milk nannies may throw some light on this issue.

There are other sicknesses which if not directly related to alcoholism are an outcome of it. These include nephritis and nephrosis, which are diseases affecting the kidneys, and again showed a large number of deaths among adults, a total of 377 (167 males and 210 females), which also included children. Table 4.3 mentions causes of death due to nephritis and nephrosis.

Alcohol affects the brain, central nervous system, heart, liver, and pancreas, which in turn leads to other problems. Drinking also makes it difficult for the brain to create long-term memories and reduces the ability to think clearly and make rational choices. Goa's death statistics show a significant number under senility, which is the highest among other causes of death. The reasons for this could be varied, such as old age, hereditary risk, mental and neurological disorders such as Parkinson's disease, depression, and, of course, alcohol abuse. So, we can infer that in Goa alcohol could be one of the reasons for such a large number of deaths under senility. Alcoholism can lead people to lose their memory and develop mental and neurological disorders. Table 4.4 shows the number of persons who died due to senility without mention of psychosis, ill-defined, and unknown causes.

Pegado also suggested the constitution of the Society of Temperance to fight against alcoholism.[44] However, the suggestion just languished until 1934, when the Society of Temperance was established due to the efforts of Dr. Baronio Monteiro.[45]

At this conference, another two delegates referred to alcoholism. J. J. Roque Correia Afonso[46] in his paper on "O Saneameto Rural da

Table 4.3 Causes of death due to nephritis and nephrosis

Age	Male	Female	Total
Adults	167	210	377
Children below 1 year	8	12	20
1 year	1	7	8
2 years	5	7	12
3 years	1	3	4
4 years	–	4	4
5–9 years	7	5	12

[Source: *Statistical Year Book, 1961*, 54–7]

Table 4.4 Senility without mention of psychosis, ill-defined, and unknown causes

Age	Male	Female	Total
Adults	565	694	1,259
Children below 1 year	5	4	9
1 year	1	2	3
2 years	–	1	1
3 years	–	–	–
4 years	–	–	–
5–9 years	–	2	–

[Source: *Statistical Year Book, 1961*, 54–7]

Índia Portuguesa na sua Relação com a Organisação Administrativa" (Rural Sanitation of Portuguese India in its Relation with Administrative Organisation)[47] viewed the village as an administrative unit for public health management and discussed various points for the improvement of rural health. The first one was on the diet, in which he proposed modification, as it consisted of "only polished rice and that too twice boiled, with chilies as curry, without any fruit or fresh salad for vitamins," which was insufficient and deficient. According to him, a clean and hygienic house along with bread is not enough for good health. He suggested that there should also be healthy entertainment that aroused a creative instinct for art amongst the workers. Since they lacked it, they went in search of entertainment in the tavern and the brothels, which acted as means to take away the fatigue of the spirit and body. He added that alcoholism was essentially a social problem associated with the lack of education of the masses. Correia Afonso concluded that "alcoholism more often is an instrument of art without honest means of satisfaction"[48] and it had ruined many and continued to do so daily amongst the people.[49]

Another essay on tuberculosis by A. Filipe Pinto Cordeiro prayed that there should be vigilance and a war against alcoholism, which is responsible for the spread of tuberculosis.[50] Interestingly, despite there being references to the problem of alcoholism in the Sanitary Conference in 1914, when the Congresso Provincial da Índia Portuguesa (Provincial Congress) was eventually formed and the issues were listed for discussion in the objectives, there was no mention of alcoholism. And this, in spite of knowing that its tentacles were reaching far and wide indiscriminately, affecting both the proletariat and elite alike.

Worst of all, alcoholics lost dignity amongst friends, colleagues, and even as heads of family, sometimes abandoning the welfare of the family to brutality. Violence against wives and children was common, bringing misery to them. It was not only the physical threat that was fearful. The financial repercussions of money earned being spent on drinking left families in dire hunger. The rich even went to the extent of selling their properties. It also caused psychological problems for the family, particularly for the children who were exposed to such violence, sometimes leaving lifelong scars. Not to forget the reaction of society, where people would point fingers at the alcoholics, making them a laughing stock, forgetting that it was not only a vice but a disease. Ermelinda adds that unfortunately, it is not only men who were affected by the vice but also women, especially those without any work, who idle their time by getting intoxicated.[51]

The Congresso Provincial da Índia Portuguesa and Its Objectives

The Congresso Provincial was conceived as an autonomous body "free from any interference, either from the government or from any faction or party."[52] The Goan intelligentsia felt that they were isolated from the renaissance movement taking place in British India, which had a brilliant history that its intellectual elite wanted to show with pride to the colonialists and others. This was done through the Indian National Congress (INC), founded in 1885, which was established as a great public manifestation led and promoted by great men and visionaries. Many seminars and conferences—scientific, economic, political, and social—were held in British India revolving around the INC, where papers presented were useful in practical life.[53]

However, Portuguese India remained away from this revival, though, after the formation of the INC, some local newspapers had discussed and proposed the formation of Congresso Provincial in Goa, which unfortunately did not materialize at that time. In 1915, arrangements were being made in Portugal to commemorate the fourth centenary of the death of Afonso de Albuquerque. Encouraged by the success of the Conferência Sanitária, the local intellectuals approached the government to support and give financial assistance for arrangements to organize a conference to discuss Goa and the different aspects of Goan life. The committee members pointed out that the British government had given this kind of support in the beginning to the INC. It was the right time for the learned members of society who, with the backing of Governor Couceiro da Costa, inaugurated the first Congresso Provincial on April 2, 1916.[54]

"The Congresso Provincial had two functions: to expose to the Government the true needs of the state and to promote through propaganda the results arrived at by the Congresso."[55] A committee was appointed to organize the Congresso, and under the presidency of the governor, Couceiro da Costa, and Miguel Caetano Dias, who was president of the municipality at the time, the first Congresso Provincial was held. Altogether, nine Congressos took place every year or every second year. The last one was held in 1931.[56]

The objectives of the Congresso Provincial were varied. A list of the issues to be discussed, directly of interest to the economic and moral development of this territory, included (1) agriculture, (2) industry and commerce, (3) public transport, (4) primary education, (5) taxes, fiscal and municipal, and (6) any other subjects not included in the list but which have a close relationship with the social needs of the people.

As seen from the list, the Congresso Provincial did not include alcoholism in its objectives. When the committee was formed and met to discuss the different problems affecting Portuguese India, alcoholism was probably not considered a priority by them. This, despite it being a major, if not the chief, problem, has reached "epidemic" proportions amongst Goans, not only in the territory but also within the emigrant community. There was an indifference to this vexed issue despite individuals voicing their concerns, and the same being raised during the first Congresso Sanitário. Besides, it was well known that the administration was not taking any action to overcome this menace for obvious reasons, as the production and consumption of alcohol filled the coffers of the government. It thus became an economic, political, and social problem for the government and the community. It is under these circumstances that the problem was debated in two of the Congresso Provincial: the second and the seventh.

The Segundo Congresso Provincial

In the Segundo Congresso Provincial, a panel on alcoholism titled "Alcoholism and *Abkari*" was included. There were four papers related to alcohol, out of which two were on *abkari*, and a general paper on wines and salt.[57] Only one paper was directly related to social problems and anti-alcoholism.[58] The two on *abkari* were related to the manufacturing and taxation of the products of the alcohol industry.[59] They mainly addressed the importance of *abkari* as an administrative and revenue-earning matter of the territory and how to solve any issues connected to it, rather than the issue of alcoholism as a social problem and its effect on the addict, his family, and those around him. However, both speakers discussed and pointed out that imposing higher taxes would reduce alcoholism.

Alcoholism went on to become a dominant issue in the twentieth century in Goa, and one of the reasons was the Anglo-Portuguese Treaty of 1878. The problem of alcoholism cannot be studied without looking into the effects of this treaty which, although it benefited the government with a higher collection of revenue, caused hardships to the people. Before it was implemented, a tax was collected only on trees used to produce spirits. The toddy collected for jaggery, vinegar preparation, and leavening of bread was exempted from tax payments.

After the treaty's implementation, a tax was imposed on all the trees. This caused unhappiness among the people who resented this tax as it would burden the ailing local manufacturing, especially that of jaggery, which substituted sugar for the locals. Vinegar was used in food preparations and was exported to British India along with palm jaggery, which earned profits for the manufacturers. However, under the treaty, the British increased the tax on alcohol so that it benefited the government irrespective of the reduced number of trees used to tap the toddy.[60] The manufacturers and the toddy tappers revolted and even stopped tapping the trees.

After the signing of the treaty in 1878, there were changes in the pattern of revenue to the government. At that point, Goa was exporting country liquor, vinegar, and toddy worth 19,320 rupees.[61] However, this export faded away due to the system of *abkari* introduced by this treaty. Instead, imports of sugar and sugarcane jaggery increased from 176,855 rupees in 1878–9 to 504,717 rupees in 1918. This led to an economic imbalance. Besides the export problems, the increase in manpower for collecting and implementing taxes as emphasized in the treaty also caused a loss to the treasury. In addition, there was the loss of manual labor, who out of frustration decided to emigrate, as they could not accrue enough income for their livelihood, owing to the heavy taxes and decrease in the export caused by the reduction in the number of coconut trees used in the industry.[62] The treaty made it easier for the people to travel, with the establishment of the railway line connecting Bombay to Mormugao Port. Those who remained in Goa had to look for an alternative income and since not much was available, they took to drinking to bury their sorrows. And then the Portuguese government went on to increase alcohol production to benefit from the added income since the revenue accrued from the spirit was substantial. This decision made even more alcohol available to the local populace.

Teodoro Miranda, in his presentation at the Segundo Congresso, suggested that if the reforms in the regime were accepted and implemented, it would reduce alcoholism. According to him, this could be achieved by not making available for sale alcohol of higher grade, which was harmful to health. It was assumed that the workforce would not be able to consume it as it was beyond their buying power and therefore would cause less damage to those who were habitual drinkers. His argument implied that the majority of alcoholics were in the labor force.[63] Another point that was discussed was the government's tax on toddy tapping based on the individual coconut tree. If this measure accrued higher returns to the government, it caused financial burdens to those producing palm jaggery, which was used as sugar by the common folk, as well as to those producing vinegar.[64] Although Miranda does not mention it in his paper, it would also affect the bread industry in a limited way since fresh toddy was used to leaven the flour batter instead of yeast. To improve their financial conditions, he suggested that family members could join in the production of jaggery and vinegar, which would give them returns. He added that the export of native liquor would bring revenue to the government and proposed that the industry of cashew liquor should be encouraged because it was less harmful and the nuts would add to the income, as they were in demand.[65] However, Miranda did not explain why and how, and nor was there any scientific evidence to prove that cashew liquor was less harmful. In fact, it was the distillation grade and not the type of spirits that was detrimental and injurious to the consumer.

Azarias Condorcet Lobo, in his presentation, recommended that the tavern owners should pay the taxes of *abkari,* and if it was accepted and implemented, then this measure would improve the production of toddy and the manufacture of jaggery. These taverns could be classified, and the tax duly imposed on them and directly collected from the owners, making it easier to coordinate the collection and also to increase it in case the government needed more revenue. Lobo had also suggested that the tax levied on alcohol could be reduced and instead, to decrease the consumption, an additional charge should be levied on tavern licenses, which amount could be used for public assistance for the sick. This measure would also help the alcoholics, who constituted a sizable number of those seeking public assistance.[66]

While Lobo suggested an increase in tax on the taverns to raise revenue, Condorcet Pereira in "Campanha Anti-alcoólica" suggested that the problem of alcoholism could be solved by decreasing the number of taverns in Goa.[67] In the introduction to his paper, he gave the example of an alcoholic who, when questioned about his drinking vice, pointed his fingers at the number of functional taverns in and around his place. The drunkard argued that "if there were no taverns, he would not drink." Pereira also argued that closing or reducing the number of taverns would not be the only solution and many people might not agree to such decisions. He was right, especially after the previous two delegates discussing this issue had suggested that taxes be imposed on the consumers and taverns. If Pereira's suggestion of decreasing the number of taverns were accepted, the government would lose revenue, which those present at the Congresso were trying to safeguard and augment. He also proposed that the government should find some other recourse to the closure of the taverns. Pereira proposed a space where people could go and enjoy some good meals and non-alcoholic drinks, and suggested a "cantina popular" (people's canteen), where other entertainments could also be provided, like a gymnasium and books for reading, the majority of which should be in Konkani.[68]

This measure, if implemented, might have solved the personal problem of the alcoholic in particular and the social problem of the community, keeping in mind that the tavern was considered to be the meeting point of the people of the village. However, the income to the government, an important issue, if not the most, would decrease with the reduction in the number of taverns; this would mean a decline in revenue, for which Pereira also suggested solutions. One was to increase the license fees of the tavern, which would add to the revenue. With the decrease of coconut trees used for the extraction of toddy, more coconuts would be obtained as the spathe of the tree would now be allowed to grow. Coconuts would add revenue for the owners of the plantation. The extra production could be exported since coconut and copra were among the main export items from Goa to British India. Likewise, copra could be used for the extraction of oil for cooking, lighting lamps, and personal grooming. He explained that the renewed energy of those who stopped drinking would give much better output in the form of work that they carried out. However, when the papers were discussed and deliberations made, Pereira's suggestion was not even considered for discussion. This was despite his request that his proposal regarding the fixing of the number of taverns be accepted and voted on. In fact, there was opposition from the delegates Isidoro Alvares and Adv. Jose Antonio Pinto do Rosario, who observed that with a fine imposed on the tavern owner, alcoholism could be reduced.[69]

In the same Congresso, the problem of alcoholism was also mentioned in a session on "Emigração" (emigration) by Socrates de Noronha, Junior, and Francisco Correia Afonso, "A Sorte do Emigrante Goês no Foco da Emigração (Alvitres para o seu Melhoramento)."[70] They brought into focus the unhygienic and inadequate conditions faced by Goans who lived in the various *cuddas* existing in Bombay, which were used by many as they could not afford independent accommodation.[71] According to the paper presenters, one of the health problems faced by the emigrants was alcoholism.[72] They added that "some of the *cuddas* were dens of vice, where alcoholism and immorality reigned within unhygienic conditions and unruly behaviour."[73] The problem of alcoholism was also broached by J. J. Roque Correia Afonso in the essay "Emigração: suas causas, seus remédios" (Emigration: Causes and Remedies), which discussed measures to reduce and stop emigration. He suggested that people in Goa should be kept busy and that the government should establish village-level industries that would employ all the available hands and provide honest recreation to them. He felt that such activities would put a stop to the tavern and *zagores*.[74] These two papers showed how the vice was carried by the emigrants across the border and instead of sobering down, saving their earnings, and helping the family back home in Goa, they spent their wages on alcohol.

José Maria de Sá had to elaborate a Relatório (report) of the session "Alcoolismo e Abcari."[75] It was clear from the report that the revenue from *abkari* was more important to the organizers than controlling or stopping the vice of alcoholism. In the very first line, he writes: "The regimen of abcari is one of the important problems of public administration of this province, linked to momentous problems."[76] He calls them "important economic-political problems, which evidently needs [*sic*] to be attended to with urgency."[77] After the papers were read and discussions and deliberations were taken by those present, a proposal was sent to the Conselho do Governo (Government Council) to tax only the taverns and not the coconut trees that were used to tap the toddy. However, this was not implemented by the Portuguese government as it was not ready to lose the much-needed revenue it obtained from *abkari*.

José Maria de Sá reported that the government should try to fill the gap of the loss of revenue through increased taxes on alcohol and that the solutions presented by the delegates Condorcet Lobo and Teodoro de Miranda should be considered. He emphasized that both speakers had ensured the interests of the Revenue Department.

It was only at the end of the session that the need to control alcoholism was discussed by the delegates. They suggested that the enhanced *abkari* taxes would solve the problem, and the Segundo Congresso Provincial voted that these should be imposed directly on the consumption of alcohol in the territory. It was also proposed that the extraction of sap from coconut trees and other products of cashew and toddy in Goa should be free from taxes to overcome the problems faced by the manufacturing units.[78] Another suggestion was to increase the fees of licenses, except for wine and beer, on non-native alcohol.[79] As can be seen, the increase in taxes was the only reference made to reduce alcoholism; other proposals were all connected to improving and organizing the services associated with the collection of taxes to benefit the Revenue Department.

Governor Jaime Morais discussed that the income would be reduced for the following main reasons, among others. The revenue accrued on *abkari* was through the *processos de previsão* (forecasting method). According to him, for the current year, it was calculated by Lobo as 600,000 rupees. On the other hand, the government had an income of 640,000 rupees, which would mean that in the very first year, the government would lose around 40,000 rupees.[80]

The local and central governments seem to have paid heed to the protests of the paper presenters and accepted some of the proposals, as has been claimed by the Report of the Committee of the Congresso Provincial, which informs that a couple of legislative diplomas were issued linking to the conclusion and proposal.

The Segundo Congresso had voted for the prohibition of the sale of intoxicating drugs outside pharmacies and drugstores and without medical prescriptions.[81] Another proposal that had the approval of the government was the application of a fine to be levied on the owners of establishments that sold alcoholic beverages and admitted to their premises, on any pretext, minors or those less than eighteen years old.[82] However, much was desired about the implementation of these laws, and the fact that the same was enacted in 1927 and 1928 shows the lethargy of the authorities to take action with regard to the orders.

The Comissão de Estudos of the Sétimo Congresso Provincial da Índia Portuguesa included alcoholism as one of the topics for study and discussions.[83] It was held in 1927 and had various themes on which to deliberate besides alcoholism—labor employment, fish industry, tourism, education, emigration, taxation, and others. However, Francisco Correia Afonso,[84] in his report on the session titled "O Alcoolismo na Índia Portuguesa," highlighted that the most important theme of the Sétimo Congresso from those selected for study was the issue of alcoholism in Portuguese India. He stated that "it was a major problem from those that so far had been studied in the earlier Congressos, as in some way or other it was connected, as either cause or outcome, of all other problems that we had to face."[85]

The very fact that the Congresso took nine years to look into alcoholism as a social problem that was so important to the community contradicts the statement of Correia Afonso. To begin with, the Congresso Provincial did not include alcoholism in its objectives despite its seriousness. It made its presence in the Segundo Congresso, as already discussed, as a politicoeconomic issue and not a social one. The need was felt to include it in the Sétimo Congresso because addiction had gone beyond the proletariat and common folk and by now was also affecting the elite and the *bhatkars* (landlords), as discussed in the press and literature.

Prohibition of the Sale of Alcohol

Was there any other reason why alcoholism was planned to be discussed, besides those elaborated by the paper presenters and delegates at the Congresso Provincial? In the 1920s, a climax was reached worldwide with people and governments opposing the manufacturing and sale of alcohol, as it was causing havoc not only among those addicted but also on their families and society. They wished to put an end to this evil drink, and the United States went a step ahead to impose prohibition. It was a nationwide constitutional ban on the production, importation, transportation, and sale of alcoholic beverages from 1920 to 1933. Though it was eventually revoked, it was found that problems such as alcoholism and family violence had reduced during that period. On the other hand, crimes related to bootlegging had increased.

Prohibition was initiated as part of the Temperance Movement, which asserted that alcohol and intoxication were responsible for crime and other negative aspects of society. However, it became highly controversial among medical professionals because alcohol was widely prescribed by that era's physicians for therapeutic purposes. The US Congress held hearings on the medicinal value of beer in 1921. Subsequently, physicians across the country lobbied for the repeal of Prohibition as it applied to medicinal liquors. The American government also decided to revoke it, as an important source of revenue was lost, and moreover, those were the years of the Great Depression.

Closer to home, in British India, Gandhi had started a movement against drinking. The Goan intellectuals were closely following what was happening there. Gandhi was a champion of the Temperance Movement and viewed foreign rule as an obstacle to national prohibition. He said alcoholism was more damning than robbery and prostitution. Sometimes, he said, it was the father of both. In the constructive program of the noncooperation movement, he enumerated five tasks, the second of which was stopping the consumption of liquor.[86] He sought the people's cooperation toward this goal and invited women and youngsters, along with men, to stand near liquor booths and try to politely enlighten the alcohol consumers to abstain.[87] This modus operandi was called picketing.

Since Gandhi was not happy with the way the Congress workers functioned in this regard, he told them that "they should shake off their lethargy and give up empty talk, demonstrations, and speeches and go on working all the time." He added that if India wished to reach this goal through nonviolent effort, then the party should not leave to the future government the fate of lakhs of men and women who were laboring under the curse of intoxicants and narcotics.[88]

Gandhi asked his workers to accept his evidence regarding the drinking problem, that the country as a whole was sick from the curse of alcohol. "The country is simply impatient of the evil itself, those unfortunate men who have become slaves to the habit required to be helped." And he invited the workers to take advantage of the wave of feeling that had been aroused against the traffic of alcohol.[89]

Sétimo Congresso Provincial (1927)

The following papers were presented during the Sétimo Congresso (Seventh Congress) in the session on alcoholism and deliberated by the delegates in the discussion that followed: "Campanha contra o alcoolismo" by Bascora M. S. Borcar, "A Repressão do Alcoolismo" by Maria Ermelinda dos Stuarts Gomes, "O Alcoolismo (causa e seus remédios)" by Nogar Prudente Lourenço, and "A Redução do Alcoolismo em Goa" by Solon de Quadros. The titles of the papers do not leave any doubt that the repression of alcoholism was the main objective of the delegates at this session.

Most of the delegates at the Congresso were of the opinion that alcoholism should be reduced and controlled. They knew that complete stoppage, which would lead to prohibition like in the United States, or attempts at it by neighboring British India, was not possible in Goa. This aspect of the problem was discussed by the delegates, and Gomes commented that "our aspirations are modest as they are limited to saving especially the youth and women falling to excess."[90] Another speaker, Lourenço, also said that "promulgation of dry law is not feasible in Goa, as long as it is ensconced in the British Territory."[91] Quadros went a step further by suggesting that the taverns should be stopped and the government should have a center for sale in each parish, after auctioning the rights in public.[92] Probably Quadros was looking at controlling the sale of alcohol, which would reduce the vice, and the measure would also give revenue to the government. Most of the speakers and delegates discussed that for the reduction in alcoholism to be achieved, limiting the number of taverns was a must, a suggestion that had been reverberating from the time of the Segundo Congresso, but was not accepted for implementation by the government for fear of loss in revenue.[93]

The local tavern had become synonymous with the ambience of a village, and many writers have portrayed them in their works. Orlando da Costa, in his novel *O Signo da Ira*, entwines the narrative around it and depicts it as the center stage for meeting, gossiping, and discussions of the poor laborers. The *mundkars* of *bhatkar* Ligôr drop in at the tavern to have a drink of local *feni* before they go home, spending part, if not the entire amount, earned for the day. He portrays Pedru as an alcoholic who wastes himself by drinking beyond his means and depicts the deplorable condition of his wife, satiating her craving for alcohol by kissing his lips: "The other one … she waits for me every night and wants to kiss my mouth like in other times, she wants to kiss me and clings to my lips until she gets the taste of feni."[94] This narrative shows the level of degradation of the alcoholic, who in this case is bedridden, but the desire to drink surmounts the physical weakness and is satisfied with the remnants and odor of the *feni* on the lips of her alcoholic husband.

Costa also uses *feni* as a metaphor for lust. Rumão, the tavern owner, offers it free to Pedru, intending to gain access to his daughter Coinção, in which he almost succeeds.[95]

Since individual efforts would have been difficult to handle successfully, in the concluding remarks at the Congresso, Pereira suggested using joint decisions by various means: from the people, by a collaboration of all the social forces, utilizing all the available means to eliminate alcohol from their habits; from the government, by reform of the regime of *abkari*, phase-wise, in which the administrators successively lost interest in the income it enjoyed at the cost of the alcohol vice.[96] However, these suggestions remained only on paper as even the laws which were promulgated were implemented only where they benefited the government.

The census report also showed a rise in deaths reported from 1885 to 1924, though there was no tangible growth in the population. Peregrino da Costa relates the cause of this high number of deaths due to alcoholism. The table below (Table 4.5) gives the figures for five years. The average for the years 1915–19 was not taken into consideration because of the deaths due to the plague in 1918.[97]

The table shows that mortality increased to 25.1, not considering emigration.[98]

The taverns had also increased in number, and Peregrino da Costa gives the example of his parish, which had around 8,000 inhabitants, where the number of taverns had increased threefold, if not more. Another reality was that alcoholism had caught up with the masses who were uneducated, and the shortage caused the wages of the *Curumbim* (*Kunnbi*) laborers to be raised. This directly affected the landlords and elite whom they served, who had to fork out more money. Peregrino da Costa also commented that instead of our people being physically fit, with a conducive warm climate,

Table 4.5 Average five-year death statistics from 1900–1909

Average for 5 years	Birth	Death	Deaths by thousand	Excess of births over deaths	By thousand
1900–1904	193	187	23,3	6	0,75
1905–9	200	183	22,7	18	2,25
1910–14	198	190	23,7	8	1
1915–19	215	238	The average is not taken into consideration because of the plague in 1918		
1919–24	220	201	25,1	19	2,36

[Source: *Sétimo Congresso Provincial da India Portuguesa*, 1927, 19]

since the needs for nutrition, environmental protection, and virulence of sicknesses are less than that in cold countries, the opposite was observed. The reason for this was the vice of drinking alcohol, which was more prevalent in the rural areas than in the city and also in contrast with the Hindu population, who were largely teetotalers. However, the population rate had not increased reasonably, as can be seen from the above table. The motto of "*A máxima de receita com o mínimo de consumo*" (maximum revenue with minimum consumption), as suggested at the Segundo Congresso, was not followed by the government.

An article by Manuel de Albuquerque that appeared in the paper *O Ultramar* blamed the Revenue Department for the increase in alcoholism.[99] He writes that in 1925, the Conselho Legislativo (Legislative Council) had voted for taverns to be located away from schools, public offices, temples, and religious institutions, far beyond 250 meters, and also for an increase in taxes. While the new taxes were implemented, the requirement of maintaining distance was not, even though it was approved unanimously by the members of the council. Albuquerque gave the example of his village, Rachol: "At a distance of 50 meters from the Church there were two taverns, on the side of the postal services, and even after complaining to the authorities to close the same, they did not take any action and continued business as before." He commented that money earned by the government goes to the treasury and to the savings of the tavern owner, who was busy buying properties belonging to the *bhatkars* who had no brains.[100]

This seems to be true, as the government did not care about reducing the taverns or for the alcohol-addicted *bhatkars* who sold their properties to satisfy their vice. In *Chivalry*, Bragança portrays the *bhatkar* as a mean person, an alcoholic who pesters his *mundkars*, and who, due to his vice, ends up selling almost all the properties. With no money left to fulfill his desire, he loses all moral value and harasses his *mundkars* to give him money, even trying to abuse the modesty of their wives.[101]

The Government Council's decision was implemented only when another Diploma Legislativo passed a law that within 1,200 meters of the institutions,[102] no taverns could be established.[103] Another clause included in the same diploma was forbidding entrance to drunken people, ladies, and minors of less than fifteen years in the taverns. Besides, the timings were also reduced from nine in the morning to eight in the evening and would be closed on Sundays except if it was a festive day. This was issued during the tenure of Governor Massano de Amorim. However, it was not successful in thwarting alcoholism or reducing the number of taverns, which went on increasing.

Thus, Peregrino da Costa sums up the moral effects that alcoholism had on the increase in crimes and vices: "gloomy and moral and material misery, manifesting itself under multiform aspects: female emigration, prostitution, robberies, perjury, and even assassinations coldly premeditated."[104] All these brought deprivation and ruin not only to the individual but also to their family and society in general, and of course to the administrators of the territory.

The paper presented by Borcar, with statistics to support his claim, showed that there was an increase every year in the production of alcohol, instead of a reduction, which aided the rise of alcoholism and defeated the purpose of eradication. He argued that the production and consequent consumption of alcohol were increasing (for the reason that, according to him, its export across the borders was smuggling and its use for industrial purposes was nil).[105] This was despite the increase of taxes on the coconut trees from two rupees to ten rupees. He also pointed out that "alcoholism was more pronounced amongst the Christians, where there was no distinction amongst the consumers: it included the rich and poor, a proprietor and a *mundkar*, the government employee and the proletariat, the teacher and the student, the director and the peon in the government department; sadly, there is no exception to the women and children."[106]

The following statistic shows (Table 4.6) the increase in coconut trees for toddy extraction, despite the rise in taxes.

Table 4.6 Year-wise coconut trees for toddy extraction

Year	No. of coconut trees for toddy extraction
1914	43,614
1915	45,848
1916	48,888
1917	46,338
1918	49,320
1919	50,545
1920	52,774
1921	52,497
1922	59,963
1923	59,623

[Source: *Sétimo Congresso*, 1927, 4]

From the above statistics, it can be seen that the number of coconut trees in the year 1914 was 43,614 and increased to 59,623 in 1923, which means the proportionate increase was 38 percent. Since the number of trees had increased, the quantity of alcohol produced had also increased. Table 4.7 below shows the increase.

The above statistics show that coconut spirit production has increased by a proportion of 39 percent. To this, the production of cashew spirits from 1918 to 1922 can be added (Table 4.8).

This shows that the increase in cashew spirit production is in the proportion of 8 percent during the five years, and it is presumed that this increased percentage will rise to 20 percent.[108] According to Borcar, the number of licenses issued to sell native spirits was 2,144, and he commented

Table 4.7 Year-wise quantity of alcohol extraction

Year	Quantity of alcohol extracted in gallons
1914	13,48,744
1915	14,55,274
1916	15,52,194
1917	14,71,231
1918	15,65,907
1919	16,04,802
1920	16,74,618
1921	16,66,776
1922	19,02,550
1923	18,93,030[107]

[Source: *Sétimo Congresso*, 1927, 5]

Table 4.8 Year-wise production of cashew spirit

Year	Quantity of alcohol extracted in gallons
1918	1,98,833
1919	1,38,025
1920	2,27,980
1921	2,18,990
1922	2,15,890

[Source: *Sétimo Congresso*, 1927, 5]

that people, especially the proletariat, could not move around in Goa without approaching a tavern. The number of taverns was increasing every year: in 1918 there were 1,143, and in 1923 it reached 1,383.[109] By 1927, the number had increased to 2,144.[110]

But what was more alarming was not only the increase in the production of alcohol and the number of taverns, but also the death rate vis-à-vis the birth rate. Statistics showed that there was an increase in deaths, and presumably, they were directly or indirectly due to alcoholism.

The sole motto of the delegates for the Sétimo Congresso, as discussed, was to decrease alcohol consumption or achieve total eradication, the latter being a very difficult, if not impossible, task in the prevalent circumstances. Domingos Roque Sousa presided over the first session, which was on "Alcoolismo em Goa—Suas causas e soluções" (Alcoholism in Goa—Its Causes and Remedies). In his speech, he stated that every effort to combat alcoholism, which has become a fatal pandemic, is appreciated, no matter how small. Until now, nothing meaningful has been done to stop the scourge, and therefore this need is felt.[111]

Sousa pointed out that it was important to understand the difference between the fight against alcoholism and the repression of drunkenness. He advocated a radical change in social habits and lifestyle to help fight alcoholism as the need of the hour. According to him, this change should be initiated by the delegates, as they are members of the educated class and in turn must pass it on to the laborers and the ignorant population. He also suggested that decisions taken by the delegates should be viable and practical, for this is the only way the government will attend to the request for reforms of the existing *abkari*, which is so important to curb alcoholism.[112]

There were also suggestions that the appeal to eradicate alcoholism should not only go to citizens and private bodies but also to the government's official and semi-official institutions.[113] According to him, their support would lend weight to the movement as exemplary behavior should begin with the higher-ups. At official functions, alcoholic beverages were served, and the masses were ready to imitate this. Another suggestion was to prohibit women and children from selling alcohol at taverns. He argued that if those dispensing medicines need to be qualified, then why not those who sell alcohol for consumption? It was not only damaging to the consumer but also affected the family and descendants. He suggested that a line be added to the deliberations: "Do not trust the sale of alcoholic beverages to minors and women."[114] And the Congresso voted unanimously that the profession of the *taverneiro* (tavern owner) should be governed by rules.[115]

According to the delegates, the present regime functioned only under the fiscal criteria and not according to the motto proposed in the report of the Segundo Congresso Provisional, which deliberated "maximum revenue with minimum consumption."[116] The delegates at this Congresso also agreed that the restriction against alcoholism faced difficulties because the government would have to stop the production and sale of alcohol, both directly and through the taverns. This would mean a major loss of revenue to the coffers as no tax would be collected on alcohol. Far from eradicating alcoholism, the government was unwilling to reduce the number of taverns, and instead, fresh licenses for new ones were issued.

However, the government failed to understand that the losses would not be great if they took into consideration the expenses incurred in administering the increase of mental illness and death due to alcoholism. This would also result in a loss of manpower for work. Human resources had already reduced alarmingly because of emigration. Besides, expenses would also be incurred for the suppression of crimes and toward assistance for those plunged into misery due to alcoholism. It was found that many a time when the alcoholic did not have money to buy a drink, he would rob things, coconuts, livestock, and anything salable. This was a known fact in the villages because the salary, even if substantial, was insufficient to kill the thirst for alcohol.[117] Usually, the tavern owner bought the stolen items at a pittance or for some alcohol in return. This showed the level of moral degradation of the alcoholic.

In the final session, the delegates at the Sétimo Congresso suggested that alcohol with a percentage above 13- or 14-grade proof should not be sold for local consumption at all. These grades were similar to *urraca* or *cajuló*.[118] Another suggestion was the reduction in the production of native liquor by 25 percent from the existing rate. They did not fail to discuss the increasing number of taverns, which was also raised during the Segundo Congresso by Condorcet Pereira. His suggestion to reduce them at that time was not even taken into consideration for discussion, let alone recommended. It was also proposed to prohibit the establishment of new taverns in localities where the public had easy access, to restrict the operating hours, and to keep them closed during festive days. Prohibiting the sale of alcohol to women and children was also mooted, and neither would they be allowed to sell. It was recommended to increase the tax amount on the import of products as well as to increase the license fee and also make effective the legislation against drunkenness.[119]

Alcoholism and the Catholics

There was a perception that the Catholics were more prone to drinking alcohol, and therefore addiction was predominant among them. Such insinuations did not go well with the Church, which decided that it was time to make a firm decision to control this menace. The religious authorities agreed that there was a problem amongst its flock. The voices at the seminars and writings in various newspapers, whether in Portuguese, Marathi, or Konkani, from Goa, Bombay (Mumbai), or even in Portugal, broached and discussed the problem of alcoholism in general and amongst the Catholics in particular. In addition, there were statistics to prove that the mortality rate was higher amongst the Catholics, and the main cause was alcoholism—directly or indirectly.[120] It was not easy for the Church to look the other way and say that nothing was wrong with the Catholic community, and hence it decided to take remedial action.

For the Church, this was not a new problem. Alcoholism existed even in the past, albeit in lesser numbers and intensity. The Church correspondence and pastoral letters show clear evidence that the problem of alcohol consumption existed within the clergy as well as amongst the laypeople.

Portaria of 1931 and the Circular of 1934 Issued by the Archdiocese

The patriarch, aware of the grave problem, supported the decisions taken by the Sétimo Congresso Provincial, which emphasized joint decisions by the people and collaboration by all the social forces to eradicate the scourge of alcoholism. Therefore, instructions were issued via a Portaria (order) prohibiting the serving of food and drinks in the sacristy or any attached room near religious buildings.[121] Such instructions were not new, as similar ones had been issued earlier by the predecessors of the patriarch. It also prohibited the use and offering of alcohol to any person in the parochial houses. Strictures were also passed regarding the celebrations of a feast in the precincts of the church. The *mordomo* (patron) of the feast was ordered not to serve food in the parochial house if ladies were present.[122]

The Portaria apparently did not make much headway, and since he was not happy with the outcome, the patriarch issued a circular to all the parish priests in the archdiocese, stating that he considered the drinking of alcohol at the celebrations of *ladainha* as a real sickness. He not only condemned but also prohibited it.[123] Lucio Rodrigues writes regarding preparations of *ladainha*: "There was the visit to the local market for gram, a bottle of *branco* (wine) … The gram … boiled to the correct degree of softness, while coconut chips were sliced to be mixed up … The inevitable bottle of coconut or cashew *fenni* (liquour) gave the preparations a touch of finality."[124] According to the circular, celebrations of *ladainha* are good traditions and should be encouraged and practiced.[125] However, the serving of *feni* at this religious function was not welcome and also hurt the patriarch's feelings, who considered this a sacrilege and a shame for the Catholics, who should give a good example of good manners, faith, and devotion to all others by drinking less. Therefore, the circular was issued.

The parish priest was held responsible for implementing and ensuring that the circular was followed. To make it more stringent, the patriarch informed that if anyone did not follow the same and this practice continued, then those not observing it would be punished according to Canon Law. Vicars and chaplains were asked to read the circular in the local language, as many times as needed, during the preaching or sermon, so that more people understood.[126] The patriarch also pointed out that while selecting and appointing staff to the different positions in the Church, the candidates should be abstemious.

The circular was criticized by the paper *O Bharat*, which had led a campaign against alcoholism and had all along pointed a finger at the Catholics, the Church, and the government authorities for denial and aversion to take any action. The editor, Hegdo Dessai,[127] spared no words when he wrote that the very fact a circular was issued showed that the patriarch, for the first time, acknowledged in a public document the problem of alcoholism and commented, "About litanies or prayers, or where these religious acts are performed, alcoholic beverages are drunk, such as *feni*, etc.," constituting "a true scandal for non-Christians."[128] According to Dessai, there was deliberate silence on the part of the Catholic newspapers and the so-called "Defensores" (defenders) and propagandists of religion. He added that the scandal of drinking that went on even during the minor acts of Catholic worship had reached such levels that it was visible to anyone. He said the religious authority could not deny and ignore the indecent spectacle of drunkenness organized on the pretext of religion on an almost daily basis. The editorial pointed out that if there were statistics maintained by the police, they would know the percentage of fights and crimes on the occasion of Catholic feast days and religious observances, which helped to cover the ignoble drunkenness.[129]

Dessai was skeptical about the circular's implementation and success. He commented that it was doubtful if this circular prohibiting alcohol at religious feasts and the penalties mentioned therein would stop or even reduce the habit of drinking, "as it is so deeply rooted amongst the Catholic population of this land, even admitting that the patriarchal circular will be executed."[130] The editor doubted the seriousness of the circular, which came so late. According to him, the authority was so indifferent to taking any action that it could have been just a "manifestação platónica" (platonic manifestation), not to be taken seriously. He also took the opportunity to take a gibe at the patriarch, who had promised a Pastoral Letter at the time of the Congresso de Acção Católica, showing that the gravity of the problem was not well thought out by the religious or civil authorities. He emphasized that the problem of alcoholism could not be settled or solved by pastoral letters, sermons, circulars, temperance leagues, or other manifestations of this type promoted with the aim to throw dust in the eyes of the public. Nor would those dependent on the revenue take any action that would prejudice them. It could not be solved by deliberately ignoring that the main cause of this illness was the unlimited production of cheap alcoholic drinks, permitted by the public administration to gain easy revenue. He concluded by saying that the circular helped in accepting the existence and immoderate use of alcohol during *ladainhas* and other religious acts and the responsibility that this custom had in the propagation of the vice of alcoholism! The editor was right in his inference that even if the circular was put into practice, there would not be much headway, as such circulars or actions were issued or proposed many times and did not produce any improvement.

On the occasion of the fourth centenary of the Archdiocese of Goa in 1933, a seminar titled Congresso da Acção Católica, the first of its kind, was organized at the Convent of S. Francisco de Assisi, at Old Goa. Various papers on different subjects relevant to Catholics were discussed at this event.[131] On the very first day, there was one on the vices of alcoholism and tobacco, titled "Alcoholism and Tobacco" by Dr. Baronio Monteiro.[132]

During the discussion after the papers were presented, Canon A. J. Heredia agreed that alcohol and tobacco were dreadful but questioned whether these could be totally banned. He opined that he was against a total ban, believing in the maxim *In medio consistit virtus*—that virtue lies in the middle and is away from the extremes. He added that the scriptures assured that man's heart is made happy by wine—*Vinum laetificat cor hominis*—and cited the example of the wedding at Cana, where Christ miraculously converted water into wine, which, according to Heredia, showed that the use of wine could be permitted at social functions.

Another church official, Canon João Paulo de Sousa, said that if medical sciences and hygiene condemned alcohol and tobacco, then they should be banned. However, he believed that alcohol in small doses was food, to which Dr. Monteiro had disagreed. Sousa added that he also read an opinion of a "médico autorisado" (authorized doctor) that alcohol in small quantities could be very useful to the human organism.[133] Heredia's argument that Christ's miracle of converting water into wine gives consent to use it for social functions was deemed not plausible since what Monteiro was discussing was the abuse of alcohol and not its use at social functions. The point raised by de Sousa that alcohol in small quantities could be very useful as food was discussed by many as not valid, as it was "bad food" and therefore unhealthy for those who consumed it.

At the valedictory function of the Congresso, the patriarch commented on Monteiro's paper, saying that the vice of alcoholism was like a cancer that had frighteningly invaded the archdiocese.[134] He acknowledged that it was grave and agreed that it was especially a moral problem, as mentioned by some of his colleagues in the press. Therefore, he said, as the head of the archdiocese, it was his responsibility to take measures to stop the vice and had, therefore, long back, begun to write a Pastoral Letter. But his busy schedule had not allowed him to finish it. However, it looked like the need and urgency to tackle the vice, as well as the criticism of Hegdo Dessai, made him write without any more delay, as he issued the Pastoral Letter while on his vacation in Wellington. It was titled "Carta Pastoral sobre o alcoolismo: D. Theotonio Manuel Ribeiro Vieira de Castro." It was dated June 8, 1934. It appears that he was looking for divine blessings, as the Letter was issued on an important day to the Catholic Church, the Feast of the Sacred Heart of Jesus.

With the Pastoral Letter on alcoholism issued, the patriarch called upon the legislators of the Conselho do Governo, who were the lawmakers, to apply the same enthusiasm to bring about the comfort and material progress of the people of Goa and to take care of their physical and moral sanitation concerning the evil vice of alcoholism. To attain this, it was suggested that rigorous implementation and perfecting of the rules relevant to the supply of alcoholic beverages be followed. Severe penalties for the transgressors were also proposed. The patriarch urged the government to overlook any loss in income if the rules were implemented, as the losses would be compensated in favor of the family and the state. He wrote that people would have strong bodies, there would be fewer crimes and mortality, an increase in births, reduced expenses on social assistance, and the honor and prestige of India Portuguesa would climb higher in stature.

In the same way, he requested the priests of the diocese to unite with him in the crusade against alcoholism and suggested the need for them to be the first to give a good example for all—the faithful and the unfaithful—with zeal and timely and prudent abstinence. Though the Church was trying to overlook alcoholism, it was not a new problem for the religious authorities. Historically, it had to face this problem amongst the clergy and the people. So, it was not surprising that the patriarch called the attention of the priests, stating that they should be the first to practice restraint as they were not above the law. Many of them were prone to drinking and became alcoholics. This trend of the past has probably continued over the years. A paper by Lopes throws some light on the problems of addiction amongst the Catholics and the clergy, which shows how the past and the present may not differ much.[135]

As far as addiction to alcoholism was concerned, the accused were, as a rule, compelled to sign a good behavior bond, make a confession, and pay a pecuniary fine. Usually, the fine imposed on those accused of alcoholism ranged from two to six *xerafins*. In rare cases, it was raised to twenty-five to thirty *xerafins*.[136] In the case of priests, the punishment was similar, made sterner by reclusion in a convent and suspension of priestly orders. This proved that the punishment was proportionate to the degree of responsibility of the individual in society. Cases of relapse were more severely punished, especially for priests, with "externment" to another parish for some time.[137] On the other hand, it is worth recalling the importance the Catholic Church assumed in Goan society and the process of acculturation that took place in the East. Notwithstanding these observations, not always favorable, the clergy seems to have responded well to their ecclesiastical duties.[138]

According to Lopes, the documentation under study brought to light the constant preoccupation and eagerness on the part of the high dignitaries of the Church to avoid, as far as possible, or to curb these excesses that were easily committed, particularly at the level of the parochial clergy, which was less subject to the control of their superiors since they were isolated in the rural surroundings.

The delicts that the priests were accused of were generally not of a dogmatic-religious nature, but mainly of social incidence and represented a clear violation of ecclesiastical statutes. Many of them were accused of not following their priestly duties properly and also of carrying on practices forbidden by Canon Law, such as engaging in business or indulging in alcoholism. Out of 128 accused among the regulars, 51 were classified as habitual drinkers, and their state of drunkenness (39.8 percent) was such that they were unable to carry out their divine obligations.

Whether the denouncers are worthy of belief or not, what were the factors responsible for such a high incidence of alcohol addiction? Could the vice have spread among the members of this society, including the clergy, following the "fashion of their parishioners"? It was noted that alcoholism assumed a high percentage, though not the highest, in the list of offenses.[139] Lopes questions the reason for so many alcoholics amongst the clergy and feels that they are attracted to alcohol as they could not have amorous relations in a society in which roughly everyone was acquainted with each other, as the deviations in sexual behavior are next in frequency on the list of offenses.

In another article, also based on pastoral visits, the author writes that the clerics are more frequently accused of the vice of drunkenness.[140] He ironically comments: "Apparently, when other pleasures of the flesh were denied to them, the clerics seem to have taken the commendation of wine by St. Paul a little too seriously." He gives the example of the parish priest of Velsao in Salcete, who was accused in 1748 of drinking so excessively as to be incapable of doing his duty of celebrating Mass for his parishioners even on Sundays and days of obligation.[141]

In the article "Poetry in the Histories of Goan Literature in Portuguese," Helder Garmes discusses a poem titled "Os desejos de um bêbado" (The Wishes of a Drunkard).[142] The poem is a satire by an anonymous poet who writes about different alcoholic beverages, connecting them to geographical identities. He dwells in the western places and then comes to the coast of Coromandel, including Cochin, Diu, and Goa. The second-to-last stanza of the poem refers to *feni* and the Mandovi River, and the last to Christianity. In the poem, the poet wishes that *feni* flows in the Mandovi:

> Wishes of a drunkard
> Oh! God! What satisfaction
> for the soul of a Christian!
> it's so happy;
> But for proof of the love
> I have for my country,
> I also fervently ask
> that the great beautiful Mandovi
> be all of Feni.[143]

Garmes comments that the poem addresses a theme that is very Goan: the drinking of alcohol, not common amongst Hindus and Muslims, functioning as a brand, in this case somewhat irreverently, of Christianity. Garmes wrote that *feni* was an alcoholic beverage distilled from cashews, mostly consumed by the Goan proletariat. He probably had not come across another important *feni*, that of the coconut palm, which was manufactured, as already mentioned, long before the Portuguese arrived. In fact, palm *feni* accounted for the majority of the quantity produced throughout the year, and its export gave huge revenue to the government.[144] Besides, it provided employment to thousands of *rendeiros*, a class by themselves, who extracted toddy from the tree.[145] Statistics show the quantities manufactured of both types of *feni*. Referring to the last verse suggests that God could also be included among drunks since he drinks wine, which would extend to the whole congregation of Catholic priests who do so in the celebration of Mass:[146] "... which you drink, my Lord, give me in hiding four chosen barrels."[147]

Garmes wrote that the theme of alcohol, treated anonymously in a subtle way in 1862, would make history and gain significant expression in Goan social history, first linked to Christianity and then to the Westernization of Goa. Indeed, in the twentieth century, alcoholism became the main scourge amongst not only the proletariat and the Catholics but also all segments of society. There is no doubt, however, that abstention being a religious precept in both Hinduism and Islam, the introduction of Western customs and increased manufacture and availability greatly facilitated the demand for alcohol.

There seem to have been no changes in the way alcoholism was perceived, as *Jornal das Comunidades* wrote what was so often being said: "The population of Goa, especially the Christian proletariat population, is overwhelmed by alcoholism. There is not a celebration, a litany, a baptism, a birth, or even a death in which the feni is not abused ... even for a silly reason, the feni! There is no sadness or joy that is not celebrated with feni"[148]

The pressure on the Church to take action against alcoholism came from all quarters, Catholics as well as Hindus, journalists, as well as intellectuals. The best example of this drive would be the conference papers and discussions of the delegates during the Congresso, where the Catholics were pointed to as the main culprits. They even blamed them for showing the way to members of other communities. Even at the Church's doorsteps during the proceedings of the Congresso, Monteiro pointed out the community's role in alcohol addiction in his paper. The criticism had to be viewed positively, as he was trying to impress upon those present and others the grave situation that was caused by this scourge. The circular issued by the Church was not enough and was also criticized by some papers. There was no option for the patriarch but to take a more serious stand. This came in the form of the Pastoral Letter, which was long overdue. In that letter, the patriarch tried to cover almost all the relevant aspects related to alcoholism and acknowledged that the problem did prevail in Goa. He also admitted that this addiction unfortunately existed not only amongst the illiterate of Goan society, but was widespread amongst different social classes, even corroding the youngsters and the adolescents. To make his point, he referred to some ignorant illiterate parents who frequently gave *feni* and other alcoholic beverages to their children of tender age.[149]

The patriarch was concerned about the bad example that the Catholic alcoholics set for people in a country which had various other religions, like Hindus, Muslims, Sikhs, and Jains, who, by rule, do not touch alcohol. To quote: "Therefore, what a big scandal they make to the followers of the only true religion, if they not only use, which is allowed to them when there are just motives, but misuse these drinks."[150] Nevertheless, the patriarch tried to fight alcoholism, and the Portarias, circulars, and pastoral letters issued by the church authorities are proof of their efforts, although most of it remained on paper and nothing much was done in practice.[151]

A committee was formed to follow up on the recommendations and proposals at the Congresso de Acção Católica, which would insist that the government fully enforce the existing law restricting the sale of alcoholic beverages, place, time, etc., in view of the moral and physical health of the population. The committee felt that a war needed to be started against the abuse of alcoholic beverages. It therefore recommended avoidance of even moderate daily use and that children and adolescents should not be allowed to drink. In this regard, support from parents, teachers, and educationists was requested.[152]

Alcoholism and the Press in Goa

One would think that after so much activism against the bane of alcoholism—by individuals and organized entities, at the Congresses, by the Church authorities, the press, and others—the government would take some concrete action, but nothing much happened. Even the laws that were enacted were not implemented to the core. However, many individuals continued the fight. Baronio Monteiro established the Liga Economico-Social da India Portuguesa (Socio-Economic League of Portuguese India) with the objective of helping the Goan community live a better life.[153] He was against alcohol and tobacco. The objective of the Liga was to simplify things, enhance moral values in life, fight alcoholism, and increase local food production. Since he was not in a position to reach people far away, he decided to start a periodical for the people to read and understand the objectives and support them in their endeavors. The first issue of *A Reforma, Revista Mensal, Orgão da Liga Economico-Social* was launched in September 1932, in the first year of the foundation of the Liga.

Although the Liga was fighting the consumption of alcohol and, in that way, alcoholism, the editor writes that they were not for the prohibition of alcohol but for moderate drinking, especially during social functions where drinks were served without any restriction. He also added that the Liga Economico-Social da India Portuguesa should not be confused with the Liga de Temperança and decided to form a Liga Anti-Tabago-Alcoólica with physicians Jacinto da Silva, Peregrino da Costa, and Baronio Monteiro at its helm for fighting against alcohol and tobacco.[154] Sometime later in 1934, the long-awaited Liga de Temperança de Goa was established, and its by-laws were published in *A Reforma*. It seems to have received a positive response from the Church authorities because the by-laws also appeared in the *Voz de S. Francisco Xavier*, which was the official organ of the Church.[155] A committee was formed, and all the members were physicians, except for Pedro Correia Afonso, who was an agronomist.[156]

This came at a time when the Temperance Movement around the world was dwindling, as in 1935, Alcoholics Anonymous started a movement against alcoholism.[157] Monteiro had hoped that through the Temperance Movement, people would be able to understand the evil that alcohol was, and this would lead them to reduce or give up drinking. However, it had a small following, and nothing much happened on this front either. Other attempts made at trying to reduce this affliction also failed in reducing alcoholism. The problem persisted because the authorities were not serious about implementation.

We find that the other newspapers were also active in criticizing the use of alcohol in Goa. *Porjecho Adar* pointed out several reasons why alcoholism was prevailing in Goa. The article, "Ladainha vo Ters. Amcheam Gaunvanim" (Litany or Rosary. In Our Villages), criticizes the serving of alcohol at these religious practices. The writer says that it is the worst practice because youngsters who accompany the elders for these practices learn to smoke and drink.[158] Drinks were also served in the villages during wedding celebrations when people had parties for a number of days and spent money, although many could not afford it. In a series of articles written by Bulhão Fratel on the tradition of wedding celebrations in the villages of Goa by the proletariat, spending money beyond their means, he advises them not to have such unnecessary expenditures, which result in a financial burden for many years, often for a whole lifetime. In these articles, he also criticizes the serving of alcohol to guests at the many functions linked to the wedding, which is detrimental to their health.[159] To emphasize how alcohol was present in all types of events—happy or sad—a write-up titled "Soro Interranc" (Liquor at the Funerals) dwelt on how no sooner the death of a person was informed, the neighbor would come over to help with the formalities.[160] He would first ask to buy a *garrafão*[161] of *feni* to serve those who come to pay condolences and to those who come to say the rosary during the seven days after the funeral. Additionally, the suggestion is made to purchase alcohol to be served to the mourners near the cemetery following the funeral.[162] This tradition benefited the alcoholics who attended a funeral because they would get free alcohol. "Inter vo Mornam" (Funerals or Death) was another one that discussed alcoholism at a funeral.[163]

The Portuguese paper *O Século*[164] from Lisbon carried an article on alcoholism in Goa, which stated that certain means had been proposed to the government of Portuguese India to resolve the problem surrounding the regulation of taverns. This revealed that there was one tavern for every 200 inhabitants, with many of them within 10 meters of one another. These comments were made in 1932, and in 1937 José Inacio de Loyola, also known as Fanchu, wrote under the title "Alcoolismo": "Alcohol is gradually poisoning the population of Portuguese India. The people are visibly weakening, losing their past physical and intellectual virility." He lamented that the damned vice of alcoholism enjoyed an unbridled reign in every stratum of society and that taverns were mushrooming at a frightful pace, selling alcohol at all times of the day or night. He also held the numerous taverns responsible for this unfortunate situation: "There are taverns—the source of irradiation of the vilest immoralities—at regular intervals, in centers, alongside roads, taverns in the heart of the towns and cities, the entire territory of Goa has been converted into a paradise of drunkenness."[165]

He blamed the state for allowing taverns, as the revenue accrued from these was one-fifth of the total income provided by *abkari*, which was the income from the alcohol industry, including distillation. This was reason enough for the state to zealously protect its interests, and it was certainly reluctant to initiate the promulgation of a law, which, though morally beneficial to society, would curtail its revenue. Loyola, therefore, made an appeal for a collective movement by the people of the state—having at its head all those men who were representatives of Indo-Portuguese intellectualism—that could persuade the government to bestow upon this problem the attention it deserved. Like others, he also felt that the fight against alcoholism by an individual would be difficult and hence asked others to join in and suggested that the government should find other means to cover the losses if the number of taverns was reduced.

This campaign against alcohol by *Portugal e Colónias* was seconded by other newspapers like *Jornal das Comunidades*, *Correio de Bardez*, and others who appreciated the effort of Loyola. *Jornal das Comunidades* wrote that the Congress government in the Bombay Presidency was determined to impose a "dry law" to control or put an end to alcoholism. Surprisingly, the British government did not oppose this move, citing loss of revenue. It instead made arrangements in the budget of the Presidency of Bombay[166] to counterbalance the losses. The paper asked why these measures could not be made applicable to Goa, which, because of the abuse in alcoholism, was called "Essencialmente Alcoólica e Taverna do Industão" (Essentially Alcoholic and Tavern of Hindustan).[167]

In fact, in the earlier decades, it was the vernacular press that was at the forefront of writing on the vice of alcohol. For example, *A Luz do Oriente—Prachi-Prabha,* of which Ramchandra P. Vaidya was the editor and Sitaram Quercar was the secretary and in-charge of the Portuguese section. Quercar wrote that the fundamental causes of Goansr ruin were illiteracy, alcoholism, unemployment, and superficial Westernization.[168] He wrote that the paper's mission was to fight against the evil of alcoholism and would constantly write about it, right from the first issue.[169] Quercar added that it was difficult for a state to prosper when the vice had completely ruined the people and the proletariat and their families by creating chaos, hunger, weakness, immorality, etc.[170] He described the taverns as "destructive agents of alcoholism."[171] He commented that nothing had been proposed by the government as if it did not mean anything and did not prejudice the people. *O Bharat*, with Hegdo Dessai, was also on a war path against the vice. He felt that the Catholic press was not doing enough. Both were prominent papers of Goa, with a good readership.

At the Sétimo Congresso, it was decided to establish the Liga de Temperançã and many of those present at the Congresso signed in its favor. However, since many were themselves followers of Bacchus, this idea fizzled out even before it could start.[172] As per an article in *O Heraldo,* the same had happened with the attempts made at Margao and Chinchinim.[173] The Government Council had appointed a committee to oversee the problem of alcoholism. The writer, who hailed from Chandor, Salcete, wrote that there were almost no living Curumbis above forty years of age in this village. Instead, one found young boys of twenty-five and above with bloated faces and bulging tummies, who were not fit to undertake any hard work. Why was this happening? The toddy tappers would sell a bottle of *feni* or *cajuri* at just four *tangas* a bottle.[174] Then, there was the deprivation of social customs, which did not anymore consider those addicted as criminals. On the contrary, it was observed that offering liquor and having a peg or two at social functions were welcome. To make matters worse, people did not attend any functions, including religious and funerals, if liquor was not served.[175] From this behavior, we can say that the circulars, Portarias, or the formal Pastoral Letter issued by the Church did not have much effect. Unfortunately, this trend was seen even in the New Conquests;

for example, in Neturlim, Rivona, and Curchorem, strong and able-bodied laborers were now into the vice of drinking. Besides the licensed official tavern, there were also those selling illegally, which increased the number of drinking dens. In Curchorem, there were three licensed taverns near the railway station and at least five other illegal places where liquor was sold.[176] Goa, with such a large number of taverns for this small territory, got the sobriquet of "Terra de Tavernas" (Land of Taverns).[177]

Libério Pereira, in an article titled "Chaga Social," refers to number 14 of article 48 of the Reforma Administrativa Ultramarina,[178] which defines stopping the production and sale of alcoholic and fermented beverages, exercising rigorously the law in vigor through agents, and having active surveillance over indigenous life, to give alcoholism a tough fight without a ceasefire. Number 5 of article 28 of the same Reforma also expected the administrative employee to fight against alcoholism.[179] But, despite these official instructions, the government had done nothing in Goa to enforce them and control the menace.

The mandates in Central Africa of the Covenant of the League of Nations recognized the need to protect the indigenous people from alcohol traffic.[180] Pereira pointed out the provision in the mandate and impressed upon the reader and the government that it was important to act to tackle this menace. He suggested that the mandate should be applied to Goa to protect the natives, who comprised the majority of the proletariat. He added that the press of British India was also following what was happening in Goa.

This adamant attitude of the government continued throughout the period of study because it was not ready to lose the much-valued revenue for the government coffers, which it felt it could not substitute by raising taxes on other items. Figures in Table 4.9 show the revenue from 1939 to 1941.

Table 4.9 Revenue from taxes collected from 1939 to 1941

Tax on the extraction of coconut toddy in Goa.	421,523:05:04
Revenue from taxes on the distillation of cashew spirit and sugarcane.	78,900:00:00
Revenue from taxes on licenses for the sale of native spirits in taverns	87,495:00:00
Of wines and non-Indian spirits	11,335:09:03
Total	599.254:04:07 rupees[181]

[Source: Maria P. Rodrigues, "Taverna and Its Socio-Economic Impact," 199]

Maria Rodrigues, in her paper, gives a comparative example of taxes collected under the provisions of Diploma Legislativo no. 551 of April 1, 1932,[182] shown under the title "Industrias em regime tributário especial" (Industries in special tax regime), and those collected based on the Diploma Legislativo no. 1770 of March 15, 1958, which was issued to approve the rules and regulations for the industrial contribution. The revenue from this contribution was much needed by the government to pay the salaries of the government employees who had been given a raise.[183] Even though the fight was taken up by the Church, intellectuals—Catholics and Hindus alike—and others, it was observed that not much was done by the government to stop alcoholism. The reason was its dependence on the revenue collected from the alcohol manufactured and sold, which was second only to the revenue from mining in Goa, even during the troubled period of the economic blockade.

5

The Economic Blockade and the Pangs of Hunger

Introduction

The Government of India did not want to use any military force against the Portuguese territories to solve the impasse created by the stubbornness of Oliveira Salazar, prime minister of Portugal.[1] His unwillingness to hand over the territories led Jawaharlal Nehru, India's first prime minister after independence, to impose an economic blockade, which impacted the Goans considerably. This action taken by the Indian government created a crisis in Goa, with everyday items rendered unavailable, and difficulties in obtaining food like rice, wheat, pulses, green vegetables, onions, potatoes, chilies, cooking oil, vanaspati (vegetable oil), sugar, and jaggery. These were some of the items that were imported from the neighboring Indian territories for local consumption.[2] This chapter examines the impact of the economic blockade from 1955 to 1961 on Portuguese India and its people.

The fact that Goans had emigrated to these areas and beyond enabled them to send home remittances.[3] These financial transfers helped both the families who received them and the government administration. However, when the blockade was imposed, postal correspondence and remittances were put on hold, and hence no money could be transferred to the relatives in Goa.[4] When Portuguese India refused to accept Indian currency as legal tender and the *escudo* was reintroduced as a monetary measure, it added to the misery of the Goans. However, the smuggling of food and other items during the period affected the successful implementation of the blockade.

Many have written about the economic blockade[5] and its historical, political, and economic aspects. However, its effect on the consumption of the different social strata in Goa has been neglected. This factor needs to be examined to understand how, during this period, a change came about in the food habits of the Goans.

It may be noted that even when diplomatic relations were not established, both governments maintained an amicable attitude, though there were undercurrents between the two. There used to be cooperation in managing the affairs between the two, especially with regard to the supply of commodities for which Goa was almost fully dependent on its neighboring territories.[6] In fact, Goa's economy was entwined with that of British India and in a special way with the then Bombay Presidency. Although the political set-ups of Portuguese India and British India differed and there were customs barriers between the two territories, trade was relatively free and population movements were unregulated. The port of Mormugao and its rail link served not only Goa but also a large hinterland within the territory.[7] Goa was not only dependent on commodities but also on jobs for its growing population. However, the undercurrents would surface at the time of the establishment of consular offices and the appointment of diplomatic representatives.

When British India attained independence in August 1947, India still had territories ruled by France and Portugal.[8] At the time, Gandhi and Nehru thought that the occupied territories would eventually be handed over to India through diplomatic efforts, without requiring any forceful action. While France[9] reluctantly gave in, Portugal refused to leave, giving various reasons for staying on.[10]

In the meantime, both India and Portugal agreed to set up diplomatic offices, and one of the important issues on the agenda for discussion, as far as India was concerned, would be the handing over of the colonial territories.[11] For Portugal, it was a non-issue. It took nearly two years to set up a legation because of India's reluctance and doubts about Portugal's sincerity in establishing relations, as well as its friendly attitude toward Pakistan and the Nizam-ruled princely state of Hyderabad. India claimed that Portugal was in discussion with the Nizam to sell Goa, a claim refuted by Portugal.[12] Another bone of contention between them was the issue of the *Padroado* between the Holy See and Portugal, by which certain privileges were given to Portugal for having rendered services in the spread of the Catholic faith. Accordingly, Portugal kept the right to intervene in some religious appointments in the Indian Archdioceses. The Government of India wished that these privileges be revoked and all dioceses be administered directly by the Holy See,[13] and also to consider the re-delimitation of the Archdiocese of Goa and its jurisdiction, which should not extend to the Indian territory.[14]

The Legation offices functioned for a short time as Nehru closed the Indian office in Lisbon on June 11, 1953, in reaction to the Portuguese government's refusal to discuss the Goa problem, that is, its integration into India.[15] The Indian government had not asked, until then, for the closure of the Portuguese legation, since they expected that it would be possible to reach a solution peacefully. As there was no breakthrough in the discussions and it was not serving any purpose, and since Portugal had rejected various offers of negotiations, coupled with the recent happenings in Goa (the anti-Satyagraha and anti-terrorist movement by the Portuguese authorities), Nehru decided to close the Portuguese legation on August 8, 1955.[16] However, he stated that it did not mean a cut-off of the diplomatic relations, as a Portuguese Consulate was maintained in Bombay and an Indian counterpart in Goa.[17] Therefore, the diplomatic ties were not closed by June 1953.[18] The ties were formally cut off when the lower diplomatic-level consulates of both the countries in Goa and Bombay and honorary consulate offices in Calcutta and Madras, respectively, closed on September 1, 1955. Nehru justified the closure, holding that the objective for which it was set up was not fulfilled, as Oliveira Salazar was adamant about not negotiating the handing over of the territories.

In the meantime, the freedom movement of Goa had picked up momentum after India's independence. Freedom fighters in Goa believed that India would take immediate action to liberate the territories of Portuguese India. However, as mentioned above, this expectation did not materialize as Nehru was obstinate in not using any force and was still hoping that the territories would be handed over peacefully. On the other hand, Salazar refused to leave and maintained that the territories were not colonies but an integral part of metropolitan Portugal. He commented that "if the 'case of Goa,' meant the transfer of sovereignty of the Portuguese territories to the Union of India, then for sure this problem would not be solved peacefully."[19]

In order to avoid the question in the future, the territories were renamed as "Overseas Provinces."[20] To add credence to this theory, Salazar introduced a new statute, "Estatuto do Estado da India," dated July 1, 1955, to counter the charge that the Portuguese administration was dictatorial. It proclaimed Portuguese India to be an autonomous unit enjoying administrative decentralization.[21]

Nehru was caught up between the ideology on which the Indian nation was built—of nonviolence—and the call of the opposition in the Parliament and the Goan freedom fighters who demanded forceful action against Portugal.[22] While the Indian National Congress unanimously approved the stand taken by Nehru, the members of the opposition and their supporters protested against his approach.[23]

Imposition of the Blockade: Stopping the Railway

With no alternative left and to avoid using military force, Nehru formally imposed an economic blockade on July 25, 1955, which continued until the liberation of the territories.[24] On that day, the railway traffic across the border into the Portuguese territory and vice versa was stopped.[25] This decision was taken without any prior intimation to the Portuguese government. Thus, Goa was isolated from the Union of India, as the railway connection between Castle-Rock and Vila de Curchorem, commonly known as Sanvordem, was stopped.[26] This meant that people and goods could not come directly from India into Goa. Under the Anglo-Portuguese Treaty, the Portuguese government had signed a contract with the British company, the West of India Portuguese Guaranteed Railway (previously designated as W.I.P.) as the concessionaire to explore the port and railways of Mormugao. But this company, with the accord of the Portuguese government, by a contract of 1902, handed over the operations of the concession to the Southern Mahratta Railway Company of British India. This contract had been regularly renewed between both parties for fifty-three years. However, when the blockade was imposed by Nehru, the Southern Mahratta Railway was asked to cease its activities as a concessionaire. It notified the Portuguese in October 1955 that it would cease to carry out its operations of the port and the railways from December 22, 1955. In doing so, it did not adhere to the period of notice of six months as stipulated in the contract.[27] The Portuguese took over the running of the Mormugao Railways on December 31, 1955.[28]

When Nehru was questioned in the Parliament on July 28, 1955, about why this unilateral measure was taken, he explained that it was due to certain difficulties regarding the functioning of the railways. The prime minister was referring to the presence of Portuguese soldiers posted at the stations. He was apprehensive that they could harm the passengers and also alleged that dynamite was used on the tracks. He added that the railway from India to the Portuguese territory would continue to operate up to Castle Rock.[29] The Portuguese authorities refuted the claim and said that soldiers were there only to protect the train and passengers from any attack. Perhaps Nehru used the safety of the passengers as a cover or justification to move away from his policy of trying to solve Goa's issue without the use of force. According to Acharya J.B. Kripalani, nothing would happen, as Nehru refused to take any action, as his only endeavor was to protect his international image, which was important to him.[30]

There are different versions regarding the enforcement of the blockade, especially concerning the timings when it was imposed. Sarto Esteves writes that after the freedom fighters liberated the territories of Dadra and Nagar Haveli, "the Portuguese, fearing military action by the Indians, sealed the border and cut off the rail link between Goa and India. India replied … by imposing an economic blockade." Further, he mentions that all trade between India and the Portuguese territories officially ended in 1954.[31] Similarly, there are other scholars who have concurred with Esteves and attributed the actions of India to Portugal's stance.[32] On the contrary, although Portugal did take measures to guard borders, it did not suspend the only rail link connecting India—almost 80 percent of daily necessities that Goa consumed were imported through railways. Moreover, Nehru's statement in the Parliament mentioned above details the actions taken by India.

According to Arthur Rubinoff, measures were taken by the Portuguese to block the march by the Praja Socialist Party on August 15, 1954—"suspension of rail and ferry services, highways and bridges were mined, trenches were dug, all foreign newspapers and journals were banned, schools were closed, and a night curfew was established."[33] Rubinoff has relied on *The New York Times,* which carried news distributed by France Press based in Bombay. However, Governor Bernard Guedes declared in a public statement that the news distributed by France Press was not true; he denied that any curfew would be clamped from August 15.[34] Rubinoff also writes that India prohibited the transfer of its currency through the mail to Goa, which was dependent on remittances.[35] However, the formal economic blockade was implemented in 1955 and not in 1954.

Some Measures before the Imposition of the Blockade

Long before the decision to close the Legation and take the crucial step of stopping train services, India had initiated some restrictions to put pressure on Portugal.[36] India had imposed the need for a permit to enter her territories with effect from September 7, 1954. By a notification dated April 10, 1954, the Government of India imposed restrictions on travel from the Portuguese territories to the Union of India. Under the new regulations, all local government officials (including Goans) of civil, military, or other departments of the Government of Portuguese possessions were required to obtain permits from the Indian Consulate General in Goa for entry into or transit through Goa. Similarly, the Government of Bombay Province imposed restrictions on motor traffic between Daman and Nagar Haveli.[37]

The Indian authorities knew the importance of rice in the diet of the Goans. It was their staple food, and yet it was not available in sufficient quantity. As written earlier, the locally grown cereal was sufficient for only five to six months, and therefore they depended on imports to meet the demand of the population. Using rice as a means to defeat the Portuguese was, therefore, a strategic decision. The reasons behind the rice insufficiency have been discussed in detail in the first chapter.

Consequently, when the governor of Goa requested seeds for cultivation, the Indian authorities took months to inform him that it would not be possible to supply them, leaving no option, as the time to initiate the cultivation had already lapsed. He claimed that the Indian authorities not only did not supply the seeds but had also imprisoned and imposed a fine on some Goans who went into the Indian territory to buy paddy.[38] The next time, even though the matter was sorted out well in advance and permission was accordingly granted, the permit issued was nullified at the last minute. This occurred despite the agreement that the Portuguese government offered to repay the seed purchase with rice, and the promised quantity of rice was proportionally beneficial to India, which claimed that times were difficult for food production. According to the governor, India's claim was not justified, and he reiterated that the solution to such problems lay in using our own resources and self-reliance. Interestingly, at this point, he had envisaged that dependence on India for seeds had to be brought to an end; if not, it would mean that they were handing over power in parts.[39]

Another incident the governor refers to is the transfer of funds to Burma (now Myanmar) for the acquisition of rice, which was made difficult by the Indian government. The governor then requested the Portuguese authorities to try to resolve the snags. Although Burma was ready to accept Indian rupees, the Reserve Bank of India refused the transfer and asked for the payment in pound sterling, which was a valuable loss of foreign currency to the Portuguese that could be used for future needs.[40] According to some Indian newspapers, the reason for such an action was that India alleged that 50 percent was used to buy weapons to send to Lisbon.[41] Others said that the decision to suspend was temporary and it was implemented because of the ongoing negotiations between both governments on the "question of Goa."[42]

The governor also warned the Portuguese government that the proposal from India to start public transport from Bombay to Goa by Bombay transporters was not viable. An objection was raised to such a move because the transport system in that city was nationalized. He feared that since the road transport was under the control of the Indian government, it would definitely jeopardize the free flow of traffic from across the territories. This would lead to severe repercussions on the movement of people and goods. This fear of the governor appears to have come true when the later political developments took place and the railway was stopped at the boundary of the Indian territory.[43] In doing so, a formal economic blockade was slapped on the Portuguese territories, which brought any kind of transportation to and from Goa to a standstill. The Indian government hoped that the stoppage of the transit of products would cause problems for the people and thereby embarrass the Portuguese.[44]

Given the scenario of rice scarcity in Goa, the problem of its unavailability was more pronounced during the economic blockade, which was intended to stop food supply and currency to the territory. In this period, food imports from the neighboring country were stopped and instead were imported from overseas. It would also be smuggled into the territory from across the border, which would increase its price and bring hardship to the Goan people. To diminish the scarcity, the Portuguese government ordered the rationing of rice.[45]

The first stanza of the poem *My Goa,* written by Manohar Sardessai in 1955, explicitly describes the scarcity that the Goans faced during the blockade period: "Land of cattle and of pastures green, Thirsty is my Goa for a drop of milk, Fertile land, land of paddy fields, My Goa goes begging for a grain of rice."[46]

The situation during the blockade was so grim that even the Portuguese military men voiced their discontent:

> In Portuguese India, life is miserable, full of starvation and terror. They (Goans) eat leaves from trees, as I have often seen, in consequence of the famine conditions created by Salazar's fascist government. The main food in India is rice, but there was not enough of it for the people, who were reduced to hunger as ourselves, the soldiers. The toilers go on without food and in torn clothes since their daily wages are of one or two rupees at the most. An orange costs eight annas and an apple twelve annas and other things are also expensive … But food is scarce and that is why we were hungry.[47]

Execution of the Blockade

An economic blockade is carried out using the termination (prohibition) of trade, financial credit, and other economic ties with the blockaded state. It may be extended simultaneously to all economic ties or only to particular forms of such ties with the blockaded country.

Scholars usually distinguish between negative and positive sanctions. Negative sanctions are the best-known economic instruments of diplomacy. They are imposed to inflict economic damage on one or more countries. Conversely, positive sanctions are measures devoted to fostering cooperation among some countries. It is possible to look at economic sanctions regarding (i) the objective; (ii) who is involved; and (iii) the object of sanctions. As regards the objectives of sanctions, following Barber,[48] it is possible to group the objectives of sanctions into three categories. There are "primary objectives" concerned with the actions and behavior of governments against whom the sanctions are directed. The "secondary objectives" are related to the status, behavior, and expectations of governments imposing sanctions. Finally, the "tertiary objectives" are concerned with broader international considerations, relating either to the structure of the international system as a whole or to some parts of it. These three categories do not exclude each other but can coexist and overlap in some cases. Sanctions may be unilateral when the initiative is taken by only one country and multilateral when imposed by more than one on the target country.

Looking at the objectives of sanctions, we can distinguish three kinds of sanctions: boycotts, embargoes, and financial sanctions.

A boycott is a restriction of imports of one or more goods from the target country. It takes place to lower the demand for certain products from that country. Moreover, it attempts to reduce the target's foreign exchange earnings and therefore its ability to purchase goods. In this case, Goa had limited exports since its industrial production was limited and it catered mainly to the local population.[49] However, there were some local products that were mainly exported to the Union of India, which refused to buy them, and therefore the producers and exporters suffered. These included coconuts, copra, coconut oil, areca nut, and salt. The government tried to overcome this problem by exporting the products overseas. A special order was issued to solve the depreciation of areca nut by exporting to some other friendly countries.[50]

Table 5.1 shows the decline in exports over the years. However, areca nut shows an increase in exports, probably because of the measures taken by the government. Cashew nuts maintained steady exports as most of them were exported beyond India and therefore were not affected by the blockade, although in 1956 and 1957 they experienced a low.

The sanctions also aimed to induce damage to a particular industry or sector of the target country. They are usually criticized as ineffective because target countries can find alternative markets or arrange triangular purchases to circumvent import controls. In the case of Goa, they were definitely ineffective since it hardly had any industry worthy of producing and exporting the end product, as Goa lacked an industrial infrastructure.

Table 5.1 Local products exported from 1955 to 1961

Year	Coconut	Mangoes	Areca nut	Copra	Salted Fish	Cashew nuts	Dry fish
1955	6,07,980	5,540	242	–	454	23,680	11,687
1956	3,86,800	35,000	21,104	3,589	227	17,472	2,975
1957	4,53,110	9,625	2,514	14,309	492	14,778	5,293
1958	2,18,328	8,140	5,510	3,159	295	21,914	9,926
1959	1,89,677	5,520	7,740	–	551	21,172	4,836
1960	16,265	8,387	7,997	–	756	35,072	8,428
1961	1,560	1,035	12,194	–	–	31,879	–

[Source: Goa, Daman and Diu, *Statistical Yearbook, 1961*, Panaji: Government Printing Press, 301–3. The figures are shown in *maunds* (15 kilos), and numbers for coconuts and mangoes]

Except for mining, on which Goa was dependent for its economy, others were producing goods that were mostly absorbed by the locals, and the surplus, if any, was exported.[51] With production being insufficient, goods were imported to make up for the deficiency.

The status of Goan manufacturing and production is best evaluated from a talk delivered by the governor of Goa at the "Feira das Indústrias Portuguesas" (Portuguese Industrial Fair), held in 1951 in Lisbon.[52] He points out that the local production, which he classified as industrial, of sugar cane, jaggery, ice, and cold drinks was all locally purchased. There was no surplus for export. Among the bigger local productions, he pointed out the export of coconut, copra, oil, and cashew nuts as giving some revenue to the government. However, the production of cashew nuts was not sufficient, and these had to be imported from Mozambique to fulfill the needs of the manufacturer. Another important manufacturing unit was that of tinned food, of which there were two in Margão, Salcete.[53] The export of salt also earned some revenue.[54] However, with the introduction of the blockade, salt could not be exported to neighboring India, which was the main market for this product. Table 5.2 below shows how the export of salt was inconsistent from 1955 to 1961. Though it was high in 1956 and 1958, in the remaining years it was negligible. The table below shows the decline during the blockade period.

To add to this, there were working units of rice and flour mills all over Goa used for husking the paddy. The cashew nut industry was perhaps the most important, after mining, and in 1961 its production was worth about 38 to 40 lakh rupees. As against this, the total industrial production that year was only 63.5 lakhs.[55]

Table 5.2 Salt export from Goa

Year	1955	1956	1957	1958	1959	1960	1961
Quantity in kilos	118	10,84,393	4,80,254	53,55,951	426	1,52,424	113

[Source: *Statistical Yearbook, 1961*, 303]

Restriction of Exports to the Target Country

An embargo also restricts the export of certain products to the target country. This is the most common technique. The prohibition on exports may be partial or complete. The Indian government kept the applications for import licenses on essential goods pending. Exports to Goa of any merchandise, as well as foodstuffs to other Indian Portuguese territories, were prohibited, and roads linking Goa, Daman, and Diu with the Union of India were blocked.

This impediment was removed only after the Liberation of Goa when the military government, which controlled the administration of the erstwhile Portuguese territories, issued a proclamation regarding the movement of goods in Goa. By this order, restrictions on both controlled and decontrolled items from the rest of India were lifted by the Government of India, and the merchants were at liberty to procure tea, coffee, cereals, potatoes, vegetables, onions, fruits, sugarcane jaggery, etc., from the Indian traders. Accordingly, appropriate instructions were given to the export, control, and customs authorities.[56] By another notification published in the Official Gazette, the government allowed free movement of all articles from the former Portuguese possessions, and no customs duty would be levied on the commodities on import into India. Areca nuts, cashew nuts, and fresh canned fruits of Goan origin were therefore permitted to be freely moved out of Goa to the rest of India.[57]

The Role of the Port and Dock Workers of Bombay

For the blockade to be successful, the sea route also had to be taken care of. Goa had access to the Indian Ocean with the natural port of Mormugao, which could be used during all the seasons, besides many other smaller ports, which were in a position to partly, if not fully, overcome the restrictions. To block this loophole, the Port and Dock Workers of India, on their own, decided to take action against the Portuguese administration. Thus, the joint workers' union in Bombay moved a resolution supporting the freedom movement of Goa and was supported by the Calcutta Port workers. The Bombay Port Trust General Workers' Union, by a decision of the general body meeting, decided not to handle any ship coming to Bombay after visiting Goa or intending to visit Goa from Bombay.[58] At the same time, the Transport and Dock Workers' Union of Bombay took a decision and directed its 20,000 members not to participate in the cargo-handling activities on ships from or to the Portuguese possessions in India, irrespective of the flags they flew.

To counteract such moves, which were only creating difficulties for them, the foreign shipping companies and agents, in order to placate the workers, gave them written assurances that their ships would not call at Goa. The agencies also guaranteed the workers' unions that their companies would not handle any ship which had called at Goa or intended to call at Goa or any of the Portuguese ports in India. However, some of the foreign shipping companies threatened to impose 35 percent surcharges to offset the so-called losses as a result of the cancellation of Goa from their trade route. Nehru reacted to this threat and, on August 22, 1955, made the following statement in the Parliament: "India could as well do without the foreign shipping lines if they enforced any surcharge on the Goa boycott issue."[59] This came as a surprise as the workers took the decision to boycott the ships and not the authorities of the Bombay Port Trust, which declared the boycott as illegal and promised action against them. However, the threat did not deter them, and they continued without giving in until December 1961.

Prohibition on the Movement of Indian Goods and Services and Various Notifications Issued by the Government of India

The Government of India issued various legislations that would help the execution of the blockade.[60] Under the Foreign Exchange Regulation Act of 1947, a notification was issued to put restrictions on the transmission by post of articles containing bank or currency notes, checks, securities, and financial instruments to Goa unless a license was obtained for the purpose from the Reserve Bank of India by the authorized dealers in foreign exchange.[61]

This notification was followed by a postal notice which said that the Post Office in India would not accept any article posted in contravention of any of these restrictions, and if inadvertently accepted, it would be returned to the sender or detained by the customs authorities empowered on that behalf, without any refund of postage or other charges paid by the sender of the said article.[62] These notifications ensured that the remittances would not reach the family in need, thereby causing them financial constraints.

Besides the above, the Ministry of Commerce and Industry issued the Export Trade Control Order under the Import and Export Control Act, 1947, prohibiting the export of goods like food grains, sugar, vanaspati, cooking oil, kerosene (used for cooking), etc.[63] Similarly, an Import Trade Control Order was issued under the same act, banning imports into India from Portuguese territories, including Goa. This meant that no food would be allowed from across the border, and scarcity would thus be created. The Indian government also instructed the customs authorities at the minor ports along the west coast not to pass shipping bills of goods meant for Goan ports.[64]

The Indian government also made arrangements to establish a physical cordon of customs personnel along the entire land border with a string of as many as 128 customs *chowkies* (outposts), manned by a sizable force.[65] The whole area affected by the blockade was headed operationally by a high-ranking officer called the assistant collector of Customs and Central Excise, who was headquartered at Castle Rock on the Ghats to the east of Goa's borders. According to Gomes (who himself was a high-ranking officer of customs, Government of India), the importance of the successful implementation of the blockade can be gauged from the appointment of an officer of the assistant collector status when, at that point in time, there were only three collectors of Central Excise for all of India![66]

In addition to these measures, a tall wall was built near Castle Rock railway station on the Ghats by the Customs and Central Excise Department, blocking the tunnel and the railway track linking Goa with the rest of India.[67] A portion of the said railway track, estimated at around 1 kilometer in length, had been removed along with its fish-plates, thus making the economic blockade of Goa a visually threatening reality and physically prohibitive to boot.[68] A Special Reserve Police Force (SRP) was set up as well, especially for this purpose, which backed up the customs authorities. The main task of the police was to deal with violations of passports, restrictions, and movement of persons from Goa in particular without valid documents, which in the first place were difficult to obtain. Such decisions of the Government of India were more harmful to the Goan people rather than the Portuguese government. It affected the people who worked and traveled across the border. Besides them, those doing business also often crossed the border. But the plight of the Goans came to the fore during the summer vacation, when hundreds of Goan emigrants came to Goa through the Manali check post. At the crossing, the Indian police harassed the emigrants, and the situation was so serious that the Goan press in Bombay criticized the happenings. It led Lambert Mascarenhas of the *Goan Tribune* to write a letter to Nehru, asking him to stop the ill-treatment and harassment meted out to the emigrants.[69]

A section of Goans who had invested money in India in various financial businesses like government securities, banks, and shares suffered because of the inability to get any income from the investment as the Government of India had frozen their accounts. Many of the investors depended on this income for their living. To make matters worse, the local government increased taxes, both direct and indirect. Customs duties were increased from 1 to 3 percent on ad valorem imports of goods from Portugal and other colonies, from 3 to 5, and on imports from 3 to 5 and 5 to 8 percent. This increase would affect all the consumers of foreign goods.[70]

In spite of these effective measures taken by the Indian government to implement a blockade on the Portuguese territories, it made a debatable statement that this was not an economic blockade but simply economic measures. This was revealed by the deputy minister for External Affairs, Anil K. Chanda, in the Rajya Sabha session on August 22, 1955. He added that while the government did not impose sanctions on Portugal, the Dock Workers Union of Bombay and other ports in India had passed resolutions not to handle ships that touched Goa.[71]

After another year, on December 6, 1956, J.V.K. Vallabh asked if the government planned on reviewing the economic blockade on Goa. Once again, Anil Chanda denied that it was a blockade and informed that economic measures had been taken, which could not be referred to as a "blockade." He said these were reviewed from time to time, but it would not be in the public interest to make the details of the measures known.

Measures to Overcome the Blockade

The Portuguese government had to save face and take action to get food for the people to overcome their hardship. More importantly, a politically motivated scenario had to be projected to show the Indian government that the blockade imposed by them was inconsequential—that neither the government nor the people were affected by the embargo. The two main problems that they had to tackle on priority were the availability of food and the accessibility of cash. The latter affected people who were fully dependent on remittances from their relatives working in the Union of

India and abroad since the postal services across the Indian territory had stopped. Those who were dependent on the income from the export of their products were also in misery.

Various measures were taken to overcome the scarcity of food to make it appear that everything was normal. Committees were appointed to help ease the shortages. These committees had to arrange the import and distribution of food to the people. To begin with, the Comissão Coordenadora de Importações e Exportações and the Comissão de Assuntos Económicos were assigned this task.[72] The latter issued ration cards that entitled the locals to collect a monthly quota. However, the people had to endure the hardship of queuing up to obtain a card. The authorities had to check any hoarding by unscrupulous persons who would take the opportunity to make money by creating a shortage of goods. This would allow them to sell their stock in the black market and make a higher profit. Therefore, measures were taken by the government to control hoarding and black-marketing by restricting the quantity of food to be sold to individuals or businessmen. One such notice informed that in order to avoid the hoarding of potatoes imported by a local businessman, the Committee, with the concurrence of the Governor, decided that the potatoes would be sold in retail.[73] To tighten control, the retailers were asked to report weekly to whom goods were sold, what quantities, and at what price, among other details such as the name and address of the buyer. We do not know how successful these measures were, but the truth is that they were hurting the people as the food supply was restricted. The sale of other essential commodities also followed regulations. These included sugar, wheat flour, tea, coffee, natural and alternative forms of milk (condensed, powdered, skimmed), and spices.[74]

In this, they were assisted by the Police Department, which had a section called Serviços Contra Assambarcamento e Especulação da Policía.[75] It would help identify any malpractices and check misconduct by the businessmen or cultivators, who were also responsible for keeping a check on the quality of food.

The local press carried various notices for the public, issued by the committees informing when and where goods would be sold. To control overcharging, the sale price was notified. To facilitate the public in buying food without hassles, shops were appointed as retailers in various parts of Goa. The government also opened several units from where rice, both imported and locally grown, was distributed to the people. It was keen to increase production and therefore various measures were taken to help local cultivators grow more rice and then buy their produce.

Licenses for importing food, especially rice, were issued to those who applied for them. The government also took steps to import food and have rice in stock for distribution to the people. It had opened 99 *postos* (centers) as per the notice issued by Comissão de Assuntos Económicos, dated May 30, 1955.[76] At some point in time, there was more stock than required, so the government decided to stop the import and close the distribution centers.[77] Was this the true position, or was the government trying to create an atmosphere to show that everything was normal?

It was not only rice that was sold by the Comissão Coordenadora das Importações e Exportações. It also imported other commodities like oranges and lemons all the way from Mozambique. Their availability and sale were publicized through an advertisement, a notice called "Aviso," so that a wider number of people could buy them. They were also available on the days of the local market fairs held in the various villages of Goa.[78] These notices also helped the government to show that there was no shortage, even if the reality was to the contrary.

While the Portuguese administration claimed that the distribution to the people was done effectively and there was no shortage, the people from the villages and remote areas maintained that food distributed through the centers did not reach them, as these were mostly located in the city, thereby causing a shortage of food.

The imports by the Comissão Coordenadora de Importações e Exportações included apples, apricots, pears, and vegetables like cabbage, tomatoes, carrots, and radishes, transported and made available for sale at its office situated in the building of the Custom House, Panjim. These were not fruits and vegetables for the common folk. This food was meant for the elite, the colonizers, and the financially well-off. The common folk did not have enough money to buy these items; they had other priorities. They had to first feed their family the essential food for sustenance before thinking of spending money on luxuries like fruits. However, they ate those grown in their orchards or the garden, or around the house, if there was an open space. The common fruit seen almost everywhere was the banana. Papayas, guavas, and sapota (chikoos) were also widely found in Goa, besides the seasonal mangoes, jackfruits, and those fruits that grew wild on the hillocks during the summer.[79]

The committees created by the government via a decree[80] to regulate imports, exports, and economic institutions were eventually amalgamated to create the Junta de Comércio Externo (JCE), which began operations on May 1, 1956.[81] From then on, the Junta controlled imports, exports, and distribution in Portuguese India. Meanwhile, some institutions and associations in Portugal started collecting food and other items to be sent to the soldiers who were posted in the Estado da Índia Portuguesa to help mitigate their problems. Cigarettes, tobacco, wines, chocolates, jams, medicines, books, tinned goods, flour, etc., were collected by Portuguese Caritas from donors.[82]

The Obra das Mães pela Educação Nacional also sent clothes for babies and 20 kilos of honey, which were needed in Diu. There were probably press releases and requests published in the Portuguese papers for food and other items needed by the soldiers in the Estado da India. This proved that the blockade was successful and caused scarcity and hunger. Others also suffered. Many Goan students went across to Bombay and Dharwad for studies, since there was not much scope in Goa, with professional education limited only to medical or pharmaceutical courses. These students needed to carry money with them, and because of the difficulties created due to the inaccessibility of Indian currency, the hoarders cashed in on the situation. The exchange rate varied depending on the person's need. Each ten-rupee note fetched eleven Portuguese rupees. Sometimes, it worked the other way around. This ongoing trend was commented on by the columnist, adding that although there were draconian laws forbidding this kind of trade in currency notes, the authorities paid no attention to such exploitation because they were too busy unearthing political plots. "This is what is happening in Goa. While the rich are growing richer, the poor and the middle-class people are being sucked completely dry and deprived of the little they have."[83]

The obstinacy of both the heads, the Indian to take forceful action, and the Portuguese not to hand over the territories to the first, was not accepted by the freedom fighters who were demanding action by the Indian government and to consider Goans as Indians and their problem as a prime national problem.[84]

Free Goa and *Goan Tribune*—The Press in Exile

Tristão Bragança Cunha, the founder of the Goa Congress, favored the merger of the Portuguese territories without delay. Since the Indian government was not taking measures in this direction, in 1953 he decided to start a fortnightly, *Free Goa*.[85] It aimed to carry the movement's voice and the problems faced by the inhabitants of Portuguese India to reach more people.[86] Another reason was the lethargic attitude of the Indian press, which did not give coverage and considered Goa and Goans as separate identities from India.[87] Therefore, *Free Goa* became "a fighter to align with the Goan patriotic forces in their struggle against the foreign usurpers."[88]

More than a few parties were active in the freedom movement of Goa, but these had very limited Catholic representation. Therefore, a group of Bombay Goan Catholic intelligentsia and elite came together to form an apolitical group called the Goa Liberation Council, with Aloysius Soares, an educationist, political thinker, and social worker, as the president.[89] They needed a platform from which they could disseminate their desires and in 1956 started a fortnightly, the *Goan Tribune,* with Soares as the editor and Lambert Mascarenhas as the assistant editor.[90] The need also arose because *Free Goa* was a political paper and therefore had a limited readership and reached few people.[91] *Free Goa* was the organ of the Goan People's Party, which had links to the Communist Party of India and was unpopular with the Catholics. Besides political issues and problems that Goa and the Goans faced, the fortnightly would also cover social functions, community news, weddings, and other features of Goan life: "It is one of the aims of the *Goan Tribune* to educate public opinion everywhere in the world in the realities of the Goan question, and thus to pave the way to that freedom and self-government which are at once our right and our responsibility."[92] The comment made by Sarto Esteves aptly defines the role of Aloysius Soares when he says that the movement for Goa's freedom would not have made so much headway without the *Goan Tribune*. He adds that "Aloysius Soares wielded his powerful pen with the skill of a craftsman to prepare the ground for the liberation of Goa."[93] Thus, *Free Goa* and the *Goan Tribune* took the mettle of addressing the issues related to the freedom movement and especially on the impacts of the blockade after this was imposed. The misery of the masses was felt and experienced by many, and some dared to voice it out in letters and articles. These were supported by editorials or comments which depicted the suffering of the common folk in Goa during the period, caused not only due to the scarcity of food but also due to other factors which were the direct outcome of the blockade.

According to Aloysius Soares, the blockade's economic effects were not meant to penalize or victimize the Goan community; rather, its primary aim was to make the maintenance of the Goan economy an increasing burden for the Portuguese rulers and also to show the dependence of Goa on the Union of India. He also writes that in such a situation, considerable discomfort and hardships were inevitable for those affected. Soares suggests a realistic approach to learning about the effects of the various measures, economic and otherwise, as the sanctions were meant to either control or ban the free movement of persons, goods, and money, obtained formerly from the rest of India.

However, he also criticized the Portuguese government's comments that the Government of India was starving the people. He refuted this argument, stating that Goa was not an enclave in the Indian territory and it had access, with a land wide open, to the sea and a first-class harbor that could take in large freighters.[94] Interestingly, Mohan Ranade made a similar statement to show that the blockade was not successful, as the territory had a huge coastline and several large ore mines, and therefore the Portuguese could import whatever they desired.[95]

There were others who also criticized it as an ineffective measure because those who suffered were the Goan people. Gerald Pereira, who, before it was enforced, argued for a "complete economic blockade,"[96] later, in a review of the situation, censured the Indian government for not taking action to solve the "Goa Problem."[97] Rendering his perspective, the situation had deteriorated economically for the people as there were restrictions on the remittances by the Goans from India. He added that the situation was so bad that even if goods were available, people had no money to buy them. On the other hand, the Portuguese government was not affected, and the blockade had not made any political advancement. According to him, the remittances amounted to more than two crores of rupees (2,00,00,000) per year.

It was not a secret that both foreign and Indian goods were available in the Goan market, which were brought by foreign steamers that directly came to Goa. In reality, the territory was flooded with foreign goods like watches, fountain pens, silk, and other luxury items, Pereira wrote in his article. However, he emphasized that the most important factor was the availability of Indian goods in Goa: cloth, spices, jaggery, cattle, and other goods found openly in the market. He questioned how these goods reached Goa and pointed out the authorities in Bombay who allowed these to be transported through with bribes being paid. Surprisingly, Pereira does not mention the availability of imported foodstuffs. However, one has to only look into the local papers of that time to find a variety of foods imported and advertised. He impressed upon Jawaharlal Nehru that the earlier the problem was solved, the better it would be for Goans, Indians, and the establishment of peace in the world.

Ranade reacted sharply against the blockade and criticized the Indian government, alleging that the implementation was intended to divert the people from the real struggle. According to him, the police posts on the border, which were asked to exercise the strictest vigilance, were just a farce. As an example, he cited the trouble that students from Sawantwadi studying in Ratnagiri had to undergo as they were not allowed to carry lunch across Goa.[98] For him, the stoppage of the import of Goan goods into India was a serious and unfortunate result of the blockade, which led to the suffering of those longing for Liberation. In reality, these people found themselves trapped in a sort of economic labyrinth. To prove his argument, he writes that the prices of areca nut, for example, crashed all at once because India was the sole market for this product. The outcome was "a desolation in the groves and it made the labourers uprooted wanderers."[99]

Ranade belonged to the Azad Gomantak Dal, the underground movement which, according to him, played the most effective role in the economic blockade of Goa, as it concentrated its energies on disrupting work in the mines, the nerve center of the Goan economy and export. He favored the use of force for liberating Goa from the colonial rule and was skeptical about achieving Goa's liberation through the imposition of the economic blockade. He felt that it brought more hardships to the people than otherwise. Ranade refers to a statement made by a Congress leader at a meeting in Sawantwadi when he was describing the situation in Goa: "This is exactly what we desire. When there is misery in Goa, the people will revolt against their Portuguese rulers!"[100] That one ought to cause destitution as a matter of policy in order to provoke the people to rise in revolt came as a shock to Ranade. For him, the economic blockade turned out to be a farce.

He recollects his days in prison and his conversation with Agente Monteiro, who jokingly remarked to him: "Your economic blockade has stopped the import of jaggery into Goa. But does your government seriously think that we Portuguese are fond of jaggery and need it badly? It is your Goan people who cannot do without it. We can get all the sugar we want from Europe."[101] What he said was a fact; the Portuguese did import their sugar and other requirements from Europe and elsewhere. Sugar was imported from Mozambique, whereas jaggery was not at all available in the Goan market due to the economic blockade.[102]

It was not only the scarcity of food and money that led to the suffering of the people. There were no jobs available locally, and to make matters worse, there was a serious problem of unemployment caused by the sealing of the Indo-Goa border. The Portuguese tried to solve this by opening new vistas for migration to Pakistan, Brazil, and African colonies. But with the number of migrants being extremely negligible, the economic problem remained unsolved.

Ironically, the Portuguese government, to garner sympathy from the emigrants who had been deported from India because they were considered its supporters, promised them placements in any of the overseas territories and friendly nations. Since it would take some time to get a placement, a subsidy was offered to them to tide over their financial problems until they got a job. By order, an "Emigrant's Fund," a subsidy to the emigrants who were expelled, was created.[103] Accordingly, a Committee of Inquiries for the Situation of Emigrants was formed to scrutinize and decide on the individuals' applications, to verify if the subsidy was admissible, the amount to be paid, the professional aptitude of the individual, and placement.[104] There is no information on how many people benefited under this scheme.

To solve the scarcity of food and paucity of money, people resorted to migrating to India, even by illegal means, without the required permit.[105] According to the press of the time, hundreds fled. Some were arrested, imprisoned, taken to court, and depending on the judgment, sometimes deported back, while others were allowed to stay after paying a fine. In this connection, the chairman of the Goa Action Committee, Dr. T. B. Cunha, protested against the deportation and externment of emigrants and refugees from the Portuguese territory.[106] In a particular case, it was reported that twenty-six Goans, who fled from hunger and tyranny, were arrested by the police and charged with entering illegally into the Indian territory. They were anxiously waiting for the decision of the magistrate and would not mind paying a fine or imprisonment because they did not want to go back to Goa, where they suffered. Fortunately, the magistrate asked them to pay a fine of fifteen rupees per person and allowed them to stay.[107] This sort of illegal migration was made possible by some agents who made a lucrative business with this modus operandi.[108] There was also an exodus from the other two Portuguese territories of Daman and Diu. When the question regarding illegal immigration came up in the Parliament, Nehru answered that in 1955, eighty-one fisherfolk, including women and children, entered India from Daman as a result of an acute shortage of food grains, other essential supplies, and lack of means of livelihood, and that they were granted facilities on compassionate grounds to remain in India.[109]

Remittances, a Secure Financial Base

Goa presented very limited job opportunities, with no industries that could generate jobs. The only solution left for the people was to migrate in search of employment.[110] Later, the landed gentry, who looked at the emigrants with contempt and had labeled them as "Bombaistas" or "Mumoicares," also joined the exodus since the land was not giving them enough to live a life of ease.[111] The problem of emigration was so important for the community, that during the Second Provincial Congress,[112] it was debated by various participants. Most of them concluded that the main reason for the exodus was economic, that is, hunger. Though rice is the staple food of Goans its production was sufficient to last for only about five to six months. For the remaining months, people depended on imported rice. For that, they required money, which was not available since the job opportunities were very limited and the vast majority of people were agricultural laborers, for whom there were only seasonal jobs available. For the rest of the year, they had to look for any other work that would give them some money with which they could buy food for themselves and their family. Several youngsters and second-generation emigrants joined schools and institutions of advanced education to better their social and professional status. This enabled them to draw higher salaries which would improve their financial position and permit them to send a higher amount of money for the family back home.

A large percentage of the money to purchase the commodities came through remittances from emigrants working outside Goa, as well as from those on the ships, who had signed Indian articles of agreement to be paid in Indian rupees, which were also legal tender in Goa.[113] Money remitted by these emigrants sustained the economy and enabled their relatives to purchase goods that were available in the market, mainly originating from India. Therefore, the problem of stoppage of remittances was a major dilemma for the Goan people. Some of them voiced their suffering in letters to the editors of newspapers. One such letter challenges the Portuguese statement that everything was normal in Goa.[114] According to the writer, they used the press and the radio to make such claims. But he points out the reality of the situation of those dependent on the remittances from their family to buy consumables and who were unable to do so because of the unavailability of money. To make matters worse, the Indian one hundred rupees, which was exchanged at a premium of twenty-five rupees, after the blockade got only three rupees as commission.[115] This meant a great loss to the family members.

It may be noted that the remittances had given a secure financial base for the families in Goa, which in most cases solely depended on this money to run the house and buy their basic needs. Hence, it was the common folk who suffered the most. In another letter, signed by an "Afflicted Indian-Goan" from Bombay, the writer questions why people should suffer and requests a change in the policy that attacks the innocent inhabitants of Goa and other enclaves, rather than the foreign government, by the imposition of controls, chiefly monetary and food.[116] The outburst was from a person, himself a victim, as he needed to send remittances to his mother, who was sick. As a rejoinder to this letter, the editor defends the blockade, saying that it is the only pressure the Government of India is in a position to apply.[117]

Food Shortage and Supplies

The availability, the shortage, the price, the production, or whatever was linked to rice, the Goans' staple, gained significant importance and was used to gauge the food situation, despite the introduction of various other imported foods to help ease the problem during this thorny period.

Thus, anything related to rice was discussed in the press. For instance, a news item informed that, though the cost of rice was much less than in the forties, people could not buy it because the purchasing power of Goans was lower than it had ever been during the past fifty years.[118] Those who could not afford to buy had to suffer starvation. It also reported that poor people, during the summer months, filled their hungry stomachs with mangoes and jackfruits, which were cheap because of the producers' inability to export. The reporter concludes by questioning what would be the outcome after the mango and jackfruit season was over, as "the poor people do not know how to keep their souls and bodies together."[119]

The production of rice had been poor in the previous year (1955) due to the floods, and therefore the government reintroduced rationing to satisfy the demands of the people.[120] They prayed for a good yield in the current year. However, there were apprehensions that until the new crop was harvested, there would not be enough stock, as rice from Pakistan was not imported due to a famine in East Pakistan.[121] On the other hand, the Portuguese authorities sought to demonstrate a show of apparent normality and used the press to give publicity to a government order that banned long queues in rice shops. According to the authorities, the queues had several meanings, the most important being that it implied the government stocks were not sufficient to guarantee a normal supply. The other was the psychological state of the people, which favored a certain type of deleterious propaganda that tried to spread rumors of the scarcity of rice in Goa.[122] The government, to assure people that everything was normal, clarified that it was wrong to say there was a shortage of rice, as there was enough stock until the next one arrived.

But then, in reality, the territory could not be maintained without stretching the beggar's bowl to its neighbors, and the rationing of the Goan staple was but a natural consequence of the interrupted economic relations of Portuguese India with the Indian mainland.[123]

Nevertheless, it was observed that the measures taken by the government to cover up the deficiency of rice were not always in line with people's needs and wishes; sometimes they even went against them. For example, people were shocked to learn that the Portuguese government had, in 1955, collected ten lakhs of rupees from a surtax on rice. This tax, fixed in the early 1930s, functioned as a protective measure for the local farmer when the price of locally produced rice had come down to less than eight rupees per *khandy*.[124] Fearing that rice cultivation in Goa would suffer from foreign competition, the government of the day had created a surtax on imported rice so that the locally produced rice would be sold at rupees twelve per *khandy*.[125] However, this measure was criticized by the local press as well as the Goan press in Bombay.[126] The *Goan Tribune* writes: "The protection given to the cultivators of rice still goes on, though the rice sells at 50 or more rupees per *khandy*. As the government needs money for its bacchanals, the consumers of rice are heavily taxed."[127]

It was reported that in the year 1959, heavy rainfall caused floods that wreaked tremendous damage and losses, particularly in the communal fields. The cause was linked to the breaches in the bunds, produced by the movement of the mining barges.[128] This was expected to affect very seriously the rice production for that year, even for those who generally produced at least sufficient rice for their own consumption. They would have to purchase imported rice,[129] but this would not be possible either, because there was no money or remittances.

The situation was so bad that the governor-general reacted by issuing an order to the Junta da Comércio Externo to decrease the price of imported rice. The second measure was a proposal to be placed before the Governor's Council authorizing the Comunidade and temples, which are the owners of the cultivable land, to forgo collection of land revenue from the cultivators who had suffered "total losses" of their crops due to the breaches in the dykes protecting the low-lying fields watered by the Mandovi and Zuari Rivers and the consequent floods.[130]

The embankments, designed to protect the low-lying rice fields along the river courses, gave way under the impact of the heavy barge movements. About 11,000 hectares (ha) were thus reduced to swamps. Heavy silting of *nalas* and rivulets also damaged the sown area. The silting of tanks reduced the irrigation facilities. All this resulted in a decrease in farm output. The local press highlighted this problem and offered solutions as the floods were creating a famine-like situation. At the same time, there was also criticism regarding the import and distribution of rice, as it was alleged that there was a racket "crying to the heavens." A letter published in the

Goan Tribune gives more or less insight into the situation in Goa regarding the above problem.

> The tremendous damage caused by the recent floods, very particularly in the communal fields, is bound to affect very seriously the rice production this year. People who generally produced at least sufficient rice for their own consumption shall have to purchase the imported rice. But, where is the money to come from? The money from the mines goes into the pockets of the exploiters of the mines and of labour, which to a large extent is from across the border.[131]

The status of rice in the diet of the Goans can also be evaluated from the importance it has gained in meetings and discussions held by the authorities of the Junta do Comércio Externo (JCE)[132] regarding the import of rice for public supply. The JCE authorities claimed that in most countries of the world, rice import is left to the government and not to private enterprises. They insisted that in Goa, the same system should be followed. However, some private entrepreneurs were interested in importing rice so that they could benefit financially from this business. Those opposing the government's control over the trade pointed out that in the past, when the government imported through the office of Direcção de Fazenda (Revenue Department), there were some incidents which the public resented, and the issue was even broached in the Conselho de Governo da Provincia.[133] This issue was discussed by the former director of Fazenda, Vasco Ferreira Martins, who argued that there was no legislation of any kind to execute the supply of imported food by the department. Taking note of the impossibility of fixing responsibility on it or any other public service, the central government thought of handing it over to an autonomous body or maybe to Junta das Importações e Exportações.[134]

During the discussions held, the management of the Junta emphasized the care needed in the storage and supply of rice to the public, and the need to take into consideration two factors:

1. Rice is the basic staple of the population. It is also of the people who live in this geographical region. Its importance is such in the idealization of politics of our neighbouring countries, that none of these *dares to trust to the private parties the supply of this item*. It is the Government that imports the rice, and, sometimes to entice the voters—fix the price at the cost of loss to the public treasury.
2. The rice is an item that is subject to price oscillations, which in our particular case, can result due to the following factors: behaviour of

> the prices in the world market; the local production; and how regular the transportation is.[135]

Therefore, the management stressed that any good policy of supply of rice should look into the above two factors before making any decision. Consequently, the authorities were reluctant to hand over the supply of rice to private dealers because they might not be able to do it regularly. They reiterated: "It can even be said that, in the current difficult situation of national life, a breakdown in the public supply of rice would have far more pernicious effects than any act of sabotage or terrorism that the detractors of the present situation could carry out."[136]

To defend its stand, the Junta also pointed out that in the past, when rice import was affected by merchants, the supply was irregular. This irregularity, aggravated by the political upheavals affecting the market situation of the main rice-supplying countries, led the Junta do Comércio Externo to take over the assignment of importing the commodity through reliable channels in large consignments to ensure regular supplies. Besides, the Junta was in a position to store the imports as it had spacious storage warehouses.[137] It also imported sugar and other foodstuffs for the districts of Daman and Diu, as well as frozen meats.

Only 4 businessmen out of 103 were opposed to the import of rice by government authorities. They claimed that the imported rice could be cheaper than the rate at which the government was buying. However, the authorities decided that fixing the price lower than the local product would act as a deterrent to local agriculture, which could not compete with the international market. In the past, the government had taken measures to protect local farmers by imposing a surtax on imported rice, and the consequences of the costlier imported rice were still hurting the people, as seen above.[138] In fact, the editorial of the BIJCE discusses the self-sufficiency of the territory, especially on the food front.[139] It stressed that instead of importing cheaper rice, the focus should be on encouraging rice cultivation, and the profits accrued with its distribution by the JCE ought to be used to improve agriculture and pisciculture. The emphasis had been on self-sufficiency. This can be said to be an outcome of the economic blockade.

The government also claimed that import by multiple businessmen was not feasible, as the simultaneous interest of various buyers would create amongst the sellers an illusion that there would be an increase in demand. Besides, transporting small cargoes would be difficult. Therefore, the Conselho do Governo deliberated and passed the following order: "The Government Council took the unanimous decision that the decree under review should be implemented, and the Junta do Comércio Externo of India Portuguesa also has the function of distribution of food."[140] The government felt that this was needed, keeping in mind the satyagraha movements and other political unrest of 1954 and the political outcome and atmosphere in which the Afro-Asiatic nations pretended to involve Portugal, and these are only two of the manifestations of evolution that times have suffered, unfortunately only to aggravate their conditions.[141]

Refusal to Accept the Indian Rupee as Legal Tender and Reintroduction of the *Escudo*

In retaliation to the economic blockade, the Portuguese government stopped the circulation of Indian currency, which was a legal tender in the territories. Reacting to this uneconomic move, a citizen, Quintino do Carmo Lobo, wrote an article criticizing the decision taken by the government.[142] Lobo argued that when issues regarding money were considered, it had to include all the monetary riches, whether in circulation or not, local or foreign, which the free trade had channeled into the country and included money brought in by the emigrants[143]:

> Our statistics show that in 1952, in India (Portuguese India), entered currency of Rs.173,170.33, with the following monetary circulation: Notes Rps. 86,727,57, Cedula Rps. 1,712, Metallica Rps. 9,12,5,500. These should include money from India which has been brought in by the emigrants, and which should be an integral part of monetary circulation, showing the value earned by our motherland (paiz).[144]

Lobo added that the problem of the circulation of the rupee had repercussions on the economic life of the people because internal commerce had been rejecting it for some months, especially for the poor people, who patriotically sided with the government in the struggle against the economic blockade.[145] Besides restricting the acceptance of the Indian rupee, monetary inflation was created by the Banco Nacional Ultramarino (National Overseas Bank), which was empowered to circulate currency cashable only in Portuguese India. It was done by depreciating the exchange rate of Indian currency from 8 to 10 percent. This move generated greater suffering for the emigrants' families, who solely depended on the rupee.[146] However, at the same time, the bank gave interest-free loans payable in debased Portuguese currency to some well-known Goan merchants, for a total amount of fifty-five lakhs (55,00,000) rupees.[147] This money would be used to procure much-needed goods from Singapore, Aden, and other places and reduce the effects of the controls imposed by the Government of India.[148] This step showed that the Portuguese were so desperate to obtain the goods to cover up the shortage in the territory and show the world everything was fine that they even waived the profit of interest.

The problem of currency continued and worsened when the Portuguese government decided to change from the rupee to the *escudo*. After the Anglo-Portuguese Treaty of 1878, Portuguese India used a currency similar to that of British India, except for the effigy.[149] This was done as the circulation of the money was important to continue to maintain the good neighborly relationship.[150] The Portuguese and the Indian rupee maintained the significance of the traditional common economy when both circulated in Goa, but the Indian rupee had a higher value given its backing of the metallic reserve. Interestingly, it continued to be used even after the Anglo-Portuguese Treaty was revoked after a decade, despite drawbacks and trouble in using the currency.

Decree 41.680 reissued the *escudo* as currency, which would have its own scale.[151] The issuing authority was the local branch of the bank—Banco Nacional Ultramarino—and it would be legal tender only in the territories of Goa, Daman, and Diu. The currency could not be used even in the other Portuguese overseas territories, and its export was prohibited. The change would be effective from January 1, 1959, irrespective of whether the new currency was issued or not. However, the bank was not in a position to recover the coins in circulation and thus allowed people to continue using the existing ones. The inaccessibility of the *escudo* created difficulties for the public, which strongly criticized the government and led the governor to issue orders to overcome them.[152] The governor of Goa issued an official communication, which also directed the Departments of Economia (Economics), along with that of Fazenda (Revenue Department) and Imprensa Nacional (Government Printing Press), to promote the posters, leaflets, and other material required to implement the laid-down clause.[153] It also directed them to affix necessary tables showing the equivalence of the transaction of rupees and its parts, vis-à-vis the *escudo* at treasury offices of departments as well as commercial establishments and various transport systems, to make people aware not to fall prey to any cheating.[154]

The change in the currency brought about a crisis for those who were visiting their hometown and added to the plight of the emigrants. Rumors made the rounds that the Indian rupee would not be accepted in the banks in exchange for *escudos,* and the people panicked because they would not be able to have money to spend or give to their relatives. This situation gave full advantage to those who illegally exchanged the money to fleece the emigrants to the extent of 24 percent of the value of the Indian paper money. This state of affairs was commented on with a warning by Dr. Jaime Rangel[155] in a letter in the *Heraldo* and transcribed in the *Goan Tribune.*[156] He wrote that the present imposition of the *escudo,* together with heavy industrial and land taxes, "not only consecrated the artificial devaluation of the rupee but came to complicate and deceive the economy of the Goan people."[157]

As if this change in currency was not enough to bring difficulties into the day-to-day life of the people, nature also lent a hand to create a miserable life for them. In the summer of 1959, there were unprecedented downpours of rain that spoiled the crop of chilies, which would have earned some sales that would have enabled them to buy food for the family. Another means of income was lost for them![158]

Fortunately, the value of the rupee was restored in May 1960, when the emigrants protested the devaluation of the rupee to the tune of 50 percent. The restoration also pretended to show the world that everything was well in the Portuguese Indian Overseas Territories.[159] Rangel pointed out that in Goa Indian currency circulated freely and everybody used the coins in day-to-day affairs. However, after the economic blockade, which was used as a political weapon, the Banco Nacional Ultramarino was caught up in a quagmire—for some time it accepted the deposits and paid the depositor in the same currency whenever they chose to withdraw. He also commented that the absence of coins in new denominations created difficulties in transactions and caused losses to the people. For example, petty agriculturists growing vegetables, bananas, and onions could not sell their products due to the unavailability of coins. The same happened with fish, which began to rot. Rangel concluded that the losses to the public must have amounted to thousands of rupees and it was, unfortunately, continuing and spreading.[160]

In such a situation, people with lesser means who were dependent on the sale of their homegrown products to meet their day-to-day expenses, and those who used horticulture as a means of living, suffered the most. The problem arose after the new currency was introduced because the shopkeepers did not agree to take the rupees, which hitherto had been accepted as legal tender, even though the new *escudo* coins were unavailable. Since some food items were cheaply priced, they were purchased using the old Indian currency.

Financial Sanctions

Financial sanctions restrict or suspend lending and investing activities in the target economy. Additionally, foreign assets of the target economy may be frozen. In this regard, the currency from the Union of India was used by the people of Portuguese India. Restrictions enforced on the transmission of Indian currency to Goa placed the Portuguese in an awkward position. We have seen how the Reserve Bank refused to send the money to make payments. At the beginning of January 1959, Banco Nacional Ultramarino ceased to accept Indian currency. Similarly, in January of the same year, the Direcção da Fazenda stopped accepting Indian currency. On January 12, the River Navigation Department affixed a notice at its ticket counter informing commuters that they would not accept any Indian currency henceforth.[161] Later, on February 2, the customs, the railways, and the businessmen stopped accepting it. Since the currency was not accepted by the bank, the local businessmen could not transact with the Indian currency nor make payments with it.[162] The outcome was that the businessmen had money accumulated with them that they could not use. Customs duties were levied on individuals crossing the Indian borders, and there were restrictions on goods taken from the Union of India to Portuguese enclaves.[163] As already mentioned, the investments by Goans were also frozen by the Indian government.

Smuggling: A Fallout of the Blockade

Clandestine trading from across the border on both sides was being carried out on a large scale and became a lucrative business, with many deciding it was a good opportunity to make money. Food grains, oil, onions, and kerosene were smuggled from the Indian territory.[164] But these, sold at high prices, simply went beyond the reach of even the average Goan, let alone the poor. Meanwhile, from Goa, imported luxury items like gold, watches, and cigarettes were much in demand.

Right from the beginning, *Free Goa* brought to the notice of the Indian government the existence of trafficking across the border, which benefited the Portuguese, because they were able to get the much-needed Indian currency that would be used to buy commodities and the much-wanted rice.[165] The currency gained importance because Portuguese money was not accepted by the foreign countries who sold supplies to them.[166] The Portuguese were in negotiations to get rice from Burma and Pakistan to supply to the people. In order to avoid scarcity, Goans were stocking rice smuggled from India with the help of the Goan customs staff.[167]

While measures were being taken by the Indian government to force the Portuguese to leave Indian soil, there were people with vested interests who interfered with these efforts, as they were benefiting materially from this situation. In fact, some Indian politicians in power protected their businessmen carrying out profitable speculation in Goa with the full connivance of the Portuguese officialdom.[168] There were allegations that Bombay merchants sabotaged government measures. Ajit Prasad Jain, the then food minister of India, referred particularly to "some traders of Bombay" who had purchased government rice and sent it to Goa and Pakistan, selling it at considerable profit. On this issue, a columnist commented on how continuously and repeatedly this issue of smuggling, especially the deliberate sabotage of the government's policy against those territories, had been reported but no action was taken.[169] Goa was considered a haven for smugglers.[170]

The problem was acknowledged by almost everybody, including Nehru, who commented that the "foreign pockets were centers of smuggling and intrigue and nests of trouble, danger spots even in times of peace."[171] Morarji Desai, the then chief minister of Bombay, while speaking at the open session of the All-India Congress Committee, held in Bombay in 1954, advised people to subject the persons engaged in smuggling across the Indo-Portuguese borders to social boycott.[172] Another writer of an article questioned the Indian government's apathy to take serious action against the perpetrators of crime and, referring to Desai's remarks, commented that the social boycott suggested by him was an imprecise thing. He claimed that the union and state governments possessed adequate machinery for dealing with them, which a private individual or the community did not possess and therefore did not hold the same advantage.[173]

It was not only the Indian press that carried reports about this immoral activity. A Singapore paper vehemently denounced some Indian merchants in that country who had been gaining from the economic blockade by importing and re-exporting to India goods from Goa and vice versa.[174] A member of the Indian Merchants' Chamber in Bombay revealed in a public statement that Indian businessmen in Tokyo and Singapore were also engaged in smuggling goods from Goa and re-exporting them to India at a good margin of profit. However, as mentioned earlier, the food was available only for those who could afford to pay for it.

This activity was going on both sides of the border on a large scale, and it became the main result of the blockade.[175] Those involved from the neighboring territories of India smuggled in foodstuffs, which would fetch them a good profit. The Indian authorities could not fully counter this despite the measures taken by customs by increasing control over the borders and even building a wall. This was mainly because the transportation of smuggled goods was done by boats and clandestinely over the border with the connivance of customs authorities who were unwilling to take action or overlooked what was happening. Many times, they profited or had a share in the smuggling. It was happening not only in Goa but also in Daman and Diu. It was evident that the Portuguese local authorities were not serious about law and order, and they, as well as their counterparts across the border, would break the rules very often, and their corrupt activities reduced the effective implementation of the economic blockade.

The prime minister told the Parliament that the Daman-based coastal vessels registered in Portuguese India were transgressing and entering Indian territorial waters. Replying to a question by Dr. Lanka Sundaram, Mr. Guha, the minister for Revenue and Defense Expenditure, replied that a certain amount of smuggling into Goa was being carried on by country crafts from the coastal ports. According to him, contraband goods valued at Rs. 1,65,553 had been seized between February and June 1956. The minister added that progressively intensive steps were being taken to stop this trade.[176] The government had received reports that goods were being transshipped to Portuguese boats on the high seas and the actual landing of the smuggled Indian goods on the Goa coast was taking place too. Answering a short-notice question by Mr. Kajrolkar, who stated that "there was reason to believe that some of the owners or masters of the country craft plying on the coast were engaged in smuggling," the minister informed that country crafts on the west coast were asked to execute bonds for obtaining the license.[177] This was required because, without them, it was difficult for the government to take action against smugglers, given the importance of anti-smuggling measures on the Goa border being made more effective.[178]

The Portuguese used smuggling to augment their economy. In fact, Morgado,[179] in his official report under the subheading "external commercial activity," cites smuggling as a favorable factor. He suggested "clandestine contraband of certain products that would give significant profits and, in exchange, food and other needed items to be sneaked into Goa for local consumption."[180]

Though the problem of smuggling had reached such proportions and was creating financial loss for the Government of India, Tristão Bragança Cunha complained that nothing had been done to curb it, despite contraband working to the detriment of the Indian economy, with great losses to state finances and administration. According to him, the huge trade deficit of Portuguese India, with imports several times higher than exports, was being met largely with the smuggling of gold, liquor, and other articles of contraband into India.[181] Earlier, he had suggested to the Government of India "to fight the smuggling business carried on to and from the Portuguese Territories."[182]

Companhia Nacional de Navegação (CNN)

The Portuguese government could not sit with their fingers crossed and pretend that nothing was wrong. In reality, Salazar had predicted that Nehru might use a blockade to force them to hand over the territories. "The question of Goa is the most delicate and serious … India has many possibilities, best said indefinite, to create difficulties and complicate the life in Goa: it has territorial contiguity, economic dependence, employment and economy of our immigrants are the weapons that can be used effectively against us."[183] Steps to provide food and pretend that everything was normal and that people were not affected by the economic blockade needed to be taken. Since the doors were closed to any import of food by road, the other two alternatives left for the Portuguese government were sea and air transport. The first was looked at as an immediate alternative, with the vast Indian Ocean encircling Goa's coast on the western side. However, it had a disadvantage, being a slow option. Ships used to come to Goa with passengers from Africa, and goods shipped by foreign businessmen were sent by this route. Many of these touched the Indian ports in transit before they arrived at Mormugao and did not come on a regular basis but only when the cargo justified the delivery. On the other hand, the ultimatum of the Dock Labour Associations of India was obstructing any delivery coming from overseas. Means and ways had to be found to circumvent this problem. Ships had to be asked to come directly to Goa with the cargo, and the onus of organizing this transportation was laid on the commercial association Associação Comercial da India Portuguesa, presently Goa Chamber of Commerce and Industry, which played a very important role during this crisis. The Associação stepped in and, to start with, succeeded in arranging a Portuguese steamer, *Timor*, to collect the goods from Europe. The ship belonged to the Portuguese shipping company "Companhia Nacional de Navegação" (CNN).[184] The company was requested by the Portuguese authorities to help the local government overcome the problem of the blockade and pressed their ships to collect and deliver goods to Goa. In 1956, it had only two annual sailings, which later increased to twelve.[185] To help with the supply of food, CNN started routing their ships from East Africa to Mormugao port, bringing goods from overseas for the merchants of India Portuguesa.[186]

The association coordinated with the committee and informed them about the cargo that needed to be transported to Goa from different foreign ports so that it could coordinate with the CNN to transport it. Although the latter went all out to help bring in goods, it also tried to gain mileage from this transportation by increasing the freight charges, which were more expensive than those of foreign ships, to which the association protested.[187]

Tables 5.3–5.5 show imports for consumption by the Estado da Índia. Under Foreign Trade, the statistics provide comparative figures in tons and values in *escudos* (1,000 *escudos*), which demonstrate the rise in the import of goods, with the highest being in 1961.

The numbers depict how many trips were made.

Table 5.3 Import for consumption in tons

	1955	1956	1957	1958	1959	1960	1961
Tons	1,69,914	1,27,237	1,74,698	1,46,090	1,45,411	1,92,744	1,98,330

[Source: *Statistical Yearbook, 1961*, 259]

Table 5.4 Import for consumption in value in escudos (1,000 escudos)

	1955	1956	1957	1958	1959	1960	1961
Escudos	7,29,221	6,84,311	8,49,935	8,74,319	7,50,678	10,30,636	12,43,839

[Source: *Statistical Yearbook, 1961*, 259]

Table 5.5 Number of ships that entered Goa and those with Portuguese flag

	1955	1956	1957	1958	1959	1960	1961
Ships in general	3,625	3,238	2,147	815	860	917	873
Portuguese	721	350	480	529	560	541	551

[Source: *Anuário Estatístico do Ultramar 1961*, 15]

Transportes Aereos da India Portuguesa (TAIP)

Transportation by sea was too time-consuming and not adequate. The faster alternative would be to use air travel. There was an airport in Goa at Mormugao, and the authorities decided to start, in August 1955, a regional airline named Transportes Aereos da India Portuguesa (Air Transport of Portuguese India).[188] Incidentally, Goa was the only colony to have its own airline. "This was considered as one of the biggest steps taken by the Portuguese administration in the Estado da India."[189] The genesis of the formation of this service was the need to break the undeclared economic blockade imposed by the Indian government, which had maintained that it would continue with the agreements that existed between Portugal and the government of British India.[190] To come to Goa, one had to use Bombay as a base for maritime, railway, as well as road transport. Many would come by road via Belgaum and Karwar. With the imposition of the blockade, communication was stopped, and the movement of people by sea, road, or railway line was prohibited. TAIP made it possible to bring goods by air from Karachi to the Portuguese territories.[191]

To add to the services and for better connectivity, which would facilitate the import of food and other items from other Portuguese colonies, an air link between Goa, Angola, and Mozambique was established, which improved commerce between them. Later, the need to have a direct connection with Lisbon was felt, and Transportes Aereos Portugueses (TAP) was introduced with direct flights from Lisbon to Goa and vice-versa from July 1961.[192] The Portuguese government also started importing goods by air from Pakistan, Malaysia, Singapore, and as far as Holland, Denmark, Australia, and Portuguese Africa.[193]

Table 5.6 shows the number of planes that have landed, passengers that have alighted, and goods transported by them. It shows the increase in all three sectors over the years and how important the air service was for providing access to food.

Table 5.6 Year-wise information of air transportation

	1955	1956	1957	1958
Planes that landed	186	422	200	304
Number of passengers	463	1,898	1,889	3,163
Cargo transported (kg)	529	4,478	16,056	80,839

[Source: *Anuário Estatístico do Ultramar 1961*, 15]

Portuguese Metropolitan and Other Portuguese Territories

India's blockade was beneficial to the Portuguese metropolitan territory as well as its other colonies. A perusal of the statistical table for the period 1956–61 of the *Statistical Yearbook, 1961* clearly shows that Mozambique was the highest exporter to Goa, amongst the other Portuguese Overseas Territories.[194] The annual import of rice itself was around an average of 20,000 tons. Mozambique wanted to use the blockade to its advantage by overcharging for the goods. Its offer to sell an excess production of 40,000 tons of rice was not accepted by the local authority because of the price. In a remark made in one of the journals of the JCE, this was pointed out: "The price of the rice should also be economical to Índia Portuguesa. None of the colonies should suffer any loss. The equilibrium of the Mozambican economy should not be made at the cost of the economy of Indo-Portuguese consumers, whose cost of living is determined, basically by the price of rice."[195]

Table 5.7 shows the imports from Portugal and its Overseas Territories, which clearly indicate the benefits accrued by metropolitan Portugal and Mozambique.

Table 5.7 Year-wise import of goods from Portugal and colonies

Year	Territories of origin	In kgs	%	Value in escudos	%
1959	Portugal	93,09,839	6.40	8,57,84,839	11.43
	Angola	9,075	0.01	2,03,570	0.03
	Macau	77,805	0.05	18,49,062	0.24
	Mozambique	9,75,847	6.71	3,44,27,650	4.59
	Timor	11,162	0.01	2,52,000	0.03
1960	Portugal	2,26,91,572	11.77	10,22,20,540	9.92
	Angola	6,330	0	1,25,900	0.01
	Macau	16,80,577	0.09	35,11,563	0.34
	Mozambique	1,18,42,991	6.25	4,25,10,993	4.13
	Timor	18,300	0.01	3,11,980	0.03
1961	Portugal	1,89,42,643	9.55	10,47,61,971	8.42
	Angola	11,682	0.01	1,53,950	0.01
	Macau	1,46,291	0.07	33,86,580	0.27
	Mozambique	1,05,81,225	5.33	3,82,09,791	3.07
	Timor	16,883	0.01	3,34,390	0.03

[Source: *Statistical Yearbook, 1961*, 266]

Food Import and Change in Habits

By the time the blockade progressed into the late 1950s and early 1960s, it looked like there was no shortage of food since the best was available. The local newspapers were full of advertisements that showed the availability of a wide range of products: tinned and frozen foods, alcoholic and non-alcoholic beverages, medicines, tonics, etc. Nevertheless, these were accessible only to the wealthy elite, the government employees whose salaries were doubled, and the colonizers. Those without money could not buy these products. They included the middle class, which depended on remittances to run the household. However, advertising does not directly reflect what people actually bought.[196] And it is unknown how this choice influenced actual practices of material consumption. At this stage, the question was of survival.

The advertisements publicized the importance of the products—their economics, taste, instructions, and time saved in preparation, among other qualities. In this regard, a correspondent made a very pertinent comment:

> Let us leave the mangoes and go to the other sector of agriculture. Have you observed the show-cases in our shops and the advertisements in the newspapers? Vegetables' soups of all kinds and for all the palates come to us from all places: Switzerland, Holland, Germany and Patagonia. You have only to open a packet and throw the powder in a cup of hot or cold water, place it on the fire and in five minutes have a soup for six persons. This is what the advertisement says.[197]

He was reviewing what was happening in Goa on the food front and picked up the thread from poor mango production, which was not only because of the climate but also due to the lack of care for the trees by the landlords, who did not work to get a good crop owing to the fall in export.

Goa now depended on imported goods for sustenance. During this period, the Portuguese government went all out to get food from almost all the continents.[198] Both *Free Goa* and the *Goan Tribune* acknowledged and criticized this action. However, it was the local Goan press that bore testimony to the products that were for sale, with pages filled with advertisements. This bounty led many people to change their eating habits due to the accessibility of a variety of products. Tinned goods replaced fresh products for cooking. For example, *tomatada* (tomato puree), tinned vegetables, and olive oil were added to the diet by many. Bacalhau—dry codfish—also flooded the market. Fruits, pulses, butter, cheeses, alcohol, etc., made their appearance in different brands from various countries. Frozen beef was imported and distributed by the government, and chicken too was flaunted in advertisements. Food enhancers like Maggi were introduced. In fact, in those days, Maggi ruled the kitchen, especially in the preparation of soups and *arroz refogado* (pulao). There were other brands, but this was the most sought-after. Tinned milk in condensed or powdered form substituted fresh milk for many. Nestlé advertised various products that changed the diets of children by replacing the traditional preparations.

Final Remarks

The blockade was a political attempt to generate an oppressive situation where Portugal would eventually give up its territories in India. It acted as a catalyst to speed up the Liberation of Goa, Daman, and Diu.[199] Nehru felt that the implementation of the blockade was the appropriate step to convey the key message that India would not accept a refusal from Portugal with regard to the integration of these territories into the Union of India. However, the common people had to bear the brunt of the blockade as food was used as a tool, despite the very discreet way it was done. In fact, closing the territorial communication and blocking the currency exchange were hidden measures to make the availability of food difficult.

The papers *Free Goa* and the *Goan Tribune* reflected the sufferings of the masses due to the scarcity of food and currency, and how the elites and the government employees largely benefited. As the salaries of the government officials doubled, they emerged as a privileged class living on imported goods.[200] The others who lived on the earnings of the exports suffered, as prices crashed owing to the ban on Goan goods in India. For example, before the imposition of the blockade, the price of betelnut was 18 to 29 rupees a *maund* (fifteen kilos), which came down to four or five rupees.[201] Due to scarcity, businessmen started selling the available food at a higher price. This meant life was tough for those who did not have enough resources. Ironically, even people with some money found it difficult to get food and had to wait in long lines!

Nevertheless, the local press only carried news that reflected the government's efforts to maintain normalcy. There are no editorials or news reports that speak about the miseries of the people. The Portuguese government notices, which appeared in the press, spoke for themselves, stating that food had to be imported from countries other than the Union of India due to shortages. Instead of garnering sympathy and support, many criticized the Government of India's policy in imposing the blockade, as it was only hurting the common people who were suffering due to the pangs of hunger. Mohan Ranade and Gerald Pereira are examples of those who protested the blockade and instead wanted India to take direct action and use military force against the territories.

It was not only rice, but potatoes, onions, chilies, and pulses on which the locals depended for their meals that were difficult to find or were very expensive. This meant that only those with more economic power could access the opportunities offered by the parallel market. Among them, we can especially include the Catholics living in urban spaces and with food habits closer to the Portuguese ones, because the alternative goods offered by the market were mainly imported from Europe. The masses with economic difficulties and who were not aligned with the Portuguese habits faced hardship in obtaining food. As the products traveled far to their destinations, they were not fresh. This was especially true of the vegetables and fruits. Another example was the availability of beef, which earlier came from the neighboring territories. The government now tried to fulfill the need for beef with imported frozen meat. This was done on an experimental basis. From the notices, it appears that it was sold only in the Panjim market, and if you wanted the best, then you had to go early in the morning to ensure you got it. The sale was not a regular feature. It depended on the arrival of the ship with the consignment.

Conclusion

Unfortunately, Goa is not self-sufficient, which leads us to import an amount almost equal to what we produce. In other words, our production is only enough for half of the population's consumption.

It is known that 320,000 people, more than half of the population, are currently enrolled for rice rations, who consumed it at a relatively much lower price than that on the black market, and even currently, the price here is higher than that of rice distributed by the CRA.[1]

The above passage from a local newspaper, *A Voz da India,* discusses the deficiency in food availability in Goa. The scarcity was more pronounced during the Second World War, and the government had initiated rationing of "artigos da primeira necessidade" (essential items) for the people. The food situation did not improve after the war because of the prevailing circumstances, yet the government wanted to stop rationing, and some newspapers backed this proposal. For example, a news item carried by *A Vida*, which had written that there was no need to continue rationing of rice, was criticized by *A Voz da India.*[2] The argument made was that even if rice was imported, it had to reach its destination and should be able to suffice to cover the deficit along with the rice produced locally. If not, the deficiency would lead to hoarding by the consumers and the black marketers, which would make high prices unsustainable for most people, with some of them unable to have even one proper meal.

To overcome such a situation, it was advisable for the government to continue rationing rice, which would allow the people to have at least one proper meal. If it was decontrolled, then some people would not be able to have rice even once a day. *A Voz da India* commented that when rice was available with a ration card, people could consume it even if it was in a smaller quantity.[3] It also writes that decontrol would lead to exploitation by the hoarders, who would buy rice directly from the producers, who would be interested in selling to them at a higher price to have a good profit. As an example, *A Voz da India* pointed out that the cultivators who obtained loans at the time of the cultivation of the *sorodio* crop last year had offered rice at Rs. 50/- per *candil*.[4] However, now,[5] they offered it at Rs. 80 or 90. The explanation given by the newspaper is that since the sale of rice was decontrolled during the second cultivation of *vangana*, they expected that during this year's *sorodio* harvest, the decontrol would continue and the price of rice would increase, bringing profit for them. In spite of knowing that the decontrol of rice would create misery, the government wanted to continue with it. Its aim was not the welfare of the people but of the *bhatkar* and Comunidades who owned vast cultivable land.

I have also argued that since there were many small land holdings, which were economically unviable, most cultivators lived a hand-to-mouth existence.[6] Whatever they cultivated may have been sufficient for a few months or just enough for the family. The others were tenant cultivators who were at the mercy of the owners of the cultivable land, be it the Comunidades or *bhatkar*. Both laid down rules and regulations that suited them to the disadvantage of the tenant cultivator. The book discussed the lease by auction and how it was detrimental to those who directly cultivated the fields. Comunidades were responsible for looking after the village's needs such as roads, *tollem* (water tanks), sluice gates, and other maintenance works, besides payment of *zonn* to the *gaunkars*, dividends to the shareholders, if any, and taxes to the government, which went on increasing. For all this, it needed income, and the maximum was made from the land lease to tenants. Since the Comunidades owned vast agricultural land, it needed to get the maximum from it. They had a system of leasing lands for which only the *gaunkars* could bid. Non-*gaunkars*, if they wanted to cultivate, had to get it on sublease from the *gaunkar*. Besides, the Comunidade did not want to lease the parcels of land to individuals and had a system where financially well-off *gaunkars* bid for large stretches and sublet to interested direct cultivators. In this way, the Comunidade collected in a single payment the amount from the bidder. However, these individuals who were called *alcistas*, sublet to the cultivator at exorbitant rates, making a profit of more than a 100 percent. The *alcista* here acted as an intermediary or broker between the Comunidade and the cultivator, and even if this arrangement was at a loss to the Comunidade, it was accepted since the money of the rent was paid in lump sum to them, whether the production was good or not. The *alcista* exploited the need of the cultivator and pretended that he was helping and doing a favor to him. On the contrary, he was enjoying at the cost of the cultivator the benefit of the extra lease money he made. However, the people were not happy with this arrangement, nor was the government, and the latter tried to put an end to this kind of malpractice by issuing legislation which included one where the leaseholder had to be a direct cultivator and no subletting was allowed. Therefore, the Governor-General issued Portaria no. 813[7] in 1930 in this regard.

It is also argued that the government's attempts to increase the cultivable area, and thereby the production, were not successful due to its lackadaisical attitude.[8] It appeared that the government was not keen to increase the production, and no strong measures were taken to implement the decisions, even when in Portugal they were successful, for a country that had introduced rice cultivation as late as the eighteenth century.[9] Measures taken by the government to protect the price of rice in the form of a "surcharge tax" on imports didn't favor the people; on the contrary, they had to pay higher prices, benefiting only the government and the *bhatkars*.[10]

A study of Goan folklore and other forms of literature in the chapter "Food, the Memory Connector," revealed many narratives of the flora and food of Goa. It discussed the relevance of various summer season fruits that bring back memories to people's minds, allowing them to recreate their past childhood and growing up. It also maintained that mangoes were the most important for the community and how they easily evoked memories for those who live in Goa and also the expatriates. Mangoes were discussed in all their varieties and forms—raw, ripe, fresh, or cooked—and how these are used to connect memories to the present. The chapter detailed how various stories, poems, and novels showed the importance of the mango to a Goan. Others included are wild blackberries (kandam), kokum, *jambhalam* (Syzygium cumini), *jangama, zamang* (Flacourtia cataphracta), and *churnam*, some of which allow the Goans to connect to the past.

I have argued that the curry, out of all the other dishes that make up the vast collection of Goan cuisine, is associated with the Goan identity and is the food that best embodies "Goanness." Goans love it; it is a quotidian part of the Goan trilogy of fish-curry-rice that adds the zing to the combo, and it is prepared with coconut and spices, to which fish or prawns are added to enhance the flavor of the cherished dish. Curry has traveled around the world as a favorite of the diaspora community. In Mozambique, the Portuguese African colony, where there was quite a marked presence of Goans, the dish was mimicked by the colonizers as well as the natives, and it is now the national dish of the colony.[11] Some studies on the food habits of the Goan community who lived in the colony show the importance of the curry.[12] I have also argued that curry has a class hierarchy, and it is shown in the way the coconut is used. Most people will grind it into a fine paste and then add enough water, according to the desired consistency, before taking the mixture to the fire to cook. The privileged well-off will grind and extract the milk of the coconut to prepare the curry. In the novel, *The Mango and the Tamarind Tree,* Leslie de Noronha writes about the hierarchy in preparing the curry.[13] The author examines curry within a literary framework, highlighting its complexities and significance in Goan households. He notes that the privileged tend to prepare a milder, less pungent version compared to that of the underprivileged.[14]

The study examines the enduring influence of colonizers on Goan cuisine, particularly Catholic culinary traditions, through the introduction of various Portuguese dishes such as *sarapatel, cabidela, vinha de alho* (vindalho), *feijoada*, and the epicurean sausage, the *chouriço*. These dishes evolved due to the spices native to the continent and those brought by the colonizers, adapting to the taste of the Goan community and now have a distinct identity separate from their original forms. The expatriate yearns to enjoy these treats, which also make them nostalgic. While some sang of the *sarapatel*, others wrote odes to the *chouriço*.

Another argument I made is about *sarapatel*, introduced by the Portuguese in Goa, which underwent a total change from the original one, and now it is a dish representative of the Goan community, especially the expatriates. While curry is a quotidian dish, *sarapatel* is prepared as a festal food. In the same study carried out by Rosales, the lady she was interviewing commented that they had to cook Goan food for Christmas and that *sarapatel* was a traditional Christmas dish.[15] A dissertation on the cultural activities of the Goans from Beira studies the annual reunions called *Encontros dos Goeses da Beira* (Reunions of the Goans of Beira) from 2000 onwards. In these get-togethers, Goan food was served to those attending the event, which included snacks like beef croquettes and samosas. It is interesting to note that *sarapatel* became the exemplary dish for these get-togethers. The list of menus is included as an appendix in the dissertation, and *sarapatel* appears to be present in all of them.[16] It was the *pièce de résistance* at the get-together served at dinner. It is a full-day celebration, and after an afternoon of music and dancing, post-lunch, high tea is served and, in the evening, dinner with *sarapatel* as the main dish.[17]

It is argued that not only through the sensuality of smells and tastes are powerful mnemonic signs transmitted, but other senses such as touch, sight, and hearing also play an important role in recalling memories. Some examples using Goan experiences show how effective these three are in constructing memories. Although there is no direct literature on Goan food and memory, the connection between the two has been expressed using different literary forms like novels, folklore, poetry, and even songs.

A study of people's customs in connection with religion and food, the traditions present in the celebrations, and the consequences thereof on the lives and families of those who borrow money to observe the existing traditions has been examined. Traditions were followed strictly by the *mordomo* (patron) who had to follow the norms laid down by the church authority, whether he liked it or not, or even worse, whether he was able to pay for the costs of observing them and patronizing the feast. People needed money to celebrate with family and friends, and those who did not have it borrowed to bear the expenses, thus creating a financial burden that was difficult to overcome for those with limited income. How to solve the problem? Those who borrowed for the expenses had to work doubly hard to repay the loans, living in indebtedness and anxiety, with the family in anguish until the loan was repaid, a tardy process in view of the then prevailing financial situation.

Alcoholism was a deep social problem for the Goan community at the beginning of the twentieth century. It had adverse effects on the consumers, the family members, and the community as a whole. The problem was increasing every year, and the government wasn't seen to be doing much, fearing the loss of revenue for the state exchequer. This problem is discussed in the chapter "Drink That 'Cheers' but Brings Tears."

Some short stories and poems have been analyzed to show how alcohol and addiction have created problems for the individual, family, and society. The intellectuals and elites tried to point out to the government the consequences of alcohol addiction and urged the government to take action and control the menace. The study analyzes the role of the Catholic community in spreading the vice and that of the Church in solving the addiction. However, the efforts of the Church authorities and the Goan educated elite were not able to resolve the problem. Those who discussed it at the Congresso Provincial were only able to propose and get enacted legislation, which was not implemented in totality by the government as it would have caused a loss of revenue to the state treasury. Even while periodicals in Portuguese, Marathi, and Konkani attempted to combat the issue, the government did not assist them.

Jawaharlal Nehru had to decide what action to take to get the Portuguese out of Goa. The territories of Goa, Daman, and Diu were for too long under the colonial regime. They colonized some of the areas in these territories for more than 400 years. Goa was for the longest time and largest area-wise. Diplomacy having failed and being pressurized by not only the Indian opposition parties and Goan freedom fighters but also by African colonies, he had to make a final decision. Not keen on using force, since India was a follower of the principle of nonviolence, Nehru decided on an economic blockade on the territories. The chapter analyzes the circumstances that led to the blockade, how it unfolded, and how the Portuguese reacted to overcome the same. Goan newspapers published from Bombay, *Free Goa,* and the *Goan Tribune* were referred to, besides other relevant literature, to highlight how the blockade affected the people of the territories, despite the Portuguese taking many steps to overcome it, including founding Goa's own airline, TAIP (Transportes Aereos da India Portuguesa). The only colony to operate an airline.

This chapter also discussed the unavailability of food, which used to come from the neighboring territories, and especially the importance of rice as the main food for the success of the blockade. The import of variety of food from overseas changed the food habits, especially among the city dwellers, the Catholic population, and government employees. However, those who depended on remittances from their families could not buy food even if it was available, as there was no money.[18] It was a tactful measure to stop the transfers. It is also argued that the blockade was not as successful as the Indian government envisaged because of the Indian and Goan industrialists who helped the Portuguese and also due to the contraband of goods between both territories, when imported luxury products to Goa were smuggled into the Indian territory and essential items, especially rice and other food, into the Portuguese territory.

Although the chapters are independent studies of different issues, inter-alia, they are all connected by food. In the first chapter, the insufficiency of rice is seen to have caused severe suffering to the Goan working class. In the second chapter, food evokes memories of the past through the various mechanisms of sensory experiences, mnemonics, nostalgia, rituals, etc. In the third chapter on celebrations of feasts, food is expressed as a votive offering or served to the devotees. This partying also brought misery caused by borrowing to keep up traditions and appearances. The fourth chapter shows how alcoholism in Goa wreaked havoc on the drinkers and their families. Rice would fall short, but alcohol was abundant. And the final chapter looks at the tense political scene in the last years of Portuguese rule in Goa and how the economic blockade caused a shortage of rice and other food, the choking of remittances to families, and a forced changeover to preserved goods.

The shortage of their staple food, rice, resulted in deprivation for the underprivileged. The manipulations of the government and elite classes, who wielded control through rice, caused socioeconomic distress to the masses who struggled to survive. The numerous feasts and traditional observances compelled the working class to keep up appearances, even at the cost of borrowing for the feasts and plunging their families into debt and austerity. Many turned to alcohol, which was available in plenty and filled government coffers with lucrative taxes. The economic blockade in the final years of colonial rule saw remittances to the people being cut off, causing a further inability to buy food. As a result, the book's analysis of the various aspects of food history concludes that the subalterns in Goa ultimately suffered the most during the final decades of the colonial rule.

Notes

Introduction

1 Orlando da Costa, *O Signo da Ira* (*The Sign of Wrath*) trans. D. A. Smith (Saligao: Goa 1556, 2017), 15.
2 Arjun Appadurai, "Gastro-Politics in Hindu South Asia," *American Ethnologist* 8, no. 3 (1981): 494–511.
3 Maria de Lourdes Bravo da Costa, "O Arroz como Metáfora em *O Signo da Ira* (1961), de Orlando da Costa," (Rice as Metaphor in Orlando da Costa's *The Sign of Wrath* (1961), *Via Atlântica* 20, no. 2 (Dez/2019): 81–100.
4 Appadurai, "Gastro-Politics," 495.
5 Ibid., 497.
6 Orlando da Costa, *Sign of Wrath*, 93.
7 Charlotte Boyce and Joan Fitzpatrick, *A History of Food in Literature: From the Fourteenth Century to the Present* (London: Routledge, 2017), 3.
8 Claude Lévi-Strauss, *The Origin of Table Manners* (New York: Harper Collins Publishers, 1978), 471.
9 Arjun Appadurai, "How to Make a National Cuisine: Cookbooks in Contemporary India," *Journal of the Society for the Comparative Study of Society and History* 30, no.1 (1988): 3–24.
10 Massimo Montanari, *Food Is Culture*, trans. Albert Sonnenfeld (New York: Columbia University Press, 2006), 133.
11 Montanari, *Food Is Culture*, 133.
12 Ibid.
13 Clifford Geertz, *The Interpretation of Cultures: Selected Essays* (New York: Basic Books, 1973), 24.
14 Anca-Luminita Iancu and Alexandra Mitrea, eds., *Food Cultures across Time: Flavours and Endeavour* (Newcastle: Cambridge Scholars Publishing, 2021).
15 Roland Barthes, "Toward a Psychosociology of Contemporary Food Consumption," in *Food and Culture: A Reader*, eds. Carole Counihan and Penny Van Esterik (New York and London: Routledge, 1997), 20–7. Barthes's ground-breaking essay *Toward a Psychosociology of Contemporary Food Consumption* (1961) was one of the first systematic approaches to foodways that influenced similar works, Iancu and Mitrea, eds., *Food Cultures*, 1.
16 Claude Lévi-Strauss, "Le triangle culinaire," *L'Arc*, no. 26 (1965): 19–29, cited in "Sustaining Meaning: Diet, Legend, and Interpretation" Plan for *Signata*, December 15, 2022.
17 Iancu and Mitrea, eds., *Food Cultures*, 1.

18 Ibid., 1.
19 Ibid., 4.
20 Ruxandra Vişan, "Culinary Lexis in Eighteenth-Century Dictionaries: The Case of the Mysterious Syllabub," in *Food Cultures across Time: Flavours and Endeavour*, eds. Anca-Luminita Iancu and Alexandra Mitrea (New Castle: Cambridge Scholars Publishing, 2021), 176–92 and Rissa L. Miller, "Eating Images and Making History: The Fruits of the Martorana Convent," in *Food Cultures across Time: Flavours and Endeavour* (New Castle: Cambridge Scholars Publishing, 2021), 153–75.
21 Maria Paula Meneses, "Food, Recipes and Commodities of Empires. Mozambique in the Indian Ocean Networks," *Centro de Estudos Sociais*, Coimbra, Oficina no. 335 (December 2009): 1–34.
22 Marta Vilar Rosales, "O Verdadeiro Caril Moçambicano. Transnacionalismo, quotidianos e materialidades goesas na Africa colonial…," in *Das Indias: Gentes, Movimentos e Pertenças Transnacionais* (Lisboa: Edicões Colibri, Centro de Estudos em Migrações e Minorias, Faculdade de Ciências Sociais e Humanas, Universidade Nova de Lisboa, Junho 2010), 59–80.
23 Fabio Parasecoli, "Food, Identity, and Cultural Reproduction in Immigrant Communities," *Social Research* 81, no. 2 (Summer 2014): 415–39.
24 Leonor Emilia Rodrigues was born in Beira and had to migrate to Portugal along with her husband and daughter after independence. The majority of those present at the event were second-generation Goans.
25 Maria Lucinda Fernandes Costa Fernandes, "Os «Encontros dos Goeses da Beira e seus Amigos» na Grande Lisboa. Património Identitário e sua Reconstrução Cultural Pós-Colonial," Mestrado em Património Histórico, diss., Universidade Nova de Lisboa, 2010. The appendices in the dissertation include a list of the annual reunions Os "Encontros Anuais" dos Goeses da Beira e seus Amigos em Portugal—Lisboa which also give the menus.
26 Marcel Proust, *In Search of Lost Time*. New York: Random, 1992. Kindle. Web. January 21, 2021. *À La Recherche Du Temps Perdu* (1913–27) with *In Search of Lost Time* being the English translation. However, it was first translated as Marcel Proust, *Remembrance of Things Past* (London: Allen Lane, 2000).
27 Jacques Revel, "Alimentação," in *A Nova História*, eds. Jacques Le Golf and Roger Chartier (Coimbra: Almedina, 1978), 24.
28 Jacques Revel, "Material Life and Biological Behaviours," in *A Nova História*, eds. Jacques Le Golf and Roger Chartier (Coimbra: Almedina, 1978), 25.
29 Ibid.
30 Ibid., 26.
31 Costa, "O Arroz como Metáfora," 86.
32 Ibid., 87.

33 Ibid., 85.
34 *Alcista* is a person in India, who is paid a *tença* or profit called *alça*. This is "a gift which was given to the middle man in a business transaction; as profits."
35 *Alçãs* is also defined as the profit resulting from the product of the lease of *mús* (floodgate), *palha*, (grass), etc. Also, as the profit that remains for the lessee of the field on the sublease.
36 *Diplomas Legislativo,* February 27, 1931; *Boletim Oficial,* March 24, 1931, *Legislação do Estado da India,* 1931, 97.
37 José C. Almeida, *Aspects of the Agricultural Activity in Goa, Daman and Diu* (Panaji: Government Printing Press, 1965), 11.
38 Please refer to *Segundo Congresso Provincial da Índia Portuguesa* (Nova Goa: Casa Luso Francesa, 1917) for the full text of the papers presented at the Congresso.
39 The land is reclaimed from the sea by putting bunds and sluice gates (*manos*). The bunds are mud walls raised above the high tide level by extracting the soft mud (*chikol*) from the river bed. Such reclaimed land is generally below the high tide level by the side of the bund. The sluice gates are erected with a special arrangement to open and close automatically and to regulate the flow of the water at every high and low tide and also during monsoons. For more information on the *khazans* please read "Alluvial and Coastal Plains" in *Fish Curry Rice: A Source Book on Goa, Its Ecology and Life-Style*, eds. Claude Alvares and Vidyadhar Gadgil (Mapusa: Goa Foundation, 2002).
40 Felippe Neri Xavier, *Descripção do Coqueiro, Arequeira, Arroz e Moedas de Goa* (Nova Goa: Imprensa Nacional, 1866), 43. For details of the various kinds of seeds used according to the type of terrain please refer to this book. It describes the types of terrains in Goa and how these are cultivated. Besides, it also gives the know-how of how to use the seeds for cultivation. Another book on this subject is A. de Bragança Pereira, *Etnografia da India Portuguesa*, vol. 2, (New Delhi: Asian Educational Services, 1991), 113–22.
41 Xavier, *Descripção do Coqueiro*, 44.
42 Ibid., 45.
43 Marcel Proust, *Remembrance of Things Past* (2000); David Sutton, *Remembrance of Repasts: An Anthropology of Food and Memory* (New York: Berg, 2001); Carole Counihan and Penny Van Esterik, eds., *Food and Culture. A Reader* edited by Carole Counihan and Penny Van Esterik, 3 ed. (New York: Routledge, 2013).
44 For further reading on the topic, please refer to works by John H. Mace, professor of psychology at Eastern Illinois University where he teaches Human Memory and Cognitive Psychology.
45 Johan Willander and Maria Larsson, "Smell Your Way Back to Childhood: Autobiographical Odor Memory." *Psychonomic Bulletin & Review* 13, no. 2 (2006): 240–4.

46 Lucio Rodrigues, *Abolim: The Flower Songs, Folk Tales and Legends of Goa. A Collection* (Saligao: Goa 1556, 2015).
47 Rodrigues, *Abolim*, 28; Sydney Mintz, "Book Review," *American Ethnologist* 30, no. 3 (August 2003): 473–5.
48 Mintz, "Book Review," 473–5.
49 Lucio Rodrigues was a professor of English literature at the University of Bombay. Lucio Rodrigues, *Abolim*, 140–4.
50 Sutton, *Remembrance of Repasts*, 170; Mintz, "Book Review," 475.
51 Jakob A. Klein and James L. Watson, ed., *The Handbook of Food and Anthropology* (London: Bloomsbury, 2016).
52 Jon D. Holtzman, "Food and Memory," *Annual Review of Anthropology* 35 (2006): 361–78.
53 José Pereira, Micael Martins and António da Costa, *Undra Muja Mama: Folk Songs of Goa. An Anthology of Dulpods. Sketches of Life in Goa in Times Past* (Saligao: Goa 1556 and Broadway Publishing House, 2011).
54 If not possible on this day, then it was offered on the death anniversary day.
55 Rowena Robinson, *Conversion, Continuity and Change. Lived Christianity in Southern Goa* (New Delhi: Sage, 1998), 19.
56 The *gaunkars* of the village of Santa Cruz, Tiswadi do not cook any meat on the occasion of the Harvest Feast that is celebrated every year on August 24.
57 Cyria C. Philalete Castelino, *Almanach Indo-portuguez para o Anno de 1886* (Nova Goa: Imprensa Nacional, 1885).
58 Filipe Neri Xavier, *Bosquejo Histórico das Communidades de Goa* (Merces, Goa: L & L, 2012), 229–34.
59 Sanitary Conference (1914).
60 Hipólito Policarpo Pegado "Suggestions to Combat the Alcoholic Hazard in Goa," in Serviço de Saúde da Índia Portuguesa, *I Conferência Sanitária. Em comemoração do 72° aniversário da Escola Médico-Cirúrgica de Nova Goa. (1-12-1914 a 6-12-1914)*, vol. 2 (Nova Goa: Imprensa Nacional, 1914), 151–8.
61 João Joaquim Roque Correia Afonso, "Rural Hygiene of Portuguese India and Its Relation with the Administrative Organization," ibid., 332–40.
62 Antonio Filipe Pinto Cordeiro, "The Tuberculosis," ibid., 171–8.
63 Antonio Teodoro de Miranda, "Regimen do Abcari para o Distrito de Goa," in *Segundo Congresso Provincial da Índia Portuguesa* (Nova Goa: Casa Luso Francesa, 1917), 14–19.
64 Azarias Condorcet Lobo, "Abcari em Goa: Antes do tratado Anglo-Luso na Índia," in *Segundo Congresso Provincial da Índia Portuguesa* (Nova Goa: Casa Luso Francesa, 1917), 1–13.
65 L. M. Condorcet Pereira, "Campanha anti-alcóolic," in *Segundo Congresso Provincial da Índia Portuguesa* (Nova Goa: Casa Luso Francesa, 1917), 119–23.
66 António Maria da Cunha, *Congresso Provincial da India Portuguesa: Subsídios para sua história* (Nova Goa: Casa Luso-Francesa-Editora, 1924).

67 Balcrisna Datarama Sinai Sacardandó, ed., *Sétimo Congresso Provincial da India Portuguesa* (Nova Goa: Tip.Bragança, 1927), 20.
68 Berta Meneses Bragança, *Tales from Goa* (Bastora: Tipografia Rangel, 1991).
69 Carta Pastoral' sobre o alcoolismo: D. Theotonio Manuel Ribeiro Vieira de Castro, dated June 8, 1934.
70 The First Treaty of Windsor, during the reign of D. João I, signed between England and Portugal, on May 9, 1386, is the oldest treaty between nations.
71 Dadra and Nagar Havel were liberated by the Indian freedom fighters in July–August 1954.
72 Sarto Esteves, *Goa and Its Future* (Bombay: Manaktalas, 1966), 87.
73 *A Vida*, July 26, 1955, 4; *Diário de Goa*, July 26, 1955, 4.
74 *Boletim Oficial* started publication on December 7, 1837, as an official paper by the Government of Índia Portuguesa, though in the beginning it also acted as a periodical, and news and articles are found in it.
75 *Legislação do Estado da Índia*, an annual publication started in 1900, is a compilation of all the legislation published in a particular year. Some official notices are also incorporated.
76 *Techno Economic Survey of Goa, Daman and Diu* (New Delhi: National Council of Applied Economic Research, 1964).
77 Government of Goa, Daman and Diu, *Report of the Goa Land Reforms Commission, 1964* (Panjim: Government Printing Press, 1964).
78 Other books important for the study of the agriculture system in Goa are José. C. Almeida, *Aspectos da Actividade Agrícola em Goa, Damão e Dio*, 2 vol. (Panaji: Government Printing Press, 1967); Claude Alvares and Vidyadhar Gadgil, eds., *Fish Curry and Rice: A Source Book on Goa, Its Ecology and Life-Style* (Mapusa: Goa Foundation, 2002); A. R. Padoshi, *Agricultural Development of India* (Bombay: Himalaya Publishing House, 1991).
79 Remy Dias, "The Socio-Economic History of Goa with Special Reference to the Communidade System: 1750–1910," PhD diss., University of Goa, 2004.
80 Remy Dias, "Some Aspects of the Consumption History of Estado da India: 1900–50," in *Goa in the 20th Century History and Culture*, eds. Pius Malekandathil and Remy Dias (Panaji: Institute Menezes Braganza, 2008), 72–121.
81 Remy Dias, "Consumption History of the Estado da India 1850–1950," in *Towards a History of Consumption in South Asia*, eds. Douglas E. Haynes et al. (New Delhi: Oxford University Press, 2010), 76–107.
82 Rodrigues, *Abolim*.
83 Pereira, Martins, and Costa, *Undra Muja Mama*.
84 *O Heraldo* founded by Messias Gomes began publication in January 1900 and continues to be published in the English language till date, with the same newspaper license—number one.

Heraldo started by António Maria da Cunha in 1908 and stopped in April 1962.

Diário da Noite, an evening paper of Goa, was started by Luis de Menezes in 1919. It also closed a few years after liberation in 1968.

Vida, A started publication in Margao in the year 1938 and closed after liberation in 1967.

India Portuguesa, founded by Jose Inacio de Loyola in 1923 and published till 1930.

Bharat, (Índia), a weekly with G.P. Hegdo Dessai as director 1912–49.

Jornal da Índia was founded by J. Damaso Rebelo in 1933 and ceased publication in 1945.

Portugal e Colónias, a weekly paper of Jose Inacio de Loyola which was published from Bombay from 1937 to 1938.

Amchó Gão edited by Luis de Menezes from 1929 to 1935.

Porjecho Adar (Auxilio do Povo) founded by Jose Batista Caetano Vas in 1930.

Chapter 1

1 Marta Vilar Rosales, "O Verdadeiro Caril Moçambicano. Transnacionalismo, quotidianos e materialidades goesas na Africa colonial …," in *Das Indias: Gentes, Movimentos e Pertenças Transnacionais*, organized by Susana Trovão e Marta Vilar Rosales (Lisboa: Edições Colibri, Centro de Estudos em Migrações e Minorias, Faculdade de Ciências Sociais e Humanas, Universidade Nova de Lisboa, 2010), 59–80.

2 Remy Dias, "Some Aspects of the Consumption History of Estado da India: 1900–50," in *Goa in the 20th Century. History and Culture*, eds. Pius Malekandathil and Remy Dias (Panaji: Institute Menezes Braganza, 2008), 91.

3 Dias, "Some Aspects," 87.

4 Ibid.

5 Vitalji Kamat, Keshav Parab Cawandy, Vithoji Sinai Dhempe, and the Mhamai brothers of Goa were some of the well-known merchants involved in the flourishing rice trade on the west coast of India. Celsa Pinto, *Trade and Finance in Portuguese India: A Study of the Portuguese Country Trade 1770–1840* (New Delhi: Concept Publishing Company, 1994), 217; Dias, "Some Aspects," 86.

6 According to José C. Almeida, if in each taluka "the cultivable fallow land" was available for agriculture purposes more than half would be brought under cereal bearing crops. The area of 44,699 Ha under paddy cultivation would have increased to about 92,367 Ha. José C. Almeida,

Aspects of the Agricultural Activity in Goa, Daman and Diu (Panaji: Government Printing Press, 1965), 11.

7 Arnaldo de Menezes (1863–1917) "Kurhtrech'm *Arrematasaum-om*," in *Song of Goa: Crown of Mandos*, eds. Jose Pereira, Micael Martins and António da Costa, (Panaji: Goa 1556, Brodway, 2010), 315. For details on auctions please see the section on "Alçãs, alcistas … and 'farcical' auctions" in this chapter.

8 Francisco João da Costa (GIP), "Jacob e Carapinho," in *Lengthening Shadows: An Anthology of Goan Short Stories*, trans. Paul Melo e Castro (Saligao: Goa 1556, 2016), 83–6.

9 Government of Goa, Daman and Diu, *Report of the Land Reforms Commission, 1964* (hereafter *Report of the Land Reforms*) (Panjim: Government Printing Press, 1964), 33.

10 *Portaria no. 4.279, Boletim Oficial do Governo do Estado da Índia* (hereafter B.O.), I series, no. 36, September 5, 1946; *Legislação do Estado da Índia* (hereafter *Legislação*),1946, 499.

11 Raghunath Vishnu Pandit, *Mhajem Utar Gavddeachem* (Bombay: Popular Prakashan, 1963), 28.

12 *Report of the Land Reforms*, 12, puts the figure at 13 percent for double-crop, and only 1 percent, for the second crop, while 86 percent is cultivated only once a year. There are two crops in a year; one is through the monsoons, between June to September called *sorodio* or *kharif*, and the other during the dry winter, between November and February, named *vangana* or *rabi*.

13 *Report of the Land Reforms*, 12; Almeida, *Aspects of the Agricultural*, 11.

14 Pandit, *Mhajem Utar*, 28.

15 Ibid.

16 Orlando da Costa, *O Signo da Ira* (Lisboa: Temas da Actualidade, 1996), 149.

17 For an overview of the laws please refer to *Report of the Land Reforms*, 25–34.

18 *Ave Maria*, July 24, 1938, 1.

19 Pedro da Costa, "Alvitres e Sugestões" (Proposals and Suggestions). *O Heraldo*, August 26, 1942, 2.

20 Ligôr *Bhatkar* comments: "During these last years, we have also not eaten more *pacharil* rice in my house, and instead of sugar we have used jaggery." Costa, *O Signo da Ira*, 148. *Pacharil* is fine rice and used to cook *arroz refogado* or pulau. For more details on it and other varieties of rice consumed in Goa, please refer to Rodolfo Dalgado, *Glossário Luso-Asiático*, vol. 1 (New Delhi: Asian Educational Services, 1988), 58.

21 *O Heraldo,* August 21, 1942, 1.

22 *Portaria* no. 4.279, established the new regime of rationing of rice, B.O., series I, no. 36, September 5, 1946; *Legislação*, 1946, 499.

23 *Voz da India*, August 28, 1948, 1; *Voz da India*, September 1 and 4, 1948, 1.

24 For more information on the *Khazans* please read the chapter "Alluvial and Coastal Plains," in *Fish Curry and Rice: A Source Book on Goa, Its*

Ecology and Life-Style, eds. Claude Alvares and Vidyadhar Gadgil (Mapusa: Goa Foundation, 2002), 86–127; Urban Lobo, "The Khazan Tragedy, I and II," *Gomantak Times*, October 27–28, 1992, 4 and "The Destructive Course, I and II," *Gomantak Times*, November 19 and 20, 1992, 4.

25 One *khandil* is equivalent to 20 *maunds*, or 3 *quintals* and 3 *arrobas*, or 480 lbs.

26 *Report of the Land Reforms*, 27; Almeida, *Aspects of the Agricultural*, 35.

27 *Techno-Economic Survey of Goa, Daman and Diu* (hereafter *Techno-Economic*) (New Delhi: National Council of Applied Economic Research, 1964), 28.

28 Ibid.

29 Alvares and Gadgil, *Fish Curry and Rice*, 87. The book may also be referred for modern agriculture practices.

30 Ibid.; for more on *tollem*, please refer to Maria de Lourdes Bravo da Costa Rodrigues, "The Reservoirs of Life-Saving Water," *The Navhind Times* (*Buzz*), April 19, 2016.

31 Alvares and Gadgil, *Fish Curry and Rice*, 87; In 1979, Lewis M. Cowardin devised a system to classify wetlands and to provide consistent terms and definitions and standard measurements for mapping them. He stated wetlands, as lands of transition between terrestrial and aquatic systems wherein the water table is usually at or near the surface or the land is covered by shallow water.

32 Ibid.

33 Ibid.

34 The Angoddi *tollem* is situated opposite the St. Alex Church and is the biggest of the existing seven in the village.

35 In Goa, the freshwater fish from Angoddi and Raitollem in Curtorim, Salcete, is famous for "*katla*" "*komin*," "*sangtam*" (catfish), "*Chonak*," "*Rohu*," "*Pitol*," and "*Kalu*." Freshwater fishing is organized with local fishermen, who use traditional methods. They venture into the knee-deep water for fishing, while others venture even deeper. The fish available in these areas is in high demand. An advertisement is published in the local press informing of the sale which is carried on for at least three days. *Herald*, April 18, 2016, 7.

36 Pantaleão Fernandes, *Goa Rare Portraits* (Goa: Author, 2018), 82; Rajendra P. Kerkar, "Goa's lost knowledge of water management," *Times of India*, February 19, 2019, 2; *Laat* is a lever system designed out of a trunk of an areca nut tree. At one end is tied a heavy stone and at the other a bamboo stick to which a bamboo basket is attached. When the stone weighs down, the bamboo basket rises filled with water. Later, the bamboo basket was replaced by a tin box, called *lata* in Portuguese, from whence the name "*laat*."

37 Shilpa J. Bhonsle and S. Krishnan, *Rices of Goa and Their Given Quality* (Goa: Goa University, 2012), 114–15. The book may be referred to for details on rice variety.

38 Felipe Neri Xavier, *Descripção do Coqueiro, Arequeira, Arroz e Moedas de Goa* (Nova Goa: Imprensa Nacional, 1866), 43. The monograph is very important as the description in it pertains to the second half of the nineteenth century and can be used for comparison with the later period agriculture status in Goa. Also read A. B. de Bragança Pereira, *Etnografia da India Portuguesa*, vol. 2 (New Delhi: Asian Educational Services, 1991), 113–22.

39 Almeida, *Aspects of the Agricultural*, 17.

40 Ibid. Comunidade land is composed of "paddy fields," "coconut plantations," "cashew plantations," "rivulets," etc.

41 Ibid.

42 A. R. Padoshi, *Agricultural Development of India* (Bombay: Himalaya Publishing House, 1991), 24. Padoshi was a Reader in the Department of Economics, Goa University when the book was published. Although the title says "*Agricultural Development of India*," it is a case study of the development of a region that discusses the trends in the various aspects of the agricultural economy of Goa.

43 *Techno-Economic*, 213–14.

44 Padoshi, *Agricultural Development*, 25. It was computed by adding together the figures of three talukas given in the *Techno-Economic* on 213–14. In fact, a number of later publications have relied upon and used the data published in the *Techno-Economic*.

45 Sen observes that in most Indian studies, holdings less than five acres of land regardless of quality are taken as smallholdings. And holdings larger than twenty-five acres are called large holdings. Bandhudas Sen, *The Green Revolution in India: A Perspective* (New Delhi: Wiley Eastern Private, 1974), 35–7; though the smallholdings numerically dominated the agrarian structure, in 1960, the area of land held by them was only 15 percent, which indicates a considerably inequitable distribution of land in Goa during the period of study. Though the holdings above two hectares formed only 14 percent of the total number of the holdings they held as much as 85 percent of the land. The number of holdings above two hectares (i.e., five acres) is found to be considerably small. These were, as mentioned, largely under the ownership of the Comunidade and a few landlords.

46 Gaudo (Gawda), the local tribal who was the *mundkar* of the *bhatkar* in the north of Goa.

47 The *mundkar* is apprehensive that he will not get enough rice even if the harvest was good, as he will be shown the arrears of the previous years that he could not pay and will be asked to make payments this year.

48 Lucio Rodrigues, "It Happens," in *Modern Goan Short Stories,* eds. Luís S. Rita Vas, (Bombay: Jaico Publishing House, 1971), 1–8.

49 Antonio Orlando da Costa was born in 1929, in Lourenco Marques, today's Maputo, the capital of Mozambique. His father was a Goan from Margão and his mother was French. As a child, Orlando's father brought

him to Goa where he lived till he was eighteen. In 1947 he proceeded to Lisbon to study at the University of Lisbon and in 1954 he got a degree in Ciências Histórico-Filosóficas. He had a notable political career during his students' days. Two years after having arrived in Portugal he joined the Movimento de Unidade Democrática (Movement of Democratic Unity), which a year before was declared illegal by the Portuguese Prime Minister Oliveira Salazar. He also lived in the Casa dos Estudantes do Império (CEI) (House of Students of the Empire) established in 1944 by the Salazar regime to support students. The need to have a common home where the colonial students could come together when they were in Portugal for higher studies, not available in their territory or those who needed to complement their academic studies in Portugal, was one of the reasons for establishing the CEI. It eventually fostered political action on the part of Black and mixed-race students present in the metropolis. Besides Lisbon, Coimbra and O Porto also had a house each. Orlando da Costa had as companions the future leaders of FRELIMO (Frente de Libertação de Moçambique), MPLA (Movimento Popular da Libertação de Angola), and PAIGC (Partido Africano para Independência de Guiné e Cabo Verde). A year after he obtained the degree, he joined the Communist Party and was even a member of the Comitê Central. He continued to be a member of the party till his death.

50 Pandit, *Mhajem Utar*, 28.

51 Winter vegetables and fruits included radish, turnip, amaranths, beans, and watermelons.

52 Costa, *O Signo da Ira*, 5.

53 Ibid.

54 Eufemiano Miranda, *Oriente e Ocidente na Literatura Goesa* (Saligao: Goa 1556, 2012), 141. For the full interview with the writer Orlando da Costa, please read, 138–44.

55 Miranda, *Oriente e Ocidente*, 142.

56 Ibid.

57 Costa, *O Signo da Ira*, 54.

58 Goa receives heavy rainfall from the southwest monsoon from June to September. The annual average rainfall of Goa is around 120 inches, which is approximately 3000 mm. The rainfall is especially heavy on the eastern side, which is around 5000 mm per year. Padoshi, *Agriculture Development*, 6; *Techno-economic*, 4; from the end of September to October the eastern monsoons are set on and are called *toddio paus*. Usually, a downpour starts in the evening with thunder and lightning. These showers are important as they add to the water harvested during the late monsoons. For more details on the weather, you may also read V. T. Gune, ed., *Gazetteer of the Union Territory of Goa, Daman and Diu* (Panaji: Gazetteer Department, 1979).

59 Filipe Neri Xavier, *Bosquejo Histórico das Communidades de Goa* (Merces, Goa: L & L, 2012) gives the number of existing water bodies under the respective Comunidade in each village. The majority of these water bodies were still in existence till 1961. Post this year many changes have taken place and many water bodies have been encroached upon and the authorities have not taken any action, on the contrary, have connived with the encroachers. The *Report of Land Reforms*, 14, puts the number of storage tanks at over 400. These are located mostly in Salcete and Bardez. In the interior tract especially in Ponda and Bicholim where rivers have a post-monsoon flow, small *kutcha* diversion works are constructed to irrigate rice fields and areca nuts' gardens. Well-irrigation is found mostly in Pernem and Bardez and low-lying areas.

60 Xavier, *Bosquejo Histórico das Communidades*, 187. This date was later changed to September 3.

61 Such applications for granting of time were part of the management of the Comunidades and ratified by the Administrador das Comunidades and after liberation, the responsibility is of the Mamlatdar of the Taluka.

62 Venancio João was interviewed in May 2016.

63 Each Comunidade decided when it would close its respective *tollem* or *tollim*. This decision was taken by the *gaunkars* who managed the affairs of the Comunidade and the procedure has been followed in the past. Xavier (1852) gives the dates on which day the sluice gate had to be closed as well as the cultivation and harvesting to be undertaken of both the *sorodio* and the *vangana*. The dates must have been decided based on the climatic conditions existing then because these (dates) have been changed later in many Comunidades an example is that of Morombim-o-Pequeno. Please read footnote no. 61.

64 Costa, *O Signo da Ira*, 10.

65 *Portaria Provincial no. 45, January 29, 1919; "A Crise de Subsistências e o Fomento—Projectos de Medidas"* (Santa Cruz, India Portugueza: Tip. Xri Ramanati, 1919).

66 Ibid. "Relatório." (Report presented by the Committee appointed by Portaria Provincial no. 45, January 29, 1918).

67 José de Freitas Ribeiro (1917–19) was the governor at the time.

68 Portaria Provincial no. 45, III.

69 Costa, *O Signo da Ira*, 106.

70 Ibid., 108.

71 Ibid.

72 Ibid., 11.

73 With people leaving Goa in hordes to get jobs since they were not available in the territory, emigration became a major issue, and the Second Congresso focused on it and related problems. The main reason for people to migrate was the need to feed themselves and save from hunger. Please refer to *Segundo Congresso Provincial da Índia Portuguesa*

(Nova Goa: Casa Luso Francesa, 1917) for full text of the papers presented at the Congresso.

74 The landlords who had to pay salaries would grumble when higher wages were demanded by the workers. The demand for a hike was always resented, even though the price of rice and other commodities increased. This resentment was discussed and means to put an end to or control the wages were felt. Therefore, in the Sétimo Congresso, a special session was organized on the "Problema de Mão d'Obra" (Labor Problem). Pedro Correia Afonso presented a seventy-seven-page report titled "Problema da Mão d'Obra Agrícola na Índia Portuguesa. Relatório," (The Problem of Agricultural Labor in Portuguese India. Report) in *Sétimo Congresso Provincial da Índia Portuguesa*, eds. Balcrisna Sinai Sacardandó (Nova Goa: Tip.Bragança, 1927), 1–77. There was also a paper on "Projecto do Regulamento de Mão d'Obra" (Draft Labor Regulation) by Cipriano da Cunha Gomes and others, ibid., 21–3 and "Problema da Mão d'Obra" (Labor problem) by Luis Jose de Souza, *Setimo Congresso*, 23–7.

75 Stella Mascarenhas-Keyes, *Colonialism, Migration and the International Catholic Goan Community* (Saligao: Goa 1556, 2011), 187.

76 Costa, *O Signo da Ira*, 121.

77 Ibid., 129.

78 Ibid.

79 Ibid., 202.

80 Ibid., 145.

81 Ibid., 149.

82 Ibid., 234.

83 For the genesis of the *Congresso Provincial da Índia Portuguesa*, please refer to the chapter on "Drink That 'Cheers' but Brings Tears."

84 For a complete list of papers and presenters at the first session please read Aleixo Manuel da Costa, *Dicionário de Literatura Goesa* (Macau: Instituto Cultural, 1997), 194–6.

85 Antonio Maria da Cunha, *Congresso Provincial da Índia Portuguesa (Primeiro)* (Nova Goa: Imprensa Nacional, 1916), 6. For more on discussions about dissolutions of the Comunidades, the following are recommended: Filipe Nery Xavier, *Defensa dos Direitos das Gão-carias, Gão-cares e dos seus Privilegios, Contra a Proposta de sua Dissolucão, e Divisão das suas Terras* (Nova Goa: Imprensa Nacional, 1856); Joaquim Heliodoro da Cunha Rivara, *Brados a Favor das Communidades das Aldeas do Estado da India* (Nova Goa: Imprensa Nacional, 1870). Both Xavier and Rivara favored the management of the Comunidade by the *Gaocars*. The issue of *desamortização* continued throughout the period of study, with some Comunidades having disentailed their assets. Orlim Comunidade in Salcete is an example. However, the last Code of 1961 maintained that there will be no more disentailment of the properties and suggested reestablishing the ones that had been dissolved and establishing new ones.

86 F. X.Teodoro de Miranda, "Crédito Agrícola," in Cunha, *Congresso Provincial* (*Primeiro*), 12.

87 The following were the other papers presented on Agricultural Credit by the delegates in the first session at the Primeiro Congresso Provincial: Aleixo Xavier de A. Godinho, "Crédito Agrícola," 7–10, F. X.Teodoro de Miranda,"Crédito Agrícola," 16–20, Quexova Ladoba Sivescar, "Crédito Agrícola, sua organização apropriada às condições económicas do país," 20–3, Sebastião da G. Pimenta,"Crédito Agrícola," 49–54, Lourenço Caetano Monteiro, "Bancos Agrícola," 90–3, Joaquim S. Pinto Carvalho, "Crédito Agrícola em Goa," 99–101, J. J.Roque Correia Afonso, "Crédito Agrícola," 101–3, Bernardino C. da Costa, "Crédito Agrícola," 103–12. For full text of the papers please refer to Cunha, *Congresso Provincial* (*Primeiro*), 1916.

88 Ricardo Micael Teles, "Crédito Agrícola," in *Segundo Congresso Provincial*, 59.

89 Ibid.

90 Jose Joaquim J. De Brito Ferrão, "Arrendamento nos Campos Comunais" in Cunha, *Congresso Provincial* (*Primeiro*), 23.

91 Ibid., 24. This topic of lease of Comunidade properties has been discussed in this chapter in the section "Alças, Alcistas … and 'farcical' public auctions."

92 Codigo of 1904, article 673. Translation by the author.

93 The other three papers are Nogar Prudente Lourenço, "Vantagens e Incovenientes de Arrendamento a Longo e Curto Prazo," Leandro X. Pereira, "Arrendamento a Curto e Longo Prazo," and J. J. Roque Correia Afonso, "Arrendamento" in Cunha, *Congresso Provincial* (*Primeiro*), 1916.

94 Pereira, Martins and Costa, *Song of Goa*, 311, 315.

95 Please refer to footnote no. 104 to see the lists of Codes.

96 In Portuguese India *sacador* is a collector of the Comunidade and the person responsible for its full annual revenue collection and his duties were included in the Code. It was equivalent to "Recebedor de Aldeia," collector of the village in Portugal. Originally, they were called *potecares* before they were designated as *sacadores*. The *sacador* had to make the payments within fifteen days from the date fixed for paying revenue to the Revenue Department, or else he would be removed from the position, Dalgado, *Glossário Luso-Asiático,* 268; We find that in the Code of 1961, the posts of *sacadores* and *vigias* are eliminated because of the ineffectiveness of their functions revealed by experience. A parallel can be drawn with the "*sopocar*" (rent collector) appointed by the municipalities to collect the *sopo* (rent) of those using the premises of the market and other places scattered around the city, wherefrom the person sold their goods or wares. These included the rents during the various fairs and festivals. In the same way, the position of *sopocar* was auctioned annually, however, in this case, the bidder with the highest

offer to pay the municipality got the lease and the system continues to date. It also covers the panchayat area.

97 Francisco Otolini de Sousa, "Alterações ao Codigo das Comunidade," in *Congresso Provincial da Índia Portuguesa (Primeiro)*, ed. Antonio Maria da Cunha (Nova Goa: Imprensa Nacional, 1916), 29.

98 Remy Dias, "The Socio-Economic History of Goa with Special Reference to the Communidade System: 1750–1910." PhD diss., University of Goa, 2004, 124–6.

99 *Sacadoria*, the position of *sacador* awarded by public auction to a person who proposes to perform it for a lower price. Before the conquest by the Portuguese, it was designated as *Pota* and *Potecar*, respectively. Dalgado, *Glossário Luso-Asiático*, 268.

100 João Baptista Amâncio Gracias, "Meios de Reduzir o nosso Deficit Cerealífero," J.J.Roque Correia Afonso, "O Deficit Cerealífero. Meios de o Reduzir," in Cunha, *Congresso Provincial*, 1916.

101 For titles of the papers and presenters, please refer to Costa, *Dicionário de Literatura*, 199.

102 Jose Maria da Costa Alvares, Presidential address of Second Congresso, in Antonio Maria da Cunha, *Congresso Provincial da Índia Portuguesa. Subsídios para a sua História* (Nova Goa: Tipografíada Casa Luso-Francesa, 1924), 2.

103 F. X.Teodoro de Miranda, "Crédito Agrícola," Roberto Bruto da Costa, "Crédito Agrícola," and Ricardo Micael Telles, "Crédito Agrícola,"in *Segundo Congresso*, 1917.

104 There are a number of books on the Comunidade, which should be read by those who wish to get detailed information about this age-old institution of Goa. Please refer to the introduction of Dias, "The Socio-economic History." The first Code was published in 1882, followed by another in 1904 where changes during the period between the two years were incorporated. In 1933 another Code was promulgated which included the legislation and changes effected during the period between both years. In 1961 another Code was promulgated before the Portuguese left Goa, incorporating the various Diplomas promulgated, effective from 1933.

105 Dias, "Socio-Economic History," 126–33; The word *arrematasaum* replaced the older native *launnim-paunnim* in Konkani. Pereira, Martins, and Costa, *Song of Goa*, 426; Later, in the auctions held in 1949, leases were given for a period of six years. Auctions were due in 1955 but were not held. Instead, the existing tenants were given the option to renew their leases for a further period of three years and this was done again in 1958. However, after the promulgation of the 1961 Code, auctions were reintroduced.

106 Dias, Remy, "Socio-Economic History," 130.

107 Ibid. Persons extraneous to a Comunidade could take part in the auctioning only in the absence of *gaunkars* and *interessados* or there being a practice to the contrary in any of the villages.
108 Francisco João da Costa (GIP), *Jacob e Dulce* (*Scenas da Vida Indiana*), 3 ed. (Panjim: Tipografia Sadananda, 1974). It was originally published in serial form in the weekly *O Ultramar*, between November 10, 1894 and June 1, 1895, and as a book in 1896. The first edition was published in Margao at the *O Ultramar* printing press. There was a second edition with a critical appreciation by Visconde de Tauney, a Brazilian writer, and GIP's reply to him. (Nova Goa: Casa Luso-Francesa, 1907). There are also two editions of the Konkani translation by Aleixo Caetano José Francisco: *Notas a Lápis de Jacob e Dulce*, 1895, and *Jacob e Dulce por Gyp. Romance* (Assagão: Tip. Moderna, 1912)
109 Costa (GIP), "Jacob ẹ Carapinho," 83–6.
110 Costa (GIP), *Jacob e Dulce*, 106–9.
111 Ibid., 109.
112 The *mando* was written by Arnaldo de Menezes (1863–1917), Pereira, Martins, and Costa, *Song of Goa*, 315.
113 Basket and mat weaving with bamboo strips is the Mahars' traditional occupation. They also play traditional musical instruments in religious festivals and marriage processions, the latter, especially in the villages. Some of them who migrated to British India became famous Western music exponents. Mahars are also known to be good cooks.
114 Pereira, Martins and Costa, *Song of Goa*, 426.
115 *A India Portuguesa* was founded in 1861 and published from Orlim, Salcete. This paper was of ownership of José Inacio de Loyola and was the archrival of *O Ultramar* which was started in 1859 by Bernardo Francisco da Costa. Both the owners were also political opponents; Pereira, Martins, and Costa, *Song of Goa*, 316 (3ab). For a fuller commentary on this *Mando,* see 426.
116 Boletim do Governo was the official organ of the Government which was published from December 7, 1837.
117 Pereira, Martins and Costa, *Song of Goa*, 311.
118 Manuel Ferreira Viegas, in *Boletim de Sociedade de Geografia de Lisboa*, xxxii, 1909, 427 indexed in Dalgado, *Glossário Luso-Asiático*, 22.
119 Costa, *Jacob e Dulce* (1974), comments about Sertório Dantas's character "thrives through *alça* … at the cost of Comunidade … at the cost of the widows and orphans," 59. Translation by the author.
120 *Alcista*: Aquele que na Índia recebe a tença ou renda, chamada alça, *Grande Enciclopedia Luso Brasileira*, vol. 1 (Lisboa: Editorial Enciclopedia Limitada, n. d.), 798.
121 Ibid., 758. *Alça* is defined as "a gift which was given to the middleman in a business transaction; as profits."

122 Ibid., 759. *Tença* ou renda na India.
123 Dalgado, *Glossário Luso-Asiático*, 20.
124 Ibid., 21. Marquês de Pombal in 1771 abolished these indecorous negotiations, which even now are effected, under the barbaric name of *Alças de bate*, buying under this denomination rice at a cheaper rate from the poor to later sell at a higher rate on behalf of Fazenda (Revenue Department); Filipe Neri Xavier, *Collecção de Bandos, e outras Diferentes Providências que Servem de Leis Regulamentares para o Governo Económico, e Judicial das Provincías Denominadas das Novas Conquistas, Precedida da Noção da sua Conquista, e da Divisão de cada huma dellas*, vol. 1 (Pangim: Imprensa Nacional, 1851), 11.
125 *Alças* (1850) also meant profit resulting from the auction of "orvanas" (retalhos [waste]), "mús" (comporta [doors of the sluice gate]), etc. Also, a percentage of the share entitled in the division of that profit to each field "vargeiro" (lessee cultivator). *O Gabinete Litterário das Fontainhas* (Nova Goa: Imprensa Nacional, 1848), iv, 113; The *regulamento* (rule) of October 17, 1516 gives the definition as pension with which services are paid. Uncertain contingency expenses and losses have ordinarily experimented, and it is also said to be the gratification that is given to the highest bidder who has increased the price of the contract; *Bosquejo Histórico das Communidades* (1852), iv, 1, defines as the profit resulting from the product of lease of "mús," "palha," (grass), etc. Also, as the profit that remains for the lessee of the field on the sublease.
126 Portaria no. 813, January 6, 1930, B. O. no.2, January 7, 1930.
127 The administrator would be the chairman of the committee and have the chief of the division of the police and the secretary of the revenue (Fazenda) office to undertake the rigorous inquiry.
128 Portaria no. 813, January 6, 1930, Art 1; *Porjecho Adar*, January 16, 1930.
129 Ibid., article 3.
130 Ibid., article 4.
131 Portaria no. 813, January 6, 1930 was signed by Governor João Carlos Craveiro Lopes.
132 Diploma Legislativo (hereafter D. L.) no. 651, March 30, 1933, B. O., no. 40, May 20, 1933.
133 D. L. no. 966, September 1, 1937, B. O. Supplement to no. 70, September 1, 1937.
134 *Report of the Land Reforms*, 28.
135 Portaria no. 813 dated January 6, 1930.
136 On September 15, 1938.
137 *A Vida*, October 10, 1938, 1.
138 Camilo Severino Rodrigues, "Depoimentos. "O Alcista," *A Vida* October 11, 1938, 1; Camilo Rodrigues "A Genese do Alcismo," October 12 and 13, 1938, 2.
139 The Comunidade continues paying to the government till today the compulsory contribution in the form of *derrama*, even though they have

no income from agricultural fields due to the Goa, Daman and Diu, Agricultural Tenancy Act, 1964, implemented with the promulgation of its Rules in 1965. The Comunidades have been forced to pay from the profits that they hold from the past and the sale of land.

140 A shareholder was asked how he owned shares of so many diverse Comunidades. He replied that it was an investment by his grandfather who had to raise five children and the dividend provided him with added income.

141 Camilo Severino Rodrigues, "A Genese do Alcismo," *A Vida*, October 13, 1938, 2; *Report of the Land Reforms*, 1964, 28.

142 *Porjecho Adar*, January 16, 1930, 1.

143 Camilo Rodrigues, "A Genese do Alcismo," *A Vida*, October 13, 1938, 2.

144 Sec. 3 no. 2 clearly establishes that "in no case should the total income of any village community be inferior to the total rent collected through the last auction." D. L. no. 1035, December 23, 1938, B. O. 102, December 23, 1938. This Diploma was superseded by another on July 15, 1948, B. O. Sr. I. no. 27, July 15, 1948, to rectify some of the clauses, in order to remedy the inconvenience stemming from them and had a better match to the end it was meant for.

145 Ibid.

146 Ibid.

147 Tristão Bragança Cunha, *Goa's Freedom Struggle* (*Select Writings of T. B. Cunha*) (Bombay: Dr. T. B. Cunha Memorial Committee, 1961), 122.

148 The government ordered that a copy of the revised rent roll be sent to the Revenue Department even before the amount of the rent was settled with the cultivators. Sec. 3, no. 6 "in order to serve as a basis for the revision of the corresponding land tax."

149 The Order no. 3645 dated February 26, 1942, B. O., Sr. I, no. 8, February 26, 1942, required the governing boards of the committee to revise the assessment (*calculo*) of the lands cultivated by them directly and accept the declaration of the previous lessee, for renewal of the leases. D. L. no. 1578 dated February 24, 1955, B. O. Sr. I, no. 8, February 24, 1955, superseded D. L. no. 1294 of July 30, 1949, B. O., Sr. I, no. 30, July 30, 1949, which had reintroduced the system of leasing by auctions for a period of six years. The basis for the bid shall be in kind and fixed by the amount of income contained in the calculations (*calculo*) organized in accordance with the D. L. 1.244 dated July 30, 1948. While D. L no. 1835 dated September 25, 1958, B. O., Sr. I, no. 39, September 25, 1958 made the assessment of rent/land revenue optional at the request of the tillers of the soil and of the Comunidade and their administrative boards.

150 D. L. no. 2070, April 15, 1961, B. O., Sr I. no. 15, April 15, 1961.

151 *Report of the Land Reforms*, 39.

152 Ibid., 35.

153 The Great Depression formed the largest financial crisis of the twentieth century. The economy started to shrink in August 1929 and the stock

market crashed in October of the same year. Although it began growing again in 1938, unemployment remained above 10 percent until 1941. It originated in the United States, but caused drastic declines in output, and affected almost every country of the world.

154 "Campanha de Arroz," Portaria no. 791, December 2, 1929, B. O. no. 97, December 3, 1929. Subsequently, another three Portarias were issued in this connection no. 78 dated September 30, 1930, B. O. no. 78, September 30, 1930; Portaria no. 1.015, November 5, 1930, B. O. no. 89, November 7, 1930, and Portaria no. 89 dated November 7, 1930, B. O. no. 95 of November 28, 1930.

155 They had a surface area of 8,101 ha, of which 7,966, as seen from a plan, were made available to the Inspection authorities of the Comunidade (Inspecção de Comunidade) by the Department of Land Survey.

156 Portaria no. 826, January 27, 1930, *Legislação* 1930, 17. Later it was also decided that uncultivated lands in Sanguem were to be given on lease for cultivation, with continuous areas of up to 20 hectares. Those in Sanquelim, Quepem, Ponda and Canacona were also to be considered at a later stage, D. L. 814, September 6, 1935, B. O. no. 72, September 6, 1935.

157 D. L. of February 27, 1931, B. O. no. 24, March 24, 1931.

158 The *Conferência Económica* is referred to in article 21 of the D. L. no. 84, April 28, 1924, B. O. no. 36, May 2, 1924, and was established by the Portuguese central government, because at that time there was serious economic disruption (nesta hora de grave perturbação economica), with a mission to study the base of the problems which are tied to the development of natural resources of the colonies, expansion of industrial activity and agricultural progress.

159 *Diário da Noite*, March 27, 1931, 1.

160 *Zonn* was paid annually to its *gaunkars* from the profit accrued by the Comunidade.

161 Ibid., March 6, 1931, 1.

162 This kind of protectionism was not new in Portuguese governance as it was applied inPortugal, where rice cultivation was introduced and cereal became one of the important staples. The government wanted to increase the output and imposed a tax on imported rice so that the local one would be protected and more people would cultivate. Other measures for higher production were improving mechanization, using better fertilizers, seeds with high yield, and the creation of experimental posts. The measure also had a support price attractive to the farmer. The protectionist stimulus initiatives improved and consolidated the growth and output of rice. However, in Goa, though similar measures were taken, there were no positive returns on the experiments carried out by the government. For more details on measures to improve rice production and the government's initiative in Portugal, please read Carlos Manuel Faísca, Dulce Freire, and Cláudia M. Viana, "The State

and Natural Resources: 250 Years of Rice Production in Portugal 18th–21st Centuries," *Ler História*, no. 79 (2021): 241–62.

163 *Diário da Noite*, March 9, 1931, 1.

164 Ibid., April 16, 1931, 1.

165 Ibid.

166 Ibid., September 30, 1931. Incidentally, *Anglo-Lusitano* was published from Bombay and though it was pro-government it criticized the proposal.

167 Ibid., March 18 and 21, 1931, 1.

168 Ibid.

169 "*Sobretaxa do equilibrio,*" D. L. no. 518, October 23, 1931; B. O. no. 85, October 23, 1931.

170 Ibid. Translation by the author.

171 Ibid., article 1°. "É criada uma taxa variável denominada 'Sobre-taxa de equilibrio,' sobre a importação, para consumo, do arroz sem casca e do arroz com casca." Translation by the author.

172 *Khandil* has a variable measure. In this case, it is equivalent to 160 liters.

173 D. L. no. 518, article 2°.

174 Ibid., article 8.

175 D. L. no. 615, December 30, 1932, B. O. no. 105, December 30, 1932.

176 Ibid. Fundo do Fomento como "Receita com aplicação especial e sob a epígrafe 'Fundo de protecção a agricultura da colonia,' não podendo, em caso algum, ser aplicado a fins diversos do prescrito fundo especial." Article 19 of 1932.

177 Ibid.

178 D. L. 732, May 4, 1934, B. O. no. 39, May 15, 1934, articles 5 and 6.

179 Ibid., Article 4. A certificate issued by the Directorate of Agriculture had to be produced.

180 Ibid. Meios de coibir qualquer abuso ou especulação pela limitação e fixação dos preços. Translation by the author.

181 Ibid., Article 10.

182 "*Sobretaxa do Equilibrio,*" D. L., no. 518 dated October 23, 1931, B. O. no. 85, October 23, 1931 modified by D. L. no. 615 dated December 30, 1932, B. O. no. 105, December 30, 1931; and subsequently D. L. no. 732, May 4, 1934, B. O. no. 36, May 4, 1934.

183 Article 1 of D. L. 615, December 30, 1932.

184 *Diário da Noite*, November 2, 1931, 1.

185 D. D. Kosambi, *Myth and Reality* (Bombay: Popular Prakashan, 1962), 153.

186 Cunha, *Goa's Freedom*, 107; Censorship was present throughout the five hundred years of Portugal's existence in different political forms. However, it became more rigid under the dictatorship of Antonio Oliveira Salazar, during the period of Estado Novo (1933–68), with Decree no. 22469 dated April 11, 1933, issued explicitly establishing prior censorship in periodical publications.

187 Jesus Gomes, "Problema de Arroz," *O Heraldo*, August 2, 1938. Gomes belonged to the elite class of Chandor in Salcete.

188 Cunha, *Goa's Freedom*, 112.

189 Ibid., 113. Cunha has discussed the issue regarding the rice problem in some articles, which includes: "The Basic Problem. An Appeal for a Customs' 'modus vivendi' with Neighbouring India," 111–20; "The Rice Problem in Goa (An Analysis of the Government's Extortionist Policy)," 120–7 and "Civil Liberties in Goa" (lecture delivered on April 7, 1946 at the Instituto Luso-Indiano Hall, Bombay at the request of the Goan Youth League), 99–109.

190 Ibid., 121.

191 Ibid.

192 Ibid.

193 Ibid. According to Cunha, not a paisa was utilized of these 30 lakhs of rupees.

194 Ibid., 116. Cunha is referring to the Anglo-Portuguese Treaty of 1878, an economic agreement regarding trade and a railway line between Goa and Bombay. It included abolition and uniformity of all customs duties on all goods imported and exported between both territories by the sea, special stipulations about salt, spirits, and opium. It was signed on December 26, 1878, at Lisbon and implemented on January 15, 1880, and expired on January 14, 1892.

195 *A Voz da India,* August 7, 10, and 11, 1948, 1.

Chapter 2

1 *Dulpod* according to Lucio Rodrigues "is virtually a documentary of Goa because it covers the human scene from birth to death, and is rooted to the native life, with greater affinity to the soil, drawing its sustenance from the rich traditions of the folk and has very negligible foreign influence." It is also a good source to depict the lifestyle in Goa as it gives brief glimpses of Goan life in its multiple aspects and has a wider scope as it embraces all life—human, animal, and vegetable. Lucio Rodrigues, *Abolim: The Flower Songs, Folk Tales and Legends of Goa. A Collection* (Saligao: Goa 1556, 2015), 64–94; Susana Sardo, *Guerras de Jasmim e Mogari: Música, Identidade e Emoções em Goa* (Lisboa: Texto Editores, 2010), 138–209; José Pereira, Micael Martins and António da Costa, *Folk Songs of Goa: Mando-Dulpods & Deknnis* (New Delhi: Aryan Books International, 2005).

2 Jon D. Holtzman, "Food and Memory," *Annual Review of Anthropology* 35 (2006): 361–78. Holtzman is a cultural anthropologist and professor in the Department of Anthropology at Western Michigan University.

3 *À La Recherche Du Temps Perdu* is a seven-volume novel. Marcel Proust, *In Search of Lost Time* (London: Allen Lane, 2002) is the English translation;

David E. Sutton, *Remembrance of Repasts: An Anthropology of Food and Memory* (New York: Berg, 2001); Carole Counihan and Penny Van Esterik, eds., *Food and Culture: A Reader* 3rd ed. (New York: Routledge 2013).

4 John H. Mace is a professor of psychology at Eastern Illinois University where he teaches human memory and cognitive psychology. His doctoral thesis is titled "Experimental Psychology-Cognition." He also researched involuntary memory, autobiographical memory recall, involuntary and voluntary recall, autobiographical memory organization, and autobiographical memory.

5 Those that occur in everyday life, those that occur during the processes of voluntary and involuntary recall, and those that occur as part of a psychiatric syndrome.

6 Rachel S. Herz, "A Naturalistic Analysis of Autobiographical Memories Triggered by Olfactory, Visual and Auditory Stimuli," *Chem Senses* 29, no. 3 (March 2004): 217–24.

7 Sydney Mintz, "Book Review," *American Ethnologist* 30, no. 3 (August 2003): 474.

8 Sutton, *Remembrance of Repasts*, 7.

9 Ibid., 6.

10 Ibid., 28; Mintz, "Book Review," 474.

11 Felipe Neri Xavier, *Descripção do Coqueiro, Arequeira, Arroz e Moedas de Goa* (Nova Goa: Imprensa Nacional, 1866), 26.

12 The Jesuit who wrote the *Arte Palmarica*, a monograph on coconut cultivation comments: "The coconut tree is the most useful, and of greater service than any other because from it is made the wine, oil, vinegar, jaggery, water, and wood. Its fruit has sales everywhere, and it is greatly esteemed and valued. It serves in the sacrifices, which the Gentiles offer to their idols, at the feasts, and weddings," in Xavier, *Descripção do Coqueiro,* 3. Translation by the author.

13 A. de Bragança Pereira, *Etnografia da India Portuguesa* (New Delhi: Asian Educational Services, 1991), 182.

14 Sebastião Rodolfo Dalgado, *Glossário Luso-Asiático* (New Delhi: Asian Educational Services, 1988), 475.

15 Pereira, *Etnografia da India Portuguesa*, 181. The book by Fragoso may also be read for details on the technique of extraction of toddy and its application for industrial purposes. Jose Joaquim Fragoso. *Technica de Lavra de Sura do Coqueiro e outras Industrias Dependentes* (Nova Goa: Imprensa Nacional, 1909).

16 Jesse Fernandes, *Toddy Tapper and His Goa* (Quepem: Mannik Publications, 2012).

17 Rodrigues, *Abolim*, 87; "Aga Muja Render Mama," in Jose Pereira, Micael Martins and Antonio da Costa, *Undra Muja Mama: Folk Songs of Goa. An anthology of Dulpods. Sketches of Life in Goa in Times Past* (Saligao: Goa 1556 and Broadway Publishing House, 2011), 20.

18 A specialty sweet made of coconut juice, little rice flour, palm jaggery, and boiled gram dal.
19 Symbolic meal for the poor.
20 On the sixth day of birth grams mixed with coconut are distributed.
21 Maria de Lourdes Bravo da Costa Rodrigues, *Tasty Goan Morsels. Food, Ingredients and Preparation*, 2nd ed. (Merces: L&L, 2000), 55.
22 Rodrigues, *Abolim*, 187.
23 Ibid. For more details, please refer to the Rodrigues, *Abolim*, "Writ of Destiny," 186–93; Sardo, *Guerras de Jasmim e Mogari*, 175–7; Franz Schubert Cotta, "A Ladainha em Goa: Uma Prática em Transformação," M.A. diss., Goa University, 2018; Maria de Lourdes Bravo da Costa Rodrigues, "*Ladainha*, a Prayer for All Seasons," *Gomantak Times* (*Weekender*), May 27, 2007, 4 and "Goa's *Ladainha* Tradition," *The Navhind Time* (*Panorama*), May 20, 2012, 2.
24 Soaked ground rice, coconut and jaggery on a jackfruit tree leaf shaped as a cone and steamed.
25 Rodrigues, *Abolim*, "The Goan Son-in-law: In Fact and Fiction," 267.
26 Rodrigues, *Tasty Goan*, 11.
27 Rodrigues, *Abolim*, "Pink and Green," 140–4.
28 Ibid., 140.
29 Ibid.
30 Fernando do Rego, *Mangas de Goa, Mangoes of Goa* (Panaji, Fundação Oriente, 2018) records more than 106 varieties up to 1961.
31 Rodrigues, *Abolim*, 142.
32 Ibid., "They Come and Go," 130–9.
33 Ibid., 134.
34 Ibid., 135.
35 *Goan Tribune*, August 16, 1956, 11.
36 Leslie de Noronha, *The Mango and the Tamarind Tree* (Calcutta: Writers Workshop, 1970), 32; Peter Nazareth, ed., *Goan Literature: A Modern Reader, Journal of South Asian Literature* (East Lansing, MI: Michigan State University, 1983),13.
37 Nazareth, *Goan Literature*, 11.
38 Noronha, *The Mango and the Tamarind Tree*, 32.
39 Ibid.
40 João de Melo de Sampaio, *A Mangueira* (Nova Goa: Imprensa Nacional, 1902), 5.
41 Translation of the poem from Portuguese to English by the author.
42 Ibid.
43 Nazareth, *Goan Literature*, 206. Manohar Rai Sardessai was a multilingual poet, who wrote in French, English, and Konkani. He is considered to have given a fillip, fresh content, and a new direction to Konkani poetry in Goa as reflected in the collection *Goem-a Tujea Moga Khatir* (For Thy Sake, Oh Goa).

44 Xavier, *Descripção do Coqueiro,* 47; Directorate of Agriculture, Goa, Daman and Diu, *Rice in Goa: High Yielding Way* (Panaji: Directorate of Agriculture, 1978), 6. Dry nursery: In this method, seed beds are made of about 10 m in length, 1.25 m in breadth, and 10 cm. in height separated by a water channel of 30 cm. The nursery should not be thickly populated so as to have vigorous seedlings. The seedlings are sowed in parallel lines across the bed and covered properly with soil. It is recommended for the rainy season. Wet nursery: Under this method, sowing is done with pre-germinated seed in a good puddle field.

45 Xavier, *Descripção do Coqueiro,* 46.

46 Ibid., 47. Various instruments used as well as the procedure carried out in the past in preparing and cultivating the rice fields are listed.

47 Sutton, *Remembrance of Repasts*, 170; Mintz, "Book Review," 475.

48 Maria de Lourdes Bravo da Costa Rodrigues, *Remembering Goa* (Merces: L&L, 2007), 72.

49 Pereira, Martins, and Costa, *Undra Muja Mama,* "Tirxem Bonder Lai Tanddela," 169.

50 Pereira, Martins, and Costa, *Undra Muja Mama,* "Sho, Sho, Joana," 194.

51 Pereira, Martins, and Costa, *Undra Muja Mama,* "Maim maim tandull haputta," 117.

52 A saying in Konkani which applies to opportunists is connected to this procedure "*Varea pormonnem, sup dorta.*" The winnowing basket is positioned according to the direction of the breeze.

53 In a year the coconuts were plucked every quarter, ideally in May, August, November, and February.

54 Mapusa, Sanquelim, Pernem, Margao, Banastari, Chaudi (Canacona) amongst others have weekly markets.

55 *Purumentachem fest* or *Festa de provisão.*

56 Rodrigues, *Remembering Goa*, 68.

57 Ibid.

58 Four *poddis* is equivalent to one *paili*, which is equivalent to 3.993 litres. *Anuário do Estado da Índia Portuguesa, 1929* (Nova Goa: Imprensa Nacional, 1929), 11.

59 There were a few villages that had their unique products, like the chilies from Harmal, Canacona, and Aldona. Parra was known for its watermelons, Moira for its bananas; sweet potatoes and brinjals in Taleigao and Goa Velha, lady's fingers (okra) in Santo Estevam, and salt in Curca; coconuts in Calangute and Benaulim; Malcorada mangoes from Chorão, and Hilário mangoes from Siolim.

60 The Catholics also fall back on *para*, a pickle made of dry fish, like mackerels, kingfish, etc. added to a sauce made of several spices ground with vinegar.

61 Pereira, Martins and Costa, *Undra Muja Mama*, 49.

62 The translations of all *dulpods* in this chapter from Konkani to English are by Jose Pereira, Micael Martins, and António Costa and published in the book *Undra Muja Mama*.
63 Rodrigues, *Remembering Goa*, 63.
64 Ibid., 64.
65 Ibid., 65.
66 Pereira, Martins, and Costa, *Undra Muja Mama*, 165.
67 Rodrigues, *Remembering Goa*, 65.
68 Ibid., 66.
69 Orlando da Costa, *O Signo da Ira* (Lisboa: Temas da Actualidade, 1996), 156.
70 Ibid., 118.
71 Ibid., 10.
72 Ibid.
73 It is a symbolic sweet, prepared by the Catholics on August 15, the feast of Our Lady of Assumption also celebrated as the harvest festival in some of the villages in Salcete. Likewise, the Hindu community makes the *pattoios* on the second day of Ganesh Chaturthi, their most important festival, to symbolize the harvesting of new ears of rice, which are tied to the *matolli*. This is a decorative wooden frame hung above Ganesh idol during celebrations and is decorated with various plants and fruits of the season.
74 The Catholics will use raw boiled rice variety while the Hindus the polished one. The latter precook the batter before spreading it on the leaf. So also, the jaggery will differ, palm for the Catholics and sugarcane for the Hindus.
75 Pereira, Martins and Costa, *Undra Muja Mama*, 28
76 Ibid.
77 For more details on ethnography and cooking please read David E. Sutton, "The Anthropology of Cooking" in *The Handbook of Food Anthropology*, eds. Jakob A. Klein and James L. Watson (London: Bloomsbury, 2016) 349–69; ibid., Klein and Watson, ed., "Introduction," 1–16.
78 Holtzman, "Food and Memory," 11.
79 In the case of *sarapatel*, the meat is first parboiled, then cut into small pieces and fried before it is cooked. For *cabidela* there is no boiling and frying, and the cut pieces of meat should not be very small. While the meat is cooking, blood is to be added carefully, stirring from time to time so that it does not get stuck to the bottom of the vessel. After 1961, the preparation of *cabidela* gradually lost its importance and at present, very few people cook or serve it. The reason may be its elitist background.
80 "On feast days it was unthinkable not to make exclusively Goan cuisine. (…) we made *pulau* rice, which takes lots of raisins, almonds and fried onions and chicken cut into pieces, sarapatel, which is a traditional

Christmas dish… The Goan food is indeed very good and has a very vast heritage. It was mandatory." Marta Vilar Rosales, "O Verdadeiro Caril Moçambicano. Transnacionalismo, quotidianos e materialidades goesas na Africa colonial…" in *Das Indias: Gentes, Movimentos e Pertenças Transnacionais* (Lisboa: Edicões Colibri, Centro de Estudos em Migrações e Minorias, Faculdade de Ciências Sociais e Humanas, Universidade Nova de Lisboa, Junho 2010), 59–80. This study was undertaken by Rosales in Portugal, interviewing Goans who had migrated from Mozambique after its independence and were called along with other Portuguese in similar situations, "retornados" (returnees) by the Metropolitan Portuguese. Translation by the author.

81 The *sarapatel* of Salvador de Bahia, State of Bahia, Brazil, which has a lot of influence on Portuguese cuisine, remains similar to the original of the colonizers, with only garlic, pepper, bay leaf, and blood as ingredients.

82 Garcia da Orta, *Coloquios dos Simples e Drogas da India* (Lisboa: Imprensa Nacional, 1891), 80.

83 Ibid.

84 Cecilia de Sousa, "Fish Curry and Goan Identity," in *Goa Today*, November 1983, 28. Pot-luck means whatever food happens to be available for a meal, especially when offered to a guest, *The American Heritage Dictionary of English Language*, 3rd. ed. (Boston, MA: Houghton Mifflin, 1996).

85 *Annaes Marítimos* (1842), 43, in Dalgado, *Glossário Luso-Asiático*, 219. Translation by the author.

86 Noronha, *The Mango and the Tamarind Tree*, 44.

87 Rosales, Marta, "O Verdadeiro Caril," 74.

88 Maria Paula Meneses, "Food, Recipes and Commodities of the Empire. Mozambique in the Indian Ocean Networks," *Centro de Estudos Sociais*, Oficina no. 335 (December 2009): 1–34.

89 Rosales, Marta, "O Verdadeiro Caril," 74.

90 Meneses, "Food, Recipes and Commodities of the Empire," 4.

91 Pepper was used before the arrival of chilies, which spread very fast unlike any other plant exchanged during and after the discoveries of the sea route. They were well accepted as a substitute for pepper as it was much cheaper, tastier, spicier, colorful, and easy to grow; Lizzie Collingham, *Curry—A Tale of the Cooks and Conquerors* (London: Vintage Books, 2006), 51.

92 Henry Yule and Arthur Coke Burnell, *Hobson-Jobson: A Glossary of Colloquial Anglo-Indian Words and Phrases, and of Kindred Terms, Etymological, Historical, Geographical and Discursive* (New Delhi: Munshiram Manoharlal, 1984).

93 Rodrigues, *Tasty Goan*, 10.

94 Mintz, "Book Review," 474.

95 *Tefflan, Zanthoxylum rhetsa* also known in vernacular as *teffal* or *triphal*, in Portuguese *limão-pimentoso,* available during the rainy season—small berry sized, green in color—is used fresh as well as dried.
96 Rodrigues, *Tasty Goan,* 33.
97 It was prepared by cooking kokum peels and onions in water, to which the cumin, turmeric, and pepper were added along with garlic and ginger. Once the onions had softened, milkfish was added to it.
98 Hog plum (*Spondias—anacardiaceae*). Publication and Information Directorate, CSIR, *The Wealth of India: A Dictionary of Indian Raw Materials and Industrial Products*. Vol. 10 (Raw Materials). (New Delhi: author, 1976), 19.
99 *Vatamba* fruit *artocarpus lakoocha*, known in English as Monkey Jack fruit.
100 Gauree Malkarnekar, "Forgotten Flavor of the Vatamba," *Times of India*, May 14, 2017, 2. Also known as *Ottamba/Ottachi/Otta Sola in Konkani and Wotomba* in Marathi.
101 Wealth of India (Raw material), vol. 1, 126.
102 Noronha, *The Mango and the Tamarind Tree*, 44.
103 Ibid.
104 Ibid.
105 Ibid., Author's note, viii.
106 Rodrigues, *Tasty Goan*, 31. During the monsoons, salted fish is a delightful substitute for a fish-crazy community, as it is a lean season for the availability of fresh stock. The Catholics also fall back on *para*, a pickle made of some type of dry fish, like mackerels, kingfish, or streak fish. The dry fish is washed in vinegar and then kept to marinate and mature in a sauce containing spices, which are also ground in vinegar. No water is added at all while preparing, which gives it a long shelf life if properly stored.
107 Nazareth, *Goan Literature*, 168. Ladis da Silva was born in Zanzibar of Goan descent and settled in Canada, where he migrated from Kenya in 1968. He was a prolific writer and author of *The Americanization of Goans,* 1976.
108 Nazareth, *Goan Literature*, 169.
109 Ibid.
110 Frank Simoes, "A Sausage with Soul," in *Frank Unedited: The Best of Frank Simoes* (New Delhi: Roli, 2003), 201–4.
111 Ibid.
112 Dom Moraes, "Sausages and Jackfruits," *Goa Today*, August 1990, 65.
113 Ibid.
114 Rosales, "O Caril Moçambicano," 73. Translated by the author.
115 Ibid.
116 Collingham, *Curry: A Tale*, 116.
117 Rodrigues, *Tasty Goan*, 36.
118 Sutton, *Remembrance of Repasts,* 6.

119 Rodrigues, *Remembering Goa*, 227.

120 It is a savory prepared for Christmas from pumpkin and raw rice, both ground together. A thin batter is made and poured in *piris* (small plates) and steamed and then removed and dried under the sun.

121 Venue where the reception was held.

122 The Goan *consoada* has a different perspective from the Portuguese, though both are linked to Christmas; for the latter, it is the supper they partake in with family and close friends on the night before Christmas. *Consoada* is *Kuthsvâr* in Konkani. Rodolfo Sebastião Dalgado, *Dicionário Português-Concani* (New Delhi: Asian Educational Services, 1988), 191.

123 In Bahia State of Brazil, *cocada* is a very common sweet sold almost everywhere and served in restaurants. However, it is different from the Goan *cocada*, which is prepared with coconut, sugar, and semolina. The original Brazilian recipe has only three ingredients, coconut, sugar, and water. The water and sugar are cooked to the desired thickness, and then grated coconut is added and cooked till the water evaporates, and the mixture leaves the side of the vessel, and is then transferred onto a plate greased with butter. It is cut into diagonal or square-shaped pieces. In some villages of Goa, *cocada* is gifted at the time of marriage as a sweet for the *ojem*, a food offering which is distributed to family and friends. In this case, several platefuls of *cocadas* are offered by the bride's family.

124 Arjun Appadurai, *Modernity at Large: Cultural Dimensions of Globalization* (Minneapolis, MN: University of Minnesota, 1996), 78.

125 Rosales, Marta, "O Verdadeiro Caril," 72. Translation by the author.

126 Holtzman, "Food and Memory," 6.

127 Sutton, *Remembrances of Repast*, 7.

128 Ibid.

129 Adeodato Barreto (1905–37) born in Margao, Goa is considered one of the most interesting personalities of modern Goan literature. He died at the young age of thirty-two, at Coimbra, where he had gone to study. Along with fellow Goans Telo de Mascarenhas and Jose Paulo Diniz, he founded the "Instituto Indiano" and the newspaper *India Nova* in Coimbra. The city honored him by having his poem imprinted on a pedestal at "Penedo de Saudades," a picturesque spot, atop a hill. His statue adorns, with other great Portuguese poets, the "Parque de Poetas," at the Jardim de Oeiras, Oeiras, Portugal.

130 Adeodato Barreto, "Natal Cristão," in *O Livro da Vida. Canticos Indianos* (Nova Goa: Edições "SWATVA," 1940), 48.

131 Alfred Rose, *Goddxem*. Translated by the author.

132 Raghunath Vishnu Pandit, ed., *Goan Poetry: An Anthology of Verse by Living Goan Poets* (Panjim: Bhagwati Prakashan, 1976), 6.

133 Rodrigues, *Abolim*, 77.

134 For example, the Goans in Lisbon organize a picnic in summertime. The newsletter of Goan Overseas Association, Vancouver (2017) includes in its activities a picnic.

135 There are a few springs with water containing minerals having medicinal values, besides several others with potable water. A list of springs grouped under the mineral is available in the *Anuário da India Portuguesa, 1933* (Nova Goa: Repartição da Estatística, 1934), 40.
136 Fr. Williams Robert Lyons was a British missionary who came to British India as an educationist.
137 St. Joseph's School was initially established by Fr. Lyons at Siolim in 1883, and later in 1887, the school was transferred to Arpora. It was the first English language school in Goa. Carlos Xavier, *Development of Sports and Games in Goa, Daman and Diu* (Panaji: Directorate of Sports and Cultural Affairs, 1976), 11.
138 Pereira, Martins and Costa, *Undra Muja Mama*, 73.
139 If not possible on this day, then it was offered on the death anniversary.
140 Nancy Munn, *The Fame of Gawa: A Symbolic Study of Value Transformation in a Massim (Papua New Guinea) Society* (Cambridge: Cambridge University Press, 1986); and Debbora Battaglia, *On the Bones of the Serpent: Person, Memory, and Mortality in Sabarl Island Society* (Chicago, IL: University of Chicago Press, 1990), in Sutton, *Remembrance and Repasts*, 36; Holtzman, "Food and Memory," 10.
141 Sutton, *Remembrance and Repasts*, 37.
142 Ibid., 39.
143 Cardamom powder is used for enhancing aroma and flavor.
144 Rodrigues, *Tasty Goan*, 21.
145 Ibid., 22.
146 Holtzman, "Food and Memory," 6.
147 Ibid., 11.
148 C. Nadia Seremetakis, "The Memory of the Senses: Historical Perception, Commensal Exchange and Modernity," *Visual Anthropology Review* 9, no. 2 (1993): 2.
149 *Canjee is* rice cooked till it becomes soft. It is part of the quotidian food of the Goans, who started their day with *canjee*. Good for digestion and is usually suggested as a meal for sick people.
150 Monserrate and Nicolau Afonso are varieties of mangoes. Both are widely available in the north of Goa. However, Salcete has no Monserrate and identifies Nicolau Afonso as Monserrate.
151 *Haap* is a sound that depicts the action of eating the food and closing the mouth. The song is in Jayanti Naik's *Amonechi Lok Geetam* (Panjim: Goa Konkani Akademi, 1993), 3. Translation of the song by Dr. Smitha Bhandari Kamat.

Chapter 3

1 Rowena Robinson, *Conversion, Continuity and Change: Lived Christianity in Southern Goa* (New Delhi: Sage Publications, 1998), 117.

2 Teresa Albuquerque, *Santa Cruz-Calapor: Profile of a Village in Goa* (Goa: Fernandes Publication, 1989), 17. The Holy Cross is the patron and titular feast celebrated at the church in the village of Santa Cruz, Tiswadi, Goa.

3 Robinson, *Conversion, Continuity*, 19–20.

4 Ibid.

5 The *gaunkars* of the village of Santa Cruz, Tiswadi, do not cook any meat on the occasion.

6 The earliest is the Church of Parra, which was a chapel before getting elevated to a church in 1649. Then we have the famous church of Santa Ana of Talaulim (1695) and Ponda (1700), Agonda, Canacona (1888), Bodiem (1946), and Olaulim (1985), the last two in Bardez.

7 *Enciclopedia Luso Brasileira*, vol. 2 (Lisboa: Editorial Enciclopedia Limitada, n.d.), 437. Anne (Arabic: حنة *Ḥannah*) is also revered in Islam, recognized as a highly spiritual woman and as the mother of Mary. The Qur'an describes her as the daughter of Faqud, who remained childless until her old age.

8 The persons with the following surnames Frias, Miranda, and Marchon were *gaunkars* at least till 1830 when Filippe Nery Xavier published the first edition of the *Bosquejo Histórico das Comunidades*. The other two surnames Meneses and Costa had ceased to exist by then. However, the heirs of the first three are known to live in Arpora (Frias) and the other two in Margão (Miranda and Marchon). The Mirandas still come to participate in the celebrations annually.

9 Xavier writes that "in the year 1557 some devotees bought the land that was on the borderline of both the Goalim-Moulá and Talaulim Comunidades and handed it over to the Jesuits, where they built a bungalow, which was on the top of the hill and therefore due to its position was healthy to live in … The priest who lived there looked after the conversion of natives of both villages and many were baptized. He was building a hermitage and was thinking about whom he would select as the patron, when the *gaunkar* Bartholomeu Marchioni (probably one of the new converts by the priest who would be Italian and would have that surname) found a matron with a cane in her hand and a hat on her head to descend from the hill to the new building, telling him that she wanted to live in that house, and soon after, an old Brahmin woman was seriously ill, also newly converted, similarly saw in her dreams a matron, who made her get up holding a hand and told that her name was Anna and that she wished to have a house around the place, whereby the priest understood that it was the glorious S. Anna that wanted to be venerated in that hermitage, and for that reason, he dedicated it to her." Such narratives are also known to have happened in some other parishes, for example, the parish of Cuncolim, where the church is in honor of Our Lady of Hope.

10 Founded in 1557 and was rebuilt by vicar Mons. Francisco do Rego (1681–9), and completed by his successor, Fr. Antonio Francisco da Cunha, in 1695, when it was elevated to a parish church; Francisco Xavier Gomes Catão, *Anuário da Arquidiocese de Goa e Damão para 1955* (Bastora: Tipografia Rangel, 1955), 107; Carmo de Azevedo, "Santana Church of Talaulim," *Purabhilekh-Puratatva* 4, no. 1 (1986): 61–70.

11 For more information on the feast and traditions please refer to Maria de Lourdes Bravo da Costa Rodrigues, *Feasts, Festivals and Observances of Goa* (Merces, Goa: L&L, 2010), 214–19; Rosario F. Rodrigues, *A Living Architectural Splendor: A Study on the Church of St. Ana* (Agassaim: Muringlyn & Muringrace Publications, 2009), 21–4.

12 Hindu Gawda in Kumar Suresh Singh, ed., *People of India: Goa* (Bombay: Anthropological Survey of India and Popular Prakashan, 1993), 100–6; A. de Bragança Pereira, *Etnografia da India Portuguesa*, vol. II (New Delhi: Asian Educational Services, 1991), 42.

13 Agriculture Officers' Association, *Important Crops of Goa* (Panaji: Agriculture Officers' Association, 1990), 62. Black gram originates in India and is also commonly found in countries in South Asia. It is also known as *udid/urad* dal. Scientific name: *Phaseolus mungo* is cultivated as a *kharif* crop, with a duration of 60–75 days. It is an important ingredient of the Indian culinary scene as it is used to create staple foods like *dals* and curries. In some parts of the country, it is also used to create bread. It is sold in its un-split forms in certain regions of the country, while in others, it is sold in its split form, showing the white fleshy insides of the gram. In Goa, it is mostly used to prepare *papads*, and as a fermentation agent in preparing *poie*, *sanna*, and some savory dishes.

14 Cyria C. Philalete Castelino, *Almanach Indo-portuguez para o Anno de 1886* (Nova Goa: Imprensa Nacional, 1885).

15 Rodrigues, *Feasts, Festivals*, 217.

16 Lucio Rodrigues, *Abolim. The Flower Songs, Folk Tales and Legends of Goa. A Collection* (Saligão: Goa 1556 and Golden Heart Emporium, 2015), 110.

17 Joseph Barros, "Religious Tradition at St. Anne's Church," a paper presented at the History Seminar, 1991 conducted by Goa University (photocopy).

18 Ibid.

19 Heman Yeshwant Karapurkar, "Agricultural Scenario in Goa," *Boletim do Instituto Menezes Bragança*, no. 176 (1996): 150–5. The traditional pulse varieties in Goa are *urid* and *moong* grown during the Kharif season.

20 Miguel de Almeida, *Jardim dos Pastores* (Rachol: Rachol Seminary, 1658).

21 Rodrigues, *Feasts, Festivals*, 40.

22 Thurnwald, L'Economie Primitive, 47 cited by Pereira, *Etnografia*, 125.

23 Pereira, *Etnografia*, 125.

24 An offering made to a god, consisting of food that is later shared among devotees.
25 Rui Gomes Pereira, *Hindu Temples and Deities* (Panaji: Printwell Press, 1978), 60.
26 Of late a small new temple has been built, devoted to Shantadurga.
27 Xavier, *Bosquejo Histórico*, 230.
28 Miguel Reis, *Portuguese Citizenship of Persons Born in the Erstwhile "Estado da India" and of Their Descendants. Practical Notes*, trans. Ave Cleto Afonso (Panjim: Broadway Publishing House, 2013), 128. Although June 3, 1975, is the date given in the book, in practice, the Portuguese government is accepting only those born before December 19, 1961, and their descendants. The citizens born in the territory of the former State of India, as it is identified by the laws of Portugal, are Portuguese, provided they were born before June 3, 1975, and they fit into any of the situations of acquisition of nationality stipulated under Law no. 2098, of July 29, 1959.
29 The Feast of Our Lady of Rosary is celebrated in the church dedicated to Her, on the last Sunday of October.
30 *Enciclopedia Luso Brasileira*, vol I, 901. The first mystery "The angel of the Lord declared onto Mary and she conceived by the Holy Spirit is celebrated in her."
31 The chapel was built in the year 1604 and was renovated and expanded in 1906. When the original Dominican church of Siridão collapsed, two statues from the church were transferred to this chapel.
32 Xavier, *Bosquejo Histórico,* 231.
33 Rodrigues, *Feasts, Festivals*, 181.
34 Vinayak Vishnu Khedekar, *Eco-culture Goa Paradigm* (Panjim: Broadway Publishing House, 2013), 93.
35 Banana and jackfruit leaves were mostly used to make *donnes* in Goa.
36 Religious conversions took place not only in Goa but also in the rest of India. With the emancipation and education of the higher-class Indians, reconversion started. In Goa, Shuddhi, a movement to reconvert Catholic Gawdas to Hinduism was started, with a purification ceremony performed. There were a large number of local Gawdas who had converted to Christianity. These were originally indigenous people of Goa and were at a lower social level. The higher caste in Goa, who were influenced by the movement across the border decided to reconvert them. Accordingly, a movement was started with the help of those in British India and was successful in reconverting in 1929, from February 16 to May end, around 7,815 Gawdas in different localities. For details, please refer to Archana Kakodkar, "Shuddhi: Reconversion to Hinduism Movement in Goa," in *Goa: Cultural Trends*, ed. Prakashchandra Pandurang Shirodkar (Panaji: Directorate of Archives, Archaeology and Museum, 1988), 242–63; Gawdas are classified as Hindu Gawdas, claiming to be descendants of

Parashuram, Christian Gawdas who were converted and Nav-Hindu Gawdas who are twice converted, once to Christianity and then to Hinduism during the Shuddhi movement in 1928; Parag D. Parobo, *India's First Democratic Revolution: Dayanand Bandodkar and the Rise of the Bahujan in Goa* (New Delhi: Orient BlackSwan, 2015), 66–70.

37 Kensor said earlier that women from Pale were also engaged in this work along with those from Siridão.

38 Khedekar, *Eco-culture Goa*, 93.

39 A local volumetric measure, each *cuddoe* is equivalent to 2 *paili* and each *paili* to 4 *podd*.

40 Rodrigues, *Feasts, Festivals*, 181.

41 The house was built on the present Mahatma Gandhi Road when they moved from Panvel near Old Goa. For details about the Dempos, please refer to Dom Moraes, *A Family in Goa* (Panjim: Vasantrao Dempo 60th Birthday Commemorative Volume, 1976). This work was commissioned by the Birthday Commemorative Committee.

42 Moraes, *A Family in Goa*, 37. How far this tradition was rooted would have to be based on Moraes, who wrote the biography based on the information he collected from the family.

43 This tradition of serving a meal was also followed by another two financially well-off families in the vicinity of one another. On the present 18 June Road was the house of the Kenis and perpendicular to this road, on Dr. Purxottam Shirgaonkar Road that of the Raos. All these three served a meal. The Raos, originally Deshpandes, were businessmen and owners of the first formal movie house in Goa, "Cine Nacional," in the capital city of Panaji. They served *canjee* to the poor. The Kenis were also businessmen and owned the first, luxury hotel in Goa, the "Hotel Mandovi" in Panaji. Some years after Liberation the Kenis and the Raos stopped serving the meal. However, the Dempos continued but from January 2016 they too stopped. When inquired as to why this tradition was discontinued, they informed me that some of those who came to eat were inebriated and misbehaved.

44 Amongst the cultured and civilized societies persist the stone cults, on interesting different aspects: in India, a stone called *shaligram*, a type of fossil from the river Gandak is consecrated to Vishnu, in the *avtar* of Krishna. The household with a *shaligram* has to compulsorily perform a *puja* every day, with or without the presence of a *bhat*. A *nivedya* needs to be presented to the deity and normally it is rice.

45 A *podd* is a volumetric measure, equivalent to 1 kg of rice. While the rice was purchased, the coconuts were from their own property. Besides rice and *ros*, there was *solkoddi,* a kokum curry with coconut milk. The dish was prepared without onion and garlic.

46 Adv. Hema S. Mhamai Kamat Priolkar, whose family also performs a daily puja of the *shaligram* in their possession, informed that they

had to cook the stipulated quantity of one *podd* rice and the *nivedya* was distributed amongst the family members, living in the house. The Mhamai Kamats were one of the most important families and significant traders of Goa, with an international reach, having the largest and one of the oldest houses in Panaji, where various families had a joint household in the past.

47 *The Laws of Manu*, trans. Wendy Doniger with Brian K. Smith (New Delhi: Penguin, 1992), 95.

48 Xavier in *Bosquejo Histórico* writes that Nerul had two parishes, the Reis Magos Church and the Our Lady of Remedios Church. Franciscans built both, the first in 1550 and the second in 1569, 452; Catão in *Anuário de Arquidiocese* writes that there are eight chapels affiliated to the church of Our Lady of Remedios, 184.

49 For details on *ladainha* please refer to Chapters 2 and 4.

50 Clams, nutritious and delicious, are collected in considerable quantities in some coastal places where they are consumed mostly by the poor. The commonest commercial species are the bay clam Meretrix, meretrix (Linn), black clam (*villorita cyprinoides*). Clams and other bivalves of their kind are usually handpicked in shallow waters at low tides. Very rarely are any mechanical devices employed, except for small bag nets or dredges operated from canoes. *The Wealth of India. A Dictionary of Indian Raw Materials and Industrial Products. Fish and Fisheries*, Raw Materials vol. iv, supplement (New Delhi: Council for Scientific and Industrial Research, 1962), 124; Maria de Lourdes Bravo da Costa Rodrigues, "'Tisreanche Fest' at St. Anthony's Chapel," *The Navhind Times (Buzz)*, May 19, 2013, 1.

51 The clams from Nerul are reddish and the inside orange or red in color and thick in consistency, besides being very tasty. Sadly, the production has dwindled a lot, because of the pollution of the river by the many boats that ply through the river. The diesel used by the boats has killed many of the ecologically viable seafood in the area. It was observed that after the lockdown (2020) by the authorities to prevent the spread of Covid-19 pandemic, and without any boat traffic in the river, there was a revival of the clams that gave a bounty to the people.

52 Preparation of the *sambarem* may vary from one *ranpin* to another. One may fry the coconut separately in oil along with some onions which are then ground together and added to the fried onions. The other may grind the coconut without frying.

53 Rodrigues, "Tisreanche Fest," 1.

54 The *dai* is used to stir up the mixtures while cooking Goan sweets, which needs continuous stirring so that the food doesn't get stuck and burnt to the bottom of the vessel. It needs to have a long handle because most of the sweets being cooked tend to splatter and can scald the skin. This long ladle is made of a single piece of wood.

55 The *vann* is also used to husk paddy and powder cereals or spices. More on the *vann* in the chapter "Food: The Memory Connector."
56 It was originally a small construction that was expanded over time through the support of devotees. The last renovation was done in 1992 by a couple on the occasion of the silver jubilee of their wedding.
57 Please refer to Catão, *Anuário de Arquidiocese* for a list of approved chapels in the village.
58 After the liberal revolution D. Maria II, Queen of Portugal, abolished the male religious orders in 1834.
59 Ricardo Micael Telles, *Freguesia de Nerul: Estudo histórico-arqueológico* (Nova Goa: Imprensa Oriental, 1925), 18.
60 Rodrigues, "Tisreanche Fest," 1.
61 Ibid.
62 Ibid.
63 Ibid.
64 Newton Sequeira, "Selflessly Sharing Shellfish by the Seashore," *Times of India*, May 14, 2017, 2.
65 Pantaleão Fernandes, "Nerul's Traditional Tisreanche Fest," *Times of India* (*Goa Times*), May 16, 2013, 1.
66 Prajal Sakardande is a writer and teaches history at a college in Panaji, Goa.
67 Please refer above to *Ufaar* practice.
68 According to Savita de Souza, whose family is from Bati and her father was the *Regedor* of the village of Nerul, only of late, in the twenty-first century, a couple of fisherfolk have moved into the ward.
69 As informed by Savita de Sousa.
70 This connotation comes from the Portuguese "Presidente."
71 *Alvorada* was played by a brass band at dawn and the band would go around the city or village till the *mordomo*'s house to announce to the people, the festive day. In Panjim city, the band would start from the church and move the length of today's 18 June Road to Caculo Island, near Pharmacy College. The band moved on foot but some years back started using a vehicle.
72 I interviewed the 91-year-old João Carmino Bragança, who is a musician himself and plays the trumpet. Bragança has his own brass band along with his two sons and grandsons.
73 This tradition of the Mahars band sadly stopped in the 1970s, probably because of the financial burden or unavailability of the musicians. Many have forgotten about its existence and confuse them with the brass band. Unfortunately, many have never experienced this unique band.
74 Rodrigues, *Abolim*, 111.
75 Confraternity is an association of lay persons. A church or a chapel may have one or more such confraternities in honor of the patron or saints. The most important were those of Confraria do Santisssimo Sacramento.

The confreres wore *opa-mursa*, the color of which depended on the affiliation to the patron, the red colored being for the most important Confraria members.

76 Leopoldo da Rocha, *As Confrarias de Goa: Seculos XVI-XX* (Lisboa: Centro de Estudos Históricos Ultramarinos, 1973), 280.

77 Orlando da Costa, *O Signo da Ira* (Lisboa: Temas da Actualidade, 1996), 77. Translation by the author.

78 Costa, *O Signo da Ira*, 88.

79 Ibid., 91.

80 Traditionally the fireworks were lit during the nine days of the novenas after the evening Mass and *salves*. However, a bigger display of fireworks was held on the vesper's evening. There was no display of fireworks on the feast day, but for a few rockets which were lit after the High Mass. In Panjim, as per tradition, for the feast of the patron, Our Lady of Immaculate Conception, there used to be fireworks. As the capital of Goa, it had the privilege of having the government administration's headquarters and the fireworks were sponsored by different offices. Lists were circulated in the government departments for collecting subscriptions from the staff for the expenses of the novenas and fireworks. The vesper's display was the most extravagant and these were sponsored by the Municipal Council, which then had the nomenclature of "Camara Municipal de Goa." The tradition of government departments celebrating continues today.

81 Costa, *O Signo da Ira*, 91.

82 Ibid.

83 Ibid.

84 Ibid., 92.

85 Rodrigues, *Abolim*, 113.

86 Ibid., 111.

87 Ibid., 112.

88 It was a tradition to engage priests of higher hierarchy like professors of the Seminary, Canon, Monsignor, or some well-known good speaker which thereby gave importance to the *mordomo*.

89 Ibid., 276.

90 *Porjecho Adar—Auxílio do Povo*, a weekly, was published by Batista Vaz from January 1930, with the sole aim of helping and defending the downtrodden (Defensor dos humildes).

91 *Vhodda tobajea zalem fest S.Lourenço, Sinquetim (Aguada). Festacho president... zannem munno-et kellem fest corunc zaitea pormonnem dourunc sogleanc khoxi. Sodanche bhaxen marleot pursau bhitor sortanam ecvis (21) nalli.*

92 Mendonças, Viegas, Mendonças with Gonzaga, Martins, Luis, Gomes, Farias, Almeidas with Falcões and Abreus. This list is according to Xavier, *Bosquejo Histórico das Comunidades* (2012), 248. At present, there are no

more Mendonças with Gonzaga nor Almeidas with Falcões. The latter two are represented individually as Almeida and Falcão.

93 For details please refer to Rodrigues, *Feasts, Festivals*, 174–7; Pereira, *Etnografia*, 116.

94 In modern times the sandbar is thrown open for navigation on the Feast of Saint Lawrence, celebrated on August 10.

95 Jose Nicolau da Fonseca, *Historical and Archaeological Sketch of the City of Goa: Preceded by a Short Statistical Account of the Territory of Goa* (New Delhi: Asian Educational Services, 1994).

96 For more on *addao* please refer to Antonio Lopes Mendes, *A India Portugueza. Breve Descripção das Possessões Portuguezas na Asia* (New Delhi: Asian Educational Services, 1989), 45; Sebastião Rodolfo Dalgado, *Glossário Luso-Asiático* (New Delhi: Asian Educational Services, 1988), 10.

97 Rodrigues, *Feasts, Festivals*, 176.

98 In recent times Mahar's band has been stopped, probably because there are no more musicians.

99 The Comunidade selects the *gaunkar* who will accompany the *mordomo*, one from each *vangor* and two nominated by the *mordomo* of his choice. There are altogether twelve *gaunkars*.

100 *Porjecho Adar*, April 30, 1930.

101 *Compromisso* can be a commitment, obligation, contract, duty, or agreement; therefore, *Compromisso* is a type of agreement that can be considered an unwritten contract, in which the parties assume certain obligations or responsibilities in this agreement.

102 *Porjecho Adar*, April 30, 1930.

Chapter 4

1 Revenue accrued from toddy tapping and related industries was known as *abkari*. It was one of the important incomes for the territory which was implemented from the beginning of the Portuguese period, under the name of *renda de urracas*. It included the spirits called *xarao*, *urraca*, and *feni*. After the Anglo-Portuguese Treaty of 1878, this tax was called *abkari*, which was the nomenclature used in British India. After the revocation of the treaty, the Portuguese government continued using the new tax tariff, as it was beneficial for them, to the detriment of the people.

2 Please see note no. 194 in Chapter 1 for the Anglo-Portuguese Treaty.

3 Daphne A. Roe, *Alcohol and the Diet* (Connecticut: Avi Publishing, 1979), 16.

4 Roe, *Alcohol*, 16.

5 Ibid., 20. Palm *feni* is used as an appetizer and it is believed that it keeps the doctor away; Biula Pereira, *One for the Road: Role of Alcohol in Goan Society* (Saligao: Goa 1556, 2015), 142.

6 Roe, *Alcohol*, 16.
7 For more on the therapeutic uses of alcohol in treating various ailments in Goa, please refer to Pereira, *One for the Road*, 141–6.
8 The Temperance Movement was a social movement dedicated to promoting moderation and, complete abstinence from the use of intoxicating liquor. The earliest temperance organizations started in Saratoga, New York, in 1808 and spread rapidly under the influence of the churches in the United States of America. This movement was required as the drinking habit amongst the people had reached overwhelming levels. It was responsible for the ratification of the Prohibition Amendment to the Constitution in 1919. This movement spread beyond the United States including several European countries, Australia, India, and southwest Africa. Temperance and abstinence became the objects of education and legislation in many regions. A World's Woman's Christian Temperance Union was formed to back the movement.
9 Roe, *Alcohol*, 16.
10 *Heraldo*, July 4, 1926, 3.
11 Ibid.
12 *Vinocarnis* was the choice of many lactating mothers. The name is derived from "wine carnis," from the Latin meaning "of meat." It is a fortified wine (17 percent) now made with a secret grape juice, malt extracts, herbs, and spices recipe but it no longer contains meat.
13 For details on Paulino Dias please refer to Aleixo Manuel da Costa, *Dicionário de Literatura Goesa*, vol. I (Macau: Instituto Cultural de Macau and Fundação Oriente, 1997), 344–8; Duarte Drumond Braga, ed., *O País de Súria: Obra Reunida do Paulino Dias* (São Paulo: Alameda, 2020).
14 *O Comércio*, October 15, 1909, 2.
15 In the olden days, the doctors prescribed what was popularly called *poção* (mixture), a liquid medicine administered in volume, by spoons or measured using a paper cutting in hexagonal shape, glued to the bottle, to show the quantity to be given to the patient. This concoction was prepared by the pharmacist and also by doctors based on pharmacopoeia and many of these had alcohol as one of the components. Some were given as restoratives to recover strength. A popular *poção* was *Tintura de Poejo*, which was given for colic, and stomach aches and prescribed for children and had Port wine as an ingredient. *Poção* was prescribed by doctors even in the 1970s. Pharmacies stopped preparing them as some of the required ingredients were unavailable locally and the Indian government disallowed imports.
16 *Heraldo*, July 4, 1926, 3. Among upper-caste Hindus, it was common practice for the nursing mother to have some wine as an appetizer for three months as it was believed that it helped during lactation and recovery from the trauma of delivery, including blood loss.

17 Francisco Correia Afonso, "O Alcoolismo na India Portuguesa–Relatório," in *Sétimo Congresso Provincial da India Portuguesa*, ed. Balcrisna Datarama Sinai Sacardandó (Nova Goa: Tip. Bragança, 1927), 13.
18 Afonso, "O Alcoolismo na India Portuguesa," 16.
19 A *boia* was a laborer employed to carry a *machila*, a carriage. Four *boias* were required to carry it on their shoulders. They were trained to carry it, with a certain pace in tandem.
20 Pereira, *One for the Road*, 142.
21 Ibid.
22 Ibid., 143.
23 Antonio Peregrino da Costa a physician who graduated from the Escola Médica de Goa, was from Aquem, Margao and was practicing at Navelim. He was popularly known as "Aquem doutor."
24 Afonso, "O Alcoolismo na India Portuguesa," 1–60.
25 Ibid., 12.
26 Ibid.
27 Please refer to the "Relatório" of Afonso where the research paper of Peregrino da Costa is often cited and details of alcoholism and its causes are given.
28 "Debts Were Paid," in Berta Menezes Bragança, *Tales from Goa* (Bastora: Tipografia Rangel, 1991), 27–38.
29 Ibid.
30 "Berta who possesses a rich heritage of talent and name has seen life in its meanest as well as in its most edifying aspects. These short stories are just an expression of these two faces of life." Preface by Prof. Dr. Manohar Rai L. Sardessai.
31 A local board game, played by two persons. For details, please refer to Maria de Lourdes Bravo da Costa Rodrigues, *Games That We Played* (Merces: L&L, 2012), 37.
32 *Porjecho Avaz*, November 6, 1930, 2. Translation from Konkani by José Lourenço, engineer, writer, and author of *The Parish Churches of Goa. A Study of Façade Architecture*, 2007.
33 Bragança, "Surrender," 15–25.
34 Alberto Osório de Castro (1868–1946) writer, poet, ethnographer, archaeologist, and botanist, he was the founder editor of *Oriente Portugues*, the scientific journal of the Archaeological Department, Índia Portuguesa. He was the Procurador da Coroa e Fazenda e Juiz de Direito (Attorney of the Crown and Revenue and Judge) in Goa.
35 Filinto Cristo Dias, *Esboço da História da Literatura Indo-Portuguesa* (Bastora: Tipografia Rangel, 1963), 68.
36 The Escola Médica de Goa was formally established in 1842 in Nova Goa. It was the pioneer in Western medicine education which had a beginning in the sixteenth century at the Royal Hospital in the City of Goa, today's Old Goa, and therefore claims to be the first Western Medical School in Asia. The Conference was held from December 1 to 6, 1914.

37 Translation by the author.

38 Serviço de Saúde da Índia Portuguesa, *I Conferência Sanitária: Em Comemoração do 72º Aniversário da Escola Médico-Cirúrgica de Nova Goa (1-12-1914 a 6-12-1914)* (Nova Goa: Imprensa Nacional, 1914), 2 vols.

39 Índia Portuguesa, *I Conferência Sanitária*, Hipólito Policarpo Pegado, "Sugestões para Combater o Risco do Alcólismo em Goa," in *I Conferência Sanitária: Em Comemoraçao do 72o Aniversário da Escola Médico-Cirúrgica de Nova Goa (1-12-1914 a 6-12-1914)* (Nova Goa: Imprensa Nacional, 1914), 149–58.

40 Ibid., 151.

41 Ermelinda Stuart Gomes, "A Repressão do Alcoolismo," in *Sétimo Congresso Provincial da India Portuguesa*, ed. Balcrisna Datarama Sinai Sacardandó (Nova Goa: Tipografia Bragança, 1927), 6.

42 Raghunath Vishnu Pandit, "Dente de Vinho?" published in *O Heraldo*, December 13, 1968, 2. Originally written on August 22, 1962 at Vengurla, Maharashtra, India.

43 *Statistical Year Book, 1961*, gives details of death according to the age, sex and their causes, 54–7.

44 Pegado, "Sugestões," 158.

45 Baronio Monteiro was a trained allopathic doctor from the erstwhile Escola Médica Cirurgica de Goa who propounded naturopathy and was even known as *médico naturista* (naturopathic doctor).

46 J. J. Roque Correia Afonso, advocate, politician, landlord, and an agriculturist, hailing from Benaulim, was a well-known personality of the time. Well-versed in the problems affecting Goa, wrote extensively on important issues like agriculture, emigration, and judicial matters, for the betterment of the territory. He was the president of the Terceiro Congresso Provincial and presented papers on different topics at the various Congressos.

47 J. J. Roque Correia Afonso "O Saneameto Rural da India Portuguesa na sua Relação com a Organisação Administrativa," in Serviço de Saúde, *Primeira Conferência*, 332–40.

48 Afonso "O Saneameto Rural da India Portuguesa," 333.

49 Ibid.

50 Ibid., 176.

51 Gomes, "A Repressão do Alcoolismo," 6.

52 Antonio Maria da Cunha, *Congresso Provincial da India Portuguesa–Subsidios para a sua História*, vol. I (Nova Goa: Casa Luso-Francesa-Editora, 1924), 3. Translation by the author.

53 Cunha, *Congresso Provincial*, 3.

54 Congresso Provincial da Índia Portuguesa (1916–31) was created by Governor Couceiro da Costa, by Portaria no. 282 dated June 22, 1915.

55 Translation by the author.

56 For details of the dates and papers presented in all the Congressos, please refer to Costa, *Dicionário de Literatura Goesa*, vol. 1, 192–202.

57 Teodoro Miranda, "Regimen do Abcari para o Distrito de Goa" and Azarias Condorcet Lobo "Abcari em Goa: Antes do Tratado Anglo-Luso na Índia." The Congresso was held on January 27, 1918.

58 L. M. Condorcet Pereira, "Campanha Anti-alcoólica," in *Segundo Congresso Provincial da Índia Portuguesa* (Nova Goa: Casa LusoFrancesa, 1917).

59 Both speakers Lobo and Miranda discussed the need to change the existing regime of *abkari* as it was outdated and not beneficial to the government, the public, nor the businessmen.

60 Maria Pia de Menezes Rodrigues "Taverna and Its Socio-Economic Impact in Colonial Goa," in *Metahistory: History Questioning History: Festschrift in honour of Teotónio R. de Souza*, eds. Charles J. Borges and Michael Pearson (Lisboa: Vega, 2007), 195. During the period of the treaty, the income derived from the *abkari* went on increasing from Rs. 65,714:04:01 before the treaty to an average of Rs.635,559/- for the period of 1885–9, which was nine times more. This increase was not due to the progress of the industry but due to the increase in the duty of toddy tapping. The maximum revenue earned from the auctioning of taverns was Rs. 277,786 in the triennium of 1886–8, when a large number of workers of railways and Mormugao Port were attracted to taverns. The treaty came to an end on January 14, 1892. The total revenue earned during the period of the treaty was Rs. 4,819,053:02:09. The toddy tapping industry suffered a lot during this period and as a result, many members of toddy tapping families were forced to migrate.

61 Palm *feni*–17.450, of cashew–950, vinegar and toddy–920 rupees.

62 José Maria Sá, "Relatório," in Antonio Maria da Cunha, *Congresso Provincial da Índia Portuguesa: Subsídios para sua História*, 5 vols (Nova Goa: Tipografia da Casa Luso-Francesa, 1924–33), 266–71.

63 Afonso, "Sétimo Congresso Provincial - Relatório," 54.

64 Ibid.

65 Ibid., 55.

66 Ibid., 56.

67 Pereira, "Campanha Anti-alcoólica," 119.

68 Ibid., 120

69 Pereira, *Segundo Congresso*, 271.

70 Ibid., Socrates de Noronha, Junior and Francisco Correia Afonso "A Sorte do Emigrante Goês no Foco da Emigração. (Alvitres para o seu Melhoramento) (Fate of the Goan Emigrant in the Focus of Emigration) (Suggestions for its improvement)."

71 *Cuddas* are rooms or a set of rooms in which the proletariat Goan emigrants lived in association and shared in paying rent and other expenses. This helped the emigrants who came for the first time to Bombay till they had a place of their own and also the seafarers who had a place to stay before starting a journey and when they returned.

72 Noronha and Afonso, *Segundo Congresso*, 2 (the papers are numbered individually).
73 Translation by the author.
74 Afonso, *Segundo Congresso*, 38. *Zagor* is defined by Sebastião Rodolfo Dalgado as a comic representation in Konkani by illiterate amateurs; a rudimentary theatre in Goa. It was prohibited by the ecclesiastical authorities under severe penalties as an immoral form of theater. The penalties included excommunication as per the Archibishopal decree of November 14, 1777, applicable to those who attended the *zagor*. In spite of this order, the *zagor* continued to be performed well into the twentieth century. Sebastião Rodolfo Dalgado, *Glossário Luso-Asiático* vol. II (New Delhi: Asian Educational Services, 1988), 436.
75 José Maria de Sá advocate, journalist, and government officer has left a sizable literature on subjects related to agriculture and Comunidades. The introduction and preliminary notes of the second edition of Filipe Neri Xavier's *Bosquejo Histórico das Comunidades Agrícolas de Goa*, 1907, can be considered an independent work and bears testimony to his scholarship. He also contributed to various journals and papers on the same topics.
76 "O regímen de abcári é um dos mais importantes problemas da administração pública desta província, concatenando-se com outros problemas também momentosos." Cunha, *Congresso Provincial*, 266. Translation by the author.
77 Ibid., 267. Translation by the author.
78 Ibid., 268.
79 Ibid., 317.
80 Ibid., 56.
81 Diploma Legislativo, hereafter D. L., no. 234, dated March 2, 1927, Boletim Oficial sr. I, no. 10, February 4, 1927.
82 D. L. no. 334 dated September 17, 1928, D. L. no. 339, dated October 17, 1928, Portaria Provincial no. 583 dated December 10, 1928.
83 Sétimo Congresso Provincial da India Portuguesa. *Relatório de Comissao de Estudos* (Nova Goa: Tipografia R. M. Rau & Irmãos, 1927), 2.
84 Francisco Correia Afonso was a professor of English literature, poet, speaker, and well-known literary personality amongst the Goan diaspora in Bombay where he taught and offered his services and knowhow for the improvement of the educational system. He also taught in Dharward and Belgaum. He was a fellow of the University of Bombay and a member of the Board of the University Journal amongst other positions that he held.
85 Afonso, "O Alcoolismo na India Portuguesa," 2. Translation by the author.
86 M. K. Gandhi, *The Collected Works of Mahatma Gandhi*, vol. 20 (New Delhi: Publications Division Ministry of Information and Broadcasting, 1958), 119.
87 Gandhi, *The Collected Works of Mahatma Gandhi*, vol. 20, 119.
88 Ibid., vol. 25, 149.

89 Ibid., vol. 20, 190.
90 Gomes, "A Repressão do Alcoolismo," 6.
91 Nogar Prudente Lourenço, "O Alcoolismo, Causas e seus Remédios in *Setimo Congresso*, 9.
92 Ibid., 7.
93 Condorcet Pereira, Ermelinda S. Gomes and Bascora S. Borcar also made this suggestion.
94 Orlando da Costa, *O Signo da Ira* (Lisboa: Temas da Actualidade, 1996), 67. Translation by the author.
95 Costa, *O Signo da Ira*, 68. Costa's tavern is like many others that populate the edge of the roads that pass the villages, ibid., 41.
96 Cunha, *Congresso Provincial,* 16.
97 *Sétimo Congresso*, 1927, 20. Please see the Table 4.5 for details.
98 Afonso,"O Alcoolismo na India Portuguesa," 20.
99 *O Ultramar* dated October 14, 1925.
100 Afonso, *Sétimo Congresso*, 36.
101 Bragança, *Tales*, "Chivalry," 3–13.
102 Schools, public offices, temples and religious institutions.
103 D. L. no. 334 dated September 17, 1928.
104 Afonso, *Sétimo Congresso*, 23. Translation by the author.
105 Bascora M. S. Borcar, "Campanha Contra o Alcoolismo," in *Sétimo Congresso Provincial da India Portuguesa*, ed. Balcrisna Datarama Sinai Sacardandó (Goa: Tip. Bragança, 1927), 3 (the papers have been individually numbered in the book).
106 Borcar, "Campanha Contra o Alcoolismo," 2. Translation by the author.
107 Ibid., 7.
108 Ibid., 8.
109 Ibid., 7.
110 Afonso, *Sétimo Congresso*, 10.
111 Cunha, *Congresso Provincial,* vol. 4, 27. Translation by the author.
112 Ibid., 29.
113 This suggestion was made by Jaganata Visnum Camotim, one of the delegates.
114 Ibid. Translation by the author.
115 Ibid., 46.
116 Ibid., 30
117 Afonso, *Sétimo Congresso*, 56.
118 *Urraca* is the first distillation from cashew apple juice fermented into alcohol, and *cajuló* the second while *feni* is the third.
119 Cunha, *Congresso Provincial,* vol. 5, 221.
120 For details on deaths according to religion please refer to Estado da Índia. Repartição da Estatística, *Censo da População do Estado da Índia em 26 de Fevereiro de 1931* (Nova Goa: Imprensa Nacional, 1935), 18–21.
121 Dated October 14, 1931. The *Portaria* no. 52 renovates the prohibition orders issued by Manuel de S. Galdino, (Pastoral of August 11, 1812), and

later by D. Antonio Valente, registered in the Diocesan Synod of December 30, 1898.

122 *A Voz de S.Francisco Xavier* (*Boletim da Arquidocese Primacial de Goa e Damão e Patriarcal das Indias Orientais*), October 2, 1931, 58.

123 Circular dated April 3, 1934.

124 Lucio Rodrigues, *Of Soil and Soul and Konkani Folk Tales* (Bombay: Laura D'Souza Rodrigues, 1974), 27.

125 *Ladainha* was sung or recited, on the occasion of an engagement, a marriage, a christening, birth or wedding anniversary, the feast of a patron saint, the return of an emigrant, or his departure on expiry of home leave. The devotion was practiced when making a vow to a popular saint or in thanksgiving for favors received. Rodrigues, *Of Soil and Soul,* 26. There are more references to the *Ladainha* in Chapter 2 "Food, the Memory Connector. A Study of the Goan Folk and Other Forms of Literature."

126 *Ave Maria,* a Bombay-based Goan paper, comments on the circular and writes that no alcoholic beverages are to be served for litany, either at the cross or at home. *Ladahinic soro pienaiye khursac vo gharan kelear. Ave Maria,* April 22, 1934, 1.

127 Govinda P. Hegdo Dessai was the founder and editor of *O Bharat.*

128 *O Bharat,* April 12, 1934, 1. Translation by the author.

129 Ibid.

130 Ibid. Translation by the author.

131 It was a two-day event held on September 12–13, 1933.

132 *A Voz de S.Francisco*, September 12, 1933, 137.

133 Ibid., 147.

134 Ibid., 170.

135 Maria de Jesus dos Martires Lopes, "Then Goan Society of the Second Half of XVIII Century Analysed by Catholic Texts of 'Pastoral Visits,'" *Boletim do Instituto Menezes Bragança*, no. 169 (1993): 225–46.

136 Lopes, "Then Goan Society," 245.

137 Ibid., 239.

138 Ibid., 232.

139 Ibid., 231.

140 Teotonio R. de Souza, "Voiceless in Goan Historiography: A Case for the Church Records in Goa," in *Indo-Portuguese History: Sources and Problems*, ed. John Correia-Afonso (Bombay: Oxford University Press, 1981), 126.

141 Souza, "The Voiceless in Goan Historiography," 126.

142 Helder Garmes, "A Poesia nas Histórias da Literatura Goesa de Língua Portuguesa," *Navegações* 9, no. 2 (2016): 136–43. The poem "Desejos de Um Bêbado" (Anonymous), published in *Tirocinio Litterário,* no. 11 (1862): 86–7.

143 Garmes, "A Poesia nas Histórias," 141.

144 In the story "Debts Were Paid," Berta de Menezes Braganza makes it a point to say that payment is made with palm *feni,* because this one was consumed by the majority of people, especially in the south. In

this part of Goa, if you ask for *feni*, you will be served palm, unless you specify cashew.

145 Toddy extraction is a tedious job for the toddy tapper, who has to climb the tree, three times a day, morning, noon, and evening. The toddy is collected from the spike of the tree and the collection is done in the mornings and evenings, whereas at noon he climbs the tree mainly to take care of the spike so as to activate the flow of sap, which is commonly known as applying *cheu*. Usually, toddy is extracted from three spikes at a time, which is tapped every day to rupture the cells and induce the flow of the sap. The first collection of toddy is normally made on the eleventh day. José Joaquim Fragoso, *Technica de Lavra de Sura do Coqueiro e outras Industrias Dependentes* (Nova-Goa: Imprensa Nacional, 1909), 1; Rodrigues, "Taverna and Its Socio-Economic Impact," 186.

146 Garmes, "A Poesia nas Histórias," 141.

147 Ibid.

148 *Jornal das Comunidades*, September 5, 1937, 1. Translation by the author.

149 Article 1. This point was also raised by others during the Congresso Provincial.

150 Translation by the author.

151 *A Voz de S.Francisco Xavier*, April 18, 1934, 368.

152 The Committee was formed of Mons.Tomaz de Aquino Barreto, Germano Correia, Antonio Maria da Cunha, Benedito Gomes and Luiz de Menezes Bragança. *A Voz de S.Francisco*, September 12, 1933, 174.

153 Liga Economico-Social da India Portuguesa was established in 1931.

154 The first meeting took place on March 5, 1931, in Margao.

155 *A Reforma* 2, no. 2 (1934): 36–8.

156 Jacinto da Silva, Inacio Manuel de Miranda, Sales da Veiga Coutinho, Baronio Monteiro, Peregrino da Costa, Jaime Rangel were the other members.

157 Alcoholics Anonymous was founded in 1935 by Bill Wilson and Bob Smith in Akron, Ohio. It is an international mutual aid fellowship whose stated purpose is to "enable its members to stay sober and help other alcoholics achieve sobriety."

158 *Porjecho Adar,* January 23, 1930.

159 Bulhão Fratel, "Cazaram Amcheam Gavanim," *Porjecho Adar*, August 7, 1930 onwards.

160 "Soro interranc," *Porjecho Adar*, April 23, 1931, 1.

161 The size of *garrafão* varies. The smallest could be of 5 liters capacity.

162 *Porjecho Adar*, April 23, 1931, 1.

163 "Inter vo Mornam," *Porjecho Adar*, October 30, 1930, 1.

164 *O Século* (Lisbon), February 19, 1932. The article was transcribed by José Inacio de Loyola in *Portugal e Colónias*, for the benefit of his local readers on March 19, 1932, 3.

165 *Portugal e Colónias*, May 19, 1937, 3.

166 *Jornal das Comunidades*, September 5, 1937, 1.

167 Ibid.
168 *A Luz do Oriente–Prachi-Prabha*, January 25, 1922, 1.
169 Ibid., May 24, 1922, 1.
170 Ibid., January 25, 1922, 1.
171 Translation by the author.
172 In Roman mythology, Bacchus was the God of wine, parties, leisure, pleasure, and revelry. Son of God Jupiter (God of the day) with the mortal Semele.
173 "Adoradores de Baco," *O Heraldo*, August 26, 1942, 1.
174 Each rupee had 16 tangas and one tanga 6 paise; J. Estevam Afonso, "Cancro Social," *O Heraldo*, August 26, 1942, 1.
175 Ibid.
176 Ibid., 2.
177 Ibid.
178 Portugal, Ministério das Colónias, *Reforma Administrativa Ultramarina, Decreto Lei. no.23.229 dated 15 November, 1933* (Nova Goa: Imprensa Nacional, 1934).
179 Decreto-Lei no. 23.229, November 15, 1933. Estatuto disciplinar dos funcionários e agentes da Administração Central, Regional e Local, a Vigorar em Todas as Colónias Portuguesas, Designadamente Angola, Moçambique, Cabo Verde, Guiné, Estado da Índia, São Tomé, Macau e Timor, a Partir do Dia 1 de Janeiro de 1934. (Disciplinary Statute of employees and agents of Central, Regional and Local Administration in force in the Portuguese colonies of Angola, Moçambique, Cabo Verde, Guiné, Estado da Índia, São Tomé, Macau e Timor, effective from January 1, 1934). Translation by the author; Libério Pereira, "Chaga Social," *O Heraldo*, September 4, 1942, 1.
180 Mandates of League of Nations, Mandate "B" "… subject only to the maintenance of public and moral order, the prohibition of abuses such as the slave trade, the arms, and beverage trade…"; The Curumbim and the Gawda are the two prominent tribes of Goa, which were most affected.
181 Rodrigues, "Taverna and Its Socio-Economic Impact," 199. For various rules and regulations on alcohol in the Portuguese period, 193. The article also gives different tariffs for taxes collected over the years.
182 D. L. no. 551 dated April 1, 1932, "Regulamento do Abcari de Goa e da Venda de Tabaco no Estado da India" in *Legislação* 1932, appendix, 21–43.
183 Rodrigues, "Taverna and Its Socio-Economic Impact," 197. In 1945, a decree was issued introducing legislative measures to be made applicable for government services and staff of different colonies, The Estado da India was covered under Article 35, by which, measures had to be taken to improve the salaries of government staff, owing to the rise of the cost of living and devaluation of rupee in relation to the escudo. In order to meet this additional expenditure, the industrial contribution of the state was to be reshaped, and the contributory regime of *abkari*, was to be merged into it. Art. 35, Decree no. 35:231 dated December 8, 1945, in *Legislação*, 1946, 83.

Chapter 5

1 Estado Portugues da India in 1947 composed of Goa, Daman, Diu, Dadra, and Nagar Haveli.

2 In a radio talk by Gerald Pereira, freedom fighter, member of the Central Committee, Goan People's Party, and trade union leader, broadcast by Bombay Radio, he remarks on the food that was imported into Goa: "Our necessaries—foodstuffs, grains, cereals come from India … All things big and small—sugar, jaggery, rice, wheat, jawar, tamarind, spices, and chillies are Indian. Even vegetables and fruits—oranges, plantains, cabbage or cauliflower always went from Belgaum." He added that "similarly, coconuts, arecanuts, salt and other goods from Goa always found a market in India," "Goa, Its Wealth and Prospects," *Free Goa* (Hereafter *F. G.*) February 10, 1958, 2.

3 The largest number of Goan emigrants was in Bombay. Other centers were Karachi, Madras, and Calcutta. They also moved to other British colonies in Asia, Africa, and Portuguese Africa.

4 When the Indian government decided to stop the postal money orders and value payable articles sent to Goa and other Portuguese settlements, *Free Goa* supported such an announcement and commented: "… comes at a time when Portuguese are feeling the pinch of shortage of Indian currency for use in making their purchases." "Goa strikes," *F. G.*, July 25, 1955, 8; Emili Marini, *Goa Tal Como a Vi* (Lisboa: União Gráfica, 1956), 147.

5 There is an extensive body of research on the impact of the economic blockade of Goa. Among them: Olivinho Gomes, "The Economic Blockade of Goa—Implication and Consequences," *Boletim do Instituto Menezes Bragança*, no. 159 (1989): 69–95. This article is based on the records from the Indian Customs and Revenue Department and some personal experience of the author, a high-ranking officer in the department in the 1970s. Though the paper includes personal woes experienced by Goans it does not talk about the impact of unavailability of food and starvation; Maria de Lourdes Bravo da Costa Rodrigues, "Economic Blockade," *Boletim do Instituto Menezes Bragança*, no. 170 (1994): 135–46 is an overview of the blockade. Maria de Lourdes Bravo da Costa Rodrigues, in *100 Years of Goa Chamber of Commerce and Industry (1908–2008)* (Panaji: Goa Chamber of Commerce and Industry, 2008), 37–46 has a chapter on "Economic Blockade" analyzing the role of the Goa Chamber of Commerce and Industry during the period. Harischandra Tucaram Nagvenkar, "Salt and the Goan Economy (A Study of Goa's Salt Industry and Salt Trade in the 19th and 20th Centuries during the Portuguese Rule)," PhD diss. (University of Goa, 1999), 409–68, includes a chapter, titled "Economic Blockade by India, the Goan Economy and Salt" which discusses the difficulties in the sale and export of salt during the said period; Murelle da Costa, "History of

Trade and Commerce in Goa: 1878–1961," PhD diss. (Goa University, 1999), 243–62, has a chapter on "Impact of the Economic Blockade and World Events on Goa's Trade." It only examines the trade and economic aspect of the period; R. P. Rao, *Portuguese Rule in Goa, 1520–1961* (Bombay: Asia Publishing House, 1963), 131–40, has a chapter titled "Economic Blockade"; Mario Cabral e Sa, *Song of the Golden Gateway—100 Years of the Port of Mormugao and the Peninsula* (New Delhi: Vikas Publishing House, 1985), 85–91, also has a chapter titled "The Blockade Years," which reflects on the port's activities during those years.

6 "The economic life of Goa is inevitably connected with India's," Nehru at the Uttar Pradesh Congress Committee in Sitapur on August 21, 1955, *Nehru on Goa* (New Delhi: Goa Freedom Publications, n.d.), 37; Nuno Alves Morgado, "Notas para um Estudo do Desenvolvimento Económico do Estado da India," *Boletim Informativo da Junta de Comércio Externo* (hereafter BIJCE), Ano I, Sr. I, 4 (1961): 6–19.

7 Morgado, ibid.; *Techno-Economic Survey of Goa, Daman and Diu* (New Delhi: National Council of Applied Economic Research, 1964), 18; Nagvenkar, "Salt and the Goan Economy," 412.

8 Pondicherry, Karikal (both in Tamil Nadu) Mahe (Kerala), Yanam (Andhra Pradesh), and Chandernagar (Bengal) were French territories. The last one was merged with India in June 1949.

9 In October 1954, the French settlements were transferred de facto to India. By 1956 an agreement was signed to give a de jure status to the transfer. For details, see "Treaty of Succession of the French Establishments of Pondicherry, Karikal, Mahe and Yanam," *Indian Yearbook of International Affairs* V (1956): 175–88.

10 Portugal claimed that the territories were under its administration for centuries, and the people were lusitanized (following the Portuguese lifestyle) and different from the rest of India, amongst others. Gonçalves Pereira, *My Personal Deposition in the Case of Goa* (Lisboa: Agencia Geral do Ultramar, 1953), 9.

11 Portugal, Ministério de Negócios Estrangeiros, *Vinte Anos de Defesa do Estado Português da India (1947–1967)* (hereafter M. N. E.), vol. I. (Lisboa: 1967), 119. Vasco Garin took charge on January 27, 1949, and later, on November 19, 1949, Parekhet Achuta Menon presented his credentials to President Carmona in Lisbon as the Indian minister. Thus, it can be seen that Portugal was the first, to set up a Legation office; Arthur Rubinoff, *India's Use of Force* (Bombay: Popular Prakashan, 1971), 48; Pratima Kamat, *Farar Far (Crossfire): Local Resistance to Colonial Hegemony in Goa, 1510–1912* (Panaji: Institute Menezes Braganza, 1999), 286.

12 M. N. E., vol. I, 7; *Hindustan Overseas Times*, September 18, 1954, 20 *apud* Rubinoff, ibid., 44.

13 An *aide-memoire* was sent by India to the Portuguese government, objecting to the Archdiocese's role in the religious affairs of India. For details, see M. N. E., vol. I, 100. Nehru even met the Pope and after his audience stated that His Holiness had confirmed that the Goa issue was purely a political question and not a religious one; *Goa. Goan Point of View* (London: The Goa League, 1956), 16.
14 M. N. E., vol. I, 135; Tristão Bragança Cunha criticized the relationship between the Church and the Portuguese government in various articles in *Free Goa*. These may also be read in his book *Goa's Freedom Struggle* (Bombay: Dr. T. B. Cunha Memorial Committee, 1961).
15 Rubinoff, *India's Use*, 49; Murli Sitaram Deora, ed., *Liberation of Goa, Daman and Diu from Portuguese Rule (Now a Territory of the Indian Union)* (New Delhi: Discovery Publishing House, 1995), 268; "O encerramento da Legação de Portugal em Nova Delhi e a suspensão do comboio," *Heraldo*, July 27, 1955, 1; *A Vida*, July 28, 1955, 1.
16 Nehru announced in the Parliament that the government had handed over a note to the in-charge of Portuguese affairs in New Delhi on July 25. The news appeared on *Heraldo* July 26, 1955, 1; Costa, "Economic Blockade," 137.
17 *A Vida*, July 28, 1955, 1. Other local papers also carried the speech of the prime minister in the Parliament; M. N. E., vol. II, 484.
18 Susheela Sawant Mendes in "Jawaharlal Nehru and the Liberation Struggle of Goa," *Indian History Proceedings* 67 (2006–7): 549–55.
19 *A Vida*, July 26, 1955, 1.
20 The *Acto Colonial* was passed by the Portuguese Parliament and became a part of the Portuguese Constitution on July 8, 1930, by Decree no. 18570. At the time Salazar was acting minister of colonies in the government of Domingos da Costa Oliveira during the period of National Dictatorship, which preceded the Estado Novo (1933–74). It was published to substitute Chapter V of the 1911 Constitution. Article 7 of the amended Act, dated May 21, 1935, specifies that this law applied to the Overseas Colonies of Portugal. This act denied civil liberties to the Goan people and designated the citizens of Goa as *assimilados* (assimilated) and *indígenas* (indigenous) or *nativos* (natives). Subsequently, by a legal change dated June 11, 1951, the Constitution was amended (Law 2.048) and Art. 134 transformed the then Overseas Territories into "províncias" (provinces) of Portugal, thus transforming the empire into a political constellation. This decentralization process aimed at guaranteeing politico-administrative autonomy to the provinces (Art. 148).
21 Portaria no. 6415 (Decree no. 40216, July 1, 1955) and implemented in Goa from August 1, 1955. *Boletim Oficial* (hereafter *B. O.*), Sr. I, Supplement to no. 28, July 18, 1955.
22 Rubinoff, *India's Use*, 48; *Heraldo*, July 26, 1955; The leader of the Praja Socialist Party, J. B. Kripalani said that the government had only

two alternatives: to permit the movement of the satyagraha (passive resistance) or to start and continue a limited war with Portugal because of Goa; the communist leader Gopalan suggested economic sanction against Goa and if necessary, policing action. A correspondent of *Observer* from Bombay also suggested that unless war is declared there is nothing that Nehru can do at this juncture and would be difficult to liberate Goa without violence. He also added that economic restrictions need to be imposed since funds that amount to 100.000 pounds are sent monthly to their relatives in the Portuguese territories, and non-receipt will cause big difficulties to women and children.

23 "We attach great importance to the basic principles governing our policies, international policies especially," Nehru at a news conference in New Delhi, on May 31, 1956, in *Nehru on Goa*, 15; "O Congresso apoia—metódos pacifícos para resolver a questão," *A Vida*, July 27, 1955, 1.

24 On December 19, 1961, the Indian Army liberated the three Portuguese enclaves of Goa, Daman, and Diu.

25 *A Vida*, July 26, 1955, 4; *Diário de Goa*, July 26, 1955, 4.

26 Ibid.; Marini, *Goa Tal Como a Vi*, 145; Alban Couto, "Economic blockade 1955—The Goan Economy." India-Seminar.com/2004/543%20alban%20couto.htm; "Goa's Changed Economy," *The Economic Weekly*, July 9, 1955; Earlier on January 26, 1955, the Indian District Traffic Superintendent asked to temporarily suspend the trains between the stations at Gorkhevadi (India) and Caranzol (Goa) because some persons wanted to cross into the Portuguese territory and had threatened to lie on the tracks. In this connection B. K. Apte under subsection "Nationalist Movement" in the *Gazetteer of the Union Territory Goa, Daman and Diu* writes: "On this date, the Government of India imposed an economic blockade on Goa and the workers of the National Congress (Goa) organized a satyagraha at Castlerock, to stop the railway traffic to Goa." Vithal Trimbak Gune, ed., *Gazetteer of the Union Territory Goa, Daman and Diu* vol. 1 (Panaji: Gazetteer Department, 1979), 203. But this was one of such random happenings that took place during the period that have been wrongly attributed to be an economic blockade; Maria Manuel Stocker, *Xeque-Mate a Goa* (Lisboa: Temas e Debates, 2005), 112.

27 *A Vida*, July 26, 1955, 4; *Diário de Goa*, July 26, 1955, 4; The former Southern Mahratta, which later had been transferred into a nationalized railway of the Indian government, unilaterally terminated the 1902 agreement from December 31, 1955, hoping decisively to prejudice the maritime and railway communications of Goa, and, consequently, the whole economy of organized State of Portuguese India. Article 4, Decree Law no. 43.517, dated February 25, 1961. *Legislação do Estado da India* (hereafter *Legislação)1961*, vol. I (Panjim: Imprensa Nacional, 1961), 237. *Diário do Governo*, Sr. I, no. 46, February 25, 1961; Supplement to *B. O.*, Sr. I, no. 11, March 17, 1961; Amaro A. Pereira,

compiler, *History of Mormugao Port*, (Vasco da Gama: Mormugao Port Trust, 1978), Appendix XXIX, 181. (A cyclostyled copy).

28 "Porto e Caminho de Ferro de Mormugao," *A Vida*, April 21, 1956, 1.

29 *A Vida*, July 28, 1955, 1.

30 Champa Limaye, ed., *Goa Liberation Movement and Madhu Limaye* preface by Jayantrao Tilak (Delhi: B. R. Publishing Corporation, 1996), xi.

31 Sarto Esteves, *Goa and Its Future* (Bombay: Manaktalas, 1966), 87.

32 Fatima da Silva Gracias, *Health and Hygiene in Colonial Goa (1510–1961)* (New Delhi: Concept Publishing company, 1994), 41; Nagvenkar, "Salt and the Goan Economy," 410.

33 Rubinoff, *India's Use*, 51.

34 *A Vida*, August 6, 1954, 1.

35 Rubinoff, *India's Use*, 51.

36 *O Heraldo*, September 1, 1954, 2; M. N. E., vol. I, 262.

37 *O Heraldo* (Suplemento), September 3, 1954, 2; *F. G.*, September 10, 1954, 5; Prakashchandra Pandurang Shirodkar. *Goa's Struggle for Freedom* (Delhi: Ajanta Publications, 1988), 108.

38 M. N. E., vol. I, 262.

39 Ibid.

40 Ibid., 264.

41 Stocker, *Xeque-Mate,* 91.

42 M. N. E., vol. I, 261.

43 On July 25, 1955.

44 *A Vida*, July 26, 1955, 1.

45 Despacho do Governo Geral–Postos de venda de arroz (normas para o seu funcionamento), dated June 29, 1956, *Legislação*, 1956, vol. II, 171.

46 *F. G.*, November 10, 1959, 8. The poem was written on May 18, 1955 in Paris. The original Devanagari version appears in a collection of poems in the book Manohar Rai Sardessai, *Goem Tujea Moga Khatir* (Mumbai: Gomant Bharti Prakashan, 1961), 23.

47 *F. G.*, October 25, 1956, 5; Antonio Correia de Lima, *O Fim dos Séculos: Goa, Damão e Diu* (Lisboa: Bertrand Editora, 1997), 193. Lima writes that there were at least ten cases of deserters, including an officer from the army who asked for shelter in India; Later in another news report, the situation in Goa is given. "Revolting! Portuguese soldier's description of conditions in Goa," F. G., September 8, 1957, 1. In the same paper news regarding the conditions in Diu is described where the poorer classes live in semi-starvation. According to the news report when the ship *Lurio* arrives in Diu the goods are pounced upon by the governor of the district and the officers, with very little left for the soldiers. As to the fate of the native population, the authorities showed very little concern.

48 James Barber, "Economic Sanctions as a Policy Instrument," *International Affairs* 55, no. 3 (1979): 367–84.

49 Goa did not have any industry worth its name. At the most, they could be designated as cottage industries. There were only a few manufacturing

units and the activity was limited to a few small-scale and cottage industries. José C. Almeida, *Goa Administration and Economy before and after 1962* (Panaji: Civitas and Broadway, 2013), 80.

50 Order of Governor-General dated July 24, 1956, *B. O.*, Sr. II, no. 30, July 26, 1956. India was the main market for areca nut.

51 Though the revenue from mining was able to support the economy, it was not declared as an industry then.

52 The governor was Fernando de Quintanilha Mendonza e Dias (1948–52), *O Heraldo*, July 11, 1951, 1.

53 Costa and Company and Monte Silva, which continue to manufacture today.

54 For more details on salt production and related topics please refer to Nagvenkar, "Salt and the Goan Economy," 409–68. Also read Reyna Sequeira, *As Dear as Salt … The Story and Neglect and Decay in a Traditional Occupation in Goa* (Saligao: Goa 1556 and Golden Heart Emporium, 2013).

55 Rodrigues, *100 years*, 55.

56 Ibid.

57 Ibid.; *Government Gazette*, Sr. I, May 24, 1962.

58 S. Maitre, "Port and Dock Workers Determined to Make Boycott Successful," in *Goan Tribune* (hereafter *G. T.*) August 26, 1956, 6. Maitre was the General Secretary of the Bombay Port Trust General Workers' Union, Bombay.

59 Ibid.

60 Gomes, "The Economic Blockade," 76.

61 Ibid. Notification No. F.E.R.A. 37/55 R.B. dated May 2, 1955 issued under the Foreign Exchange Regulations Act, 1947.

62 Ibid. Postal Notice issued under No. C.69.5/55 based on the Director-General, Posts and Telegraphs, endorsement No. N.C.69–5/55 dated August 25, 1955, and later endorsed by the Central Board of Revenue letter No. 90/56/55 L.C. dated September 10, 1955 from its Land Custom's Wing.

63 Ibid.; Custom's Manual, Central Board of Revenue, 1955, New Delhi.

64 Ibid., 78.

65 Ibid.

66 Ibid.

67 Ibid.

68 Ibid.

69 *G. T.* The letter was published on the first page to make a stronger statement.

70 *G. T.*, July 29, 1956, 1.

71 The Bombay Port Trust General Workers Union decided to boycott all ships going to Portuguese territories from August 12, 1954, even though Bombay Port Trust declared that refusal to handle any particular ship on political grounds was a serious breach of discipline. *G. T.*, August 26, 1956, 6.

72 Co-ordinating Committee for Imports and Exports and the Committee for Economic Affairs.
73 The limit was set at not more than sixteen arrateis (one arrátel about 450gms).
74 As mentioned in the notice issued by Comissão de Assuntos Económicos dated February 1, 1955.
75 Police Anti-Hoarding and Speculation Services.
76 *B. O.*, Sr. III, no. 22, July 1, 1956.
77 *B. O.*, Sr. II, no. 31, August 2, 1956.
78 The district of Goa was divided into Concelhos, known as talukas after 1961. From 1917 there were altogether eleven, with each having an administrative headquarters in the important city or villa of the Concelho. The other two Concelhos were of Daman and Diu. The imported foods were sold in the offices of the Concelhos de Administração of Salsete, Bardes, Mormugão, and Ponda. Pears, apples, prunes, cauliflowers, carrots, tomatoes, turnips. The price of the pears and apples was Rs.5 and 4 a dozen, respectively. Tomatoes were sold for one rupee and turnips at 10 annas a pound, *G. T.*, September 9, 1956, 13.
79 An average agricultural laborer got a wage of Rs.2 to 2.50 and a mine worker Rs.5 to 7 per day; a government clerk Rs.250 and a school teacher Rs.350 to 600 per month. Data was taken from the *Techno-Economic survey*, 8; an agricultural laborer's lowest wage was 12$00 and the highest 18$00 for a man. Women were paid the lowest at 6$50 and the highest at 10$00. According to the exchange rate, one rupee was equivalent to 6 escudos, Goa, Daman and Diu, General Statistics Department, *Goa, Daman and Diu, Statistical Yearbook, 1961* (Panaji: Government Printing Press, 1963), 193.
80 Decree of May 5, 1937.
81 Decree of April 12, 1956.
82 *A Vida*, September 16, 1954, 2.
83 *G. T.*, July 15, 1956, 5.
84 *F. G.*, October 10, 1953, 1.
85 The first issue of the fortnightly is dated October 10, 1953, and the editor was Antonio Furtado, followed by Bragança Cunha. On his death, Berta de Menezes Bragança became the editor. Initially, it was bilingual, English and Portuguese.
86 *F. G.*, ibid.
87 Ibid., 3.
88 Ibid.
89 Irene Heredia, "Liberating Goa: The Laudable Role of the Goa Liberation Council in Securing Goa's Liberation," *Goa Today*, June 2005, 41. Francisco Correia Afonso, L. J. de Souza and Prof. Wellingkar were Vice Presidents. J. N. Heredia was the secretary along with J. M. Pinto and Nicolau Menezes.

90 The first issue is dated June 17, 1956. J. S. Sousa took over as editor from Soares from July 13, 1958, till December 13, 1959. Lambert Mascarenhas became editor on January 10, 1960 and continued till the end in May 1962. In the intervening period Cajetan Lobo, who was the publisher for some years, was the editor.
91 José Clemente Vaz, *Profiles of Eminent Goans, Past and Present* (New Delhi: Concept Publishing Company, 1997), 264.
92 *G. T.*, June 17, 1956, 2.
93 Esteves, *Goa and Its Future*, 81.
94 Ibid.
95 Mohan Ranade, *Struggle Unfinished* (Ribandar: Vimal Publications, 1988), 88.
96 Pereira, "Last Phase of Goa's Struggle," *F. G.*, July 25, 1955, 4.
97 Pereira, "Economic Blockade-A Fiasco!," *F. G.*, January 25, 1956, 4.
98 Ranade, *Struggle Unfinished*, 87.
99 Ibid., 88.
100 Ibid.
101 Casimiro Emérito Rosa Teles Jordão Monteiro was a military intelligence and law enforcement officer during the Estado Novo. He was entrusted with the interrogation of those involved in the independence movement in the Portuguese Territories. In Goa, he tortured the freedom fighter prisoners and suspects and was feared by the people for his inhuman behaviour.
102 Ranade, *Struggle Unfinished*, 89.
103 "Despacho–Subsídios aos emigrantes expulsos da União Indiana e Comissão de Inquérito a Situação dos Emigrantes" signed by Governor General, *Legislação de 1956*, vol. II, 173.
104 Ibid., clause 2.
105 Aurel Mendonça, *India's Policy and Goa* (Bangalore: Author, 1957), 7.
106 Cunha criticized the Indian government for not considering the political implications of these deportations and requested that the refugees be given the same status as those from Pakistan and other countries; Mendonça, ibid., 8.
107 *G. T.*, September 9, 1956, 1.
108 Ibid.; Gomes, "Economic Blockade," 82.
109 *G. T.*, December 30, 1956, 14.
110 Berta Menezes Bragança, *Landmarks in My Time: Selected Writings* (Margao: Author, 1992), 28.
111 John Baptist Pinto, *Goan Emigration* (Saligão, Goa: author, 1962), 3.
112 The Congresso Provincial was established by the Goan intelligentsia to discuss various problems that affected Goa and Goans. For details on the Congresso, please refer to the chapter on "Drink That 'Cheers' but Brings Tears."
113 Gomes, "Economic Blockade," 76.

114 *G. T.*, July 15, 1956, 11.
115 Ibid.
116 Ibid., September 23, 1956, 2.
117 Ibid.
118 Ibid., August 26, 1956, 11.
119 Ibid.
120 "Despacho do Governo Geral–Postos de venda de arroz (normas para o seu funcionamento)," dated June 29, 1956. *Legislação*, 1956, vol. II, 171.
121 *G. T.*, August 12, 1956, 4.
122 Ibid., August 26, 11; *Legislação*, 1956, vol. II, 171.
123 *G. T.*, July 15, 1956, 11.
124 Equivalent to 20 *maunds*.
125 *G. T.*, December 2, 1956, 11.
126 *Heraldo*, November 13, 1956. A letter by a consumer, titled "O preço do arroz," writes that the production was not good because of untimely and excessive rains in 1956 and the tax was uncalled for.
127 *G. T.*, December 2, 1956, 11.
128 Ibid., September 20, 1959, 3; Silvia de Mendonça-Noronha, "The Economic Scene in Goa (1926–1961)," in *Goa through the Ages: An Economic History*, vol. ii, ed. Teotonio R. de Souza (New Delhi: Concept Publishing House, 1990), 267.
129 *G. T.*, July 12, 1959, 5.
130 Ibid., September 20, 1959, 3.
131 *G. T.*, June 28, 1959, 11.
132 Board of External Commerce
133 Government Council of the Province. The Government governing body.
134 Established in this Estado by Decree no. 35.849 dated September 6, 1956.
135 BIJCE 1, Série I, no. 3 (1961), 10. Italics as in the original text.
136 Ibid. Translation by the author.
137 Ibid., 11.
138 For more on the sur-tax please read Chapter 1.
139 BIJCE 1, Série I, no. 3 (1961), 1.
140 Ibid., 11. Translation by the author.
141 Ibid.
142 Lobo was a well-known philatelist and contributor to *Heraldo*, *O Heraldo* and *A Vida* in which he wrote on different topics. Post-Liberation he also contributed to the *Navhind Times* with a column on philately.
143 "A Não Circulação de Notas da União Indiana é um Flagelo Economico-social," *A Vida*, February 11, 1956, 1.
144 Ibid. Translation by the author.
145 Ibid.
146 *G. T.*, November 4, 1956, 1.
147 The following names were listed: Damodar Mangalji, Tarcar, Furlencar, Neogi, Timblo, and Abdul Latif.

148 Ibid.
149 Decree no. 41.680 dated June 16, 1958.
150 Ibid., Art. 1.
151 Ibid.
152 Order dated December 29, 1958; *Heraldo*, January 3, 1959, 4.
153 Order dated December 1958. A comment to solve the difficulties faced by the people appeared in the *Heraldo*, January 3, 1959, 4.
154 Ibid.
155 Jaime Rangel, physician, journalist, and president of Bardez Municipality had occupied many official positions and represented Portugal at some international Labour Conferences.
156 "Monetary Crisis. Wanted Immediate Action," *G. T.*, June 14, 1959, 7.
157 Ibid.
158 *Heraldo*, November 13, 1956.
159 *F. G.*, May 25, 1960, 8.
160 *G. T.*, June 14, 1959, 7.
161 Rodrigues, *100 years*, 39.
162 Ibid.
163 Ibid.
164 Gomes, "Economic Blockade," 81.
165 *F. G.*, November 8, 1953, 2.
166 Ibid.; M. N. E., vol. I, 264.
167 Ibid., 7.
168 Read "Portuguese Occupation of Goa Supported by Indian Merchants," *F. G.*, July 25, 1958, 1, which lists names of those involved: Chowgule & Co. Ltd., Damodar Mangalji & Co. (India) Ltd., Gangadhal Agrawal, Hiralal Khodidas, Khantilal & Co. Ltd., Mineira Nacional Ltd., Shantilal Khushaldas & Brothers, Subraya & Co., Timble Brothers Ltd., V. M. Salgaonkar & Brother Ltd., V. S. Dempo & Co. Ltd., Joao Hugo Siqueira, Madev Sinay Talaulikar, A. Abdul Razak, Sesa Goa Ltd. (Germano-Italian), W. I. P. Railway (British), Mingoa Society (Italian).
169 *F. G.*, May 25, 1956, 4.
170 Rubinoff, *India's Use*, 106.
171 *F. G.*, October 10, 1953, 1; Speech made by Nehru, September 17, 1953, in *Nehru on Goa*, 3.
172 *F. G.*, June 10, 1954, 4.
173 Ibid., June 10, 1956, 6.
174 Ibid., June 10, 1954, 4.
175 Bragança, *Landmarks*, 29.
176 *G. T.*, August 26, 1956, 15.
177 Ibid., September 23, 1956, 14.
178 Ibid.
179 Nuno Alves Morgado was appointed to conduct a survey by Governor Vassalo e Silva. Morgado, a Law graduate from the University of Lisbon

attended the reputed Instituto de Estudos Superiores Ultramarinos. The latter delivered higher education in "Overseas Sciences," preparing the frameworks for overseas administrations, and cultivating an investigation of scientific problems related to the valuation of the overseas territories, their population, and the study of people and their languages. He held various senior management positions, such as Provincial Secretary of the Angolan Economy, Director of Technical Secretariat, Vice-Governor of the Bank of Angola, and Secretary-General of the Presidency of the Council of Ministers. He has several publications to his credit.

180 Translation by the author.

181 Teotónio de Sousa comments on this affair: "Pascoal Menezes, represents the Goan business class that benefited from the economic blockade of the Union of India, from 1954, and from the smuggling that this blockade promoted." Teotónio de Sousa, "Lógicas Imperiais e Processos Contemporâneos: Analisando Algumas Memórias Coloniais Recém-publicadas em Goa e em Portugal," *Babilónia*, Dossier Mestiçagem Linguística e Cultural, no. 4: 55–70.

182 Cunha, *Goa's Freedom Struggle*, 169.

183 Salazar in his speech delivered on October 20, 1949, M. N. E., vol. I, 157. Translation by the author; Shrikant Ramani, *Operation Vijay: The Ultimate Solution* (Panjim: Broadway Book Center, 2008), 21.

184 Rodrigues, *100 years*, 41.

185 Ibid., 42.

186 During the period several ships belonging to CNN were included in the transportation of goods from abroad: Lurio, India, Zambezia, Rovuma, São Tome, Timor, and Moçamedes were some of them.

187 Rodrigues, *100 Years*, 43.

188 "Transporte Aereos da India Portuguesa" (TAIP). Started on August 10, 1955 with one plane. Later, on September 28 another plane was added to the fleet, which would fly from Goa to Daman then Diu and from here to Karachi and back. Initially, it was called "Serviços de Transporte Aereos da India Portuguesa."

189 "TAIP—do primeiro ao Último Voo," February 1, 2018, 1. Translation by the author.

190 Ibid.

191 The Chief of TAIP, Solano de Almeida, in an interview with the local newspaper, informed that "in the first three months they had done 90.905 kilometres, more than two times around the world. The planes transported 4.787 kilos of postal matter between Estado da India, the Metropolis and other overseas provinces …"

192 Rodrigues, *100 Years*, 42.

193 Ibid.; Sá, *Song of the Golden*, 86.

194 Goa, Daman and Diu, *Statistical Yearbook, 1961*, 266. For details, please refer to the table.

195 BJCE, I, Série No. II. no. 9, October 1961, 23. Translation by the author.
196 Douglas E. Haynes and Abigail McGowan, *Towards a History of Consumption in South Asia* (New Delhi: Oxford University Press, 2010),13.
197 *G. T.*, May 3, 1956, 6.
198 For details of trade of Portuguese India, please refer to Goa, Daman, and Diu, *Statistical Yearbook, 1961*, 259–305.
199 The other two enclaves of Dadra and Nagar Haveli were liberated by the Freedom Fighters on July 22 and August 7, 1954, respectively.
200 *G. T.*, August 12, 1956, 11; Estatuto do Funcionalismo Ultramarino e Remodelação de Vencimentos. Decree no. 40.708 and 40.709, July 31, 1956.
201 Ranade, *Struggle Unfinished,* 88.

Conclusion

1 "Mercado Livre," *A Voz da India*, August 7, 1948, 1. CRA is Comissão de Racionamento de arroz (Committee for Rationing of Rice). Translation by the author.
2 Ibid.
3 Ibid.
4 Ibid.
5 Year 1948.
6 A. R. Padoshi, *Agricultural Development of India* (Bombay: Himalaya Publishing House, 1991), 25. Out of the total number of the holdings, as many as 85 percent were less than two hectares each, that is, less than five acres each.
7 Portaria no. 813, January 6, 1930, *B. O.* no. 2, January 7, 1930.
8 J. C. Almeida, if in each taluka "the cultivable fallow land" was available for agriculture purposes more than half would be brought under cereal bearing crops. The area of 44,699 ha under paddy cultivation would have increased to about 92,367 ha. José C. Almeida, *Aspects of the Agricultural Activity in Goa, Daman and Diu* (Panaji: Government Printing Press, 1965), 11.
9 Carlos Manuel Faísca, Dulce Freire, and Cláudia M. Viana, "The State and Natural Resources: 250 Years of Rice Production in Portugal 18th–21st Centuries," *Ler História* 79 (2021): 241–62.
10 "*Sobretaxa do equilibrio,*" D. L. no. 518, October 23, 1931; *B. O.* no. 85, October 23, 1931.
11 Maria Paula Meneses, "Food, Recipes and Commodities of the Empire: Mozambique in the Indian Ocean Networks," *Centro de Estudos Sociais*, Universidade de Coimbra, Oficina no. 335 (December 2009): 1–34.

12 Marta Vilar Rosales, "O Verdadeiro Caril Moçambicano: Transnacionalismo, quotidianos e materialidades goesas na Africa colonial ...," in *Das Indias: Gentes, movimentos e pertenças transnacionais* (Lisboa: Edicões Colibri, Centro de Estudos em Migrações e Minorias, Faculdade de Ciências Sociais e Humanas, Universidade Nova de Lisboa, Junho 2010), 59–80.

13 Leslie de Noronha, *The Mango and the Tamarind Tree* (Calcutta: Writers Workshop, 1970), 44.

14 Noronha, *The Mango and the Tamarind Tree*, 44.

15 Rosales, "O Verdadeiro Caril Moçambicano," 74.

16 Maria Lucinda Fernandes Costa Fernandes, "Os «Encontros dos Goeses da Beira e seus Amigos» na Grande Lisboa. Património Identitário e sua Reconstrução Cultural Pós-Colonial," Mestrado em Património Histórico, diss., Universidade Nova de Lisboa, 2010. The appendices in the dissertation include a list of the annual reunions Os "Encontros Anuais" dos Goeses da Beira e seus Amigos em Portugal—Lisboa which also give the menus.

17 Ibid.

18 The exact amount of remittances is unknown as the money was sent by various means like banks, postal orders, and through a third person. Gerald Pereira puts it to more than two crores of rupees (Rs.2,00,00,000/-) per year. Gerald Pereira, "Economic Blockade-A Fiasco!," *Free Goa*, January 25, 1956, 4.

Bibliography

Published Primary Sources

Anuário da India Portuguesa, 1933. Nova Goa: Repartição da Estatística, 1934.

Anuário do Estado da Índia Portuguesa, 1929. Nova Goa: Imprensa Nacional, 1929.

Anuário Estatístico de Goa, Damão e Diu, 1926–61. Goa: Imprensa Nacional, 1926–61.

Anuário Estatístico do Estado da India, 1959. Lisboa: Tipografia Portuguesa, 1960.

Anuário Estatístico do Ultramar, 1959. Lisboa: Instituto Nacional de Estatística, Bertrand (Irmãos), 1960.

Anuário Estatístico do Ultramar, 1961. Lisboa: Instituto Nacional de Estatística, Bertrand (Irmãos), 1962.

Boletim Oficial do Governo do Estado da Índia 1837–1961. Goa: Imprensa Nacional, 1837–1961.

Codigo das Comunidades.1904 (Portaria Provinvincial no. 315, December, 1904; 1933 (Dipolma Legislativo no. 651, March 30, 1933), and 1961 (Diploma Legislativo no. 2070, April 15, 1961).

Estado da Índia. Repartição da Estatística. *Censo da População do Estado da Índia em 26 de Fevereiro de 1931*. Nova Goa: Imprensa Nacional, 1935.

Estatuto do Estado da Índia. Portaria no.6415 (Decreto no.40216, 1 de Julho, 1955). *Boletim Oficial*, Sr. I. Supplement to no. 28, July 18, 1955.

Government of Goa, Daman and Diu. *Report of the Goa Land Reforms Commission, 1964*. Panjim: Government Printing Press, 1964.

Government of Goa, Daman and Diu. *Statistical Yearbook, 1961*. Panjim: Government Printing Press, 1963.

Government of India. *Goa and the Charter of the UN*. New Delhi: Ministry of External Affairs, 1960.

Governo de Goa. *Regulamento do Abcari de Goa e da Venda do Tabaco no Estado da India* (Aprovado por Diploma Legislativo no. 551, de 1 de Abril de 1932 e Legislação Correlativa). Nova Goa: Imprensa Nacional, 1932.

Governo Geral do Estado da Índia. *Divisão Administrativa do Estado da Índia: Diário do Governo*, Decreto no. 35:229 and 35:230, December 8, 1945.

Governo Geral do Estado da Índia. *Organização da Polícia Internacional e de Defesa do Estado*. Goa: Imprensa Nacional, 1954.

Governo Geral do Estado da Índia. *Reforma Tributária. Boletim Oficial*, Diploma Legislativo no. 1761, 1958.

Gune, Vithal Trimbak, ed. *Gazetteer of the Union Territory of Goa, Daman and Diu*. Panaji: Gazetteer Department, 1979.

Khera, Prem Nath *Operation Vijay: The Liberation of Goa and Other Portuguese Colonies in India (1961)*. Delhi: Government of India, Ministry of Defense, 1974.

Kunt, Bhalchandra Gajanan, ed. *Goa Freedom Struggle vis-à-vis Maharashtra 1946–1960*. Bombay: Gazetteers Department, 1978.

Legislação do Estado da Índia, 1900–1961. (Not published from 1936 to 1945).

Portugal, Ministério das Colónias. *Reforma Administrativa Ultramarina, Decreto Lei. no.23.229 dated November 15, 1933*. Nova Goa: Imprensa Nacional, 1934.

Portugal, Ministério dos Negócios Estrangeiros. *Vinte Anos de Defesa do Estado Português da India (1947–1967)*. Lisboa: 1967.

Recenseamento Geral da População da Índia Portuguesa de 1900, 1910, 1940, 1950 and 1960. Goa: Imprensa Nacional.

Ribeiro, Orlando. *Goa em 1956: Relatório ao Governo*. Lisboa: Comissão Nacional dos Descobrimentos, 1999. *Tratado Anglo-Portugues de 26 de Dezembro de 1878*.

Xavier, Filipe Neri. *Collecção de Bandos, e outras Diferentes Providências que Servem de Leis Regulamentares para o Governo Económico, e Judicial das Provincías Denominadas das Novas Conquistas, Precedida da Noção da sua Conquista, e da Divisão de cada huma dellas*, vol. 1. Nova Goa: Imprensa Nacional, 1851.

Xavier, Filipe Neri. *Leis Peculiares das Communidades Agricólas das Ilhas, Salcete e Bardez*. Nova Goa: Imprensa Nacional, 1852–5.

Journals and Periodicals

Amcho Gao, 1929–33.

(O) Amigo do Povo, 1916–17.

(O) Amigo dos Operários, 1938–40.

(O) Anglo-Lusitano, 1925–35.

(O) Aryano, 1908–15.

Ave Maria, 1934–75.

Ave Maria (Weekly), 1929–51.

Bardesano, 1904–6.

Bharat, 1912–49.

Boletim da Sociedade de Geografia de Lisboa, 1938.

Boletim do Comércio, 1922.

Boletim do Instituto Meneses Bragança, 1963–96.

Boletim do Instituto Vasco da Gama, 1926–61.

Boletim Eclesiástico da Arquidiocese de Goa, 1942–50.

Boletim Informativo da Junta de Comércio Externo, 1961.

Bombaense, 1901–7.

Colloquium, 1978–9.

(O) Comércio, 1909–12.
(A) Convicção, 1900–12.
Correio de Bardez, 1929–47.
Correio de Bicholim, 1931–2.
(O) Debate, 1912–19.
Diário da Noite, 1919–61.
Diário da Tarde, 1925–33.
Diário de Goa, 1953–64.
Dudhsagar, 1955–60.
Echo da India, 1905–7.
Época (A), 1924–9.
Era Nova (A), 1900–03.
Estado da India, 1924–33.
Free Goa, 1953–61.
(O) Futuro, 1910–15.
(*O*) *Gabinete Literário das Fontaínhas*, 1846–52.
Garcia de Orta 1956, 1957.
(The) Goa Mail, 1929–36.
Goa Times, 1933.
Goa Today, 1966–2020.
Goan Tribune, 1956–62.
(O) Goano, 1908–10.
Goenchim Jasmin Fhulam, 1948–52.
Govapuri, 1998–2000.
(O) Heraldo, 1900–2016.
Heraldo, 1908–62.
Heraldo (Sup. Mensal), 1921–31.
Heraldo (English), 1956.
(O) Hindu, 1924–30.
(O) Ideal, 1933.
(O) Independente, 1933–7
India Portuguesa, 1926–30.
(The) Indo-Portuguese Review, 1919–33.
(O) Jornal, 1920–1.
Jornal da India, 1933–42.
Jornal das Colonias, 1927–31.
Jornal das Comunidades, 1933–5.
Jornal do Comercio, 1930–1.
Jornal do Povo, 1914–18.
Konkani Daily News Bulletin, 1946.
(A) Luta, 1935.
(A) Luz, 1900–16.
Luz do Oriente (Prachi Prabha), 1921–6.
Mascote, 1933–7.
(O) Nacionalista, 1904–10.

The Navhind Times, 1963–2016
(O) Oriente, 1905–49.
(O) Oriente Português, 1904–20 and 1931–41.
(O) Paiz, 1926–7.
(A) Patria, 1901–28.
(O) Pigmeu, 1910.
Porjecho Adar, 1930–58.
Portugal e Colónias, 1931–8.
(O) Povo, 1902–12.
Pracasha, 1928–31.
Prachi-Prabha, Luz de Oriente, 1912–26.
(O) Progresso, 1917–19.
Purabhilekh-Puratatva, 1983–2010, 2020.
(A) Reforma. Revista Mensal. Orgão da Liga Economico-Social, 1932–42.
(O)Tempo, 1931–44.
(A) Terra, 1917–35.
(The) Times of India, (Goa edition) 2007–16.
Tribuna, 1920–6.
(O) Ultramar, 1900–41.
(A) Vanguarda, 1955–8.
Vauradeancho Ixtt, 1935–58.
(A) Verdade, 1923–6.
(A) Vida, 1938–67.
(A) Voz da India, 1946–50.
(A) Voz de S. Francisco Xavier, 1931–42.

Secondary Sources

Achaya, Konganda Thammu. *A Historical Dictionary of Indian Food*. New Delhi: Oxford University Press, 2002.

Achaya, Konganda Thammu. *Indian Food: A Historical Companion*. New Delhi: Oxford University Press, 1998.

"Adoradores de Baco." *O Heraldo*. August 26, 1942, 1.

Afonso, Francisco Correia. "O Alcoolismo na India Portuguesa—Relatório." In *Sétimo Congresso Provincial da India Portuguesa*, edited by Balcrisna Datarama Sinai Sacardandó, 1–60. Nova Goa: Tip. Bragança, 1927.

Afonso, João Joaquim Roque Correia "O Saneameto rural da India Portuguesa na sua relação com a organisação administrativa." In Serviço de Saúde da Índia Portuguesa, *I Conferência Sanitária. Em Comemoração do 72o Aniversário da Escola Médico-Cirúrgica de Nova Goa. (1-12-1914 a 6-12-1914)*, 332–40. Nova Goa: Imprensa Nacional, 1914.

Afonso, J. Estevam. "Cancro Social." *O Heraldo*, August 26, 1942.

Agriculture Officers' Association. Important Crops of Goa. Panaji: Agriculture Officers' Association, 1990.

Albuquerque, Braz, ed. *Commentários do Grande Afonso d'Albuquerque*. Lisboa: Imprensa Nacional, 1921–6.

Albuquerque, Condorceth J. R. de.*Questão Caranzalem*. Nova Goa: Tip. Colonial, 1911.

Albuquerque, Teresa. *Santa Cruz Calapor: Profile of a Village in Goa*. Goa: Fernandes Publication, 1989.

Alexandrowicz, Charles Henry,"Treaty of Succession of the French Establishments of Pondicherry, Karikal, Mahe and Yanam," *Indian Yearbook of International Affairs* V (1956): 175–88.

Ali, B. Sheik, ed. *Goa Wins Freedom, Reflections and Reminiscences*. Bambolim: Goa University, 1986.

Almeida, José C. *Alguns Aspectos Demográficos de Goa, Damão e Dio*. Panaji: Government Printing Press, 1965.

Almeida, José C. *Aspectos da Actividade Agrícola em Goa, Damão e Dio*, 2 vol. Panaji: Government Printing Press, 1967.

Almeida, José C. *Aspects of the Agricultural Activity in Goa, Daman and Diu*. Panaji: Government Printing Press, 1965.

Almeida, José C. *Goa Administration and Economy before and after 1962*. Panaji: Civitas and Broadway, 2013.

Almeida, Miguel de. *Jardim dos Pastores*. Rachol Seminary, 1658.

Almerico, Gina M. "Food and Identity: Food Studies, Cultural, and Personal Identity." *Journal of International Business and Cultural Studies* 8 (June 2014): 1–7.

Altekar, Anant Sadashiv. *A History of Village Communities in Western India*. Madras: Oxford University Press, 1927.

Alvares, Antonio Francisco Xavier. *Mandioca: O Valor do Producto da sua Cultura Superior ao de todas outras Plantas Frutiferas*. Bastora: Tip. Rangel, 1917.

Alvares, Claude, and Vidyadhar Gadgil, eds. *Fish Curry and Rice: A Source Book on Goa, Its Ecology and Life-Style*. Mapusa: Goa Foundation, 2002.

The American Heritage Dictionary of English Language. Boston, MA: Houghton Mifflin, 1996.

Angle, Prabhakar S. *Goa: Concepts and Misconcepts*. Bombay: The Goa Hindu Association, 1994.

Angle, Prabhakar S. *Goa: An Economic Review*. Bombay: The Goa Hindu Association, 1983.

Antunes, José Freire. *Kennedy e Salazar: O Leão e a Raposa*. Lisboa: Difusão Cultural, 1991.

Appadurai, Arjun. "Gastro-Politics in Hindu South Asia." *American Ethnologist* 8, no. 3 (1981): 494–511.

Appadurai, Arjun. "How to Make a National Cuisine: Cookbooks in Contemporary India." *Journal of the Society for the Comparative Study of Society and History* 30, no. 1 (1988): 3–24.

Appadurai, Arjun. *Modernity at Large: Cultural Dimensions of Globalization*. Minneapolis, MN: University of Minnesota, 1996.

Arte Palmarica, Escrita por um Padre de Companhia de Jesus. Nova Goa: Imprensa Nacional, 1918.

Avelar, Pedro. *História de Goa: de Afonso de Albuquerque a Vassalo e Silva*. Portugal: Texto Editores, 2012.

Axelrod, Paul, and Michelle A. Fuerch. "Flight of the Deities: Hindu Resistance in Portuguese Goa." *Modern Asian Studies* 30, no. 2 (1996): 387–421.

Axelrod, Paul, and Michelle A. Fuerch. "Living on the Edge: The Village and the State on the Goa-Maratha Frontier." *Indian Economic Social History Review* 45, no. 4 (2008): 553–80.

Axelrod, Paul, and Michelle A. Fuerch. "Portuguese Orientalism and the Making of the Village Communities of Goa." *Ethnohistory* 45, no. 3 (1998): 439–76.

Ayalla, Frederico Diniz. *Goa Antiga e Moderna*. Nova Goa: Livraria Coelho, 1927.

Azevedo, Antonio E d'Almeida. *As Comunidades de Goa: História das Instituições Antigas*. Lisboa: Viúva Bertrand e Successores Carvalho, 1890.

Azevedo, Cândido do Carmo. *Goa, Damão e Diu. Factos, Comunidade e Lazer nos Meados do Século XX*. Macau: Instituto Cultural de Macau, 1998.

Azevedo, Carmo de. "Glimpses of the Past: The Communidades." *Goa To-day*, March 1969, 8.

Azevedo, Carmo de. "Santana Church of Talaulim." *Purabhilekh-Puratatva* 4, no. 1 (January–June 1986): 61–70.

Baden-Powel, Baden Henry. *The Indian Village Community*. London: Longmans, Green, and Co., 1896.

Baden-Powel, Baden Henry. *The Land System of British India: Being a Manual of the Land-Tenures and of the Systems of Land-Revenue Administration Prevalent in the Several Provinces*. Delhi: Oxford Clarendon Press, 1974.

Baden-Powel, Baden Henry. *The Origin and Growth of Village Community in India*. London: Swan Sonnenschein; New York: Charles Scribner's Sons, 1899.

Baden-Powel, Baden Henry. "The Villages of Goa in the Early Sixteenth Century." *The Journal of the Royal Asiatic Society*, 32, no. 2 (April 1900): 261–91.

Bal, Mieke. "Food, Form, and Visibility: Glub and the Aesthetics of Everyday Life." *Postcolonial Studies* 8, no. 1 (2005): 51–73.

Bandyopadhyaya, Jayantanuja. *The Making of India's Foreign Policy*. New Delhi: Allied, 1980.

Barber, James. "Economic Sanctions as a Policy Instrument." *International Affairs* 55, no. 3 (1979): 367–84.

Barbosa, Talita Prado. "Antropologia e Gastronomia: a Identidade de ser Brasileiro a partir da Alimentação." *Sociological Review* 42, no. 4 (June 2008): 664–85.

Barreto, Adeodato. *Civilização Hindu seguido de O Livro da Vida (Cánticos Indianos)*. Lisboa: Hugin Editores, 2000.

Barreto, Adeodato. "Natal Cristão." In *O Livro da Vida: Canticos Indianos*, 48. Nova Goa: Edições "SWATVA," 1940.

Barros, Joseph. "Glimpses of Portuguese Colonialism in Goa." In *Goa Wins Freedom: Reflections and Reminiscence*, edited by B. Sheik Ali, 73–7. Goa: Goa University, 1989.

Barthes, Roland. "Toward a Psychosociology of Contemporary Food Consumption." In *Food and Culture: A Reader*, edited by Carole Counihan and Penny Van Esterik, 20–7. New York and London: Routledge, 1997.

Basham, Arthur Llewellyn. *The Wonder That Was India*. London: Sidgwick & Jackson, 1954.

Bastos, Matins. *Tempo de Falar: Diário da Invasão de Goa*. n.p: author, 1962.

Battaglia, Debbora. *On the Bones of the Serpent: Person, Memory, and Mortality in Sabarl Island Society*. Chicago, IL: University of Chicago Press, 1990.

Bègue, Sandrine. *La Fin de Goa et de l'Estado da Índia: Décolonisation et Guerre Froide dans le Sous-Continent Indien (1945–1962)*. Portugal: Ministério dos Negócios Estrangeiros, 2007.

Bhandari, Romesh. *Goa*. Varanasi: Lotus Collection, Roli Books, 1999.

Bhattacharya, Brindavan C. *Indian Images, the Brahmanic Iconography Based on Genetic, Comparative and Synthetic Principles*. New Delhi: Cosmo Publications, 1978.

Bhonsle, Shilpa J., and Sellappan Krishnan. *Rices of Goa and Their Given Quality*. Goa: Goa University, 2012.

Boman-Behram, Boman Kavasji. *Goa and Ourselves*. Bombay: New Book Company, 1955.

Borcar, Bascora M. S. "Campanha Contra o Alcoolismo." In *Sétimo Congresso Provincial da India Portuguesa*, edited by Balcrisna Datarama Sinai Sacardandó, 1–8. Goa: Tip. Bragança, 1927.

Bossa, José. *Estado da Índia*. Lisboa: Agencia Geral do Ultramar, 1965.

Boyce, Charlotte, and Joan Fitzpatrick. *A History of Food in Literature: From the Fourteenth Century to the Present*. London: Routledge, 2017.

Braga, Duarte Drumond, ed. *O País de Súria: Obra Reunida do Paulino Dias*. São Paulo: Alameda, 2020.

Braga, Isabel M. R. Mendes Drumond. *Portugal a Mesa—Alimentação, Etiqueta e Sociabilidade, 1800–1820*. Lisboa: Hugin Editores, 2000.

Bragança, Berta Menezes. *Landmarks in My Time: Selected Writings*. Margao: Author, 1992.

Bragança, Berta Menezes. *Tales from Goa*. Bastora: Tipografia Rangel, 1991.

Bragança, Luis de Menezes. *Prosas Dispersas—Politica, Administração, Ensino*. Panjim: Comissão de Homenagem, 1965.

Brass, Paul R. *The Politics of India since Independence*. Cambridge: Cambridge University Press, 1990.

Brito, Raquel Soeiro de. *Goa e as Praçās do Norte*. Lisboa: Junta de Investigações do Ultramar, 1966.

Brito, Raquel Soeiro de. "Notas para o Estudo dos Modos de Vida em Goa." *Garcia de Orta*, Special number on India Portuguesa (1956): 183–202.
Brito, Raquel Soeiro de. "Notícia do Inquérito das Aldeias de Goa." *Garcia de Orta* 5, no. 4 (1957): 659–69.
Brito, Raquel Soeiro de. "A Terra e a Gente na Índia Portuguesa." *Colóquio sobre Problemas Humanos nas Regões Tropicais*. Lisboa: Junta de Investigações do Ultramar, 1961.
Caetano, Marcelo. *Minhas Memórias de Salazar*. Lisboa: Verbo, 1977.
Campos, Joaquim Inacio. *Goenchem Xetcamotponn [Agricultura de Goa] ani Gorjêchi Xicounn Xetcamteam, Gauncaranc, Bhattcaranc ani Zomin Vossoinnaranc*. Bastora: Tipografia Rangel, 1931.
Castelino, Cyria C. Philalete. *Almanach Indo-portuguez para o Anno de 1886*. Nova Goa: Imprensa Nacional, 1885.
Castro, Augusto Emilia de. *Preparados Práticos da Cosinha*, 1st ed. Margão: 1909.
Catão, Francisco Xavier Gomes. Gomes. *Anuário da Arquidiocese de Goa e Damão*. Bastorá: Tipografia Rangel, 1955.
Chrisafis, Angelique. *Paris and agencies@achrisafis*. October 19, 2015.
Collingham, Lizzie. *Curry—A Tale of the Cooks and Conquerors*. London: Vintage Books, 2006.
Confêrencia Económica do Império Colonial. Delegação da India Portuguesa. *Propostas*. Nova Goa: Imprensa Nacional, 1936.
Congleton, Adam. R., Niels Peter Nielsen, Dorthe Berntsen. "Through the Gateway of the Senses: Investigating the Influence of Sensory Modality-Specific Retrieval Cues on Involuntary Episodic Memory." *Psychological Research*. (March 2, 2020). doi: 10.1007/s00426-020-01304-5. Epub ahead of print. PMID: 32124005.
Correia, Carlota Mesquita. *Livro da Cozinha Goesa*. Margão: Tipografia Progresso, 1963.
Correia-Afonso, Pedro. "A Cor Local na Obra de Orlando da Costa." 1961. http://archiveofgoanwritinginportuguese.blogspot.in.
Costa, Adelyna da. *Social Change in Goa*. Panjim: W. D'Costa, (n.d).
Costa, Aleixo Manuel da. *Dicionário de Literatura Goesa*. Macau: Instituto Cultural de Macau e Fundação Oriente, 1997.
Costa, Constancio Roque da. *O Tratado Anglo-Portuguez de 26 de Dezembro de 1878. O Sr. João de Andrade Corvo e os Povos da India Portugueza seguido da tradução do Bombay Akbary Act 1878*. Margão: Ultramar, 1879.
Costa, Cosme da. "Khajans I & II." *Herald*, July 1 and 2, 1993, 4.
Costa, Cosme da. "Konkan Railway Controversy I & II." *Herald*, June 24 and 25, 1993, 4.
Costa, Francisco João da (GIP). "Jacob e Carapinho." In *Lengthening Shadows: An Anthology of Goan Short Stories*. Translated by Paul Melo e Castro, 83–6. Saligao: Goa 1556, 2016.

Costa, Francisco João da (GIP). *Jacob e Dulce (Scenas da Vida Indiana)*, 3rd ed, edited by Jeremias Xavier de Carvalho. Panjim: Tipografia Sadananda, 1974.

Costa, João António Jacinto da. *A History of Goa*. Mapusa: Author, 1982.

Costa, Murelle da. "History of Trade and Commerce in Goa: 1878–1961." PhD diss., University of Goa, 1999.

Costa, Orlando da. *The Sign of Wrath*. Translated by D. A. Smith. Saligao: Goa 1556, 2017.

Costa, Orlando da. *O Signo da Ira*. Lisboa: Temas da Actualidade, 1996.

Costa, Pedro da. "Alvitres e Sugestões." *O Heraldo*, August 26, 1942.

Costa, Pedro Joaquim Peregrino da. *A Expansão de Goês pelo Mundo*. Goa: Tipografia Sadananda, 1956.

Costa, Roberto Bruto da. *Valorização do Porto de Mormugão*. Nova Goa: Tipografia do Heraldo, 1927.

Cotta, Franz Schubert A. de Miranda. "A Ladainha em Goa: Uma Prática em Transformação." M.A. diss., University of Goa, 2018.

Counihan, Carole, and Penny Van Esterik, eds. *Food and Culture: A Reader*, 3rd ed. New York: Routledge, 2013.

Couto, Maria Aurora. *Goa: A Daughter's Story*. New Delhi: Penguin, 2004.

Couto, Maria Aurora. "Literature and History." In *Metahistory: History Questioning History: Festschrift in Honour of Teotónio R. de Souza*, edited by Charles Borges and Michael Naylor Pearson, 175–84. Lisboa: Vega, 2007.

Cunha, Antonio Maria da. *Congresso Provincial da Índia Portuguesa (Primeiro)*. Nova Goa: Imprensa Nacional, 1916.

Cunha, Antonio Maria da. *Congresso Provincial da Índia Portuguesa: Subsidios para sua História*. Nova Goa: Casa Luso-Francesa, 1924–33.

Cunha, Tristão Bragança. *Goa's Freedom Struggle (Select Writings of T. B. Cunha)*. Bombay: Dr. T. B. Cunha Memorial Committee, 1961.

Cunha, Tristão Bragança. "The Rice Problem (1936)." In *Goa's Freedom Struggle (Select Writings of T. B. Cunha)*, 121–8. Bombay: Dr. T. B. Cunha Memorial Committee, 1961.

D'Costa, Anthony. *The Christianisation of the Goa Islands 1510–1567*. Bombay: Heras Institute, St. Xavier's College, 1965.

D'Souza, Bento Graciano. *Goan Society in Transition: A Study in Social Change*. Bombay: Popular Prakashan, 1975.

D'Sylva, Andrea, and Brenda L. Beagan. "'Food Is Culture, but It's Also Power': The Role of Food in Ethnic and Gender Identity Construction among Goan Canadian Women." *Journal of Gender Studies* 20, no. 3 (September 2011): 279–89.

Dalgado, Sebastião Rodolfo. *Dicionário Português-Concani*. New Delhi: Asian Educational Services, 1988.

Dalgado, Sebastião Rodolfo. *Glossário Luso-Asiático*. New Delhi: Asian Educational Services, 1988.

Damodar R. Sardesai and Anand Mohan eds. *Legacy of Nehru: A Centennial Assessment*. New Delhi: Promilla, 1992.
Deora, Mohan Singh, ed. *Liberation of Goa, Daman and Diu from Portuguese Rule (Now a Territory of The Indian Union)*. New Delhi: Discovery Publishing House, 1995.
Desai, Nishtha. *Liberation vs Armed Aggression: The Media Response to Goa's Liberation*. Goa: Government of Goa, Directorate of Art and Culture, 2011.
Desai, Suresh S. "An Ethnological Study of Goan Society." In *Goa: Cultural Trends (Seminar Papers)*, edited by Prakashchandra Pandurang Shirodkar, 34–45. Panaji: Government of Goa, Directorate of Archives, Archaeology and Museum, 1988.
"Desejos de Um Bêbado" (Poem) (Anonymous). *Tirocinio Litterário*, no. 11, (April 1862): 86–7.
Devi, Vimala. *Monção*. Lisboa: Dédalo, 1963.
Devi, Vimala, and Manuel de Seabra. *A Literatura Indo-portuguesa*. Lisboa: Junta de Investigações do Ultramar, 1971.
Dhume, Anant Ramkrishna Sinai. *The Cultural History of Goa from 10,000 B.C–1352 A.D.* Panaji: R. A. S. Dhume, 1985.
Dias, Filinto Cristo. *Esboço da História da Literatura Indo-Portuguesa*. Bastorá: Tipografia Rangel, 1963.
Dias, Remy. "Consumption History of the Estado da India: 1850–1950." In *Towards a History of Consumption in South Asia*, edited by Douglas E. Haynes et al., 76–107. New Delhi: Oxford University Press, 2010.
Dias, Remy. "The Socio-economic History of Goa with Special Reference to the Communidade System: 1750–1910." PhD diss., University of Goa, 2004.
Dias, Remy. "Some Aspects of the Consumption History of Estado da India: 1900–50." In *Goa in the 20th Century History and Culture*, edited by Pius Malekandathil and Remy Dias, 72–121. Panaji: Institute Menezes Braganza, 2008.
Dicionário de História dos Descobrimentos Portugueses. Lisboa: Circulo de Leitores, 1994.
Doshi, Saryu, ed. *Goa: Cultural Encounter*. Bombay: Marg Publication, 1984.
Enciclopédia Luso-Brasileira. Vol. 2. Lisboa: Editorial Enciclopédia Limitada, n.d.
Estatutos da Associação Denominada Kazan. Nova Goa: 1870.
Esteves, Sarto. *Goa and Its Future*. Bombay: Manaktalas, 1966.
Esteves, Sarto, and Souza, Vatsala de. *This Is Goa*. Bombay: Source Publishers, 1983.
Faísca, Carlos Manuel, Dulce Freire, and Cláudia M. Viana. "The State and Natural Resources: 250 Years of Rice Production in Portugal, 18th–21st Centuries." *Ler História* 79 (2021): 241–62.
Fernandes, Agostinho. *Batcara*—Part I. Bombay: L. M. Furtado and Sons, 1909.

Fernandes, Agostinho. *Batcara*—Part II. Bombay: Victoria P. Works, 1916.

Fernandes, André Rafael. *When the Curtains Rise ... Understanding Goa's Vibrant Konkani Theatre*. Panaji: Goa 1556, 2010.

Fernandes, Avertano Correia. "Emigração Indo-Portuguesa." *Boletim da Sociedade de Geografia de Lisboa* 56, no. 7–8 (1938): 1–32.

Fernandes, Avertano Correia. "A Renovação Económica da Índia Portuguesa." *Boletim do Instituto Vasco da Gama*, no. 45 (1940): 1–37.

Fernandes, Constancio Patricio. *Gancarias de Goa: Hoje Chamadas Communidades Agricolas*. Margao, 1932.

Fernandes, Francis Ernesto Xavier. *India Portugueza: Estudos Economico-Sociaes*. Bastorá: Tipografia Rangel, 1906.

Fernandes, Jaime. *In Quest of Freedom*. New Delhi: Concept Publishing Company, 1990.

Fernandes, Jason Keith. "Invoking the Ghost of Mexia: State and Community in Post-Colonial Goa," *Ler História* 58 (May 1, 2010): 9–25.

Fernandes, Jesse. *Toddy Tapper and His Goa*. Quepem: Mannik Publications, 2012.

Fernandes, Maria Lucinda Fernandes Costa. "Os «Encontros dos Goeses da Beira e seus Amigos» na Grande Lisboa. Património Identitário e sua Reconstrução Cultural Pós-Colonial." Mestrado em Património Histórico, diss., Universidade Nova de Lisboa, 2010.

Fernandes, Pantaleão. *Goa Rare Portraits*. Goa: Author, 2018.

Fernandes, Pantaleão. "Nerul's Traditional Tisreanche Fest." *The Times of India*, May 16, 2013.

Fernandes, Pantaleão. *Traditional Occupations of Goa*, edited by Isabel Santa Rita Vás. Benaulim: The Word Publications, 2015.

Fernandichém, São Francisco. *Pustoc Randitoleac*. Margao: Tip. Nacional, 1926.

Ferrão, Jose E. Mendes. *The Adventure of Plants and the Portuguese Discoveries*. Lisbon: Institute of Tropical Scientific Research, 1994.

Ferrão, Jose Joaquim J. De Brito. "Arrendamento nos campos comunais." In *Congresso Provincial da Índia Portuguesa* (*Primeiro*), edited by Antonio Maria da Cunha, 23–6. Nova Goa: Imprensa Nacional, 1916.

Figueira, Maria Inês, and Oscar de Noronha. *Episódio Oriental: Readings in Indo-Portuguese Literature*. Panjim: Fundação Oriente & Third Millenium, 2007.

Fleet, James Fergusson. "The Village Communidades of Goa." *Goan Tribune*, October 6, 1957, 7.

Foley, Wendy. "Tradition and Change in Urban Indigenous Food Practices." *Postcolonial Studies* 8, no. 1 (2005): 25–44.

Fonseca, Jose Nicolau da. *An Historical and Archaeological Sketch of the City of Goa: Preceded by a Short Statistical Account of the Territory of Goa*. New Delhi: Asian Educational Services, 1994.

Fragoso, Jose Joaquim. *Technica de Lavra de Sura do Coqueiro e outras Industrias Dependentes*. Nova Goa: Imprensa Nacional, 1909.

Frenz, Margret. *Community, Memory, and Migration in a Globalizing World: The Goan Experience, c.1890–1980*. New Delhi: Oxford University Press, 2014.

Furtado, António. "As Comunidades no Passado, no Presente e no Futuro. (Conferência)." *Boletim do Instituto Vasco da Gama*, no. 59 (1944): 1–62.

Furtado, A. D. *Goa Yesterday, Today and Tomorrow an Approach to Various Socio-economic and Political Issues in Goan Life and Re-interpretation of Historical Facts*. Goa: Furtado's Enterprise, 1981.

Gaitonde, Pundalik D. *The Liberation of Goa: A Participant's View of History*. Panaji: Rajhauns Sankalpana, 2016.

Gandhi, Mohandas Karamchand. *Christian Missions: Their Place in India*. Ahmedabad: Navjivan Publishing House, 1941.

Gandhi, Mohandas Karamchand. *The Collected Works of Mahatma* Gandhi, vol. 20. New Delhi: Publications Division Ministry of Information and Broadcasting, 1958.

Gandhi, Mohandas Karamchand. *Goan Struggle for Freedom*. Ahmedabad: Navajivan Publishing House, 1954.

Garmes, Helder. "Colonialismo e Conflito Cultural em *O Signo da Ira* de Orlando da Costa." In *Goa Portuguesa e Pós-colonial: Literatura, Cultura e Sociedade*. Organized by Everton Machado, Duarte Braga, 95–106. V. N. Famalicão: Húmus, 2012.

Garmes, Helder, ed. "Dossiê: Goa—Literatura e Cultura." *Via Atlântida* 12, no. 19 (2011). São Paulo: USP—Universidade de São Paulo, 2011.

Garmes, Helder. "A Poesia nas Histórias da Literatura Goesa de Língua Portuguesa." *Navegações*, Porto Alegre 9, no. 2 (July–December 2016): 136–43.

Gecser, Ottó. "Some Like It Hot: Piquant Taste between the Middle Ages and Modern Times." In *My Favorite Things: Object Preferences in Medieval and Early Modern Material Culture,* edited by Gerhard Jaritz and Ingrid Matschinegg, 87–102. Münster, Vienna, and Zurich: LIT, 2019.

Geertz, Clifford. *The Interpretation of Cultures: Selected Essays*. New York: Basic Books, 1973.

George, Evágrio. *Goa's Awakening*. Pangim: Prafulla Press, (n.d.).

George, Evágrio. *The Goa Case*. Goa: National Campaign Committee, 1961.

George, Evágrio. *Salazar's Rule in Goa and the Goa Case*. Delhi: E. F. George, 1959.

Gizbug, Lidiya. *Blockade Diary*. Translated by Alan Myers. Manhattan: Harvill Press, 1995.

Goa. Goan Point of View. London: The Goa League, 1956.

"Goan Catholics Are not Anti-national." *Herald*, February 2, 1987, 2.

The Goan Overseas Association (GOA). Newsletter. Vancouver, 2017.

Goldstein, Darra. "Talking Food History." *Gastronomica* 2, no. 1 (Winter 2002): iii–iv. University of California Press Stable URL: http://www.jstor.org/stable/10.1525/gfc.2002.2.1.3.

Gomes, Ermelinda Stuart. "A Repressão do Alcoolismo." In *Sétimo Congresso Provincial da India Portuguesa*, edited by Balcrisna Datarama Sinai Sacardandó, 1–6. Nova Goa: Tipografia Bragança, 1927.

Gomes, Francisco Luís. *A Liberdade da Terra e a Economia Rural da Índia Portugueza*. Lisboa: Typografia Universal, 1862.

Gomes, João Filipe Olivinho. "The Economic Blockade of Goa—Implication and Consequences." *Boletim do Instituto Menezes Bragança*, no. 159 (1989): 69–95.

Gomes, João Filipe Olivinho. *The Goan Village Communes*. Panaji: Vasantrao Dempo Education & Research Foundation, 2006.

Gomes, João Filipe Olivinho. *The Religious Orders in Goa (XVIth-XVIIth Centuries)*. Chandor: Konkani Sorospot Prakashan, 2003.

Gomes, João Filipe Olivinho. *Village Goa (A Study of Goan Social Structure and Change)*. New Delhi: S. Chand, 1987.

Gomes, Jesus. "Problema de Arroz." *Heraldo*, August 2, 1938, 1.

Gonçalves, Caetano. *O Estado da Índia: Passado e Presente*. Lisboa: Sociedade de Geografia de Lisboa, 1947.

Gonsalves, Jeanette. "Food and Foodways in Transition (A Socio-cultural Study of Domestic Dining in Goa)." PhD diss., Goa University, 2007.

Gough, Kathleen Eleanor. *Rural Society in Southeast India*. Cambridge: Cambridge University Press, 1981.

Government of Goa, Daman and Diu. *Rice in Goa: High Yielding Way*. Panaji: Directorate of Agriculture, 1978.

Gracias, Caetano F. Xavier. *Catálogo Descriptivo dos Produtos Economico-industriais da Flora da Índia Portuguesa*. Lisboa: Tip. Literária, 1922.

Gracias, Fatima da Silva. *Cozinha de Goa—A Glossary on Food*. Panjim: Broadway Publishing House, 2019.

Gracias, Fatima da Silva. *Cozinha de Goa: History and Tradition of Goan Food*. Panjim: 1556 and Broadway, 2011.

Gracias, Fatima da Silva. *Health and Hygiene in Colonial Goa (1510–1961)*. New Delhi: Concept Publishing Company, 1994.

Gracias, Fatima da Silva. "Into the Melting Pot." *Marg—A Magazine of the Arts* 64, no. 2 (December 2012): 88–93.

Gracias, Fátima da Silva. *Kaleidoscope of Women in Goa: 1510–1961*. New Delhi: Concept Publishing Company, 1996.

Gracias, Fatima da Silva. "Merendas: Teatimes Delights in Goa." In *India, the Portuguese and Maritime Interactions: Religion, Language and Cultural Expressions*, edited by Pius Malekandathil, Lotika Varadarajan, and Amar Farooqui, 467–80. New Delhi: Primus Books, 2019.

Gracias, João Baptista Amâncio. *História Económico-Financeira da India Portuguesa (1910–1947)*. Lisboa: Agência Geral das Colónias, Divisão de Publicações e Biblioteca, 1950.

Gracias, João Baptista Amâncio. *Portugal na Índia*. Nova Goa: Edição da Repartição de Estatística e Informação, Instituto Vasco da Gama, 1946.

Gracias, João Baptista Amâncio. *Subsidios para a História Economico-Financeira da Índia Portuguesa*. Nova Goa: Imprensa Nacional, 1909.

Halligan, Marion. *The Taste of Memory*. Australia: Allen & Unwin, 2004.

Halloran, Vivian Nun. "Recipes as Memory Work: Slave Food, Culture." *Theory and Critique* 53, no. 2 (2012): 147–61.

Haynes, Douglas E. Abigail Mcgowan, Tirthankar Roy and Haruka Yanagisawa, ed. *Towards a History of Consumption in South Asia*. New Delhi: Oxford University Press, 2010.

Henn, Alexander. "The Becoming of Goa: Space and Culture in the Emergence of a Multicultural Lifeworld." Lusotopie 7, no. 1 (2000): 333–9.

Henn, Alexander. *Hindu-Catholic Encounters in Goa: Religion, Colonialism, and Modernity*. Indiana: Indiana University Press, 2014.

Heredia, Irene. "Liberating Goa: The Laudable Role of the Goa Liberation Council in Securing Goa's Liberation." *Goa Today*, June 2005, 40–2.

Herz, Rachel S. "A Naturalistic Analysis of Autobiographical Memories Triggered by Olfactory, Visual and Auditory Stimuli." *Chem Senses* 29, no. 3 (March 2004): 217–24.

Holtzman, Jon D. "Food and Memory." *Annual Review of Anthropology* 35 (2006): 361–78.

Iancu, Anca-Luminita, and Alexandra Mitrea, eds. *Food Cultures across Time: Flavours and Endeavour*. Newcastle: Cambridge Scholars Publishing, 2021.

Ibrahim, Faizul H. "Kitchen Anthropology: Understanding Food, Cooking and Eating in Bruneian Middle-Class Families." *Institute of Asian Studies*, Universiti Brunei Darussalam, Gadong, Working Paper no. 38 (2018): 1–28.

A Índia Portuguesa. Nova Goa: Imprensa Nacional, 1923.

Índia Portuguesa, Serviço de Saúde. *I Conferência Sanitária: Em Comemoração do 72º Aniversário da Escola Médico-Cirúrgica de Nova Goa. (1-12-1914 a 6-12-1914)*, vol. 2. Nova Goa: Imprensa Nacional, 1914.

Isalita. *Doces e Cozinhados—Receitas Escolhidas por Isalita*. Lisboa: Livraria Bertrand, 1935.

Kakodkar, Archana. "Shuddhi: Reconversion to Hinduism Movement in Goa." In *Goa: Cultural Trends* (Seminar Papers), edited by Prakashchandra Pandurang Shirodkar, 242–62. Panaji: Directorate of Archives, Archaeology and Museum, 1988.

Kamat, Pratima. *Farar Far (Crossfire): Local Resistance to Colonial Hegemony, 1510–1912*. Panaji: Institute Menezes Braganza, 1999.

Karapurkar, Heman Yeshwant. "Agricultural Scenario in Goa." *Boletim do Instituto Menezes Bragança*, no. 176 (1996): 150–5.

Kelekar, Ravindra. *Panthasth: Memories of Goa's Freedom Struggle*. Panjim: Rajhauns, 2000.

Kerkar, Rajendra. "Goa's Lost Knowledge of Water Management." *Times of India*, February 17, 2019.

Kerkar, Rajendra. *Natural Heritage of Goa*. Panaji: Broadway, 2016.

Khedekar, Vinayak Vishnu. *Eco-culture Goa Paradigm*. Panjim: Broadway Publishing House, 2013.

Klein, Jacob A., and James L. Watson, eds. *The Handbook of Food and Anthropology*. London: Bloomsbury, 2016.

Klougen, Denis Cottineau de. *An Historical Sketch of Goa*. New Delhi: Asian Educational Services, 1988.

Kosambi, Damodar Dharmanand. *Myth and Reality: Studies in the Formation of Indian Culture*. Bombay: Popular Prakashan, 1962.

Larsen, Karin. *Faces of Goa: A Journey through History and Cultural Revolution of Goa and Other Communities Influenced by the Portuguese*. New Delhi: Gyan Publication House, 1998.

Lawrence, Leo. *Nehru Seizes Goa*. New York: Pageant Press, 1963.

The Laws of Manu. Introduction, Notes and Translation by Wendy Doniger with Brian K. Smith. New Delhi: Penguin, 1992.

Lemos, Mário Matos e. "Goa, o Principio do fim do Império. Alguns Documentos." *Estudos do Século XX: colonialismo, anticolonialismo e identidades nacionais*, no. 3 (2003): 271–87. Coimbra.

Lévi-Strauss, Claude. *The Origin of Table Manners*. New York: Harper Collins Publishers, 1978.

Lévi-Strauss, Claude, "Le Triangle Culinaire." *L'Arc*, no. 26 (1965): 19–29.

Lima, Antonio Correia de. *O Fim dos Séculos: Goa, Damão e Diu*. Lisboa: Bertrand Editora, 1997.

Lima, Edward de. *Luis de Menezes Bragança—Goan Thinker and Visionary*. Panaji: Institute Menezes Braganza, 2010.

Limaye, Champa, ed. *Goa Liberation Movement and Madhu Limaye*. Delhi: B. R. Publishing Corporation, 1996.

Lobato, Alexandre. "Pequena História da Índia Portuguesa." *Ultramar, Revista da Comunidade Portuguesa e da Actualidade Ultramarina Internacional*, no. 7–8 (Janeiro–Junho 1962): 11–40.

Lobato, Alexandre. *Sobre a Índia Portuguesa, a sua Cultura e a sua História*. Lourenço Marques: Imprensa Nacional, 1973.

Lobato, Alexandre. "Sociologia Política da Expansão." *Revista de Gabinete de Estudos Ultramarinos*, no. 16 (1957): 1–13. Lisboa: Junta de Investigação do Ultramar.

Lobo, Amaro Pinto. *Memória Histórico Eclesiástica da Arquidiocese de Goa (1533–1933)*. Nova Goa: A Voz de S. Fransisco Xavier, 1933.

Lobo, Azarias Condorcet. "Abcari em Goa: Antes do tratado Anglo-Luso na Índia." In Segundo Congresso Provincial da Índia Portuguesa. Nova Goa: Casa Luso.

Lobo, Sandra Maria C. A. "O Desassossego Goes, Cultural e Política em Goa do Liberalismo ao Acto Colonial." PhD diss., Universidade Nova de Lisboa: 2014. run.unl.pt/bitstream/ … /Lobo.

Lobo, Urban. "The Destructive Course I and II." *Gomantak Times*, November 19–20, 1992, 4.

Lobo, Urban. "The Khajan Tragedy I and II." *Gomantak Times*, October 27–8, 1992, 4.
Lohia, Ram Manohar. *Action in Goa*. Bombay: August Publication House, 1947.
Lopes, António Martires. *Portugal na India*. Lourenço Marques: Imprensa Nacional de Moçambique, 1973.
Lopes, Maria de Jesus dos Martires. "Then Goan Society of the Second Half of XVIII Century Analysed by Catholic Texts of 'Pastoral Visits'." *Boletim do Instituto Menezes Bragança*, no. 169 (1993): 225–46.
Lopes, Maria de Jesus dos Martires. *Tradition and Modernity in Eighteenth Century Goa (1750–1800)*. New Delhi: Manohar, 2006.
Loyola, José Inacio de. "Batcares e Mundcares." *Portugal e Colónias*, June 26, 1937.
Lupton, Deborah. "Food, Memory and Meaning: The Symbolic and Social Nature of Food Events." *Sociological Review* 42, no. 4 (June 2008): 664–85.
Mace, John H. *Involuntary Memory*. New Jersey: Wiley-Blackwell, 2008.
MacPherson, Kenneth. "A Secret People of South Asia: The Origins, Evolution and Role of the Luso-Indian Goan Community from the Sixteenth to Twentieth Centuries." *Itinerário* II, no. 2 (1987): 72–86.
Mahajan, Malati. *A Cultural History of Maharashtra and Goa*. New Delhi: Sundeep Prakashan, 1989.
Malekandathil, Pius, and Remy Dias, eds. *Goa in the 20th Century History and Culture*. Panaji: Institute Menezes Braganza, 2008.
Malkarnekar, Gauree. "Forgotten Flavor of the Vatamba." *Times of India*, May 14, 2017, 2.
Maria, Emma. *Women in Portuguese Goa 1510–1835*. Tellicherry, Kerala: Institute for Research in Social Sciences and Humanities MESHAR, 2002.
Marini, Emili. *Goa Tal Como a Vi*. Lisboa: União Gráfica, 1956.
Martins, José Francisco. *In Search of Self-Fulfilment*. Panaji: Rajhauns Vitaran, 1997.
Martins, Luis Filippe d'Almeida. *Recreio Economico Contendo Variados Preparativos de Doces e Viandas Para Facilmente Executar*, 2nd ed. Bombaim: Nicol's Printing Works, 1892.
Mascarenhas, Antonio. *Goan Life and Outlook*. Lisboa: Ed. Paulistas, 1958.
Mascarenhas, Constancio. "Curumbins de Goa: Estudo Antropo-social," *Trabalhos de Antropologia e Etnologia* 17, no. 1–4 (1959): 315–28.
Mascarenhas, Filipe F. *A Luta Anti-tuberculosa em Bardez* (*Estudo Medico-Social*). Nova Goa: Tip. Bragança, 1925.
Mascarenhas, Lambert. "Goan Freedom Movement Outside Goa." In *Goa Wins Freedom: Reflections and Reminiscence*, edited by B. Sheik Ali, 123–37. Goa: Goa University, 1989.
Mascarenhas, Mira. "Social Life as Reflected in Goan Christian Folksongs." In *Goan Society through the Ages*, edited by Balakrishna S. Shastry, 79–92. New Delhi: Asian Publication Services, 1987.

Mascarenhas, Telo. *Goa, Terra Minha Amada. Sonetos*. Panjim: Esmeraldo, 1972.

Mascarenhas-Keyes, Stella. *Colonialism, Migration and the International Catholic Goan Community*. Saligão: Goa 1556, 2011.

Mascarenhas-Keyes, Stella. "International Migration: Its Development, Reproduction and Economic Impact on Goa upto 1961." In *Goa through the Ages*, vol. II, edited by Teotonio R. de Souza, 242–62. New Delhi: Concept Publishing Company, 1990.

Mathew, Kuzhippalli Skaria. *Portuguese Trade with India in the Sixteenth Century*. New Delhi: Manohar, 1983.

Mathew, P. A., D. G. Dhandar, and S. Subramaniam. *Mangoes of Goan Origin*. Old Goa: Indian Council of Agricultural Research (ICAR)—Goa Research Center, 1997.

Mattoso, António Gonçalves. *Compêndio de História de Portugal*. Lisboa: Livraria Sá da Costa, 1949.

Melo, Froilano de. "O Caso da Índia: Discurso, na Assembleia Nacional." In *Diário de Sessões*. Lisboa: Assembleia Nacional, 1949.

Mendes, Antonio Lopes. *A Índia Portuguesa. Breve Descripção das Possessões Portuguezas na Asia*. New Delhi: Asian Educational Services, 1989.

Mendes, Sushila Sawant. "Jawaharlal Nehru and the Liberation Struggle of Goa." *Indian History Proceedings* 67 (2006–7): 549–55.

Mendes, Sushila Sawant. *Luis de Menezes Bragança, Nationalism, Secularism, and Free-Thought in Portuguese Goa*. Panjim: Directorate of Art and Culture, 2014.

Mendonça, Aurel. *India's Policy and Goa*. Bangalore: Author, 1957.

Mendonça, Délio. *Conversions and Citizenry: Goa under Portugal 1510–1961*. Delhi: Concept Publishing Company, 2002.

Mendonça–Noronha, Silvia de. "The Economic Scene in Goa (1926–1961)." In *Goa through the Ages: An Economic History*, edited by Teotonio R. de Souza, 263–96. New Delhi: Concept Publishing House, 1990.

Meneses, António. *Goa: Notas Históricas*. Pangim: Author, 1977.

Meneses, Maria Paula. "Food, Recipes and Commodities of Empires: Mozambique in the Indian Ocean Network." *Centro de Estudos Sociais* (*CES*), Universidade de Coimbra, Officina no. 335 (December 2009).

Menezes Bragança Memorial Committee. *Biographical Sketch: Menezes Bragança*. Panaji: Menezes Bragança Memorial Committee, 1972.

Menezes, Julião. *Goa's Freedom Struggle*. Velim (Goa): Alzira da Almeida Charitable Trust, 2011.

Menezes, Maria Tereza. *The Essential Goa Cookbook*. New Delhi: Penguin Books India, 2000.

Miller, Rissa L. "Eating Images and Making History: The Fruits of the Martorana Convent." In *Food Cultures across Time: Flavours and Endeavour*, edited by Anca-Luminita Iancu and Alexandra Mitrea, 153–75. Newcastle: Cambridge Scholars Publishing, 2021.

Ministério do Ultramar. *Notas sobre o Estado Portugues da Índia*. Lisboa: Agência Geral do Ultramar, 1954.

Ministry of Information and Broadcasting. *World Opinion on Goa*. New Delhi: Ministry of Information and Broadcasting, 1957.

Mintz, Sydney. "Book Review." *American Ethnologist* 30, no. 3 (August 2003): 474–5.

Miranda, Antonio Teodoro de. "Regimen do Abcari para o Distrito de Goa." In *Segundo Congresso Provincial da Índia Portuguesa*, 14–19. Nova Goa: Casa Luso Francesa, 1917.

Miranda, Eufemiano. *Oriente e Ocidente na Literatura Goesa*. Saligao: Goa 1556, 2012.

Miranda, Francisco Xavier Teodoro de. "Crédito Agrícola." In *Congresso Provincial da Índia Portuguesa (Primeiro)*, edited by Antonio Maria da Cunha, 16–20. Nova Goa: Imprensa Nacional, 1916.

Miranda, Jose Antonio da Piedade. *Excelencia da Vida Agricola*. Nova Goa: Tip. "Xri Manguesh", 1922.

Mitragotri, Vithal Raghavendra. *A Socio-cultural History of Goa from the Bhojas to the Vijayanagara*. Panaji: Institute Menezes Braganza, 1999.

Modesto, Maria de Lourdes. *Cozinha Tradicional Portuguesa*. Lisboa: Editorial Verbo, 1998.

Monís, Álda. *Preparados Práticos da Cozinha (Goesa ou Luso-Indiana)*. Margao: Tipografia Nacional, 1926.

Montanari, Massimo. *Food Is Culture*, Translated by Albert Sonnenfeld. New York: Columbia University Press, 2006.

Moraes, Dom. *A Family in Goa*. Panjim: Vasantrao Dempo 60th Birthday Commemorative Volume, 1976.

Moraes, Dom. "Sausages and Jackfruits." *Goa Today*, August, 1990.

Moraes, Frank. *Jawaharlal Nehru—A Biography*. New York: Macmillan, 1956.

Moraes, George M. *A History of Christianity in India: From Early Times to St. Francis Xavier: A.D. 52–1542*. Bombay: P. C. Manaktala and Sons, 1964.

Morais, Carlos Alexandre. *Cronológia Geral da Índia Portuguesa -1498-1962*. Lisboa: Sociedade de Geografia, 1997.

Morais, Carlos Alexandre. *A Queda da Índia Portuguesa*. Lisboa: Editorial Estampa, 1995.

Moreira, Adriano. *Imperialismo e colonialismo da União Indiana*. (Discurso Inaugural do Curso de Instituto Superior de Estudos Ultramarinos). Lisboa: Agência Geral do Ultramar, 1955.

Moreira, Adriano. *Intransigência*. (Discurso proferido no encerramento dos trabalhos do Concelho Ultramarino). Lisboa: Agência Geral do Ultramar, 1962.

Moreira, Adriano. *Política da Integração*. (Discurso na Associação Comercial do Porto). Lisboa: Bertrand, 1961.

Moreira, Adriano. "Política Ultramarina." *Estudos de Ciências Política e Sociais*, vol 1, no. 1, 4th ed. (1961).

Moreira, Adriano. "Projecção Internacional de Goa." *Garcia de Orta*, Special issue dedicated to Índia Portuguesa, (1956).

Morgado, Nuno Alves. "Notas para um Estudo do Desenvolvimento Económico do Estado da India." *Boletim Informativo da Junta de Comércio Externo*, Ano I, Sr. I, 4 (May 1961): 6–19.

Munn, Nancy D. *The Fame of Gawa: A Symbolic Study of Value Transformation in a Massim (Papua New Guinea) Society*. Cambridge: Cambridge Uiversity Press, 1986.

Nagvenkar, Harischandra Tucaram. "Salt and the Goan Economy: A Study of Goa's Salt Industry and Salt Trade in the 19th and 20th Centuries during the Portuguese Rule." PhD diss., University of Goa, 1999.

Naik, Jayanti. *Amonem ek Lokjin*. Panjim: Goa Konkani Akademi, 1993.

Naughton, John. "How the Madeleine Will Help with Remembrance of Smells Past." *The Guardian*, October 2013.

Nazare, José Maria de Carmo. "Camaras Agrárias e Communidades Agricólas: Contribuintes da Fazenda Pública." *O Oriente Portugues* 1 (1904).

Nazareth, Peter, ed. *Goan Literature: A Modern Reader*, Issue of the *Journal of South Asian Literature*. East Lansing, MI: Michigan State University, 1983.

Nehru, Jawaharlal. *The Goa Problem*. New Delhi: Ministry of Foreign Affairs, 1956.

Nehru, Jawaharlal. *Jawaharlal Nehru: An Autobiography*. New Delhi: Oxford University Press, 1989.

Nehru on Goa. New Delhi: Goa Freedom Publications, n.d.

Newman, Robert S. *Goan Anthropology: Festivals, Films and Fish*. Saligao: Goa 1556, 2019.

Newman, Robert S. *Of Umbrellas, Goddess and Dreams: Essays on Goan Culture and Society*. Mapusa: Other India Press, 2001.

Noronha, Antonio Floriano. *Os Hindus de Goa e a República*. Nova Goa: Imprensa Nacional, 1923.

Noronha, Antonio Floriano. *Pareceres (1913–1914)*. Nova Goa: Imprensa Nacional, 1915.

Noronha, Leslie de. *The Mango and the Tamarind Tree*. Calcutta: Writers Workshop, 1970.

Oliveira, Barradas. *Roteiro do Oriente: Na viagem do Ministro do Ultramar, Comandante Sarmento Rodrigues, às Províncias Portuguesas da Índia, Timor e Macau, no ano de 1952*. Lisboa: Agência Geral do Ultramar, 1954.

Oliveira, Hermes de Araújo. *O Problema da Índia Portuguesa*. Lisboa: Ministério do Exército, 1958.

Orta, Garcia da. *Colloquies on the Simple and Drugs of India*. Delhi: Sri Satguru Publications, 1987.

Orta, Garia da. *Coloquios dos Simples e Drogas da India*. Lisboa: Imprensa Nacional, 1891.

Padki, Madhav Balakrishna, S. H. Pore and S. W. Muranjan. *Utilization of Local Resources: A Case Study of Goa*. Poona: Gokhale Institute of Politics and Economics, 1967.

Padoshi, A. R. *Agricultural Development of India*. Bombay: Himalaya Publishing House, 1991.

Panandiker, Vithal Anant Pai, and Prabhat Narayan Choudhuri. *Democratic Transition in Goa and Its Policy Implication*. New Delhi: Uppal Publishing House, 1983.

Pandit, Raghunath Vishnu. "Dente de Vinho?" *O Heraldo*, December 13, 1968, 3.

Pandit, Raghunath Vishnu. *Mhajem Utar Gavddeachem*. Bombay: Popular Prakashan, 1963.

Pandit, Raghunath Vishnu. *My Goa and Other Poems*. Panaji: Antonio Caetano Fernandes, 1971.

Pandit, Raghunath Vishnu. *Voices of Peace*. Translated by Thomas Gay. Goa Velha: Bhagawati Prakashan, 1967.

Panikkar, Kavalam Madhava. *Asia and Western Dominance: A Survey of the Vasco da Gama Epoch of Asian History, 1498–1945*. London: George Allen and Unwin, 1953.

Parasecoli, Fabio. "Food, Identity, and Cultural Reproduction in Immigrant Communities." *Social Research* 81, no. 2 (2014): 415–39.

Parobo, Parag D. *India's First Democratic Revolution: Dayanand Bandodkar and the Rise of Bahujan in Goa*. New Delhi: Orient Blackswan, 2015.

Passos, Joana. *Literatura Goesa em Portugues nos Séculos XIX e XX: Perspectivas Pós-coloniais e Revisão Crítica*. Famalicão: Edições Húmus, 2012.

Pawar, Rajay. "Konkani Poetry—Fonte of Goan History." In *Goa in the 20th Century History and Culture*, edited by Pius Malekandathil and Remy Dias, 294–306. Panaji: Institute Menezes Braganza, 2008.

Pearson, Michael Naylor. *Coastal Western India*. New Delhi: Concept Publishing Company, 1981.

Pearson, Michael Naylor. *Merchants and Rulers in Gujarat*. New Delhi: Concept Publishing Company, 1976.

Pearson, Michael Naylor. *The Portuguese in India*. Hyderabad: Orient Longman, 1990.

Pegado, Hipólito Policarpo. "Sugestões para Combater o Risco do Alcólismo em Goa." In *I Conferência Sanitária: Em Comemoração do 72º Aniversário da Escola Médico-Cirúrgica de Nova Goa. (1-12-1914 a 6-12-1914)*, 149–58. Nova Goa: Imprensa Nacional, 1914.

Pereira, A. de Bragança. *Etnografia da India Portuguesa*. New Delhi: Asian Educational Services, 1991.

Pereira, Amaro A. compiler. *History of Mormugao Port*. Vasco da Gama: Mormugao Port Trust, 1978.

Pereira, Angelo. *Goa Remembered: Vignettes of Fading Traditions*. Bombay: Michael Lobo, 1995.

Pereira, Biula V. Cruz. *One for the Road: Role of Alcohol in Goan Society*. Saligão: Goa 1556, 2015.

Pereira, Catarina Valdigem. "Postcolonial Memories of Media Reception and Construction of Collective Belongings: The Case of Portuguese Muslim Women of Indian and Mozambican Origins." In *Media, Gender and the Past: Qualitative Approaches to Broadcast Audiences and Memories*. http://www.livroslabcom.ubi.pt/book/106: 179–222.

Pereira, Gerald. "Goa, Its Wealth and Prospects." *Free Goa*, February 10, 1958.

Pereira, Gerald. "Goa Strikes." *Free Goa*, July 25, 1955.

Pereira, Gonçalves. *Informe Personal sobre el Caso de Goa: Prefacio de uma Monografia sobre la India Portuguesa*. Lisboa: Agência Geral do Ultramar, 1954.

Pereira, Gonçalves. *My Personal Deposition in the Case of Goa*. Lisboa: Agência Geral do Ultramar, 1953.

Pereira, Hugo Silveira, and Ian J. Kerr. "Caminhos de Ferro e Desenvolvimento Econômico na Índia e em Portugal: Uma Comparação Entre as Linhas de Mormugão e do Tua, c.1880–c.1930 e adiante." *Revista Brasileira de História*, São Paulo 39, no. 81 (May–August 2019): 1–24.

Pereira, Jose, and Pratapaditya Pal, eds. *India & Portugal: Cultural Interactions*. Mumbai: Marg Publications, 2001.

Pereira, Jose, Micael Martins, and António da Costa. *Folk Songs of Goa: Mando-Dulpods and Deknnis*. New Delhi: Aryan Books International, 2005.

Pereira, Jose, Micael Martins, and António da Costa. *Song of Goa: Crown of Mandos*. Panaji: Goa 1556, Brodway, 2010.

Pereira, Jose, Micael Martins, and António da Costa. *Undra Muja Mama: Folk Songs of Goa. An Anthology of Dulpods. Sketches of Life in Goa in Times Past*. Saligao: Goa 1556 and Broadway Publishing House, 2011.

Pereira, L. M. Condorcet. "Campanha Anti-alcoólica." In *Segundo Congresso Provincial da Índia Portuguesa*, 119–23. Nova Goa: Casa Luso-Francesa, 1917.

Pereira, Libério. "Chaga Social." *O Heraldo*, September 4, 1942.

Pereira, Rui Gomes. *Goa: Gaunkari (The Old Village Association)*. Panaji: Print Well Press, 1981.

Pereira, Rui Gomes. *Goa: Hindu Temples and Deities*. Panaji: Print Well Press, 1978.

Pereira, Rui Gomes. *Questões da India. I. Jonos Perante o Problema de Vocação Sucessória e o de Prescrição Aquisitiva*. Bastora: Tip. Rangel, 1958.

Perez, Rosa Maria et al., ed. *Histórias de Goa*. Lisboa: Museu Nacional de Etnologia, 1997.

Perez, Rosa Maria. *O Tulsi e a Cruz, Antropologia e Colonialismo em Goa*. Maia: Autora, Círculo de Leitores e Temas e Debates, 2012.

Perez, Rosa Maria, (coord.) *Os Portugueses e o Oriente, História, Itinerários, Representações*. Lisboa: Publicações D. Quixote, 2006.

Phal, Suresh R. *Society in Goa (Some Aspects of Tradition and Modern Trends)*. Delhi: B. R. Publishing Corporation, 1982.

Phaldesai, Pandurang. *Goa: Folklore Studies*. Saligão: Goa 1556 and Broadway Publishing House, 2011.

Phaldesai, Pandurang. *Kaleidoscopic Goa: A Cultural Atlas*. Panaji: Dempo Education and Research Foundation, 2004.

Pinto, Celsa. "Between Two World Wars: 'Normalcy in Goan Economy.'" In *Indo-Portuguese History: Global Trends. Proceedings of XI- International Seminar on Indo-Portuguese History-Silver Jubilee Session*, edited by Fátima da Silva Gracias, Celsa Pinto, and Charles Borges, 381–96. Panaji: Maureen & Camvet Publishers, 2005.

Pinto, Celsa. *Goa: Images and Perceptions: Studies in Goan History*. Panaji: Rajhauns, 1996.

Pinto, Celsa. *Trade and Finance in Portuguese India: A Study of the Portuguese Country Trade 1770–1840*. New Delhi: Concept Publishing Company, 1994.

Pinto, John Baptist. *Goan Imigration*. Saligão, Goa: author, 1962.

Pinto, Jaime Nogueira. *Portugal, os Anos do Fim: de Goa ao Largo do Carmo*. Lisboa: Difel, 1995.

Pinto, Rochelle. *Between Empires: Print and Politics in Goa*. New Delhi: Oxford University Press, 2007.

Pinto, Rochelle. "The Foral in the History of the Comunidades of Goa." *Journal of World History* 29, no. 2 (June 2018): 185–212.

Pinto, Rochelle, Sidh Losa Mendiratta, and Walter Rossa. "Reframing the Nineteenth Century." *Revista Crítica de Ciências Sociais* 115 (May 2018): 93–112.

"Porto e Caminho de Ferro de Mormugao." *A Vida*. April 21, 1956, 1.

Portaria no.45, January 29, 1919. "*A Crise de Subsistências e o Fomento—Projectos de Medidas.*" Santa Cruz, India Portugueza, Tip. Xri Ramanatii, 1919.

Portugal, Ministério das Colónias. *Reforma Administrativa Ultramarina, Decreto Lei. no.23.229 dated 15 November 1933*. Nova Goa: Imprensa Nacional, 1934.

Pratt, Jeff. "Food Values: The Local and the Authentic." *Critique of Anthropology* 27, no. 3 (2007): 285–300.

Primeira Conferência Económica do Império Colonial Português. *Propostas da Delegação da Índia Portuguesa*. Nova Goa: Imprensa Nacional, 1936.

Priolkar, Anant Kakba. *Goa: Facts and Fiction*. Bombay: Sudha Joshi, 1962.

Priolkar, Anant Kakba. *Goa Re-discovered*. Bombay: Author, 1961.

Proust, Marcel (1913–27). *In Search of Lost Time*. London: Allen Lane, 2002.

Proust, Marcel. *Remembrance of Things Past*, trans. C. K. Scott Moncrieff and Terence Kilmartin, rev. D. J. Enright. New York: Modern Library, 2000.

Rajkumar, Narayana Vaman. *The Background of India's Foreign Policy*. Delhi: Indian National Congress, 1952.

Ramani, Shrikant. *Operation Vijay: The Ultimate Solution*. Panjim: Broadway Book Center, 2008.

Ranade, Mohan. *Struggle Unfinished*. Ribandar: Vimal Publications, 1988.

Rangel, Vicente João Janin, ed. *Regulamenlo das Communidades Agricolas de Goa, 30.10.1886*, vol. I, and Appendice ao Regulamenlo das Communidades Agricolas de Goa, vol. 2. Bastora: Typografia Rangel, 1904.

Rao, Ramesh P. *Portuguese Rule in Goa, 1510–1961*. Bombay: Asia Publishing House, 1963.

Rego, Antonio da Silva. "A Índia Portuguesa e a posição de Portugal." Offprint of *Pontos de Doutrina*. Coimbra: Comunidade Distrital de Coimbra, 1967.

Rego, Fernando do. *Mangas de Goa. Mangoes of Goa*. Panaji: Fundação Oriente, 2018.

Reis, Miguel. *Portuguese Citizenship of Persons Born in the Erstwhile "Estado da India" and of Their Descendants. Practical Notes*. Translated by Ave Cleto Afonso. Panjim: Broadway Publishing House, 2013.

Repartição Central de Estatística e Informação. *Here It Is Portugal*. (Colecção Divulgação e Cultura, no. 17). Nova Goa: RCEI, 1950.

Representações das Comunidades Agrícolas do Estado da Índia. Nova Goa: Imprensa Nacional, 1861.

Revel, Jacques. "Alimentação." In *A Nova História*, edited by Jacques Le Golf and Roger Chartier, 24–6, 45–8, 129. Coimbra: Almedina, 1978.

Ribeiro, Orlando. *Originalidade da Expansão Portuguesa*. Lisboa: Edições João Sá da Costa, 1994.

Rivara, Joaquim Heliodoro da Cunha. *Brados a Favor das Comunidades das Aldeias do Estado da India*. Nova Goa: Imprensa Nacional, 1870.

Robinson, Rowena. *Christians of India*. New Delhi: Sage Publications, 1998.

Robinson, Rowena. *Conversion, Continuity and Change: Lived Christianity in Southern Goa*. New Delhi: Sage, 1998.

Robinson, Rowena. "Sixteenth Century Conversions to Christianity in Goa." In *Religious Conversion in India: Modes, Motivations, and Meanings*, edited by Rowena Robinson and Sathianathan Clarke, 291–322. New Delhi: Oxford University Press, 2008.

Rocha, Leopoldo da. *As Confrarias de Goa: Seculos XVI–XX*. Lisboa: Centro de Estudos Históricos Ultramarinos, 1973.

Rocha, Leopoldo da. *O Signo da Ira de Orlando da Costa*, 1961. Disponível em. http://archiveofgoanwritinginportuguese.blogspot.in.

Rodrigues, Camilo Severino. "Depoimentos: 'O Alcista.'" *A Vida*, October 11, 1938, 2.

Rodrigues, Camilo Severino. "A Genese do alcismo." *A Vida*, October 13, 1938, 2.

Rodrigues, Lucio. *Abolim: The Flower Songs, Folk Tales and Legends of Goa. A Collection*. Saligão: Goa 1556 and Golden Heart Emporium, 2015.

Rodrigues, Lucio. "It Happens." In *Modern Goan Short Stories*, edited by Luís S. Rita Vas, 1–8. Bombay: Jaico Publishing House, 1971.

Rodrigues, Lucio. *Of Soil and Soul and Konkani Folk Tales*. Bombay: Laura D'Souza Rodrigues, 1974.

Rodrigues, M. M. Sarmento. *Aos Portugueses da União Indiana*. Lisboa: Agência Geral do Ultramar, 1954.

Rodrigues, M. M. Sarmento. *Portugal in India*. Lisboa: Agência Geral do Ultramar, 1954.

Rodrigues, M. M. Sarmento. *The Portuguese Overseas Provinces*. Lisboa: Agência Geral do Ultramar, 1955.

Rodrigues, Maria de Lourdes Bravo da Costa. "O Arroz Como Metáfora em O *Signo da Ira* (1961) de Orlando da Costa." *Via Atlântica* 20, no. 2 (December/2019): 81–100.

Rodrigues, Maria de Lourdes Bravo da Costa. "Economic Blockade." *Boletim do Instituto Meneses Bragança*, no. 170 (1994): 135–46.

Rodrigues, Maria de Lourdes Bravo da Costa. "Feast of the Betrothal of Our Lady." *The Navhind Times*, (*Buzz*), January 26, 2014, 1.

Rodrigues, Maria de Lourdes Bravo da Costa. *Feasts, Festivals and Observances of Goa*. Merces: L&L, 2010.

Rodrigues, Maria de Lourdes Bravo da Costa. *Games That We Played*. Merces: L&L, 2012.

Rodrigues, Maria de Lourdes Bravo da Costa. "Goa's Ladainha Tradition." *The Navhind Time* (*Panorama*), May 20, 2012, 2.

Rodrigues, Maria de Lourdes Bravo da Costa. "Ladainha, a Prayer for All Seasons." *Gomantak Times* (*Weekender*), May 27, 2007, 4.

Rodrigues, Maria de Lourdes Bravo da Costa. *Lifestyle Goa (1908–2008)*. Pangim: GCCI, 2008.

Rodrigues, Maria de Lourdes Bravo da Costa. *100 Years of Goa Chamber of Commerce and Industry*. Panaji: Goa Chamber of Commerce and Industry, 2008.

Rodrigues, Maria de Lourdes Bravo da Costa. *Remembering Goa*. Merces: L&L, 2000.

Rodrigues, Maria de Lourdes Bravo da Costa. "The Reservoirs of Life-Saving Water." *The Navhind Times* (*Buzz*), April 19, 2016, 1.

Rodrigues, Maria de Lourdes Bravo da Costa. *Tasty Goan Morsels—Food, Ingredients and Preparation*, 2nd ed. Merces: L&L, 2004.

Rodrigues, Maria de Lourdes Bravo da Costa. "'Tisreanche fest' at St.Anthony's Chapel." *The Navhind Times* (*Buzz*), May 19, 2013, 1.

Rodrigues, Pia de Menezes. "Interactive Relationship between Goa and Bombay Journalism." In *Goa's External Relations*, edited by Prakashchandra Pandurang Shirodkar, 90–101. Panaji: Rajhauns Offset, 1992.

Rodrigues, Pia de Menezes. "Taverna and Its Socio-Economic Impact in Colonial Goa." In *Metahistory: History Questioning History: Festschrift in*

Honour of Teotónio R. de Souza, edited by Charles Borges and Michael Naylor Pearson, 185–202. Lisboa: Vega, 2007.

Rodrigues, Rosario F. *A Living Architectural Splendor: A Study on the Church of St. Ana*. Agassaim: Muringlyn & Muringrace Publications, 2009.

Roe, Daphne A. *Alcohol and the Diet*. Connecticut: Avi Publishing, 1979.

Rosales, Marta Vilar. "O Verdadeiro Caril Moçambicano: Transnacionalismo, quotidianos e materialidades goesas na Africa colonial . . .," In *Das Indias: Gentes, Movimentos e Pertenças Transnacionais*. Organized by Susana Trovão e Marta Vilar Rosales, 59–80. Lisboa: Edições Colibri, Centro de Estudos em Migrações e Minorias, Faculdade de Ciências Sociais e Humanas, Universidade Nova de Lisboa, 2010.

A Rota das Especiarias. Lisboa: Edições INAPA, 1989.

Rubinoff, Arthur. *The Constructions of a Political Community: Integration and Identity in Goa*. Thousand Oaks, CA: Sage Publications, 1998.

Rubinoff, Arthur. *India's Use of Force*. Bombay: Popular Prakashan, 1971.

Rubinoff, Arthur. "Integration Theories and the Case of Goa." In *National Unity, the South Asian Experience*, edited by Milton Israel, 165–208. New Delhi: Promilla, 1998.

Rubinoff, Janet Clare Ahner. "Casta and Communidade: The Transformation of Corporate Agrarian Structures in Goa, India." PhD diss., University of Toronto, 1992.

Rubinoff, Janet Clare Ahner. "Pink Gold: Transformation of Backwater Aquaculture on Goa's Khazan Lands." *Economic and Political Weekly* 36, no. 13 (March 31–April 6, 2001): 1108–14.

Sá, Mario Cabral e. "Mandovi Masala." *Goa Today*, October, 1994, 50–4.

Sá, Mario Cabral e. *Song of the Golden Gateway 100 Years of the Port of Mormugao and the Peninsula*. New Delhi: Vikas Publishing House, 1985.

Sacardandó, Balcrisna Datarama Sinai, ed. *Sétimo Congresso Provincial da India Portuguesa*. Nova Goa: Tip. Bragança, 1927.

Saksena, Ramesh N. *Goa into the Mainstream*. New Delhi: Abhinav Publishers, 1974.

Salazar, António de Oliveira. *O Caso de Goa*. Lisboa: Secretariado Nacional de Informação, 1954.

Salazar, António de Oliveira. *Discursos e Notas Políticas*, vol. vi. Coimbra: Coimbra Editora, 1935–67.

Salazar, António de Oliveira. *Goa e a União Indiana*. Lisboa: Secretariado Nacional de Informação, 1954.

Salazar, António de Oliveira. *Goa e a União Indiana, Goa e o Mundo, Goa e o Cristianismo na Àsia, Goa e Nós Próprios, Goa e o Futuro*. Lourenço Marques: Imprensa Nacional, 1954.

Salazar, António de Oliveira. *Invasão e Ocupação de Goa pela União Indiana*. Lisboa: Secretariado Nacional de Informação, 1962.

Salazar, António de Oliveira. *Portugal and Its Overseas Provinces: The Case of Goa*. Lisboa: Agência Geral do Ultramar, 1953.

Salazar, António de Oliveira. *Portugal e a Campanha Anticolonialista*. Macau: Imprensa Nacional, 1961.

Saldanha, Cláudio F. *A Short History of Goa*. Bombay: Anglo-Lusitano, 1952.

Saldanha, Gabriel. *História de Goa (Política e arqueológica)*. Nova Goa: Livraria Coelho, 1925.

Saldanha, Mariano. "A Lusitanização de Goa." *Rumo: Revista de Cultura Portuguesa* (1947): 1–28.

Sampaio, João de Melo. *A Mangueira*. Nova Goa: Imprensa Nacional, 1902.

Saraiva, José Hermano. *História Concisa de Portugal*. Mem-Martins: Publicações Europa-America, 1978.

Sardessai, Manohar Rai. *Goem Tujea Moga Khatir*. Mumbai: Gomant Bharti Prakashan, 1961.

Sardessai, Manohar Rai. *My Song, Ma Chanson, O Meu Canto*. Goa: New Age Printers, 2008.

Sardo, Susana. *Guerras de Jasmim e Mogari: Música, Identidade e Emoções em Goa*. Lisboa: Texto Editores, 2010.

Sarin, Manohar Lal. "The Case of Goa (1961) and the Controversy Regarding Gandhian Non-violent Resistance (Satyagraha), and International Law Involved in It." (Inaugural-Dissertation Marburg/Lahn University, 1973).

Scholberg, Henry. *Bibliography of Goa and the Portuguese in India*. New Delhi: Promilla, 1982.

Scholberg, Henry. "The Goan Crisis Seen by the American Press." In *Goa Wins Freedom: Reflections and Reminiscences*, edited by Sheikh Ali, 205–24. Bambolim: Goa University, 1986.

Secretariado Nacional da Informação. *Cultura Popular e Turismo: Invasão e Ocupação de Goa*. Lisboa: SNI, 1962.

Segundo Congresso Provincial da Índia Portuguesa. Nova Goa: Casa Luso-Francesa, 1917.

Sen, Bandhudas. *The Green Revolution in India: A Perspective*. New Delhi: Wiley Eastern Private, 1974.

Sen, Colleen Taylor. *Curry a Global History*. London: Reaktion Books, 2009.

Sen, Coleen Taylor. "The Portuguese Influence on Bengal Cuisine." In *Food on Move-Proceedings of the Oxford Symposium on Food and Cookery* (1996), edited by Harlan Walker, 118–32. Devon: Prospect Books, 1997.

Sequeira, Alito. "Post Colonial Portugal, Post Colonial Goa: A Note on Portuguese Identity and Its Resonance in Goa and India." *Lusotopie* 9, no. 2 (2002/3): 211–13.

Sequeira, Newton. "Selflessly Sharing Shellfish by the Seashore." *Times of India*, May 14, 2017, 2.

Sequeira, Reyna. *As Dear as Salt ... The Story and Neglect and Decay in a Traditional Occupation in Goa*. Saligao: Goa 1556 and Golden Heart Emporium, 2013.

Seremetakis, C. Nadia. "The Memory of the Senses: Historical Perception, Commensal Exchange and Modernity," *Visual Anthropology Review* 9, no. 2 (1993): 1–18.

Serrão, Joaquim Veríssimo. "Portugal e a Índia." In *Vasco da Gama e a Índia*, edited by Teotónio R. de Souza e José Manuel Garcia. Conferência Internacional, Paris, 1998, vol. 2, 11–21. Lisboa: Fundação Calouste Gulbenkian, 1999.

Serrão, Joel, ed. *Dicionário de História de Portugal*. Porto: Livraria Figuerinhas, 1961–71.

Serviço de Saúde da Índia Portuguesa, *I Conferência Sanitária. Em Comemoração do 72o Aniversário da Escola Médico-Cirúrgica de Nova Goa (1-12-1914 a 6-12-1914)*, 2 vols. Nova Goa: Imprensa Nacional, 1914.

Serviços de Informação do Governo Geral. *Em volta do Caso de Goa: Heraldo responde ao Examiner*. Goa: Serviços de Informação do Governo Geral, 1954.

Sétimo Congresso Provincial da India Portuguesa. *Relatório de Comissão de Estudos*. Nova Goa: Tipografia R. M. Rau & Irmãos, 1927.

Shah, Amritlal Balkrishna. *Goa: The Problem of Transition*. Bombay: Manaktalas, 1965.

Shastry, Bhagamandala Seetharama, ed. *Goan Society through the Ages*. New Delhi: Asian Publication Services, 1987.

Shastry, Bhagamandala Seetharama. "Land-Holdings under the Communidades of Goa: An Historical Perspective." In *Proceedings of the Indian History Congress*. Forty-Ninth Session Karnatak University, Dharwad, 1988, 411–19. New Delhi: Indian History Congress, 1989.

Shastry, Bhagamandala Seetharama, ed. *Socio-economic Aspects of Portuguese Colonialism in 19th and 20th Centuries*. New Delhi: Asian Publication Services, 1987.

Shastry, Bhagamandala Seetharama. *Studies in Indo Portuguese History*. Bangalore: IBH Prakashan, 1981.

Shirodkar, Prakashchandra Pandurang, ed. *Goa Cultural Trends*. Panaji: Directorate of Archives, Archaeology and Museum, Government of Goa, 1988.

Shirodkar, Prakashchandra Pandurang. *Goa's Struggle for Freedom*. Delhi: Ajanta Publications, 1988.

Shirodkar, Prakashchandra Pandurang, ed. *Trial of T. B. Cunha*. Panaji: Goa Gazetteer Department-Government of Goa, 1991.

Silva, Manuel António Vassalo e. "*Dossier*" *Goa*. Lisboa: Liber, 1975.

Simoes, Frank. *Frank Simoes' Goa*. New Delhi: Roli Books, 2004.

Simoes, Frank. *Frank Unedited: The Best of Frank Simoes*. New Delhi: Roli, 2003.

Singh, Kumar Suresh, ed. *Goa: People of India* Series, vol. XXI. Bombay: Anthropological Survey of India/Popular Prakashan, 1993.

Singh, Khushwant. *A Family in Goa*. Goa: Vasantrao Dempo 60th Birthday Commemorative Volume, 1976.

Sinha, Arun. *Goa Indica: A Critical Portrait of Postcolonial Goa*. New Delhi: Bibliophile South Asia, 2002.

Soares, Mário. *Portugal Amordaçado: Depoimento sobre os Anos do Fascismo*. Lisboa: Arcádia, 1974.

Sociological Review 42, no. 4 (November 1994): 179–222.

Sousa, Cecilia de. "Fish Curry and Goan Identity." *Goa Today*, November 1983, 28.

Sousa, Francisco Otolini de. "Alterações ao Codigo das Comunidade." In *Congresso Provincial da Índia Portuguesa (Primeiro)*, edited by Antonio Maria da Cunha, 29. Nova Goa: Imprensa Nacional, 1916.

Sousa, Maria Fernanda Noronha Costa. *Cozinha Indo-Portuguesa-Receitas da Bisavó*. Lisboa: Assirio e Alvim, 1998.

Sousa, Maria Fernanda Noronha da Costa and Inês Gonçalves. *Sabor de Goa: Cozinha Indo- Portuguesa*. Lisboa: Assírio & Alvim, 2004.

Souza, Carmo de. *Legal System in Goa-Laws and Legal Trends 1510–1961*. Panaji: New Age Printers, 1995.

Souza, Carmo de. "The Village Communities—A Historical and Legal Perspective." In *Goa and Portugal History and Development*, edited by Charles J. Borges, Óscar G. Pereira, and Hannes Stubbe, 111–28. New Delhi: Concept Publishing Company, 2000.

Souza, Shaila de. "Health Practices and People's Identity: Re-Locating Identity." *Lusotopie* (2000): 455–68.

Souza, Teotonio R. de. "Capital Input in Goa's Freedom Struggle: The Bombay Connection." *Rojnishi*, I, no. 2, Poona University, Dept. of History (1983): 8–15.

Souza, Teotónio R. de. *Goa: Roteiro Histórico-Cultural*. Lisboa: Grupo do Trabalho do Ministério da Educação para as Comemorações dos Descobrimentos, 1996.

Souza, Teotonio R. de, ed. *Goa through the Ages: An Economic History*, vol. II, New Delhi: Concept Publishing Company, 1990.

Souza, Teotonio R. de. *Goa to Me*. New Delhi: Concept Publishing Company, 1994.

Souza, Teotonio R. de. "Goan Agrarian Economy in Crisis," *Itihas* I (1976): 55–70.

Souza, Teotonio R. de. "Goan Catholicism and the Liberation." *Goa Today*, December 1986, 47–51.

Souza, Teotonio R. de, ed. *Indo Portuguese History: Old Issue, New Questions*. New Delhi: Concept Publishing Company, 1985.

Sousa, Teotónio R. de "Lógicas Imperiais e Processos Contemporâneos: Analisando Algumas Memórias Coloniais Recém publicadas em Goa e em Portugal." *Babilónia, Dossier Mestiçagem Linguística e Cultural*, no. 4: 55–70.

Souza, Teotónio R. de. "Lusofonia e Lusotopia no Oriente: O caso do folklore goês." *Universidade Lusófona de Humanidades e Tecnologias* em. http://revistas.ulusofona.pt.

Souza, Teotonio R. de. *Medieval Goa*. New Delhi: Concept Publishing Company, 1979.

Souza, Teotonio R. de."Voiceless in Goan Historiography: A Case for the Church Records in Goa." In *Indo-Portuguese History: Sources and Problems*, edited by John Correia-Afonso, 114–31. Bombay: Oxford University Press, 1981.

Spina, Daniela. "Goa e as Dobras da História Literária em Língua Portuguesa: *o como e o porque*." PhD diss., Universidade de Lisboa, 2020.

Srinivasan, Sheela. *Goa a Social History, 1640–1750*. Panaji: Rajhauns, 2012.

Stocker, Maria Manuela. "O Processo Politíco-militar de Integração do Estado Português da Índia no território da União Indiana." In *Vasco da Gama e a Índia*, edited by Teotónio R. de Souza e José Manuel Garcia. Conferência Internacional, Paris, 1998, vol. 2, 341–57. Lisboa: Fundação Calouste Gulbenkian, 1999.

Stocker, Maria Manuela. *Xeque-mate a Goa*. Lisboa: Temas e Debates, 2005.

Subrahmanyam, Sanjay. "O Romântico, o Oriental e o Exótico: Notas sobre os Portugueses em Goa." In *Histórias de Goa*, edited by Rosa Maria Perez et al., 29–43. Lisbon: Museu Nacional de Etnologia, 1997.

Sukthankar, Vishnu Sitaram. *Tales and Tellers of Goa*. Bangalore: Atelier Sukthankar, 1974.

Super, John C. "Food and History." *Journal of Social History* 36, no. 1 (Autumn 2002): 165–78.

Sutton, David E. "The Anthropology of Cooking." In *The Handbook of Food Anthropology*, edited by Jacob A. Klein and James L. Watson, 349–69. London: Bloomsbury, 2016.

Sutton, David E. *Remembrance of Repasts: An Anthropology of Food and Memory*. New York: Berg, 2001.

Swinson, Richard P., and Eaves, Derek. *Alcoholism and Addiction*. Plymouth: Macdonald & Evans, 1978.

Techno Economic Survey of Goa, Daman and Diu. New Delhi: National Council of Applied Economic Research, 1964.

Teixeira, Rui de Azevedo. "*O Signo da Ira* (*The Sign of Anger*): Ethno-literature and Neo-realism in a Case of Literary Excellence." In *Goa and Portugal History and Development*, edited by Charles J. Borges, Óscar Guilherme Pereira, and Hannes Stubbe, 398–401. New Delhi: Concept Publishing Company, 2000.

Telkar, S. *Goa-Yesterday and To-Day*. Bombay: States People Press, 1962.

Telles, Ricardo Micael. "CréditoAgrícola." In *Segundo Congresso Provincial, da Índia Portuguesa*, 59–61. Nova Goa: Casa Luso-Francesa, 1917.

Telles, Ricardo Micael. *Freguesia de Nerul: Estudo histórico-arqueológico*. Nova Goa: Imprensa Oriental, 1925.

Tendulkar, Suresh S. P., and Shankar B. Dhaimodkar. *Vegetable Cultivation*. Panaji: Agriculture Officers' Association, 1994.

Thapar, Romila. "Dana and Daksina as Forms of Exchange." *Indica* 13, no. 1 & 2 (March–September 1976): 37–48.

Thomas, Hugh. *An Unfinished History of the World*. London: Hamish Hamilton, 1979.

Tombat, Nishta. "Tristão de Bragança Cunha (1891–1958) and the Rise of the Nationalist Conscious in Goa." PhD diss., University of Goa, 1995.

Trichur, Raghuraman S. *Refiguring Goa: From Trading Post to Tourism Destination*. Saligao: Goa 1556, 2013.

Usgaokar, Kumudini, and Shama Sardessai. *Traditional Taste of Goa*. Goa: Fomento Foundation, 2000.

Vale, Regina Célia Fortuna do. "A literatura de Goa em língua portuguesa e *O Signo da Ira*." Dissertação de Mestrado em Letras. Faculdade de Filosofia, Letras e Ciências Humanas da Universidade de São Paulo, 1999.

Vaz, José Clemente. *Profiles of Eminent Goans, Past and Present*. New Delhi: Concept Publishing Company, 1997.

Velinkar, Joseph. *India and the West: The First Encounters (Particularly in Goan Salcete): A Historical Study of the Early Indo-Portuguese Cultural Encounters in Goa*, 2nd rev. ed. Margão, Goa: CinnamonTeal Publishing, 2016.

Velinkar, Joseph. "Role of the Catholic Church in Twentieth Century Goa." In *Goa in the 20th Century History and Culture*, edited by Pius Malekandathil and Remy Dias, 22–38. Panaji: Institute Menezes Braganza, 2008.

Venkatarangaiya, Mamidipudi. *The Indian Year Book of International Affairs, 1956*, vol. v. University of Madras: Indian Study Group of International Affairs, 1956.

Viagem do Francisco Pyrard de Laval, edited by Magalhaes Bastos. Porto: Tipografia Domingos de Oliveira, 1944.

Vicente, Filipa Lowndes. *Outros Orientalismos: A Índia entre Florença e Bombaim, 1860–1900*. Lisboa: ICS, Imprensa de Ciências Sociais, 2010.

Vişan, Ruxandra. "Culinary Lexis in Eighteenth-Century Dictionaries: The Case of the Mysterious Syllabub." In *Food Cultures across Time: Flavours and Endeavour*, edited by Anca-Luminita Iancu and Alexandra Mitrea, 176–92. Newcastle: Cambridge Scholars Publishing, 2021.

Wealth of India. A Dictionary of Indian Raw Materials and Industrial Products. Supplement. *Fish and Fisheries*. Raw Materials vol. IV. New Delhi: Council for Scientific and Industrial Research, 1962.

Whiteway, Richard Stephen. *Cambridge History of India*. Delhi: Cambridge, 1963.

Whiteway, Richard Stephen. *The Rise of the Portuguese Power in India (1497–1550)*. New Delhi: Asian Educational Services, 1989.

Willander, J. Larsson M. "Smell Your Way Back to Childhood: Autobiographical Odor Memory." *Psychonomic Bulletin & Review* 13, no. 2 (2006): 240–4.

Xavier, Alberto. *A Índia Portuguesa à Face da Razão e do Direito*. Lisboa: Edições SNI, 1950.

Xavier, Ângela Barreto, and Ines G. Županov. *Catholic Orientalism: Portuguese Empire, Indian Knowledge (16th–18th Centuries)*. New Delhi: Oxford University Press, 2015.

Xavier, Caetano Francisco. *Catálogo Descritivo dos Productos Económico Industriais da Flora da India Portuguesa*. Lisboa: Biblioteca Nacional, 1922.

Xavier, Carlos. *Development of Sports and Games in Goa, Daman and Diu*. Panaji: Directorate of Sports and Cultural Affairs, 1976.

Xavier, Filipe Neri. *Bosquejo Historico das Communidades das Aldeas dos Concelhos das Ilhas, Salsete e Bardez*. Revista e acrescentada por Jose Maria de Sá. Bastora: Typographia Rangel, 1907.

Xavier, Filipe Neri. *Bosquejo Histórico das Communidades de Goa*. Merces, Goa: L & L, 2012.

Xavier, Filipe Neri. *Defensa dos Direitos das Gão-carias, Gão-cares e dos seus Privilégios, Contra a Proposta de sua Dissolucão, e Divisão das suas Terras*. Nova Goa: Imprensa Nacional, 1856.

Xavier, Filipe Neri. *Descripção do Coqueiro, Arequeira, Arroz e Moedas de Goa*. Nova Goa: Imprensa Nacional, 1866.

Xavier, P. D. "Role of the Press in the Freedom Struggle in Goa." In *Goa Wins Freedom, Reflections and Reminiscences*, edited by B. Sheik Ali, 79–107. Bambolim: Goa University, 1986.

Yule, Henry, and Arthur Coke Burnell. *Hobson-Jobson: A Glossary of Colloquial Anglo-Indian Words and Phrases, and of Kindred Terms, Etymological, Historical, Geographical and Discursive*. New Delhi: Munshiram Manoharlal, 1984.

Index

About the Author

Maria de Lourdes Bravo da Costa retired as Assistant State Librarian from the Krishnadas Shama State Central Library, Goa, India. She was Reference Librarian specializing in Indo-Portuguese history, focusing on Goa.